Richard B. M
Caribbean Militant in Harlem

Blacks in the Diaspora
Darlene Clark Hine and
John McCluskey, Jr., General Editors

RICHARD B. MOORE, CARIBBEAN MILITANT IN HARLEM

Collected Writings 1920–1972

EDITED BY

W. BURGHARDT TURNER AND
JOYCE MOORE TURNER

WITH BIOGRAPHY BY

JOYCE MOORE TURNER

INTRODUCTION BY

FRANKLIN W. KNIGHT

INDIANA UNIVERSITY PRESS
Bloomington and Indianapolis

PLUTO  PRESS
London

First Midland Book Edition 1992

Manufactured in the United States of America

Library of Congress Cataloging-in-Publication Data

Moore, Richard B. (Richard Benjamin)
Richard B. Moore, Caribbean militant in Harlem : collected writings, 1920–1972 / edited by W. Burghardt Turner and Joyce Moore Turner with biography by Joyce Moore Turner ; introduction by Franklin W. Knight.
p.   cm. — (Blacks in the diaspora)
Bibliography: p.
Includes index.
ISBN 0-253-31299-X
1. Caribbean Area—Politics and government—1945-   2. Nationalism--Caribbean Area.   3. Afro-Americans—History.   I. Turner, W. Burghardt, 1915-   . II. Turner, Joyce Moore, 1920-
III. Title.   IV. Series.
F2183.M66 1988
970.004'96—dc19   87-37382
                                                                          CIP
ISBN 0-253-20759-2 (pbk.)

2 3 4 5 6 96 95 94 93 92

To Mitchell, Sylvia, Richard,
who, in the Age of Media,
must not forget the message.

CONTENTS

ACKNOWLEDGMENTS

The eighty-five-year lifespan and wide interests of Richard B. Moore required extensive research, which was aided by librarians, archivists and scholars from widely distant areas such as Barbados, Britain, The Netherlands, California, Massachusetts, New York, and Washington, D.C. While it is impossible to mention all who were helpful at the Schomburg Center for Research, the National Archives, the Moorland-Spingarn Research Center at Howard University, and the Frank Melville, Jr. Memorial Library at the State University of New York at Stony Brook, recognition and appreciation is acknowledged for the expert assistance in locating materials extended by E. Christine Matthews, Chief, and Michael Chandler, former Chief of the Barbados Archives; Alan Moss, Librarian at the University of the West Indies at Cave Hill, Barbados; Esther J. Walls, Associate Director of Libraries, and Irvin Kron and Jacob Lipkind, Librarians at State University of New York at Stony Brook; Ernest Kaiser at the Schomburg Center; and Carl Seaburg, Archivist at the Unitarian Universalist Association.

The scholars who were very generous in sharing materials included Philip S. Foner, Irma Watkins-Owens, Jeffrey B. Perry, Anthony De V. Phillips, Wilfred D. Samuels, and Elinor Des Verney Sinnette. We were especially grateful to Robert A. Hill, Theodore Kornweibel, Jr., and Mark D. Naison, who made a substantial number of records available that were critical to this study. It is impossible to express adequately our indebtedness to friends of Richard B. Moore who, through conversations, correspondence, and interviews provided invaluable insights and encouragement: Errol W. Barrow, Reginald G. Barrow, Wynter A. Crawford, Alice T. Moore, Jill Sheppard, Hilton A. Vaughn, and John Wickham of Barbados; Herbert Aptheker, John H. Clarke, Eulalie M. Domingo, Richard Hart, Harry Haywood, Louise T. Patterson, and Edith Segal. We wish to express special appreciation to Hermie Dumont Huiswoud and Reginald St. Aubyn Pierrepointe, who not only provided enthusiastic and warm support along with substantial data but read the manuscript for accuracy for the periods with which they were most familiar. Thanks are also due Ingeborg B. Knight, who typed all of the selections from Richard B. Moore's writings and translated German documents.

The editors gratefully acknowledge permission granted by the Schomburg Center for Research in Black Culture to quote from the letter of August 7, 1922, from Richard B. Moore to Arthur A. Schomburg.

The editors accept full responsibility for the selection and editing of Richard B. Moore's works and the preparation of the manuscript. The project, however, could not have been completed without Franklin W. Knight, to whom we are most indebted for his prodding and guidance, as well as for his incisive introduction to this volume.

INTRODUCTION
THE CARIBBEAN BACKGROUND OF
RICHARD B. MOORE
Franklin W. Knight

Richard Benjamin Moore was strongly representative of a Barbadian and English Caribbean colonial society that no longer exists. Tall, gaunt, with penetrating eyes, stentorian voice, and a natural gift for oratory, Moore was a commanding figure. His background paralleled in many ways those of a number of his contemporaries who shaped the political evolution of the Commonwealth Caribbean during the major part of the twentieth century: William Alexander Bustamante of Jamaica, Vere Bird of Antigua, Albert Marryshow of Grenada, Grantley Adams of Barbados, and Captain Arthur Andrew Cipriani of Trinidad. Politicians all, they combined a fierce insular loyalty with an ardent vision of political office as the principal engineer for social change. All except Moore sought and achieved significant political office in their respective territories. Yet Moore, as the "man of words," was a presence that could not be avoided during the first five decades of the century. His voice was frequently heard, not only in North America but also in Europe, extolling the virtues of political emancipation for his native English-speaking islands. This cause and an unrelenting opposition to racial injustice were the twin pursuits of his life.

Like his better-known contemporary and staunch adversary in the Harlem of the 1920s, Marcus Mosiah Garvey (1887–1940), Richard B. Moore was a typical turn-of-the-century Anglophone Caribbean product. His formative years were spent on the small, quaintly English-speaking island of Barbados before the First World War.

Barbados at the beginning of the twentieth century was a remote British imperial outpost. Encompassing 430 square kilometers (166 square miles), it was the earliest English settlement colony in the Americas. Its early history—before the sugar revolutions of the 1640s and 1650s—resembled that of the mainland settler colonies, especially Virginia and the Carolinas, with which it was closely related by trade and migration. By 1680 it was, in the words of Richard S. Dunn, "the richest colony in English America."[1] Its strategic geographical location made Barbados the first port of call for sailing ships traveling between Europe or Africa and North America. But

1

since it was more difficult for sailing ships to tack against the wind, the island did not face many hostile attacks from competing European colonizers in its formative years.[2] Barbados, then, remained British from its initial settlement in 1627 until its formal grant of political independence in 1966.

With its first recorded assembly in 1639, the Barbados legislature ranks as the third oldest representative body in the Americas, falling behind the legislature of Bermuda and the House of Burgesses of Virginia. This rare unbroken exercise in constitutional government continues to exert a strong influence on the island's political culture.

The heavy involvement in sugar cultivation with imported African slaves for two centuries fundamentally affected the development of its political culture. Englishmen in Barbados, no matter how they tried, simply could not duplicate the patterns of their metropolitan culture. The Barbadian reputation as the premier English settlement colony was short-lived. Compared with English North America, English settler society did not flourish in Barbados in the seventeenth century, and the relative failure of Englishmen to thrive on the island helped establish the myth that white people could not survive in the tropics.

By the 1660s Barbados had become a multi-ethnic, multi-cultural, sugar-plantation dominant structure held together with English laws, English institutions, and English military force. The population was a highly transient one, and the island was more a springboard for other settlements than a magnet for the hopeful.

That Barbados could recover to be deemed the "richest colony in English America" by 1680 reflected the rapid prosperity brought about by the sugar revolutions of the preceding twenty years.[3] The social structure of the island was transformed. With the onset of the sugar revolutions, a minority of Europeans managed a preponderant majority of workers of African descent as best they could, producing primarily sugar and sugar by-products such as rum and molasses for export to Europe and North America. Sugar production formed the base of Caribbean economies until the middle of the twentieth century.

The agro-industrial complex of sugar created a rigid social order in the Caribbean and throughout the tropical American world.[4] Based less on lineage than on relationship to the structure of production on the sugar estate, the society contained three overlapping, proportionally uneven divisions of castes and classes. Until the abolition of slavery during the middle years of the nineteenth century, the legal divisions consisted of three castes: superordinate whites, intermediate free persons of color, and subordinate masses of slaves. After the emancipation of the slaves in the nineteenth century, the caste structure yielded to a simple threefold division based primarily on race and color. Caribbean caste divisions, however, were never as rigid as the classical forms found in India, and passing from one caste to the other was feasible.

By the middle of the nineteenth century the white classes in Barbados contained only about 13,000 individuals—down from a high of 20,000 in 1680—constituting some 13 percent of the island's population. The abolition of slavery in the nineteenth century grouped the nonwhites together to form the differentiated masses against whom the whites fought doggedly to exclude or restrict their political participation. Given the disintegration of the plantation society, political participation by the numerically superior nonwhites could be delayed but it could not be avoided. By the later part of the nineteenth century nonwhites were aggresively challenging the whites both for the right to vote and be elected assemblymen and for the right to decide what should be priorities of the emerging state.[5]

The economic legacies of the sugar plantation lasted until well into the twentieth century. While sugar expansion did not entirely destroy the small landholding group, it severely restricted its expansion, especially in the aftermath of slavery, when a large number of ex-slaves sought to establish themselves as independent peasants. As late as 1970, the top 10 percent of Barbadian landholders controlled 77 percent of all the land on the island. Until the diversification into tourism and small manufacturing in the 1970s, sugar and sugar products accounted for nearly 90 percent of the export earnings of Barbados.[6] The island was, to all intents and purposes, still one vast subdivided sugarcane plantation.

The persistent pattern of sugar monoculture discouraged competing forms of agricultural enterprises. With a limited resource base for manufacture and mining, and a growing population after the nineteenth century, even the most buoyant resurgence of sugar could not provide adequate employment for the labor force. Moreover, sugar prices continued to fluctuate, as they have throughout its bittersweet history, and the increasing competition from beet sugar meant that cane-sugar producers have always been on the defensive, always extremely sensitive to their market vulnerability. The result for Barbados was continual high unemployment and a continuous stream of migrants away from the island. Indeed, by the beginning of the twentieth century outmigration had become an economic imperative for most of the aspiring classes.[7]

Economic and market sensitivity represented only one of the enduring legacies of the sugar plantation. The other was the predominant African population. Introduced as the major working force along with the rise of the sugar plantation in the middle of the seventeenth century, Africans soon outnumbered their masters and the rest of the free population. As early as 1680 African slaves outnumbered free whites by two to one, and by 1834 Africans and persons of African ancestry accounted for more than 87 percent of the entire population. This proportion was approximately the same in 1986.[8]

It is clear that a preponderantly Afro-Barbadian society would eventually modify the norms and manners of the original English settler society. Nevertheless, the English influence remained strong in Barbadian life, not merely in the manifestations of political culture but also in the affinity for individual industry, a sense of politeness and orderliness, and what the visiting American journalist William Sewell described in 1860 as "neatness and tidiness."[9] Sewell described the capital, Bridgetown, as "European." By contrast, Anthony Trollope, the literary English civil servant who visited Barbados the same year, was less impressed by its natural beauty and charming Europeanness than Sewell. Yet Trollope wrote that it could pass, except for the heat, as "an ordinary but ugly agricultural county," and Bridgetown, "a second or third-rate English Town."[10] James Anthony Froude, the Oxford University historian who visited Barbados in 1887, found the island to be "thoroughly English." "The language of the Anglo-Barbadians," he wrote, betraying his rather narrow circle of acquaintances,

> was pure English, the voices without the smallest transatlantic intonation. On no one of our foreign possessions is the print of England's foot more strongly impressed than on Barbados. It has been ours for two centuries and three quarters, and was organized from the first on English traditional lines, with its constitution, its parishes and parish churches and churchwardens, and schools and parsons, all on the old model, which the unprogressive inhabitants have been wise enough to leave undisturbed.[11]

Despite the variations in these descriptions, the vision of Barbados during the later years of the nineteenth century was one of an unmistakable English colonial society, and that is an important consideration in evaluating the background of Richard B. Moore. But, as was the case elsewhere in the English Caribbean, it was a society in the vicious throes of economic distress.

Throughout the 1890s Barbados suffered from a series of droughts, plant disease, and poor harvests. Sugar prices continued to fall as the market became more competitive. Between 1884 and 1905 world sugar production of beet and cane increased from a total of about 4.7 million tons to approximately 14 million tons. At the same time, the price for sugar on the world market fell by approximately 65 percent.[12] Producers using inferior technology simply ceased to exist. In many of the smaller eastern Caribbean islands such as St. Vincent, Saint Martin, Dominica, Grenada, and Montserrat, the cane-sugar industry virtually disappeared. In Barbados the industry survived but paid a very high price. Wages for laborers fell dramatically and the impetus for Barbadians to leave their island to find employment abroad gained considerable momentum. Since the local economy was so inextricably linked to the export economy, the repercussions of the prolonged decline in the price of sugar produced a severe crisis among the middle and lower classes.

Neither economic hardship nor migration was new to the Barbadian experience. Barbadians formed a major part of the English-speaking Caribbean tide that moved hither and yon around the neighboring islands and throughout the Americas. They were found in especially large numbers in Trinidad and British Guiana (now Guyana), where they comprised the first corps of policemen and elementary schoolteachers. They spread to Venezuela and engaged in a variety of activities ranging from ranching to gold mining. They formed one of the largest components of the laborers building the Panama Canal, and Bonham Richardson confidently claims that the financial returns from that migration virtually resurrected the economy and began a social revolution on the island.

Richard B. Moore and his family apparently did not share in the economic bonanza brought on by the canal construction in Panama, for as we shall see, it was precisely at this time that he chose to leave Barbados for the United States in order to improve his personal economic circumstances.

The Barbadian character that Moore so strongly illustrated was forged during those trying years of the late nineteenth and early twentieth centuries. Barbadians seemed to adjust well to adversity and to place great confidence in education, planning, and hard work. Certainly in the case of Moore his self-acquired education and his penchant for hard work cannot be questioned. Those were attributes of his native land. In a biography of Sir Grantley Adams, the first Barbadian prime minister as well as first prime minister of the ill-fated West Indian Federation, the historian F. A. Hoyos described that spirit, that character:

> A former governor of Barbados had once said that, if the island experienced
> a series of poor harvests, emigration or pestilence would be the only alterna-
> tives to starvation. The people of Barbados seemed to realize the truth of this
> remark. They worked industriously wherever they went and sent back large
> sums of money to their hardpressed relatives at home. And the significant
> thing was that the latter used this new income not to purchase the pleasures
> of the moment but to buy property and to give to their children a better
> education than they themselves had enjoyed.[13]

As early as the 1820s several hundred West Indians (including an unspecified number of Barbadians) began to emigrate to the United States, forming a Caribbean counterpart to Manifest Destiny.[14] This Caribbean immigration is dwarfed by the flood of Europeans who were then arriving in the United States before the first immigration law of 1924 brought some order to the event. The Caribbean contribution was a steady stream of about one thousand per year for the half century or so before 1924. And while it is difficult to sort out the Barbadians from the other West Indians arriving in the United States, it can be ascertained that between 1913 and 1924 more than 104,506 Barbadians left their homeland.[15] Considering that at that time the total population of the island was only about 200,000, this figure represented a major exodus.

Research is currently under way to find out who were those emigrating Barbadians and what were their chosen destinations.[16] It seems that a large proportion of those who went to the United States—immigrants like Richard B. Moore—ended up in or gravitated toward Harlem, then fast becoming the greatest black diaspora community in the world.

By the 1920s Harlem had become, as Jervis Anderson so graphically described in *The New Yorker*, and later in his book, "A Black metropolis."[17] Harlem was a mecca not only for the massive black migration northward from the southern states, but also for Africans and people of African descent throughout the world. The big night clubs such as Edmond's, where Eubie Blake and Ethel Waters began their careers, had relocated there from midtown Manhattan, and so did such celebrated meeting places as Barron Wilkins's café. Above all, the black churches reestablished themselves in Harlem following the movement of their congregations: the Abyssinian Baptist Church, described as "the largest and richest Negro Baptist congregation in the world," and the pulpit that catapulted Adam Clayton Powell, Sr., and his son, Adam Clayton Powell, Jr., to fame;[18] the St. Philip's Protestant Episcopal Church; the Union Baptist Church; Mother A.M.E. Zion; St. Cyprian's Episcopal Church, with its "large West Indian membership"; Mount Olivet Baptist; and St. Benedict the Moor Catholic Church, significant for its interracial congregation.

The Harlem in which so many West Indians began their American odyssey in the 1920s was undergoing the "Harlem Renaissance," to use the phrase common in the period and the title of a study by Nathan Huggins.[19] This renaissance was artistic, intellectual, and political. An enthusiastic and inspired outpouring of music, poetry, novels, and drama treating the black American experience with greater confidence and greater sensitivity delighted audiences across America and throughout the world. In music and the theater great names emerged in Harlem: Eubie Blake, Florence Mills, Fletcher Henderson, Louis Armstrong, Ethel Waters, Paul Robeson, Marian Anderson, and Duke Ellington. In poetry and prose the names of Claude McKay (who arrived from Jamaica in 1912—three years after Moore and four years before Marcus Garvey—), Alain Locke, Langston Hughes, Arna Bontemps, Countee Cullen, Wallace Thurman, Jessie Fauset, Jean Toomer, and Nella Larsen emerged to delight the public for decades.

Politics, too, constituted an integral part of the Harlem Renaissance as various groups of Afro-Americans gave vitality to such organizations as the National Negro Business League, organized by Booker T. Washington in Boston in 1900; the National Association for the Advancement of Colored People, founded in New York City by W. E. B. Du Bois and others in 1909; the National Urban League, founded in 1910; and the most dynamic, flamboyant, and political of them all, the Universal Negro Improvement Association of the expatriate Jamaican Marcus Mosiah Garvey, founded in Jamaica in 1914 and transferred to New York in 1916.[20]

The phenomenon of Garvey—who had his share of confrontations with Richard B. Moore—can only be properly understood by looking at the social and intellectual environment in the British West Indies at the turn of the century.[21]

Harlem did not evoke a similar response in the blacks moving from the

South and those moving from the Caribbean. If blacks came from the American South to discover themselves in Harlem, the same was not exactly true of the majority of English-speaking West Indians. West Indians who came to Harlem, or anywhere else in the United States, certainly discovered more about themselves. But what they discovered most was a consciousness and an identity of being West Indian, rather than a collection of Jamaicans, or Barbadians, or other islanders; of sharing a West Indian nationalism and a pan-African solidarity. This pan-African solidarity, albeit with an accentuated preference for Ethiopia, is still strongly evident among the Ras Tafari movement throughout the Caribbean.

Above all, West Indians who came then to Harlem did not arrive with the same degree of personal self-consciousness and collective sensibility of being part of a minority as did their fellow Afro-Americans from the South. They came from islands that did not practice overt racism or encourage legal segregation. Even those who first discovered that they were "black" in Harlem—and sometimes were surprised at some of those who called themselves "black"—shared an awareness that in their home societies, nonwhites constituted the overwhelming majority of the population, and the old plantation system of mutually reinforcing social cleavages was crumbling. In their home islands West Indians of all origins were socially and politically on the move.[22]

Except at the highest level of politics and economics, the white society back in the West Indies found itself in slow retreat. A new generation of educated, literate, and sometimes prominently certified Afro-West Indians had emerged since the 1880s to challenge the nature of English colonialism, with its disproportionate privileges for the heirs of the old plantations and the dwindling minority of European descent. Some had been accepted into the political system but that was not enough. Everywhere throughout the English Caribbean nonwhites steeped in a British elementary education, versed in the language of William Shakespeare and the King James version of the Holy Bible, and adept at British parliamentary procedure, agitated for more reforms that would permit them to broaden the base of political power. Although restricted to the educated emerging classes, this new political consciousness flowed in two streams. One was patently populist, independent, and inspired by a semi-millennial spiritual return to Africa. From this stream came such individuals as John J. Thomas, the articulate sociolinguist and formidable literary opponent of James Anthony Froude, and the political leaders George Padmore, the grey eminence of Kwame Nkrumah of Ghana, and Marcus Garvey. The other stream was orthodox, reformist, and restrained by the moderate tutelage of the activist Fabian Society, and especially the Fabian supporters within the then newly formed British Labour Party. The most ardent representatives of this group were individuals like Sandy Cox and J. A. G. Smith in Jamaica, or Andrew A. Cipriani in Trinidad, or D. M. Hutson of British Guiana. Although they did not depend on the masses for political support (since the masses did not yet have the vote), they knew how to incorporate the masses into political action and strongly supported legal recognition of the fledgling trades union movement.[23]

The West Indies produced an unusual number of individuals who, regardless of whether they worked within the system, like Cirpiani, Cox, Hutson, and Smith, or outside the system, like Williams, Padmore, and Garvey, were exceptionally articulate, politically sophisticated, and energetic. Whether they stayed at home or they adventured abroad, they actively used the local Caribbean press to publish fiery letters and provocative articles on a variety of subjects. Their attack on British colonialism was relentless, and they refused to concede that anything short of self-government—or in the case of Marcus Garvey, world government—would serve the best interests of the Caribbean masses. The organizational talents of this generation were also extraordinary. Although success for their efforts was fleeting before the Second World War, their zeal never flagged. They laid the groundwork for the generation that eventually succeeded to political office and who made history in their individual territories: these later politicians included Norman Manley and Alexander Bustamante in Jamaica; Robert Bradshaw in St. Kitts; Vere Bird in Antigua; Eric Matthew Gairy in Grenada; Grantley Adams in Barbados; Uriah Butler, Albert Gomes, and Eric Williams in Trinidad; Cheddi Jagan and Forbes Burnham in British Guiana; and George Price in British Honduras (now Belize).

What distinguished these men, and others whose names are less illustrious but whose roles in the political and social evolution of the Caribbean cannot be overestimated, was their ability to transcend the limitations of their socioeconomic status and locale. They grasped whatever small opportunities were offered and in serving themselves they served their countries well. They were men of the moment, with determination, stamina, and vision. Not all were saints or prophets. But collectively their virtues overshadowed their weaknesses, and their personal histories remain an irrefutable testimony to the advantages of the open society. Richard B. Moore belonged to this generation.

If, in the case of Moore, the history that he helped create left him somewhat bewildered in his old age, we do well to remember that his was a full as well as a long life. To the very end his zeal for battle remained undiminished. Nor did he waver from the two causes that he had espoused in his youth, justice for the racially oppressed and political independence for his beloved Caribbean states.

This edited version of the papers of Richard B. Moore serves three interrelated purposes. In the first place, Moore is an important political figure in both Caribbean and United States history. While he did not create the vast political organization of his fellow West Indian expatriate, Marcus Garvey, his political activism was long, focused, and consistent.[24] Moore fervently believed that in furthering the cause of political independence for the English-speaking Caribbean he could simultaneously inspire dignity and pride in all Afro-Americans. He considered both goals to be inextricably entwined, so that one way or another they formed the basic thread that connected all his writing, his speeches, and his political activism. The quest for personal and political freedom as well as individual dignity permeated his thought from his early evangelical phase, through the period of self-doubt, the espousal of socialism, and finally his nonactivist final years.

More than any other individual, Moore educated the American public in the proper semantic distinctions between "black," "Negro," and "Afro-American," terms used interchangeably in the Afro-American community until the 1960s. Moore himself used the terms interchangeably and unselfconsciously until the 1950s. (See selections in chapters 7 and 9.) But some time after he parted company with the Socialist Party and began his extensive reading and collection of African history, his consciousness was altered. Whether from his own reading and reflection or as a reaction against the pejorative use of "Negro" and "Black" by the public media in the United States, Moore arrived at the conclusions expressed in *The Name "Negro"—Its Origin and Evil Use,* published in 1960, that persons born in the Americas of African descent ought to be more accurately referred to as Afro-Americans. (See chapter 10.) He was evangelistic about this change. Year after year he would raise the issue at the annual meetings of the Association for the Study of Negro Life and History, until finally he was instrumental in getting the association to modify its official name.

In the second place, the career of Richard B. Moore offers an illustration of the typical Caribbean immigrant to the United States during the early decades of the twentieth century. Although their number was small, they had an inordinate impact on local politics and events. As such the picture of the racial political activity and erratic occupational existence of Richard Moore certainly parallels that of other outstanding West Indian expatriates such as Marcus Garvey, W. A. Domingo, Claude McKay, George Padmore, Cyril Briggs, Otto Huiswoud, and Hermie Dumont Huiswoud. On the one hand we have here an intimate and detailed account of a small, vocal, active community of radicals centered in Harlem but whose interests were without national boundaries. On the other hand, their stories provide an essential window into the general social history of Afro-Americans both in the United States and throughout the Caribbean.

W. Burghardt Turner has written elsewhere on the remarkable backgrounds and the long tradition of oratory, polemicism, newspaper publishing, and strong moral outrage at the injustices of racism, segregation, and discrimination among Afro-Americans.[25] In his book about the Harlem Renaissance, Nathan Huggins describes the political position of W. A. Domingo as outlined in A. Philip Randolph's *The Messenger* and Marcus Garvey's *Negro World,* stating that "few other Negro spokesmen talked in terms of a labor party as a viable political vehicle".[26] Yet the number of Afro-American adherents to the socialist and other prolabor parties was certainly not "few," and in this volume Joyce Moore Turner and W. Burghardt Turner describe some of the articulate spokesmen involved in the agitation of the 1920s, thereby significantly modifying our knowledge of this long-neglected dimension of life in Harlem. This knowledge is valuable for all Americans, regardless of color or race. By knowing these past experiences better we not only expand our own historical horizon but we also know ourselves a little better too.

In the third place, Richard B. Moore and his associates (mainly in Harlem but not exclusively there) played a significant role in fostering West Indian nationalism. George Padmore had made this perfectly clear in a column in *The Negro Champion* (vol. 1, no. 14, p. 3):

> Those in this country can be depended on to play an important role in helping their countrymen to foster such a forward movement as the Federation of the Islands. Their group life in America has tended to unite them and establish a common fellowship, for it is the first time in the history of these peoples that they have been brought together and out of this contact has come a unity of feeling and sentiment, that could well be utilized in promoting a movement for their common good.

As the documents in chapter 11 illustrate, Moore kept the issue of the political future of the Caribbean islands constantly before English, American, and local Caribbean audiences. His group badgered organizations with memoranda, letters, and addresses while constantly sending money and correspondence to the leading political groups and daily newspapers in the larger islands of Jamaica, Barbados, and Trinidad.

The issues of political reform for the Caribbean had loomed as a major preoccupation of the British government during the 1930s. A series of social and economic outbursts throughout the English territories—euphemistically called "disturbances" in the official reports—forced the English government to introduce universal adult suffrage, beginning with Jamaica in 1944 and gradually extending to all the other colonies.[27] Political reforms ushered in a new group of political participants, a group that had been, in most cases, at the head of the recently organized trades and workers unions throughout the region. Politics in the Caribbean and Harlem were not much different. The nostalgic recollection of those days and their activities by Norman Manley for his Jamaica could quite easily have been made by Richard B. Moore for his Harlem:

> The early years when young volunteers were out six nights a week, not seeking or even thinking about achieving power, but totally dedicated to changing the political structure of Jamaica, totally dedicated to the task of political education, seeing with total clarity that political education was a function of political action in every field of life.[28]

Mr. Manley went on to say that his "generation had a distinct mission to perform. It was to create a national spirit with which we could identify ourselves as a people for the purposes of achieving independence on the political plane."[29] Moore, the contemporary of Manley, accepted that mission with tremendous enthusiasm.

In the years immediately after the Second World War, the general political inclination was for a federation of all the English-speaking territories in the Caribbean. The conference held at Montego Bay, Jamaica, in 1947 created the blueprint for a new political association.[30] Some common institutions such as the University College of the West Indies resulted, and ten years later arrangements for a political system were put in place with ten island units, excluding the mainland enclaves of British Honduras (Belize) and British Guiana (Guyana).

Moore and his colleagues were ardent supporters of this federation (see chapters 6, 11, and 12). They could not have been otherwise. More so than the populations remaining in the region, they had forged a strong political consciousness in the crucible of exile. In the United States—and in Canada or England—they were considered collectively as West Indians and to them it seemed at last that the political reality had finally caught up with the convenient designation. They saw absolutely no incompatibility between being Jamaicans or Barbadians or Guyanese and being West Indians, and they combined readily, harmoniously, and delightfully their insular or territorial and their regional identity.

Unfortunately, the euphoria of a political federation was short-lived. Federation was a paltry, insecure structure that collapsed after four years. In 1961 Jamaica held a referendum to leave the ten-unit body and opt for its own independence, which it attained the following year. Eric Williams, the scholarly premier of Trinidad, declared that "In political arithmetic, one from ten leaves nothing," so Trinidad and Tobago also sought and gained their political independence in 1962 as a unified state. That officially ended the experiment in federation. The creation of mini-states caught on like wildfire in the region. Barbados, Moore's birthplace, and Guyana became independent in 1966 with the other territories following in the years afterward.

Although disappointed by the political fiasco of the federal experiment, Moore accepted the new nation-states with unrestrained enthusiasm (see "Independent Caribbean Nationhood"). He shared no illusions about their abilities to sustain their economies, but his abhorrence of colonialism was stronger by far than any misgivings about the future. Political independence was sufficient to take him back to his native land. It was a poignant homecoming, as his daughter describes in her biographical essay here, and he had considerable difficulty grasping the changes that had taken place in his absence. Yet to the very end he remained proud of the achievement of his people and of his contribution to their struggle.

Not much emerges here of Richard B. Moore the private man. He was extremely reticent to speak about himself, even in the twilight of his long life when his sharp mind needed small provocation to recall with astonishing detail the events of nearly half a century before. He had exceedingly strong opinions, but they were tempered by a versatile intelligence and an insatiable curiosity. Given his career, he probably did not and could not distinguish between his private and public lives. This does not suggest that Moore was not, or was incapable of being, sentimental. His letter to his only granddaughter (chapter 13) amply supports his sensitivity. But Moore did not allow himself to dwell on sentiment. He was an individual of over-whelming singlemindedness, whose ability was narrowly channeled into political commitment. To the end of his life he served his political causes with missionary zeal and single-minded effort.

The writings and speeches of Richard B. Moore address themes that are deeply rooted in the Caribbean and wider American experience. He shared fully and actively the preoccupations of his time as well as those of the black minority in the United States and the colonized majorities throughout the Caribbean. He articulated his sentiments with clarity, with eloquence, with vision, and with humor. His large library he left to his native island. His thoughts and his public experience, as far as they can be captured, belong to all who share his deep sense of history. This edited work is merely a small tribute to a valiant warrior. It is important to understand that the Turners have not attempted to provide an intellectual analysis of his thinking or textual criticisms of his writing, for Moore was, above all, an agitator and polemicist. He had to be listened to, not read. Although these selections cannot capture the magnetism of his oratorical skills, they do reflect the mainstream of his thinking, and the wide span of his interests. Richard B. Moore was a courageous man, a loyal citizen, and a dedicated foe of all forms of injustice. While he might not have kept the religious faith, he fought a good political fight and delighted in the fact that in some ways the world caught up with his ideas.

NOTES

1. Richard S. Dunn, *Sugar and Slaves. The Rise of the Planter Class in the English West Indies, 1624–1713* (Chapel Hill: University of North Carolina Press, 1972), p. 83.

2. Spanish attempts to discourage permanent settlements by rival powers may be followed in Carl and Roberta Bridenbaugh, *No Peace Beyond the Line. The English in the Caribbean, 1624–1690* (New York: Oxford University Press, 1972), pp. 22–33. Early non-Spanish settlement may be followed in Samuel Eliot Morrison, *The Oxford History of the American People* (New York: Oxford University Press, 1965), pp. 59–100. See also Franklin W. Knight, *The Caribbean. The Genesis of a Fragmented Nationalism* (New York: Oxford University Press, 1978), pp. 50–66; and Cyril Hamshere, *The British in the Caribbean* (Cambridge, Mass.: Harvard University Press, 1972), pp. 9–125.

3. The sugar revolutions have been chronicled in many accounts. Beside Dunn and Bridenbaugh, cited above, see Noel Deerr, *The History of Sugar*, 2 vols. (London:

Chapman and Hall, 1949–50); Sidney Mintz, *Sweetness and Power. The Place of Sugar in Modern History* (New York: Viking Press, 1985); and J. H. Parry and P. M. Sherlock, *A Short History of the West Indies* (London: Macmillan, 1956), pp. 63–80.

4. See Knight, *The Caribbean*, pp. 93–120; Barry W. Higman, *Slave Society and Economy in Jamaica 1807–1833* (New York: Cambridge University Press, 1976). The literature on the free coloreds is large and growing. See William G. Sewell, *The Ordeal of Free Labor in the British West Indies* (New York: Harper and Brothers, 1861); Jerome Handler, *The Unappropriated People. Freedmen in the Slave Society of Barbados* (Baltimore: The Johns Hopkins University Press, 1974); Gad J. Heuman, *Between Black and White. Race, Politics and the Free Coloreds in Jamaica, 1792–1825.* (Westport, Conn.: Greenwood Press, 1981); Mavis Christine Campbell, *The Dynamics of Change in a Slave Society. A Sociopolitical History of the Free Coloreds of Jamaica, 1800–1865* (New Jersey: Fairleigh Dickinson University Press, 1976); Edward L. Cox, *Free Coloreds in the Slave Societies of St. Kitts and Grenada, 1763–1833* (Knoxville: University of Tennessee Press, 1984); and *Neither Slave Nor Free: The Freedmen of African Descent in the Slave Societies of the New World,* ed. David W. Cohen and Jack P. Greene (Baltimore: Johns Hopkins University Press, 1972).

5. See Bridget Brereton, *Race Relations in Colonial Trinidad 1870–1900* (London: Cambridge University Press, 1979); and *Trade, Government and Society in Caribbean History 1700–1920,* Essays Presented to Douglas Hall, ed. Barry W. Higman (Kingston: Heinemann Educational Books, 1983).

6. Virginia R. Dominguez and Jorge I. Dominguez, *The Caribbean. Its Implications for the United States* (New York: Foreign Policy Association, 1981), p. 38. See also Ransford Palmer, *Caribbean Dependence on the United States Economy* (New York: Praeger, 1979).

7. The savage effects of repeated recession in the sugar industry and the intimate connection with migration may be followed in the excellent monograph by Bonham Richardson, *Panama Money in Barbados, 1900–1920* (Knoxville: University of Tennessee Press, 1985).

8. All the data on race and color for the Caribbean are imprecise, and considerable divergence exists in the sources. For example, The Gleaner Company's *Directory of Caribbean Personalities in Great Britain and North America* (Kingston, Jamaica: The Gleaner Company, 1985), p. 305, comments: "Barbados is less racially diverse than most of the other West Indian territories. 80 percent are of direct African descent, 5 percent are of European descent and 15 percent are mostly of mixed Afro-European origin."

9. Sewell, *Ordeal of Free Labor,* pp. 15, 22–23. Note that Sewell also observed: "The distinctions of caste are more strictly observed in Barbados than in any other British West India colony. No person, male or female, with the slightest taint of African blood, is admitted to white society" (p. 67).

10. Anthony Trollope, *The West Indies and the Spanish Main* (New York: Harper and Brothers, 1860), pp. 200–201.

11. James Anthony Froude, *The English in the West Indies* (New York: Charles Scribner's Sons, 1888), p. 38.

12. *Crisis and Change in the International Sugar Economy, 1860–1914,* ed. Bill Albert and Adrian Graves (Edinburgh: ISC Press, 1984), pp. 1–7.

13. F. A. Hoyos, *The Rise of West Indian Democracy* (Bridgetown, Barbados: Advocate Press, 1963), p. 10.

14. For Caribbean migration, see *Migration and Development in the Caribbean. The Unexplored Connection,* ed. Robert Pastor (Boulder: Westview Press, 1985), p. 7; *Female Immigrants to the United States: Caribbean, Latin American and African Experiences,* ed. Delores Mortimer and Roy S. Bryce-Laporte (Washington: Smithsonian Institution, 1981); and *Return Migration and Remittances: Developing a Caribbean*

Perspective, ed. Roy Bryce-Laporte, et al. (Washington: Smithsonian Institution, 1982).

15. *International Migrations. Volume 1. Statistics*, ed. Walter Wilcox (New York: National Bureau of Economic Research, 1929), p. 515.

16. Dawn Marshall of the University of the West Indies, Barbados, is currently engaged in research along these lines. For more on Caribbean migration, see *A Bibliography of Caribbean Migration and Caribbean Immigrant Communities* compiled and edited by Rosemary Brana-Shute (Gainesville: University of Florida Libraries, 1983).

17. Jervis Anderson, "That was New York," *The New Yorker*, June 29, 1981, pp. 38–79; July 6, 1981, pp. 55–85; July 13, 1981, pp. 38–79; July 20, 1981, pp. 42–77. The quotations in this paragraph are all from the articles. The book was published by Farrar, Straus & Giroux, New York, in 1982, with the title *This Was Harlem. A Cultural Portrait, 1900–1950*.

18. Adam Clayton Powell, Jr., was born in New Haven, Connecticut, in 1908. He succeeded his father as pastor of the Abyssinian Baptist Church in 1937. By then a leading Harlem politician, Powell won election to the New York City Council in 1941 and to Congress in 1945, serving until 1970. Flamboyant and slighthly eccentric, Powell chaired the House Committee on Education and Labor between 1960 and 1967, when he was excluded on a series of charges pertaining to both his personal life and his professional duties. Reelected in 1967 and 1968, Powell was eventually seated in 1969 but lost his reelection bid the following year. He died in 1972.

19. The phrase "Harlem Renaissance" was commonly used in the 1920s, and Richard B. Moore himself makes reference to the term as early as 1920. In a personal communication to me dated January 26, 1986, Mrs. Joyce Turner wrote: "I have checked a few sources re 'Harlem Renaissance.' It is unfortunate that Huggins in his study on the era, failed to give a derivation of the term. At least I could not find such a discussion. While his study is about the period and therefore appropriately the title of a book, you may want to consider referring to Alain Locke who 'acted as a sort of spiritual father for the Renaissance,' according to Houston A. Baker, Jr. *Black Literature in America*. In the issue of *Survey Graphic* which served as the basis for the book, *The New Negro*, Locke wrote an article on Harlem in which he stated: 'The special significance that today stamps it as the sign and center of the renaissance of a people lies, however, layers deep under the Harlem that many know but few have begun to understand.' In the foreword to his book he concludes, 'Justifiably then, we speak of the offerings of this book embodying these ripening forces as culled from the first fruits of the Negro Renaissance.' Part I of the book is labelled, 'The Negro Renaissance.' . . . I still find it fascinating that Cyril Briggs wrote in 1918 that his magazine, *The Crusader*, would be dedicated to a 'renaissance of Negro power and culture throughout the world.' " Compare Nathan Huggins, *Harlem Renaissance* (New York: Oxford University Press, 1971).

20. See Richard A. Long, *Black Americana* (Secaucus, N.J.: Chartwell Books, Inc., 1985); and *The Marcus Garvey and Universal Negro Improvement Association Papers*, ed. Robert A. Hill, vols. 1–4 (Los Angeles: University of California Press, 1983–).

21. See the splendid introductory essay by C. L. R. James, "The West Indian Intellectual," in the new edition of J. J. Thomas, *Froudacity. West Indian Fables Explained* (London: New Beacon Books, 1969), pp. 23–48. Biographical works on Garvey are numerous. Among the best, see Tony Martin, *Race First. The Ideological and Organizational Struggles of Marcus Garvey and the Universal Negro Improvement Association* (Westport, Conn.: Grenwood Press, 1976).

22. The best general history of the period is Gordon K. Lewis, *The Growth of the Modern West Indies* (New York: Monthly Review Press, 1968).

23. See, for example, Bridget Brereton, *A History of Modern Trinidad* (Kingston,

Jamaica: Heinemann Educational Books, 1981); and Walter Rodney, *A History of the Guyanese Working People* (Baltimore: The Johns Hopkins University Press, 1981).

24. The Garvey Research Center at the University of California at Los Angeles has generated more than 15,000 items on Garvey's worldwide activities. Richard B. Moore was not careful about preserving his record—and in some cases probably wanted no records at all—a wish continually betrayed by the surveillance and often imaginary reporting of the Federal Bureau of Investigation.

25. W. Burghardt Turner, "The Polemicists: David Walker, Frederick Douglass, Booker T. Washington and W. E. B. Du Bois," in *Black American Writers. Bibliographical Essays*, ed. M. Thomas Inge, Maurice Duke, and Jackson R. Bryer, pp. 47–132 (New York: St. Martin's Press, 1978).

26. Huggins, *Harlem Renaissance*, pp. 53–54. The quotation is on p. 54.

27. See Ken Post, *Arise Ye Starvelings* (The Hague: Nijhoff, 1978), and Post, *Strike the Iron*, 2 vols. (New York: Humanities Press, 1981); Trevor Munroe, *The Politics of Constitutional Decolonization. Jamaica, 1944–62* (Mona, Jamaica: Institute of Social and Economic Research, 1972); Sabadeo Basdeo, "Walter Citrine and the British Caribbean Workers Movement during the Moyne Commission Hearing, 1938–1939," and Brinsley Samaroo, "The Trinidad Labor Party and the Moyne Commission, 1938," in *Politics, Society and Culture in the Caribbean*, ed. Blanca G. Silvestrini, pp. 239–73 (San Juan, Puerto Rico: University of Puerto Rico, 1983).

28. *Manley and the New Jamaica. Selected Speeches and Writings, 1938–1968*, ed. Rex Nettleford (London: Longman Caribbean, 1971), p. 363.

29. Ibid., p. 365.

30. The sad episode of the West Indies Federation may be followed in Lewis, *Modern West Indies*, pp. 343–86, which cites letters from Moore and Domingo to Caribbean newspapers.

I.

Richard B. Moore and His Works

Joyce Moore Turner

I

FROM BARBADOS TO HARLEM

Richard Benjamin Moore's embracement of radical views could not have been predicted on his arrival in New York on July 4, 1909. Although not quite sixteen, Moore had already worked for four years and viewed himself as a man prepared to assume responsibility as head of the family. As the steamship S.S. *Cuthbert* entered the harbor, he eagerly anticipated embarking on a promising career in the land of opportunity. His father had died when he was eight years old, and as the small family watched their resources continually dwindle, they had decided that New York held the most promise. His two older sisters, Marie and Lucille, who had left Barbados a year earlier, had already demonstrated that jobs were to be found.

As immigrants entering the United States prior to the establishment of severe restrictions on nationals of the British Caribbean colonies, Moore and his stepmother were spared the trauma of Ellis Island. Following the completion of immigration documents, including those prepared in Barbados showing proof of financial assets, they were quickly reunited with his sisters and his stepmother's sisters who had preceded them. It was a joyous occasion, yet the deafening firecrackers evoked alarm. He wondered, what kind of people carried on like this? To the serious, deeply religious young man such behavior was a bit of a shock. While the Independence Day celebration marked a discordant entrance upon the American scene, it did not dampen his expectations. It did cause him, however, to reflect on his years in serene, bright Barbados.

The Moore family had lived in Hastings, Christ Church, where Richard was born on August 9, 1893. Although he hardly knew his mother, Josephine Thorn Moore, he always regarded her death when he was three as a great loss. His father, Richard Henry Moore, was a building contractor who constructed various types of buildings throughout the island, including the home in which the family resided and a home for the Robert Barrow family with specifications to withstand all hurricanes. This latter building was so sturdy that it not only withstood the hurricane of 1898 but exists today as a landmark, serving as the Rectory of St. Augustine Anglican Church in St. George Parish.[1] In addition to carrying out custom building and repairs, his father tried to maintain a regular operation by constructing homes that he would then sell and operating a bakery and grocery.

Hastings and the area to the east where the Moore family resided after 1896 were typical linear residential communities situated along the southern coastal main road between the capital city, Bridgetown, and the fishing village of Oistins. Moore described the location of his home as "a comfortable middle-class area." At the turn of the century the colony was experiencing a serious economic downturn, but Moore's family was able to operate a business and purchase land. Both Richard Henry and his wife, Josephine, were parties to contracts transferring property as well as investing in the Barbados Building and Loan Association. Their status is reflected in the popular jingle chanted in the neighborhood as a result of Moore's father showing his concern for the people of the community by selling a loaf of bread for four cents instead of the usual six cents: "R. H. Moore, six for four, / Keep starvation from the door."

In Moore's memory, the house in which they lived following his father's remarriage to Elizabeth McLean was a two-story stone house with a large living room, dining room, and three or four bedrooms, located on Stream Road east of Hastings. This structure contrasted with the temporary chattel houses of most of the people. The yard had provisions for a horse and buggy, chickens, and a vegetable garden. At one time his father had a fashionable landau in which he would drive the family to services in Oistins.[2]

His father was a lay preacher of a small sect, The Brethren, with congregations in Bridgetown and Oistins. They had withdrawn from the Anglican church, which they considered "the whore of Babylon." On Sundays evangelican prayers and sermonettes inspired by the spirit of the Lord were conducted during the morning and evening by converted lay members who sat together in the front. There were no trained ministers, although Moore recalls two English preachers visiting his father and conducting some services. His father attended to the children's baptism by dipping them in a four-foot cement cistern behind the house.

While the baptism seemed rather unceremonious, almost traumatic to Richard, or "Benny" as he was called by the family, the preaching had a profound effect. His sisters, and at times the servants, became his congregation as he fashioned sermons that he conceived as real rather than play. He had not experienced any "psychological shaking experience commonly called conversion," but as a result of his exposure he assumed the role of preacher.

His formal education began with classes conducted by Jacob Price, a retired elementary school headmaster. The students were Price's two sons and the three Moore children, who were fairly close in age. Price was a perfectionist who insisted that if anything was worth doing, it should be done well. When he decided that Moore was a good candidate for the Empire-wide penmanship competition conducted by the John Jackson Institute in England, he coached his young pupil, administering strong scoldings if a stroke went the least bit below the line. His high standards resulted in Moore's winning first prize for his age division in 1902 and again in 1903, and the experience instilled in Moore strict attitudes toward writing in particular and work in general. The proud family decided that the prize of 2 shillings should go toward the purchase of new suits for Benny. He recalls that being neat and clean was part of the teaching—that one had to appear as "befitting persons of worth."[3]

In 1902 Moore experienced his second great loss. By the time he was ready for more advanced education, his father had died. Fortunately, his father had previously made an agreement with James J. Lynch to educate his son in payment for Moore's repairs on Lynch's house. His stepmother arranged for him to live with her sister in Bridgetown so that he could attend Lynch's Middle Class School. In later years the name of the school evoked great mirth, but at the time, it seemed very appropriate to be joining a larger group of students at the middle level.

After Price's class, Lynch's school seemed large, with a staff of three: Lynch; his son, Albert; and his daughter, Marie. It served poor families with middle-class aspirations but primarily sons of the upper class who had not succeeded in gaining entrance to Combermere School or Harrison College. Moore performed well under the demanding tutelage of Lynch, and as he advanced he helped instruct the younger students. While Lynch honored the agreement for three years, he claimed that advanced subjects taught by his son were not part of the agreement. On April 12, 1905, at the age of eleven, Moore graduated, the proud owner of a book presented for winning the first prize for English grammar, and determined to go to work.

He soon got a position on Lynch's recommendation at C. F. Harrison & Co. as a junior charge clerk. This department store conducted most of its business on credit and it was Moore's job to convert the price of the item being charged from pounds and shillings to dollars and cents, the decimal system in which accounts were maintained and calculated. He worked as an apprentice without compensation for one and a half months, then was paid four dollars per month. Within three years he managed to earn increases to six and eight dollars per month; he then shifted to Alleyne, Arthur & Co. as junior clerk in the office for nine dollars, with an increase to ten dollars per month by the time he left Barbados.

During the period that he lived in Bridgetown he had contact with his father's brother, a carriage painter, and another family, also named Moore but not related as far as can be determined. He grew quite attached to Mrs. Josephine Moore, calling her "Muds." She treated him like a member of her family and nursed him following an attack of typhoid fever.[4]

In Bridgetown he attended revival services held by a Euro-American evangelist, James M. Taylor of Knoxville, Tennessee. He did not fully comprehend the preacher's reference to the South and the "War Between the States" or the agitation among older Afro-Barbadians caused by Taylor's objections to being housed with them. Moore, however, did heed the sermons and was especially moved by the hymn played by Mrs. Penny, the mission organizer's wife, on the hand organ: "Tell Mother I'll Be There." He still carried a memory and love for his mother even though his stepmother, who had not had any children of her own, was in every way a mother to him and his two sisters.

Following one of the hell-fire sermons, he could sense during the long night his bed sinking and flames rising around him. He determined that he would have to avoid hell if he were ever to see his mother in heaven, and the next evening, when sinners were called to the mourners' bench, he presented himself and gave up his worldly belongings—his silver watch and chain. After a while he considered that he had been saved and became one of eight young converts of the Christian Mission who were given special indoctrination and encouraged to spread the gospel. His stepmother tried to get him to continue as a member of the Brethren sect, to which she and his father had been dedicated, but his newfound religion was central to his being. He and his fellow converts, Lewis Braithwaite, Clement Clarke, Edwin Clarke, Marcus Jordan, Henry Nurse, Edgar Phillips, and Cheltenham Smith, went about Barbados preaching.[5] They gained attention more because of their youth than their message.

Elizabeth Moore had been married only a few years when she was faced with the sole care of three stepchildren and an abrupt change in income. On the death of her husband, the merchant from whom he had obtained money and building materials seized properties owned by Moore in order to recover the outstanding debts, leaving the family without assets from their father. According to Bishop Reginald G. Barrow, who knew Moore's father, the elder Moore was one of the best builders in the island and had a comfortable income but would not have accumulated savings because of his generosity and concern for the poor. "There was a lot of poverty in the island at the time. Anybody who had money and had sympathy could not keep what they had. . . . He was the type of person who always wanted to be helpful."[6]

The only property left was that which had not been involved in the business: Mrs. Moore's six acres, acquired from the proceeds of the small plantation that had been distributed among the heirs upon her father's death, and an adjacent two-acre plot with a two-story stone house in Bath Village on the road between Hastings and Oistins, which had been willed to the children by their natural mother, Josephine Thorn Moore.[7] To economize, Elizabeth Moore moved the family out of the large house. She managed well but the sale of portions of the property for income continually reduced the available resources.

When Moore insisted upon going to work instead of continuing his education, she was concerned. He was young and very bright and should be in school. The girls were also eager to work. She consulted her sisters, who advised going to America, where opportunities for the children would be better. She moved to Fairchild Street opposite the railroad station in

Bridgetown, and for a short time the children all worked to save money for the trip to the United States. She was not sure what Mr. Moore would have wished, but she felt she had to do something before the income reached a point where mobility would no longer be possible.

In 1908 Marie and Lucille left Barbados, and in June of 1909 Moore and his stepmother set sail, leaving behind the childhood name of "Benny." It proved to be a permanent move for the children, but Mrs. Moore remained in New York about ten years—just long enough to see all the children married.

In 1909, "destination, New York" did not mean Harlem for passengers of African descent. Harlem had not yet developed as a "Negro Mecca," and Caribbean immigrants joined relatives in various areas of the city. Mrs. Moore's sister and her son lived on West 99th Street, and room was found there for the two new arrivals along with Lucille.[8]

The task of locating a job began immediately, as Moore joined the nephew who was seeking employment with the Fall River Line. Instead of a job, he ended up with tonsillitis. A physician detected a lung condition, possibly tuberculosis, for which he prescribed medicine to build the body against the rigors of the coming winter. He also recommended fresh air in the park. Moore was crushed by this turn of events. After a few outings in nearby Central Park, he rejected the diagnosis of tuberculosis, pitched the medicine as far as he could, and went home to announce to his mother that there was nothing wrong with him and he was going to work.

Another of his stepmother's nephews recommended him for a job as office boy with an advertising firm. His tasks consisted of cleaning and dusting the office in the morning, answering the switchboard, and filing for four dollars per week. For several months he got along well until he showed an interest in one of the stenographers. He left on her desk a sketch of her he had drawn with the verse of a current song, "Lonesome," written in shorthand. When he returned from lunch he was met with many scowls and much advice from the bookkeeper: "Richard, I know you weren't born here. You don't understand this situation. Colored young men don't have anything to do with white young ladies. You might lose your life."[9] The nephew who worked in the building learned of the transgression and delivered a severe lecture later that evening. It did not end there. The young woman's boyfriend became menacing and the mood so untenable that he decided to leave the job.

The architectural design of Manhattan created jobs for which Caribbean immigrants and southern Afro-Americans had no preparation but quickly mastered. Every skyrise building required elevators, and often their operation was assigned to the "colored boys." Moore's next job, in a men's clothing firm on 14th Street, was a prelude to a series of jobs as an elevator operator and was similar to those resorted to by colleagues he was to meet. He remained on that job long enough to receive increases over the initial five dollars per week, then operated an elevator for higher wages in a department store on the corner of Sixth Avenue and 14th Street for about one year.

In an effort to utilize skills he had acquired in Barbados and obtain work in a different line, he applied to the YMCA for courses in typing and shorthand. He had been taught shorthand by Bruce Price, son of his schoolmaster Jacob Price, who recorded the House of Assembly proceedings in Bridgetown. He wrote one hundred words per minute but needed typing. At the 57th Street YMCA he was met with evasive questions such as, "Why don't you go to the free evening high school?" and finally was denied admission on the basis that the students would not accept him. He insisted he only wanted to listen to the teacher and did not plan to have any contact with the students; they insisted they would not enroll him. He left with the retort that this was not a Christian institution and they should have the word "Christian" chiseled off the lintel over the entrance.[10]

He then tried some courses at Harlem Evening High School and New York Preparatory School, a private institution that prepared students for college, but the subsequent jobs as bellhop in a hotel and elevator operator in an apartment house required such hours and changing shifts that he could not maintain his studies. The long hours and arduous work taken to improve his earnings seemed to require a physique greater than his 140 pounds. His stepmother was not well or prepared to work. They had moved in with a friend of his stepmother's but really needed an apartment, even though the original plan to unite the family was no longer pressing with his sisters' marriages.

What Moore considered his first good job developed when a neighbor, John A. Ross, recommended him for a job with a silk manufacturing firm. After operating the elevator for a while, he was given a position as a raw silk clerk and in time became the head of the department responsible for the stock. He remained with the firm about ten years, from before the war until about 1923.

While efforts to find and maintain employment and take courses were his major concern and consumed most of his time and energy, he attempted to reach out for other activities and relationships. Soon after his arrival he attempted to locate a religious group of the same persuasion as the Christian Mission he had joined in Bridgetown. He located the Christian Missionary Alliance on Eighth Avenue, which seemed similar to his Barbados group, and determined to attend services. He soon discovered that they were segregating people of color in the gallery. This observation evoked no overt reaction; he simply left quietly and never returned. Internally, however, his indignation raged and burning questions began to plague him. Instead of hell in the hereafter, he began to discern a hell on earth.

For a brief period recreational interests attracted him. He sought out other members of the New York Barbadian community and became involved in the formation of the Ideal Tennis Club in 1911. He was acquainted with the sport in Barbados but not as a participant. There had been no opportunity to play, for it was still a "gentleman's sport" confined to the Euro-Barbadian Belleville and Strathclyde Tennis Clubs. He indicated that he served as president and that the club established the first tennis courts in Harlem.[11]

He also joined with a small group desirous of establishing a printing business in Harlem. In 1916 he became a partner with Isaac Newton Braithwaite, a court stenographer; Orlando M. Thompson, an accountant; and one or two others in the Cosmo Letter Company, which brought to Harlem the first multigraph machine, and subsequently, the Cosmo Printing Company, which introduced the first linotype machine.[12] Later, in keeping with his interest in a socialist society, he was a chief founder and served as treasurer of the Pioneer Co-operative Society. The grocery and delicatessen conducted on the Rochdale Co-operative Plan featured southern and West Indian products. Unfortunately this venture met with disaster when the business manager speculated in coconuts that spoiled before they could be sold. These enterprises demonstrate Moore's interest in communication and business at an early stage, but they failed to develop into full-time operations and they certainly did not answer the questions plaguing him or satisfy the growing urge to respond to the injustices he discerned.

A description of Harlem in 1916 by Rev. Charles Martin reveals the more positive developments within the emerging community to which Caribbean immigrants like Moore would be attracted. In a church publication he commented upon the increase in the numbers of West Indians and their fraternal societies, the orators of radical and "socialistic" bent who were beginning to appear on street corners, the new Negro bookstore, and the growing number of private libraries with fine collections on racial topics.[13] This was the milieu that lured Moore and other immigrants from the Caribbean as he moved to make Harlem his home.

The rejection at the YMCA school, the Jim Crow section of the Christian Missionary Alliance, the daily rebuffs and insults at work were the personal barbs that underscored the news of more serious and tragic attacks upon persons of African ancestry throughout the land. Lynching, a phenomenon unknown in the Caribbean, was particularly horrifying. It revealed attitudes that were contrary to everything Moore understood about Christianity and had envisioned regarding the United States. As he recoiled from these negative aspects of American life, he began a quest for an understanding of the pained relations, as he termed it, and a basic philosophy by which he might guide his behavior. It was clear he had to seek counsel from sources other than family and church, on which he had relied previously. As he went about the city two avenues to understanding seemed available: the street philosophers and books.

When he was not following the arguments of the Madison Square Park polemicists at Madison Avenue and 23rd Street, he was rummaging through bookstores on Lexington Avenue, 23rd, and 25th Streets. Often the bookstore was substituted for a restaurant and he returned to work with books rather than lunch. He felt he had to read and seek answers to the "way out." The first key was provided when he came upon C. F. Volney's *The Ruins: or A Survey of the Revolutions of Empires*. As Volney traced the development of man, society, government, and religion, he explained how man, rather than God, sows the seeds of despotism and destruction. Moore had never been exposed to such a discussion on the differences and similarities between various religions as Volney presented in a fictional meeting of world nations. The young Barbadian evangelist was struck by the portrayal of a religion that "consecrated the crimes of despots, and perverted the principles of government." In addition to discovering that religion could be used to justify the distinction of persons and thereby impose the tyranny of slavery, Moore was intrigued by glimpses of ancient Ethiopia, where "a people since forgotten, discovered the elements of science and art, at a time when all other men were barbarious, and that a race, now regarded as the refuse of society, because their hair is woolly and their skin dark, explored among the phenomena of nature, those civil and religious systems which have since held mankind in awe."[14] This triple revelation published in London in 1792 struck at the base of his religious understanding, clarified the development of the system of exploitation, and opened his eyes to a new view of Africa.

A second book that marked a significant breakthrough was Frederick Douglass's autobiography, *Life and Times of Frederick Douglass*. Moore's discovery that Douglass was successful not only in freeing himself from the horrors of chattel slavery but in helping to free his fellow slaves by utilizing the tools of communication that were denied slaves, also had a profound influence. The strength of Douglass's character, the courage of his defiance, the power of his oratory, the wisdom of his pronouncements, and the magnitude of his deeds all seemed to establish a model of leadership to be emulated by those who were oppressed. Douglass's life became a standard reference for his entire life, as illustrated in chapter 9. Ultimately he became a specialist on Douglass, writing and speaking about him, drawing analogies and quoting passages frequently, naming organizations and a bookstore in his honor, and publishing an edition of *Life and Times*, which had been out of print for forty years.

While other books directly associated with socialism were also very influential during this period, a little-known volume, *The Call of the Carpenter* by Bouck White, pastor of the Church of the Social Revolution, played a particular role in creating a bridge between Moore's evangelical view of Christianity and a broader humanitarian outlook. This socialist interpretation of Jesus as a worker made it possible for him to accept socialism as a philosophy and to distinguish between so-called Christians of the Bible belt who were lynchers and others who had greater respect for their fellow man regardless of race, color, and class. Ku Klux Klan activities in the South and a representative of the Klan speaking in the white Calvary Baptist Church in New York evoked rage as well as incomprehension, and he needed a new outlook on religion as well as history and social structure.

This quest for answers to questions regarding a political system that permitted, in fact perpetuated, such injustices and a society where groups burned people as well as crosses in the name of Christ, led directly to the embracement of socialism. It was not difficult to learn about socialism or to meet socialists. They and their message were right on the street. Moore's first contact was listening to the speakers in Madison Square Park on his lunch hour. Noon heralded the hour for the soapboxers to share their truth on various subjects. Moore listened carefully to one and then another.

When he happened upon an Afro-American socialist, Hubert H. Harrison, speaking in the park, he was particularly impressed. He continued to seek out this great orator whenever he learned Harrison would be speaking at 96th Street off Broadway, near where he lived, or in Harlem. He was also attracted to the socioeconomic analysis that the Afro-American socialists A. Philip Randolph and Chandler Owen applied to the Negro question, as it was called then. Under the banner of socialism they raised the issue of the treatment of the Afro-American in the United States and the expectation that there was a socialist answer to the barrier created in the United States on the basis of race. When the formation of the 21st Assembly District Branch of the Socialist Party was announced in the July 1918 issue of *The Messenger* magazine, Moore could be counted as a member.[15]

What indeed were the socialists proposing that seemed to make sense? To one from the Caribbean, where social status was based largely upon class, and economic stagnation had stimulated migration, it was a revelation to discover an ideology that clarified the relationship between classes in relation to the economic structure. Later the success of the Russian Revolution demonstrated the possibility of not only changing the economic structure but eliminating discrimination against ethnic groups. The Afro-American socialists' fascination with the Russian model was expressed clearly by W. A. Domingo, a close associate of Moore's in the 21st AD Socialist Club:

> The question naturally arises: Will Bolshevism accomplish the full freedom of Africa, colonies in which Negroes are the majority, and promote human tolerance and happiness in the United States by the eradication of the causes of such disgraceful occurrences as the Washington and Chicago race riots? The answer is deducible from the analogy of Soviet Russia, a country in which dozens of racial and lingual types have settled their many differences and found a common meeting ground, a country which no longer oppresses colonies, a country from which the lynch rope is banished and in which racial tolerance and peace now exist.[16]

Thus Marxism became not another academic exercise but a drama of hope emerging before their very eyes.

As war erupted among imperialist European nations, the stand of the socialists against the war and particularly against the involvement of the United States was in keeping with Moore's growing objection to support for any nation exerting domination over the Caribbean and Africa, which shared the same colonial experience. Maintaining his position against British imperialism, Moore and other socialists took vehement exception to Du Bois's advice to "close ranks" and support the war. Ever strident and militant with words, they battled against service on behalf of the British colonialists while worrying about being drafted for military duty. A Department of Justice informant offered an explanation of one socialist's efforts to avoid being drafted: "Crosswaith . . . a native of Santa Cruz . . . is said to have taken out his first papers just prior to our entry into the war, when war was declared, to have cancelled them and by feigning sickness to have obtained exemption from the British Draft."[17]

That does not clarify how so many of the group escaped service. A notice of the British and Canadian Recruiting Mission reprinted in *The African Times and Orient Review* of October 1918 reveals that the British had not sought to fully utilize their West Indian resources early in the war:

> Within 70 days all British West Indians between the ages of 18 and 45 must enlist in the service of Great Britain or be inducted into the United States Army. . . . Owing to the limited number of coloured subjects who volunteered . . . it was not necessary for such action to be taken before. But . . . it has been decided to fill the depleted white regiments with Negro soldiers instead of having all-coloured or all-white regiments.[18]

Moore was actually spared making a choice by the sudden victory of the Allies. He has indicated that, had the war lasted longer, he would certainly have faced induction.

In the 21st AD Socialist Club he found Afro-Americans and Afro-Caribbeans of various backgrounds. Native-born members were well aware of W. E. B. Du Bois's prophecy that their time would be known as the century of "the problem of the color-line,—the relation of the darker to the lighter races of men. . . ."[19] They felt the need to break out of the accommodationist milieu prevailing despite Booker T. Washington's death in 1915 and to seek equality through new political alignments. The foreign-born members, who had been lured to northeastern cities with dreams of economic and social improvement over the conditions prevailing in the various islands they were fleeing, shared this reaction against inequality and denial of opportunity.

As it had for Moore, the land of opportunity had failed to live up to their expectations. Not only were they barred from decent jobs, in some cases denied access to education, forced to live in particular neighborhoods, and insulted by white clerics and their congregations, but they read daily of lynchings and other brutalities heaped upon blacks in the United States.

This cultural shock is well described by Claude McKay, a friend of Moore's who had come to the United States from Jamaica in 1912.

> It was the first time I had ever come face to face with such manifest, implacable hate of my race, and my feelings were indescribable. . . . I had heard of prejudice in America but never dreamed of it being so intensely bitter; for at home there is also prejudice of the English sort, subtle and dignified, rooted in class distinction—color and race being hardly taken into account. . . . In the South daily murders of a nature most hideous and revolting, in the North silent acquiescence, deep hate half-hidden under a puritan respectability, oft flaming up into an occasional lynching—this ugly raw sore in the body of a great nation. At first I was horrified, my spirit revolted against the ignoble cruelty and blindness of it all. Then I soon found myself hating in return but this feeling couldn't last long for to hate is to be miserable. Looking about me with bigger and clearer eyes I saw this cruelty in different ways was going on all over the world.[20]

For Moore and his fellow Caribbean socialists, prejudice and discrimination based upon race had been heaped upon a sensitivity forged out of the experience with class discrimination and colonialism.

It is somewhat ironic that Moore, Frank R. Crosswaith, Wilfred A. Domingo, Otto E. Huiswoud, and others from the Caribbean joined a political club. They could not officially enroll in a party, sign petitions for candidates, run for office, or vote. They were not citizens. But they recognized the significance of political struggle and power and cast their lot with Afro-Americans who did have the priviledge of voting.

Moore described the 21st AD Socialist Club as a unique branch of the Party—a Harlem variety of socialism made up of militant, vocal young men and one woman (Grace P. Campbell), all of African descent except for one Jewish American. By this time Hubert Harrison had disassociated himself from the Socialist Party and was not a member, even though he had inspired many of these members to embrace socialism. While Randolph and Owens undoubtedly played a key role in establishing the club at the time of Morris Hillquit's campaign for mayor on the Socialist ticket, they did not continue as active participants in the meetings of the group. According to Moore, they were very involved with the publication of *The Messenger* and maintained contact directly with the Socialist Party downtown.

The Harlem group, on the contrary, had little connection with headquarters and developed their study group and educational forum according to their own ideas. On Sunday mornings they gathered without benefit of an instructor to read, study, and comment upon pertinent theoretical works such as *The Communist Manifesto* by Marx and Engels and *Socialism—Utopian and Scientific* by Engels. There was no particular leader; they shared responsibility for maintaining the study group.[21]

A group of members including Grace Campbell, W. A. Domingo, Otto Huiswoud, and Moore organized the People's Educational Forum as a means of educating themselves and the public. Meetings were held every Sunday afternoon in a room in Lafayette Hall on Seventh Avenue and 131st Street. The format called for a speaker's presentation, a period for questions followed by discussion, and then a summary by the speaker. The motto was "Lay on McDuff and damned be he who cries, 'Hold, enough.' " Moore characterized it as an "intellectual battleground," "an arena" where "he who came there would have to be ready to battle for his ideas."[22] Featured speakers included David Berenberg of the Rand School, Franz Boas, W. E. B. Du Bois, Fenton Johnson, William Ferris, Elizabeth Gurley Flynn, Hubert Harrison, Norman (?) Thomas, and Walter White.

On one occasion, when Du Bois spoke on the position and role of labor in the postwar period and recommended that Afro-Americans should not align themselves with either the capitalists or labor but should stand in the middle of the road, prepared to take whichever side offered the most at the time, he was challenged by Moore as tendering impossible advice. Moore insisted that when two trains were approaching each other on the same track, to instruct the people to get in the middle was to tell them to commit suicide. Du Bois countered with the comment, "As for that young man who waves his hands and froths at the mouth, I didn't come here to engage in this sort of exchange. I thought you wanted to learn something but you know everything."[23]

The discourses extended well beyond the Sunday forums. By 1918 Moore was preaching socialism on the streets of Harlem. The socialists were out on some corner almost every night except Sunday. Black Harlem was a relatively small section extending no more than fifteen short city blocks traversed by three broad avenues. While the elevated train structure on Eighth Avenue created a periodic din and shut out the light, Seventh and Lenox Avenues were excellent assembly areas, especially at the junction of 135th Street, the hub where some small businesses were located. The announcements that appeared regularly in *The New York Call* established clearly that the Hyde Park speakers' area was not confined to the northeast corner of Lenox Avenue and 135th Street; by 1921 the socialists were rotating their soapboxes among nine different sites. On the same evening Moore, Ethelred Brown, and H. Leadett would be speaking at Lenox Avenue and 128th Street, while Domingo, John Patterson, and Frank Poree were holding forth at Lenox Avenue and 133rd Street.[24]

Once the stepladder was hauled from a fellow socialist's tailor or cigar shop on 135th Street, the comrades assembled for a street meeting put a standing question to one another: "Well, what shall it be tonight? Shall it be propagate straight socialism or shall we talk Negro-ology?"[25] They were prepared to discuss the meaning and significance of socialism or to deal with the problems and suffering of the Afro-American people and the potential solutions to those problems. Since the Socialist Party had not been able to come to grips with the "Negro Question," there remained two separate topics rather than an integrated approach.

In the era of television domination, it is difficult to imagine the appeal of the street speakers. Ira Reid has pointed out that they were thrust into a new role. "Street-corner speaking became the device through which loyalties were analyzed, interpreted and resolved into group action. The minister, the physician, the lawyer and the soap-box orator became group leaders, either because of the prestige of their positions or because of their vocal audacity in a new societal setting."[26] While several of the socialists, especially Randolph, Owens, and Domingo, expressed their audacity with both pen and voice, in 1918 Moore concentrated more on developing his oratorical skills. The socialist stepladder launched him into a lifetime career of oratory.

Political campaigns to promote Socialist candidates intensified the activity. Heckling by Morris Hillquit's supporters at a meeting in November 1917 at the Palace Casino in support of the fusion mayoral candidate, John Purroy Mitchell, was one of the first activities reported in the literature.[27] Moore recalled, however, that it was Chandler Owen who appealed for order when members of the audience harangued and booed Theodore Roosevelt as he attempted to speak for the Bull Moose Party. Owen asked them to let Roosevelt state his case so that they could answer it.[28]

The initial strategies on Hillquit's behalf were utilized in time on behalf of Socialist candidates including Afro-Americans who were members of the local club. In 1918 Randolph, Owen, and George Frazier Miller were the first of the Harlem socialists to be placed on the ballot. Subsequently other members of the 21st Assembly District Branch such as Grace Campbell, Frank Poree, and W. B. Williams were candidates along with Randolph and Owen, requiring campaign activity. Moore worked feverishly for the local Socialist Party candidates in 1918 and 1920 and later reported that they had been successful in gaining twenty-five percent of the Afro-American vote.[29]

Harlem was in ferment. The Socialist Club was only one example of organized radical reaction. The sense of frustration shared by others in the community is evident from the number of organizations and publications emerging from such a tiny enclave. It was a matter of steps between the offices of Randolph and Owen's *Messenger* at 2305 Seventh Avenue, William Bridges' *Challenger* at 2305 Seventh Avenue, Cyril V. Briggs's *Crusader* at 2299 Seventh Avenue, and Marcus Garvey's *Negro World* at 56 West 135th Street, and no more than a few blocks to homes, soapboxer corners, and meeting halls of the African Blood Brotherhood, Universal Negro Improvement Association, the Liberty League, and other militant organizations.

The intense radical activity in Harlem from 1917 to 1919 could hardly go unnoticed by the government. Campaigns against socialists had already resulted in surveillance and arrests. With the growing red-scare hysteria in

1919, federal and state legislators were pressed to investigate propaganda and agitation in the Afro-American community, even though there was some doubt that Negroes were intelligent enough to mount aggressive campaigns and write militant magazines on their own. Investigations were launched by both the Sixty-sixth Congress, with the assistance of the Department of Justice, and the State of New York Joint Legislative Committee Investigating Seditious Activities (referred to as the Lusk Committee), which culminated in reports filled with accounts of *The Messenger, The Crisis, The Crusader, The Challenger,* and *The Emancipator* and their editors.

It is purely an accident of timing that *The Emancipator* was brought into the historic limelight. By coinciding with the Lusk Committee investigations, the publication received attention that was out of proportion to its duration and impact. Domingo had served as editor of *The Negro World* from its inception in August 1918 to July 1919 and as contributing editor of *The Messenger* commencing with the July 1919 issue. Despite the intense activity of the local press, he and his colleagues decided to enhance their voice with a weekly publication located at 2295 Seventh Avenue, in the midst of the other radical publications. Almost as a response to the federal investigations, he and Moore launched *The Emancipator* in March of 1920 with the assistance of other socialists including Frank Crosswaith and Thomas Potter. Chandler Owen, A. Philip Randolph, Cyril V. Briggs, Anselmo Jackson, and Moore were listed as contributing editors with Domingo as editor.

Explaining their "Reason for Being," the first editorial decried the lack of vision and comprehension of world events among existing Negro newspapers, especially as those events related to the Negro race in America, the West Indies, and Africa. The editors warned of the "wave of reaction and patriotic hysteria," which, "if unchecked, augurs the destruction of all constitutional guarantees and time-honored democratic traditions," and proclaimed *The Emancipator* had come into being "because the very destiny of our toiling race, in whatever land and under whatever flag found, is inextricably bound up with the future of those whose labor produce the wealth of the world. . . ."[30] The struggling publishers were able to release only ten issues during a three-month period, despite attempts to combine the distribution of the newspaper with that of *The Messenger* and *The Crusader.* It is not likely that they achieved the 10,000 circulation alleged in the Lusk Report.[31]

The Emancipator is notable not only for its radical stance but for its attacks on Garvey. By 1920 the widening ideological differences between the socialists and Garvey had resulted in open conflict. A movement to remove Garvey from the scene had been initiated by such figures as Randolph, Owen, and Domingo, and *The Emancipator* was one of several periodicals that attempted to expose Garvey. Moore has recounted Domingo's clever strategy of obtaining advertisements from Garvey's Jewish tailor for *The*

Emancipator, thereby revealing Garvey's "undeniable contradiction between preachment and practice."[32]

The Emancipator was Moore's only association with a publication while involved with the socialists. There is no evidence that he contributed to *The Messenger, The Crusader,* or Dusé Mohamed Ali's *African Times and Orient Review* and its sequel, *Africa and Orient Review,* as reported in various recent publications. He served, rather, as an agent for the distribution of *The Crisis* and *Africa and Orient Review.*[33] During this period he was much more involved as an orator than as a writer and came under lifetime surveillance by the Department of Justice primarily because of his revolutionary oratory.

Regular surveillance of dissidents in Harlem was established as a result of the government reports on the radical Afro-American press. From his office on 135th Street, Agent P-138 could easily observe the socialists stuffing circulars in doors and letter boxes, encouraging men around the Primary Election Booth to vote their ticket, conferring and debating at Martin Luther Campbell's Tailor Shop, "the 'hot bed' of all these radical ideas." He noted that "step ladder orators infested Lenox Avenue," urging the "advisability of casting their ballots this year for the Socialist Party."[34] Reports included a description of a meeting at Socialist headquarters at 116 West 133rd Street, where Domingo spoke on the "Fear of Bolshevism" and

> Moore followed up the discussion by telling the people that they should not lose faith in themselves because they felt themselves a minorative issue. He claimed that Bolshevism did not require adherence of the majority as never has there been a majority. . . . He claimed that the embittered and desperate souls of the minority would reach forth from the most daring agitators of Bolshevism, as long as the continuance of unjust oppression of the present political and economic conditions exist. One old gentleman . . . rose from his seat with tears in his eyes and said that it was unfair of any government to allow their people to be oppressed, receiving no comfort or happiness from their labor but poverty and increasing anxiety at every turn.[35]

While Moore and his colleagues were unaware of the increasing number of individuals serving as informants for the Department of Justice, they were suspicious of some observers. A report in *The Emancipator* on a meeting of the People's Educational Forum at which Chandler Owen was the speaker indicated that Owen made frequent sharp sallies at the three Department of Justice operatives, and that all the speakers denounced them as "snooping spies and suggested that they had worked overtime and should join the bookkeepers' and stenographers' union."[36] Special Agent WW, however, singled out Moore's comments for his report:

> Mr. Moore of the Emancipator bitterly denounced the Department of Justice and termed the Government contemptible that would employ men to spy

upon people in their homes, for the [purpose] of satisfying their curiosity
and inquisitiveness.

He called the men in the employ of this department as Secret Service Men
a bunch of skunks, who always left an unpleasant odor behind them when
they came in contact with people who were clean. After he denounced this
department 3 men of the Department of Justice who were present left the
room.[37]

The enormous energy and anger pent up in men like Moore and
Domingo was not released completely in full-time employment and Socialist Party activities. They continuously sought vehicles through which the
cause of the Afro-American might be advanced. While Hubert Harrison
had their great respect and they responded to his efforts to build the
Liberty League, involvement in the African Blood Brotherhood was more
compelling.

According to Moore, Cyril V. Briggs was not a member of the 21st AD
Socialist Club but frequented their programs. As editor of the *Amsterdam
News,* he expressed a militant stance regarding the plight of Afro-
Americans, West Indians, and Africans. His views were in accord with
those espoused by Moore and others with whom he would become closely
associated, but were evidently less and less acceptable to political figures
able to influence the owners of the newspaper. Not long after the founding
of the 21st AD Club, Briggs was pressured to leave the *Amsterdam News* and
founded his own magazine, *The Crusader,* "dedicated to the honorable
solution to the 'Negro Problem', and to a renaissance of Negro power and
culture throughout the world."[38]

While Moore has been linked by historians to the establishment of both
The Crusader in 1918 and the African Blood Brotherhood, he has always
stressed Briggs's responsibility for their inception. Rather than speak of
"we," he has referred to his role as a response to Briggs's invitation to him
to join the African Blood Brotherhood after it had been formed.[39] The
dates when Briggs initiated the ABB and Moore joined and chaired certain
committees remain shrouded in mystery. The confusion exists largely
because the organization was conceived along the lines of the secret
fraternal orders so popular in that day. It was not until October 1919 that
advertisements for the ABB began to appear in *The Crusader.* When Moore
was queried in the 1970s regarding the ABB's inception, he could not
remember exactly when it was founded but was adamant that it preceded
Garvey's UNIA.

The intriguing puzzle as to whether credence should be given to 1917,
the year given by Briggs to Carl Offord, who conducted an interview in
1939 for the Federal Writers Program of New York City, or 1919, based
upon more compelling evidence, should not detract, however, from
recognition of the role it served. For Moore the ABB was initially a response not to the Garvey movement but to the need for the Afro-American
community to protect itself and to work for the "liberation of people of

African descent all over the world and certainly in the United States."[40] The promotion of the concept of self-protection can be noted as early as 1918 in Briggs's "Aims of *The Crusader*" and 1919 in Domingo's editorials in *The Messenger.*[41]

Moore had been greatly disturbed by the series of "race riots," which he termed "wholesale massacres," occurring across the country. A mass attack on Afro-Americans had taken place in East St. Louis in July 1917, and the pattern repeated from Washington, D.C., to Longview, Texas, with estimates running as high as twenty-five riots in 1919.[42] (For the earliest-known article written by Moore, a tribute to the white workers who died defending a black fellow worker in Bogalusa, Louisiana, on November 23, 1919, see "Bogalusa.") These massacres evoked vehement outcries from the Afro-American community, especially the radicals, whose response included programs for self-defense such as that of the ABB.

The ABB provided a dimension that the Socialist Club could not possibly offer. Ira Reid has identified three factors around which special-interest groups of foreign-born Afro-Americans tended to coalesce: "(1) economic and political adjustment in the United States, (2) mutual benefit organizations, and (3) organizations to foster and perpetuate desirable conditions in, and relations with the homeland."[43] Moore and his associates tried to cover all bases.

The socialists addressed the first need but offered no group benefits or immediate protection to Afro-Americans. The ABB considered self-help the only defense against physical attacks on Afro-Americans, especially when the police failed to protect or supported the attacks. Obviously protection had to be organized secretly from within the community. This concept was not unique to the ABB, but such an organization could promote "fraternal, economic, educational, physical, social benefits" and protection through "calisthenics, workers' co-operative enterprises, forums, co-operations with other Darker Peoples," etc., in various communities.[44]

Last but not least, the ABB offered an opportunity, which the socialists had failed to consider seriously, to address the concerns of those of African descent from an international perspective. The fate of the Caribbean was tied to that of the African nations since the root cause of the problem was imperialism. Moore has stated that, following the development of the Russian Revolution, Briggs became quite interested in Lenin's statement on the right of self-determination of suppressed nations as a basic policy position from which the world could go forward.[45] The appeal of such a concept was not lost on Moore and others from the Caribbean, who were all too familiar with colonialism. If their islands could be aided by the promulgation of self-determination, and the link between Africa, the Caribbean, and the United States made clearer, then the program of the ABB should be supported. Self-determination became the central theme in the lifelong organizational pursuits of Moore and his colleagues.

Early statements of the ABB's aims are not available. Briggs's "Race

Catechism," published in 1918 or 1919, has been accepted as an expression of the organization's aims and serves as a comparison to those statements available for 1920, 1922, and 1923. To the question "How can you further the interest of the race?" he responded:

> By spreading race patriotism among my fellows; by unfolding the annals of our glorious deeds and the facts of the noble origin, splendid achievements and ancient cultures of the Negro Race to those whom alien education has kept in ignorance of these things; by combatting the insidious, mischievious and false teaching of school histories that exalt the white man and debase the Negro, that tell of the white man's achievements but not of his ignominy, while relating only that part of the Negro's story that refers to his temporary enslavement and partial decadence; by helping race industries in preference to all others; by encouraging race enterprise and business to the ends of an ultimate creation of wealth, employment and financial strength within the Race; by so carrying myself as to demand honor and respect for my Race.[46]

Moore certainly subscribed to these tenets, but his interest in the ABB extended beyond its dedication to correcting African and Afro-American history to its militant stance on self-protection and economic adjustment along socialist lines.

The organization was structured with a Supreme Council, of which Briggs was Executive Head, and posts located in various areas of the United States, Africa, and the Caribbean. Moore was a member of both the Supreme Council, whose headquarters were in Harlem, and Post Menelik, the branch that served the New York area. Reports from 1921 reveal that his leadership roles included Educational Director of the parent body and Secretary of Labor Unions and Co-Operatives of Post Menelik, where he also administered the oath to new members along with Post Grand Master Arthur Reid, W. A. Domingo, and Thomas Potter.[47]

The initiation ritual described by Harry Haywood, who joined the Chicago Post in 1922, has been utilized to give an exotic connotation to the word "Blood" in the name of the organization. Moore claimed he did not know about such a rite, which supposedly required the mingling of drops of blood. A Department of Justice informant participating in an initiation administered by Moore failed to mention such a practice.[48] The significance of the name is to be found in the intent of the members to construct an organization consisting of individuals who were "of African blood." In 1920 Briggs stated, "the organization is to be formed of men of African blood for the purpose of liberating Africa from the white race and restoring 'it to its rightful owners.' " He insisted upon organizing "quietly and secretly as other groups have done in the past. . . . We do not believe that you can play effectively against the other man while allowing him to see 'your hand.' "[49]

It is perhaps for this reason that the activities of the early years are not documented. Moore claimed not to know the detailed historical develop-

ment of the ABB.[50] Aside from publicity associated with interactions with
Marcus Garvey, the ABB came to public attention principally when the
Tulsa Post was accused of "fomenting and directing" the race riot in Tulsa,
Oklahoma, in May 1921.

Accusations against the victims placed the ABB in a unique position of
protest and precipitated an intensification of activity by the various ABB
posts. The July *Crusader* reported on three mass meetings organized in
New York:

> All posts of the African Blood Brotherhood were galvanized into renewed
> activity. . . . Mass meetings were held in many cities, notably in New York
> City, where Post Menelik . . . and the Supreme Council co-operated in
> bringing before the public the real facts in the Tulsa riot and enlightenment
> as to the wholly protective purpose of the A.B.B. At a mass meeting on July
> 12, at Palace Casino, New York, over two thousand people turned out and
> were addressed by Comrade Richard Moore, secretary of Labor Unions and
> Co-Operatives of Post Menelik. Comrade Fanning . . . acted as chairman, and
> Comrade W. A. Domingo . . . made an appeal for funds to carry on the work
> of the organization. . . . [A]nother mass meeting is being advertised for June
> 19 at St. Mark's Hall. Comrade W. A. Domingo is slated as the principal
> speaker, with Post Commander Reed (Menelik) as chairman. Still another
> mass meeting is planned for June 29 at Lafayette Hall, with Comrades
> Moore, Domingo and Grace Campbell as speakers. . . . At the Palace Casino
> meeting, the report of the Commander of the Tulsa Post was read. . . . The
> Tulsa Post Commander though present was not introduced as the In-
> telligence Department of the A.B.B. reported the presence in the hall of
> several spies from the Department of Justice.[51]

The riots struck a strident chord in Moore and triggered his emerging
impassioned revolutionary zeal. A Department of Justice agent was indeed
present and made a rather detailed report:

> In view of the fact that Cyril Briggs has got a serious impediment in his
> speech, Domingo and Moore conducted the meeting which was well
> attended. . . . I listened to Moore, who spoke for about one and one-half
> hours . . . and so far I have never heard anyone who spoke so defiantly and
> disrespectfully of the U.S.A. and the flag. Among the things he said were:
> "When I look down at the stripes in the American Flag (pointing down at the
> large flag which draped the bottom of the rostrum on which he stood) I can
> only remember and they only remind me of the stripes in the negroes'
> backs". He said that the home of the free and the land of the brave should be
> "the home of the savages" as to his mind the Americans were savages. After
> reading a newspaper clipping from President Harding's speech before the
> negro college in Pa. Moore told the audience that now they can see what use
> a President is to them and a government, who openly said to negroes that he
> can't and won't do anything for them. He criticized President Harding and
> said it was the privilege of anyone to critize him. "Now," said Moore, "ne-
> groes, Harding told you plainly that he can't and won't do anything for you.

Go out and do something for the protection of your life and properties. Be prepared to fight the white mob who tries to lynch and start a race riot. Fight for yourself and don't wait on the Government." He said he was glad to be a member of the African Blood Brotherhood whose object and teaching was: "Self-defence by negroes and preparation to fight back." He said, that after [this] race riots would be more serious as negroes were now able to fight back after the U.S.A. had trained and armed them and sent them to fight the Germans in France for a democracy which they never received at home; that his watchword to them is: "Get ready—be prepared so that you can fight back when attacked." He concluded by reciting a poem by Claude McKay, "If We Must Die". Moore . . . is the most pronounced Communist and has really become the most outspoken, daring and radical among all the other negro "Reds" in Harlem. He is a regular "fire-eater" and aspires to outshine all the other radicals.[52]

Historical accounts of the ABB have been associated with studies of the Garvey or the Communist Party movements. Without a study from the perspective of the ABB that examines the development of the ABB along with the numerous organizations of the period and their interactions during their formative stages, it is difficult to evaluate the impact of the group and its key members. Moore's accounts are sketchy, but it is clear that he viewed the organization as one of many responses during the period and not one constructed as a counterforce to Garvey or a recruitment vehicle for the Communist Party.[53]

From Moore's perspective, he and his fellow radicals were already in New York debating the causes and effects of oppression against peoples of African descent and constructing their philosophical positions when Garvey arrived on the scene. They became involved in the political thrust of the Socialist Party and certainly did not consider Garvey a radical. Moore had gotten to know Garvey not only through Domingo, who had been associated with Garvey in S. A. G. Cox's National Club in Jamaica and in time became the first editor of Garvey's *Negro World*, but through the Cosmo-Advocate Publishing Company. He has recounted:

Garvey got a desk space from us . . . and we used to have long talks as to what he was after. He was not as aggressive then as he later became, as power excited him. He had not yet started the UNIA; he was struggling to get that going somehow. . . . He soon got it organized with some of the dissidents of Hubert Harrison's organization, the Liberty League.[54]

There is no question that members of the ABB attempted to influence the direction of Garvey and the UNIA, but the philosophical differences sharpened as the ABB and UNIA developed. When the diverging views became infused with personal enmity between Domingo and Garvey and later Briggs and Garvey, it was inevitable that both the ABB and *The Emancipator*, with which Moore was associated, would become embroiled with Garvey. To some degree Moore shared Briggs's and Domingo's opposition to Garvey, but he took an entirely different position as the "Garvey Must Go" campaign mounted.

Moore stated that the major conflict arose when Garvey "endorsed the statement made by President Harding that there were inescapable differences between the races which would make it impossible for them to live together on the basis of equality," in which case "the so-called white man should be the ruler."[55] The socialists discussed Garvey's stand at the People's Educational Forum and adopted a resolution condemning Harding and criticizing Garvey for endorsing Harding. Moore viewed this action and the strong reaction to Garvey's meeting with the leader of the Ku Klux Klan as an opposition on the basis of a philosophical and political position, not as a matter of contest for power, rivalry between leaders, or personal antagonism.

When Domingo and Briggs joined A. Philip Randolph, Chandler Owen, and others to pressure the government to deport Garvey, Moore objected. The names of many of his close associates can be found on the stationery and rolls of the Friends of Negro Freedom, which spearheaded the campaign against Garvey in 1920, but "Richard B. Moore" is singularly missing.[56] Moore stated that when Randolph moved from opposing Garvey's endorsement of racism to the attack on Garvey, "I broke relations with Randolph."[57] He also disagreed with Hubert Harrison when Harrison demanded Garvey's deportation and organized a meeting of the People's Educational Forum in which he discussed the question "Back to Africa or Back to Jamaica?" He argued against both as contrary to the best interests of the Afro-American people. He opposed many of Garvey's ideas and activities at the same time that he fought against the unprincipled "joining with the oppressors of your own people" and the "betrayal of the right to speech."[58] Although critical of his friends' involvement with the government's deportation case and convinced that Domingo sent a telegram congratulating the New York District Attorney for having "bayed the tiger" without consulting him because Domingo was aware of his disapproval, his friendship with Domingo, Briggs, and Harrison survived the difference in positions.[59]

The ABB also managed to endure the confrontation with Garvey and the government charges stemming from the Tulsa riot and eventually became allied with positions of the Workers Party. As with its origin, the facts of the organization's demise are unknown. There is evidence that Moore's involvement lasted as late as 1925.[60] Moore judged that there was not any possibility of collaboration between the ABB and Garvey, and they each went their way. Nevertheless, some writers like Robert Allen have recognized the efforts of Moore and his colleagues as a "search for a synthesis between nationalism and socialism."[61]

Moore's involvement in the Socialist Party, the African Blood Brotherhood, publication of *The Emancipator*, and his recent marriage did not prevent him from responding to a call by Domingo to organize a church in the early months of 1920. The Reverend E. Ethelred Brown, ordained as a Unitarian minister at Meadville Theological School, had decided to try to establish a Unitarian Church in Harlem following a disappointing two-year effort in Kingston, Jamaica. As a close friend of Mrs. Domingo's family in Jamaica, Brown had contact with W. A. Domingo, resulting in a meeting to which Moore was invited.

Brown's history of The Harlem Unitarian Church recounts:

> The historical fact is that eight days after my arrival in New York I called a meeting to consider the advisability and feasibility of organizing a Unitarian Church in Harlem. That meeting was held in a room of the Lafayette Hall, 131st Street and Seventh Avenue, New York City, on Sunday evening, March 7, 1920. The question was carefully discussed and it was then and there decided to organize such a church. The following nine persons signed the roll as Charter Members, namely, Martin Luther Campbell, Grace P. Campbell, Hayward Shovington, Ella Matilda Brown, Wilfred A. Domingo, Frank A. Crosswaith, Thomas A. Potter, Richard B. Moore and Lucille E. Ward. The church was named "The Harlem Community Church" primarily in recognition of the marked interest shown at that early stage of the venture by the Reverend Dr. John Haynes Holmes, Minister of the Community Church of New York.[62]

Moore was one of several socialists who supported the church, and throughout the decade he participated in services and programs. In 1919 he had been married at the Lenox Avenue Unitarian Church in Harlem and was familiar with the tenets of the denomination. He said that he joined Brown's church because he considered it more rational than other churches and would be able to express his views there. He saw his involvement with the church and a socialist political party not as a contradiction but as two aspects of his development. "Socialism developed as a critique of the existing society and what I preached in the Unitarian Church was also critical of society."[63]

In 1926 Brown wrote to Unitarian Headquarters: "I have often spoken to capacity attendances and so has my lay colleague Richard Moore."[64] One of Moore's notable sermons in 1929 responded to Brown's sermon "How I Found Jesus" with "How I Lost Jesus," in which he detailed his personal experiences with the un-Christianlike behavior of the churches and questioned the record of the Christian church as a force for improving the conduct of men. He drew upon Volney's *Ruins of Empire* and Ingersoll's lectures as well as his extensive knowledge of the Bible. It was clear that he had "lost Jesus" not in a political party but in the church.

Brown's report raised but left unanswered an intriguing question, "What relation if any did the fact that the foundation members of the church were socialists bear to the early trials of the movement?" The church remained small and it was a constant struggle for Brown and the church to survive. The socialists employed Brown part-time when he lost his job as an elevator operator. The callous treatment and poor support by Unitarians, with the exception of John Haynes Holmes, further convinced Moore of the hypocrisy of the church.

Moore drifted away from the church, however, not for philosophical reasons. His growing agnostic conviction was not completely out of harmony with the ethical considerations of Unitarianism. The members of the church were broad enough to tolerate his critical position, but pressure was exerted by some of his radical comrades outside the church who feared the church might be more successful in influencing him than vice versa.[65] Even though Moore had come to view organized religion as the "opiate of the people" by the late 1920s, his association with the Harlem Unitarian Church was considered inappropriate by associates in the Communist Party. Not only had Moore traversed the spectrum from the evangelical to the liberal church; by the end of the decade his involvement with organized religion had come to an end.

Moore's relationship with Brown extended beyond the church. In the early twenties both could be found on the socialists' soapbox and in secret meetings of the African Blood Brotherhood, and later with organizations supporting Caribbean independence. Brown's history notes that the first meetings of the church were held at Lafayette Hall, and that "soon after, sometime in 1921, we transferred them to the Lodge Rooms of the American West Indian Association, 149 W. 136th Street." Not recorded in his account is the fact that this building also served as the meeting place for the ABB, and Brown as the organization's chaplain.[66]

It was at a meeting of the People's Educational Forum that the affiliation with the socialists came to a head for Moore and some of his associates. In their Sunday morning study group they had reached the point where they were not satisfied with straight socialist theory because it did not address their questions regarding the status of the Afro-American. At first they had assumed on the basis of the theory they read and statements made by some Socialist Party speakers that socialists were deeply concerned about the plight of the Afro-American people. But as they proceeded they discovered that this was not the case. One of their members, Thomas Potter, had complained in a letter to *The Call* as early as 1911 that the socialists "were as silent as a clam on every question that affects the negro," and charged "if there is one blot on the record of the Socialist Party, it is that of its utter apathy."[67] On the basis of the group's study, they were ready for socialism, but was socialism ready for them?

They determined to force the issue with the leadership of the Socialist Party by inviting Algernon Lee, director of the Rand School of Social Science, to be guest speaker at the People's Educational Forum. They planned a series of questions to elicit the basic position of the Party in respect to the struggles of the Afro-American people, such as lynchings, discrimination, and employment, and to ask about the Party's plans to organize Afro-Americans especially in the South, which they put to Lee during the question period. He replied that the Socialist Party was the party of the proletariat, and by "proletariat" Marx meant workers in industry, but most Negroes were sharecroppers or peasant toilers on the land. The Socialists had a big enough task organizing workers in industry and certainly would have neither funds nor personnel to conduct a campaign to organize Afro-Americans. Such a reply was hardly what the group wanted to hear, even though they had become increasingly familiar with the Socialists' perspective. In the heated encounter, they protested that this admission of no program meant that the Socialist Party had nothing to offer them, and they could not accept such a philosophy and strategy for political action.

This turn of events necessitated a meeting of Moore and his associates after the Forum had adjourned, but before they could determine their next move, they were summoned to the New York office of the Party by Julius Gerber, the Executive Secretary of Local New York, and criticized for having subjected a comrade to such attacks in public. They were warned that if they repeated such behavior, disciplinary action, possibly expulsion, would have to be taken. They countered that there would be no opportunity to discipline them because they could not support an organization that did not consider the importance of supporting the Afro-American's struggles.[68] Interestingly enough, Du Bois echoed these sentiments in 1924, when he declared that "If American socialism cannot stand for the American Negro, the American Negro will not stand for American socialism."[69]

This encounter with the Socialist Party should be viewed in conjunction with Domingo's manuscript, "Socialism Imperilled, or the Negro—A Potential Menace to American Radicalism," prepared to advise Socialists that they endangered their cause by not incorporating a program designed particularly for the education and recruitment of Afro-Americans. Almost a decade earlier Hubert Harrison had pressed the Party to conduct "special work" among Negroes, and in February 1911 he had experienced the bitter disappointment of cancellation of a project characterized by Gerber as one of "great promise" to employ "an organizer who shall devote his entire time to the work of propaganda and the holding of meetings and circulation of suitable literature and addresses."[70]

Domingo's lengthy argument in 1919 for a stand and program by the Socialists, whether Left or Right, pointed to the inadequate efforts of the 21st AD Branch and stressed the need to utilize "specially prepared propaganda" and "competent paid negro speakers . . . touring the country" and to support "radical negro publications."[71] The pressure exerted by Domingo individually, through his essay and direct contact with the Rand School, and in conjunction with his associates in the 21st AD Club failed to have the intended effect. The Socialist Party's response served as a signal to Moore, Domingo, and others that it was time to seek an alliance with activists who were more responsive to the Afro-American's oppression.

It is unknown exactly when and under what circumstances Moore became acquainted with the core of socialists with whom he would spend so many years of agitation. It is clear, however, that the involvement in the 21st AD Club forged a comradeship that traversed many organizations and many years. As the crossroads bringing together a vast mobile population from the South and the Caribbean, Harlem served as a staging area for unique networks forming to act upon the burgeoning ideas. While the membership rolls of the 21st AD Club and the ABB are not available and little is known about the twenty socialists identified by Moore in his writings, such a diverse group could have congregated only in New York during that period (see "Afro-Americans and Radical Politics" and "Africa Conscious Harlem"). Grace Campbell, Frank Crosswaith, W. A. Domingo, Otto Huiswoud, and Moore became known leaders and close friends. Moore, slightly younger than the others except Huiswoud, became closest to Domingo, Huiswoud, and later Cyril Briggs. Perhaps the fact that they had not known one another previously and represented different areas of the Caribbean—Barbados, Jamaica, Dutch Guiana, and Nevis—was symbolic of the Pan-Caribbean interests the four were to espouse in the future.

As this cadre of socialists from different English and Dutch Caribbean areas found one another and new ways of thinking that had not been available to them as colonial subjects, their voices and pens grew more articulate and vehement, and their sense of organization more sophisticated. They cried out and they organized; they organized and they cried out. They became the orators, lecturers, and pamphleteers of Harlem and over the years established untold numbers of organizations despite the fact that they had not had the benefit of higher education. Jervis Anderson has described them as among the young agitators who,

> even without college degrees . . . were about the brightest intellectuals in Harlem. . . . In night schools and in private study, they had trained themselves in literature, history, economics, philosophy, and political theory—all of which they spouted with a natural gift of oratory and, it seemed, a natural talent for pamphleteering. In one capacity or another, they exerted a significant influence on aspects of the racial and political militancy that later evolved in Harlem.[72]

They certainly contributed to the reputation of Harlem as "the most militant community in the black world."[73]

Insight can best be gained from Domingo's description of the perspective of Moore and other fellow Caribbean socialists:

> Unlike their American brothers, the islanders are free from those traditions that bind them to any party and, as a consequence, are independent to the point of being radical. Indeed, it is they who largely compose the few political and economic radicals in Harlem; without them the genuinely radical movement among New York Negroes would be unworthy of attention. . . .

In facing the problem of race prejudice, foreign-born Negroes, and West Indians in particular, are forced to undergo considerable adjustment. Forming a racial majority in their own countries and not being accustomed to discrimination expressly felt as racial, they rebel against the "color line" as they find it in America. . . . Color plays a part but it is not the prime determinant of advancement; hence the deep feeling of resentment when the "color line," legal or customary, is met and found to be a barrier to individual progress. For this reason the West Indian has thrown himself whole-heartedly into the fight against lynching, discrimination and the other disabilities from which Negroes in America suffer.

It must be remembered that the foreign-born black men and women . . . were dissatisfied at home, and it is to be expected that they would not be altogether satisfied with limitation of opportunity here when they have staked so much to gain enlargement of opportunity. . . .

The outstanding contribution of West Indians to American Negro life is the insistent assertion of their manhood in an environment that demands too much servility and unprotesting acquiescence from men of African blood. This unwillingness to conform and be standardized, to accept tamely an inferior status and abdicate their humanity, finds an open expression in the activities of the foreign-born Negro in America.

Their dominant characteristic is that of blazing new paths, breaking the bonds that would fetter the feet of a virile people. . . . [74]

II

RADICAL POLITICS

Moore's intense political activities and job at the silk firm had not removed him completely from the social scene. The handsome, neatly groomed, well-spoken, serious young man who carried himself erect with a bearing of pride and purpose was quite attractive and considered a fine "catch" for some young lady. The one who really caught his eye was Kathleen James, who had come to New York from Jamaica in October 1914. She was a beautiful woman with hazel eyes and fair complexion, a talented seamstress and draper, but, more important, an intelligent woman of about his age who seemed disposed toward socialism while not espousing the cause. After a brief courtship, a traditional wedding took place on June 24, 1919, at the Lenox Unitarian Church in Harlem.

The couple established their residence on 140th Street, close to the apartment Moore had maintained with his mother. His mother moved in with the bride and groom but soon decided that she was no longer needed in New York. His sisters had married and started their families. She begged Lucille to allow her to take her little granddaughter to Barbados for a while, but Lucille and her husband were not prepared to have their first-born at so great a distance. Sadly, Elizabeth returned to Barbados to live with relatives. Many times, she would say that she would do anything to see Benny again, but Moore was not to return to Barbados until twenty years after her death.

In August 1920, his daughter, Joyce Webster, was born. Moore was delighted with his expanded family but considered babies strictly their mother's responsibility. His was the world of work, ideas, and struggle; his time and attention were never allotted to parenting and domestic chores. He maintained throughout his life that his domestic awkwardness stemmed from his mother's insistence that he stay out of the kitchen. While the men were struggling to improve the world and provide for their families, Mrs. Moore and Mrs. Domingo, who had become friends, pushed the baby carriages to the stores. Often the families attended the Unitarian Harlem Community Church with little Karl Domingo and Joyce falling asleep long before the discourse ended.

By 1920 the Americanization process was well under way. While many Caribbean residents in New York did not seek to become naturalized, both Moore and his wife applied for United States citizenship. They had an excellent command of English and their Caribbean accents became modified so that in later years one could hardly discern that their childhoods had been spent in Barbados and Jamaica respectively. The names used in the islands were also lost as employers and fellow workers substituted common nicknames for their given first names. Moore was now addressed as "Dick" for Richard instead of Benny. Likewise, his wife, whose family had called her "Sula" for her middle name, Ursula, was now dubbed "Kitty" for Kathleen. It was not many years before she joined the many women working in downtown factories to help support the family.

Moore's work as stock clerk ranked as "a good job" in the early 1920s. He became disillusioned and disgusted, however, when the firm continued to have him train white workers who were then given training and promotions beyond Moore's level, for which he was never considered. No doubt his organizational involvement reduced his efficiency on the job at times. The mutual dissatisfaction resulted in the loss of his job. For a few years he worked as a receiving clerk for a clothing manufacturer, then found himself back to operating an elevator.

He had built a considerable library, managing to create a milieu similar to the view he observed when he visited Arthur Schomburg's home. His description of Schomburg's books filling the living and dining rooms from ceiling to floor was not too different from his own dining room with china cabinets stuffed with books.[1] He supplemented his income by selling books to friends who were searching for particular volumes.

The break with the Socialists in 1921 left a vacuum despite the intensification of activities with the ABB. Having failed at stirring the sensibilities and sensitivities of the Socialist Party on the "Negro Question," the cadre of the ABB struck out in various directions to influence other movements to incorporate their thinking. During the early twenties Moore and his colleagues faced the critical choice of which radical road to travel.

His friend Otto Huiswoud made his decision early enough to have been the only delegate of African descent to attend the National Left Wing Conference in New York City in June 1919 and was considered, therefore, a founding member of the Communist Party.[2] Both Huiswoud and Arthur Hendriks, a theology student from British Guiana who also left the Socialist Party to join the Communist Party in 1919, urged Moore to join the newly organized radical party, but Moore hesitated. Later, Lovett Fort-Whiteman, who had been active with the Socialists, and Cyril Briggs joined. Moore was still skeptical. He was impressed with the success of the Russian Revolution but disillusioned by the failure of the American Socialists, some of whom were now leaders of the Communist movement, to come to grips with the "Negro Problem."

When the Fourth Congress of the Communist International was called late in 1922, an opportunity was seized to test the position of the international Communist body on the "Negro Question" and possibly create pressure on the recalcitrant American contingent. Otto Huiswoud, attending as an official member of the American delegation under the name of Billings, served as chairman of the Negro Commission. When he introduced the "Theses of the Fourth Comintern Congress on the Negro Question" for adoption by the Congress, he pointed out the necessity of taking into consideration "the psychological factors which enter into the Negro problem," and characterized it as fundamentally an economic problem, "aggravated and intensified by the friction which exists between the white and black races." He declared that the question of race does play an important part. "The Negroes in America and the West Indies are a source of cheap labour supply" and are used by the capitalist class "to suppress the white working class in its every-day struggle." He attacked the unions for their exclusionary policies based upon race and the resulting attitude of black workers against labor unions.[3]

Claude McKay, with the encouragement of Max Eastman, had also made his way to Russia and was considered as a representative of the ABB.[4] To help defray the cost of McKay's trip, Moore and Grace Campbell had mounted a campaign to raise funds in August. In soliciting Arthur Schomburg's assistance, Moore wrote:

> This trip of his should mean a great deal to our race. First of all, he will investigate at first hand the actual condition of the Jews and other minority groups to determine just what advantages or disadvantages have accrued to them under the new regime. Then, he will be able to ferret out what opportunities may exist for the race in the South of Russia where the climate is favourable, and where social conditions may conduce to that welfare which is our age-old quest. Russia, as you know, a virgin country of rich and vast resources, is regarded by many, capitalist and all, as the new land of opportunity. And last but not least he should be able to put his finger upon the pulse of that political movement in the interest of the subject peoples which has been centering thereabouts. Irish, Indian, Turk, Persian, Egyptian, all have been participating in this activity but we of the Western World have not even had an observer there to apprise us of these events and trends which are destined to affect the status quo most profoundly.
>
> Do you think that we ought to get a competent man there at whatever cost, and can you think of anyone better suited than McKay?[5]

Huiswoud was not free to discuss plans and positions of the delegation with McKay, but each man's statement was basically supportive of the other's position. McKay underscored that his race belonged "to the most oppressed, exploited, and suppressed section of the working class of the world," but was the "trump card in their [the capitalists'] fight against the world revolution." He went on to complain about the "great element of prejudice among the Socialists and Communists of America. They are not willing to face the Negro question." He spoke of the attempt by the American Negro radicals to spread information on the Third International Manifesto regarding exploited colonies but warned that the American Communists "first have got to emancipate themselves from the ideas they entertain towards the Negroes before they can be able to reach the Negroes with any kind of radical propaganda."[6] While McKay displayed animosity toward Huiswoud in describing the Russian experience in his 1937 auto-biography, *A Long Way From Home,* it should be noted that in 1922 the two men, who had been associates just prior to their departure for Moscow, were serving as ambassadors in the cause against racial oppression in the United States and throughout the world.[7]

Huiswoud's and McKay's efforts evoked a response; the resolution unan-imously adopted by the Congress declared the Negro problem as "a vital question of the world revolution." It tied the world struggle of the Negro race to the struggle against capitalism and imperialism. The "Theses on the Negro Question" made it the special duty of Communists to apply the "Theses on the Colonial Question" to the Negro problem, recognized the necessity of supporting every form of the Negro movement that un-dermined or weakened capitalism, pledged to fight for the equality of the white and black races and to help force trade unions to admit black workers, and projected a world Negro congress or conference—all activi-ties that Moore and his colleagues had been trying to promote for years.[8]

McKay remained in the USSR for seven months and prepared a report, *The Negroes in America,* in which he quoted at length Domingo's article, "The Maintenance of the Spirit of Radicalism Among White Radicals," which built an argument for the points he and Huiswoud had made at the Congress. He reiterated his admonition that

> every Negro worker knows that, whatever the party, when it refuses to take a stand on social equality to that extent, it also refuses to approach the Negro question. The Workers' party must go further than President Harding on the Negro question. It must . . . establish a completely clear revolutionary program . . . which first attracts to its side progressive Negro leaders and afterwards the wide masses of American Negroes, who are duped by the leaders of the "Back to Africa" movement and by bourgeois reformers.[9]

Briggs informed the Afro-American community through his Crusader Service of the statements made at the Congress without identifying Huiswoud.[10] The ABB members were ecstatic; their cry had at last been heard. Encouraged by the resolutions of the Congress, in 1923 they mounted a more extensive campaign to solicit membership and financial support from left-wing labor organizations, including the Trade Union Educational League in Canada.[11] Huiswoud and Domingo visited other cities to encourage the development of ABB posts. They reported gaining over 300 members and that all of their expenses had been paid for by the posts they visited. Huiswoud also made a trip to Chicago to make contact with the Farmer-Labor Party.[12]

Moore seems to have confined his activities to New York City, serving as secretary of the Harlem Educational Forum, the successor to the People's Educational Forum. Announcements in the local press for the renamed forum did not mention a sponsoring organization, but there is evidence that it represented the efforts of the ABB at that time.[13] The organization experienced considerable difficulty finding a place to rent for meetings and the Crusader Service. Briggs, who was by this time a member of the Workers Party, sought their financial assistance. In September the Workers Party refused to help, but by November Briggs and Huiswoud had forged an agreement for the Harlem Branch of the Workers Party and the ABB to rent quarters for an office and a forum that would "meet jointly for the good of both organizations."[14]

The developing relationship between the ABB and the Workers Party was symbiotic. To move forward the ABB needed the support of the Workers Party pledged at the Fourth International Congress, and the Workers Party needed an Afro-American cadre. Allegations that the ABB was the official Communist organization among Negroes had already surfaced earlier in the year. In July Briggs issued a statement that "The African Blood Brotherhood is not affiliated with the Workers' Party of America, or with any other political party, for that matter, and is not the official Communist organization among Negroes," but such a denial could no longer diminish the perception among former socialist comrades that the leaders of the ABB were communists.[15]

The change in the relationship of the ABB to other organizations can be noted in the development of the Sanhedrin Conference. In January 1923 the ABB announced that it was prepared to respond to the invitation issued by Dr. M. A. N. Shaw of the National Equal Rights League for a conference of Afro-American civil rights organizations. Cooperative planning for an all-race conference began on March 23 and 24, when Briggs, Domingo, Huiswoud, and Moore, representing the ABB, met with representatives of five other organizations: Kelly Miller of The National Race Congress, James Weldon Johnson and R. W. Bagnall of the NAACP, Dr. Shaw and William Monroe Trotter of the National Equal Rights League, Dr. Campbell of the International Uplift League, and George Schuyler of the Friends of Negro Freedom. At the conclusion of the sessions a "Concordat Signed by Six Leading Civil Rights Organizations" was issued, which sought "the closest cooperation and the most harmonious relationship possible among all the agencies working for the civil and citizenship rights of Negro Americans." It pledged that each organization would do nothing to cause friction among the groups and would make every effort to achieve "the greatest possible correlation and concentration of all our forces, that we may present to the common enemy, a united front and inspire in the whole race united action." Briggs and Moore were active spokesmen, Briggs served as secretary, and Domingo signed the Concordat for the ABB. In June the four ABB representatives were still reportedly engaged in planning with the expanded Committee on the All-Race Conference.[16]

During the year the alliance between the ABB and the Workers Party became more apparent, and the editors of *The Messenger* anticipated un-reconcilable differences between the radicals and the more conservative Afro-American leaders. In October, while casting snide references regarding the ABB's "six members," they warned that "whatever conference is held among Negroes it must be à la Negroes and not according to the gospel of St. Zinoviev of the Third International of Soviet Russia."[17]

When the projected All-Race Conference, referred to in the Call to Conference by Kelly Miller as the "Negro Sanhedrin," finally took place in Chicago in February 1924 with representatives from sixty-one organizations, the two delegates of the ABB were reported as working in concert with the five delegates of the Workers Party. They could not maintain the spirit of cooperation in the face of the weak stance taken by the conference against segregated unions. Fort-Whiteman later reported at the Fifth Congress of the Communist International that the conference was dominated by ecclesiastical and petty-bourgeois Negroes and claimed: "Nevertheless we were successful in the last two day of the congress in provoking a split."[18]

Moore's role in the Chicago conference is unclear because he is not mentioned in the daily accounts of the Sanhedrin printed in the *Daily Worker*.[19] It is obvious, however, that the lofty vision of uniting Afro-American leaders, to which he had subscribed early in 1923, had become an event that future historians would rarely mention in accounts of the civil rights movement. Of greater significance to the radicals was the prospect that they were no closer to their goal of the world Negro congress that had been projected in Moscow in 1922.

By mid-decade all the early Harlem militants had assumed their positions on the widening spectrum of radical alignments. Frank Crosswaith and Ethelred Brown had chosen to remain with the Socialist Party; A. Philip Randolph had shifted his concentration to the development of the Brotherhood of Sleeping Car Porters and drifted from his radical socialist stance; Chandler Owen had gone to Chicago, leaving his militancy behind. McKay had remained in Europe and disengaged from politics in order to concentrate on his writing. Likewise, another Jamaican writer, J. A. Rogers, who had lived with the Moore family after settling in New York and joining the *Messenger* group in 1922, had decided not to be a "joiner" but to devote himself completely to research, writing, and publishing historical facts on Africans around the world. Grace Campbell had joined the Communist Party, but Domingo, like other members of the ABB, had decided against any political affiliation. Domingo had faced the fact that radical journalism would never support a family. With the encouragement of his wife, a successful classical pianist and music teacher, he launched a wholesale West Indian produce business.

Moore has stated that his caution and doubts about movements dominated by European Americans, which had been created by the confrontation with the Socialists, had begun to ebb and that he tried the Farmer-Labor

Party before joining the Communist Party.[20] "Our idea was to go over these radical movements to find out just what their position was in respect to the Afro-American people."[21] It is not clear whether he found the Farmer-Labor Party more acceptable as he continued his search for a satisfactory political base concerned with the problems of Afro-Americans, or was pressed to join as part of the effort of the ABB or Workers Party to gain influence within that constituency. Ultimately he cast his lot with the Communists.

The year that Moore made the decision to join the Workers Party is obscure. He consistently placed the year as "late 1920s" or "around the beginning of 1930," while writers describing the movement have guessed the early part of the twenties. Reports of the formation of the West Side Harlem Branch of the Workers Party at the American West Indian Association Hall (site of ABB meetings and the Harlem Community Church services) on June 13, 1922, and the subsequent election of provisional officers including Huiswoud as organizer; Briggs as recording and financial secretary; and Moore, Campbell, and McKay as members of the Propaganda and Educational Committee have given credence to the earlier date.[22] The question may well be moot, for it matters more what philosophy was emerging in Moore's mind and through which activities and organizations he sought to implement those ideas. He explained: "I was becoming more and more militant . . . and I was looking for a more militant means of action against this system. Finally I was impelled to join the Communist Party because I considered that to be the most militant in acting against the conditions which were quite distressing."[23]

The Department of Justice had more than a scholar's curiosity about Moore's association with the Party and attempted on several occasions to establish that he was a member prior to his naturalization on September 11, 1924. The earliest date they could document, however, was 1926, a date provided in testimony by his wife in 1931.[24] The year 1926 is significant not because it may represent his espousal of communism; he had been moving in that direction throughout the decade. Rather it seems to signal his acceptance of the Party as employer. Moore would hardly have described his situation in that manner. In referring to his work for the American Negro Labor Congress and later the International Labor Defense, he said, "My awareness of the viciousness of the society in which I lived became clearer in my mind. I became more involved in the movement in order to change the situation, to improve it."[25]

It is obvious that by 1925 Moore had moved into a position of leadership among the Harlem Communists. When the American Negro Labor Congress was organized in Chicago, October 25–31, 1925, he served on the Resolutions Committee along with Huiswoud, made addresses on at least four occasions, and was elected to the twenty-five-member General Executive Board and the nine-member Council of Directors. Moore registered as a representative not of the ABB but of the obscure Ethiopian Students'

Alliance. In fact the ABB delegates came solely from Montgomery, West Virginia; there was not one from New York.[26]

While Moore was identified by the Department of Justice informant as belonging to the Workers Party contingent, and his rhetoric was compatible with their sentiments, his behavior demonstrated an independent streak. At the open sessions he challenged the wording of the resolutions, insisted that the seven council directors provided for in the constitution be increased to nine, and took the national organizer, Fort-Whiteman, to task for releasing information to the press on Afro-Americans in Russia for training. The resolutions and number of directors were altered along the lines recommended by Moore.[27] The Congress established a newspaper, *The Negro Champion,* with Briggs as editor and Moore, Huiswoud, Fort-Whiteman, and seven others as contributing editors. In 1927 Moore was elected general secretary and national organizer.

It is not only the establishment of the ANLC but the reorganization of the Party structure that marks 1925 as a watershed. In tracing the development of Afro-American work within the Communist Party in Harlem, Mark Naison credits "bolshevisation" of the Party structure in 1925 as enhancing the outlook of the small Afro-American cadre.

> In the reorganized Party, they emerged publicly as spokesmen for an interracial movement. . . . Within a newly centralized, interracial Party, black leaders could mobilize the entire movement behind the struggle for Negro rights rather than only the miniscule black membership. They would have to fight for such an orientation against significant white resistance, but they felt confident that the Comintern would support them in such a struggle.[28]

A conference of the ANLC in 1926 marked Moore's last employment in private industry when his responsibilities in Chicago caused a delay in his returning to work. Even though he notified his employer that he was delayed one day, the job was gone when he reported for work. The ANLC then put Moore on their limited, irregular payroll, and he continued as a paid organizer until the early forties. Records of 1927 reveal that he received forty dollars per week, the same amount as Jay Lovestone, Max Bedacht, Alexander Bittelman, William Foster, and Benjamin Gitlow.[29]

His skill as an orator provided the radical movement with one of its most forceful, compelling, convincing, and eloquent voices. He could hold an audience spellbound for hours. Typical of the reactions to his oratory was McKay's poem "You are the thunder," dedicated and presented to Moore, or Harry Haywood's description: "Richard B. Moore brought the house down with an impassioned speech which reached its peroration in Claude McKay's poem, 'If We must Die.' I was spellbound by Moore; I had never heard such oratory."[30] Fifty years later comrades still recalled Moore's bold, scathing speech delivered as hundreds staged a protest when the Congressional Committee headed by Representative Hamilton Fish, Jr., investigated Camp Nitgedaiget near Newburgh, New York, in July 1930. Described by the New York *World* as "an eloquent and graceful figure despite the trousers rolled up around his knees, the shirt open at the throat," Moore was reported as having said: "American workers will not submit to your tyranny. If this be treason make the most of it. You gentlemen from the South may be interested to know there are no lynchings or pogroms in the Soviet Union. Send your own damned effete parasite sons to the next war. We'll tell you to go to hell."[31] Moore required no written draft or notes; he could be counted on to speak extemporaneously on short notice. This gift made him a valuable asset to the Party. His assignments always included speaking engagements.

Support of Afro-American motion-picture operators in their quest for employment at the Lafayette Theater in Harlem certainly fell within the goals of the ANLC, but Moore's involvement in 1926 developed as a result of a Socialist campaign. Frank Crosswaith had been involved but was reluctant to speak on behalf of the projectionists in the face of a court injunction. When the projectionists sought Moore as their spokesman, he consented and conducted a mass campaign stressing the actions of management and the courts as attacks on the employment and civil rights of the Afro-American. Perhaps there was some satisfaction in pulling Crosswaith's chestnuts out of the fire. Crosswaith, however, was spared arrest, while Moore was dragged off to jail, found guilty of obstructing traffic, and given a suspended sentence.[32]

The most exciting and rewarding experience came in 1927, with the assignment to represent the ANLC at the International Congress Against Colonial Oppression and Imperialism in Brussels, February 10–15 (the founding conference of the League Against Imperialism and For National Independence). Sufficient funds had to be raised. Friends not associated with the ANLC also assisted. When Moore informed Arthur Schomburg of his plans in a casual conversation on the street, Schomburg hastened into a store and presented Moore with a valise.[33]

For some unknown reason, Moore and a few colleagues were able to get the New York UNIA to agree to have Moore represent their organization as well as the ANLC. The subsequent disclaimer and announcement in the *Negro World* that "Moore was never empowered to appear as its representative" was issued too late to prevent listing Moore as a delegate of the ANLC and the UNIA in the official proceedings of the Congress.[34]

The Congress attracted 174 delegates from over 21 countries, including such figures as Henri Barbusse of France, Albert Einstein of Germany, Jawaharlal Nehru of India, and Madame Sun Yat-sen of China. Moore served as *rapporteur* or secretary of the committee on the Negro question. The Common Resolution on the Negro Question, largely drafted by Moore, was introduced to the Congress by five members of the committee: Lamine Senghor (Senegal), who acted as chairman, Max Bloncourt (French Antilles), Carlos Deambrosis Martins (Haiti), J. T. Gumede (South Africa), and Moore, who read the resolution following his introductory remarks. The resolution was adopted unanimously. (For Moore's statement and the text of the resolution, see Chapter 7).

The intelligence memorandum on the conference addressed to the secretary of state of the United States singled out this resolution, "which particularly interests our Government," and went on to report: "This same document makes a demand for the support of the Patriotic Union and Haiti in a powerful campaign to expose to the world the terrible suppression of the Haitian people. . . . This document further speaks of propaganda with a view of inciting rebellious action in the Caribbean Islands and colonies and in Latin America."[35]

Delegates did indeed attack the foreign policy of the "American empire." Apart from the resolution on the Negro question, Moore joined with other delegates from the United States, Latin America, and China in a declaration that stated in part that it was the task of all labor, farmer, and other progressive forces in the United States:

> 1. To fight side by side with nationalists and national liberation movements of the countries under the heel of U.S. imperialist domination, for:
> a. Immediate, complete and absolute independence for the Philippine Islands and Porto Rico; self-determination for all colonies and semi-colonies;
> b. Abrogation of the unequal treaties making virtual protectorates of Panama, Cuba and the other countries of the Caribbean area; c. Withdrawal of U.S. military and naval forces from Caribbean, Central and South American territory, and from China . . . 4. Giving wide publicity to the outrages accompanying U.S. imperialism in Haiti, Santo Domingo and elsewhere.[36]

Imanuel Geiss has pointed out that despite the Comintern's role in initiating and financing the Congress, the communist element kept in the background. "This Congress brought about for the first time collaboration between communist and bourgeois-nationalist forces irrespective of race . . . at a time when European colonialism was still almost unchallenged."[37] This broadly based representation inspired Moore not only because of the receptivity to his concerns but because the Congress seemed to harness the potential of a successful international onslaught on colonialism. Except for Senghor's gloomy prediction that the French were plotting his death, the Brussels Congress was exhilarating.[38]

Moore did not return home immediately. Le Havre, where the French ship *La France* had landed February 5, was also his port of embarkation, but he detoured to Paris, Marseilles, and Antibes to locate Claude McKay. Leaving McKay with all the money he could spare, he returned to Le Havre in time to board *La Savoie* to complete his journey one and one-half months later. He then hastened to distribute copies of the resolution and to make addresses on the Congress and the projected program of the League Against Imperialism.

Participation in the Brussels conference was only one indication of the concern of ANLC leaders for issues beyond the domestic scene. In fact, the ANLC had been projected as an organization "to rally the Negro world: Africa, America and the West Indies, for a struggle against world Imperialism."[39] Articles on conditions in Africa and the Caribbean were constantly featured in the organization's publications, *The Negro Champion* and *The Liberator*. As field organizer, Otto Huiswoud's territory included the Caribbean, where not only did he and his wife report on conditions in the islands, but he aided in the organization of unions. He reported, for example, in 1929:

> Recently the American Negro Labor Congress through its Field Organizer, aided the workers in Jamaica to organize a union. . . . The need for a real strong union, fighting in their behalf, was long felt by the masses. A number of mass meetings were held and the workers demonstrated their interest and appreciation in attending in hundreds. Committees comprising thirteen trades and occupations, such as carpenters, longshoremen, bakers, dressmakers, trainmen, etc., were formed and charged with the task of organizing local unions in their respective occupations. . . . Out of these committees has developed a permanent organization, "The Jamaica Trades and Labor Union."[40]

It is not surprising that Moore and Huiswoud attended the Fourth Pan-African Congress held in New York in August 1927. True to form, they pressed for a more radical position. Moore criticized the Congress for not delving sufficiently into the problems of black workers, urged their organization into trade unions, and proposed alliance with other groups working against imperialism. The report on the Brussels Congress was given by William Pickens, who had been designated as the delegate to represent the NAACP but had not made it to Brussels. He attempted to include Moore on the interim international executive committee, "to give a special report on the Brussels Anti-Imperialist Conference," but W. E. B. Du Bois, in his role as chairman, resisted broadening the representation to include Moore and Huiswoud. Their contribution can be noted, however, in several resolutions, particularly one urging the Caribbean peoples "to begin an earnest movement for the federation of these islands; . . . the broadening of educational facilities on modern lines and labor legislation to protect the workers against industrial exploitation."[41]

The most noteworthy of Moore's accomplishments with the ANLC was organizing the Harlem Tenants League in January 1928. Few Harlemites worked in the community, and organizing around the housing problems of residents was more effective than promoting equality in the trade unions. As president of the League, Moore led protests against evictions, rent increases, and violations of housing codes, and lobbied in Albany on housing legislation. He and his fellow workers, including Hermie Dumont (Mrs. Otto Huiswoud), who served as the first secretary, Grace Campbell, Elizabeth Hendrickson, and Cecil Hope, maintained a barrage of strategies that went beyond the usual literary and legal protests to boycotts, strikes, and mass demonstrations. Among the tenants who supported the League in its fight against rent increases and helped call for a rent strike were W. A. Domingo and George Padmore.[42] Padmore was more, however, than a tenant-member. During the four years that he worked in New York with the Communist Party, he was associated with Moore in the work of the ANLC, including the publication of *The Negro Champion*.[43] Periodically the work of the ANLC was deemed inadequate and ineffective, but the Harlem Tenants League was cited by the Comintern as an example of "joint organizations of action which may serve as a means of drawing the Negro masses into struggle."[44]

The examination of the Negro question by the Comintern had not ended with the Theses of the Fourth International Congress adopted in 1922. In 1924 Fort-Whiteman made another appeal at the Fifth Congress, emphasizing the radical aspect of the problem and seeking a special approach to the Afro-American. He "argued that the Negro problem was psychological as well as economic, and covered all classes of Negroes."[45] The interest demonstrated by the Russians and the resulting influence on the American Party had continued to encourage the small Afro-American leadership. When the discussions in New York and Chicago became particularly difficult and frustrating, Huiswoud would remind the comrades, "If you don't settle it here, we'll settle it in Moscow"[46] They were unprepared, however, for the direction that the Negro question was to take in Moscow at the Sixth Congress in 1928.

A review of Negro work by the thirty-two-member Negro Commission produced a fundamental change in the theoretical outlook and direction of work in the United States. Harry Haywood, who had been attending school in Russia, became one of the proponents of self-determination for the "Black Belt." In propounding the new thesis he attacked not only previously developed theory but also the work of the American Party and individuals, including Moore, despite the fact that he had been out of the United States for four years and, in fact, had never been on the New York scene. This thesis, ascribing the characteristics of nationhood, and thereby the right of self-determination, to Afro-American residents of the southern states, caught the American delegation off guard and presented the Afro-Americans particularly with a dilemma. Four of the five Afro-American members of the Negro Commission resisted. James W. Ford and Otto Hall (Haywood's brother) spoke against it, but the resolution to adopt carried.[47]

Moore, Huiswoud, Briggs, and others had difficulty with the revised approach. The debate and decision had indeed elevated the Negro question to a major position for Party work, but it savored of Garveyism and they feared that its separatist appearance would have little appeal, despite the nationalist consciousness already developed in the Afro-American community. They struggled to comprehend the merits of the argument and, as disciplined members, strove to incorporate the controversial concept into their campaigns.

The enlarged significance of Negro work also brought a response to the pressure that the Afro-American members had been exerting for greater representation on decision-making bodies. In March of 1929, at the Party's Sixth National Convention, Briggs, Huiswoud, Otto Hall, John Henry, and Ed Welsh were elected to the Party's Central Committee. Briggs was appointed as director of the "Negro Department," Harold Williams (Aubrey Bailey) was appointed section organizer of the Harlem section, and Negro work committees were established in every Party district.[48] Moore continued as general secretary and national organizer of the ANLC until its demise in 1930.

He was also nominated to run as candidate on the ticket of the Communist Party on three occasions: the races for the congressional seat representing the 21st District in 1928, attorney general of the state of New York in 1930, and the New York State Assembly representing the 19th Assembly District in 1931.[49] Electioneering was not without risks, especially during the campaign in the fall of 1929 when the police escalated their attacks at street meetings conducted by the Communists. The determination of the police to deter public speaking and assembly was matched by that of the Communists, who viewed the assaults as inspired by Tammany Hall and a breach of civil rights. Night after night a battle for the streets would be waged as speakers were hauled from ladders or platforms, beaten along with bystanders who objected, and arrested. Moore was arrested at least twice and spent three days in jail for lack of funds to pay the fine.[50]

The criticism of the ANLC launched in 1928 raised questions as to whether the organization should be continued. It was recognized that faulty design, limited budget, and caustic confrontations with potential member groups had weakened the Congress. In addition political and personal differences within the party created problems. For example, the Foster-Lovestone struggle for leadership had played havoc with the Harlem Tenants League when Ed Welsh and Grace Campbell sided with Lovestone and tried to steer the League into the Lovestone camp. Moore successfully resisted their efforts to take over the group, then had to contend with the confrontation and expulsion of long-term friends and comrades.[51]

The militancy of the Tenants League and the confrontations with the police during election campaigns had not only demonstrated the loyalty of Moore and his associates to the Party during its internal turmoil under Lovestone; it had impressed the community with the Party's commitment to redressing problems in Harlem. Mark Naison cites the tenants' movement and the election campaign as indicators of considerable political momentum when the Depression struck. He claims:

Its small black cadre, although reduced by the expulsion of the Lovestone group, included people who had been active in Harlem movements since the early twenties and who possessed ability as writers, orators, and community organizers. In their years in the Communist movement, they had waged a successful struggle to make Negro work a central task in the Party and to promote black comrades to important Party posts. They now knew that the entire apparatus of the Party would be mobilized behind their efforts to build a political base in the community. Equally important, the last year and a half of organizing in Harlem had shown them "that the Negro masses can be drawn into revolutionary struggle when the Party intensifies its activities among them in their everyday struggle."[52]

As part of the dialogue on the Negro question, Ford and William Wilson (William L. Patterson) had written that the ANLC was too narrow and proposed that it be replaced with a League of Struggle Against Prejudice and Racial Inequality.[53] In November 1930 at the meeting of the ANLC in St. Louis the Congress was transformed into a new organization, The League of Struggle for Negro Rights. Moore was elected general secretary with Langston Hughes as president.

The new decade brought many changes in Moore's personal and professional life. His wife had become increasingly dissatisfied with his lack of attention to home and his meager, irregular earnings. Her decision to obtain a legal separation was in part a reaction to the lifestyle of agitation and meetings conducted late at night, which Moore and his friends developed to accommodate the long working hours spent downtown during the day. After extolling on the soapbox or deliberating in a meeting, Moore would settle into a stuffed chair to ferret out more ammunition from his books as the cigarette smoke curled above his head. His wife found his missionary zeal, which she did not share, and the inadequate income from the ANLC work unacceptable. She returned to work in the garment industry and became a sample-maker working with the designer in a dress factory. She was able to maintain this more privileged steady employment even during the Depression because of her skill and her fair complexion. She felt obliged to support herself and young daughter but drew the line at supporting her husband. A divorce was never obtained. She continued to work and managed quite well, considering that she had no family in New York, until she became ill with cancer and died in 1946. Years later Moore claimed that he had never left his family but was "put out." Even after forty years he did not want to admit that it was really his decision to pursue radical causes that had led to a broken marriage.

Within a year of the formation of the LSNR, Moore's major assignment was shifted to the International Labor Defense, which in time would have him constantly on the move. The ANLC and the LSNR had been established to involve Afro-Americans and their unions or community groups in addressing problems exacerbated by racial prejudice. The ILD, on the other hand, was designed to respond to legal problems growing out of labor and community confrontations. Even though communists believed there could be no true justice in a capitalist nation, the defense of radicals experiencing conflict with the law was essential.

In March two cases broke that called upon Moore's skills. The first was not a case in the traditional sense, nor even an ILD project, but a trial growing out of the attempt to reeducate Party members regarding racial prejudice. The long-standing complaint of chauvinism on the part of white comrades had never left the agenda of the Afro-American comrades. The 1930 Resolution of the Communist International on the Negro Question had boldly stated that "In the struggle for equal rights for the Negro, . . . it is the duty of the *white* workers to march at the head of this struggle. . . . The white workers must jump at the throat of the 100 per cent bandits who strike a Negro in the face."[54] The eagerness to demonstrate that such resolutions were intended to change behavior as well as recognize a problem reached a crescendo with the Yokinen trial.

August Yokinen, a member of the Finnish Workers Club with health and recreational facilities in Harlem, defended the discriminatory actions by members of the club against three Afro-Americans who had attempted to attend a dance at the hall. The Party chose to try him for white chauvinism in an open "workers' court" at the Harlem Casino. Moore was asked to act as prosecutor for the District Committee but at the last minute was switched to defense attorney. Difficult as it was, he managed to build a case for clemency for Yokinen on the basis that the chief criminal was the capitalist system, which spread the poison of racial and national hatred throughout every stratum of society.

He pointed out that "capitalist imperialism not only doubly oppresses the Negro Masses . . . but . . . also the foreign born workers." After the capitalists, certain Afro-American leaders came in for their share of blame: "Together we must also combat the opportunist Negro bourgeois nationalist misleaders, the DePriests, Du Boises, Garveys, Randolphs, etc. who are . . . attempting to stir up the Negro masses against the white workers and are attacking the foreign-born workers, Negro as well as white."[55] He particularly stressed, however, the guilt of the members of the Party in not rooting out chauvinism.

His characterization of the disgrace of expulsion has often been quoted. In appealing to the court not to destroy Yokinen, he dramatically declared: "We must remember that a verdict of expulsion in disgrace from the Communist Party is considered by a class-conscious worker as worse than death at the hands of the bourgeois oppressors. As for myself, I would rather have my head severed from my body by the capitalist lynchers than to be expelled from the Communist International."[56] The question will never be answered as to whether he felt that expulsion meant political death when he met the same fate as Yokinen. It is clear, however, that the

Yokinen trial did not put an end to chauvinism. Despite the Party's unique stance against chauvinism, and favorable policies and programs on Negro work, white chauvinism continued to plague the Party.

More significant to Moore, the ILD, and the Party was the true case of the Scottsboro Boys, which hit the headlines later in the month when nine Afro-American youths aged thirteen to twenty were arrested in Scottsboro, Alabama, and charged with the rape of two white women riding on the same freight car. To some there would not seem to be a direct link between the Yokinen trial in Harlem and the criminal case in Alabama, but to Earl Browder, general secretary of the Communist Party at the time, the Party's attempt to purge white chauvinism was a prelude to the Scottsboro campaign. He stated:

> If we had not previously had the experience of the Yokinen trial, probably the Scottsboro boys would have become merely another item in the long list of Negro lynchings which disgrace America daily. . . . But because the Communist Party had been politically armed and prepared, this made it possible to seize upon the Scottsboro case for a national mobilization of protest and struggle which aroused large masses throughout the country, and even throughout the world.[57]

The ILD defended cases from 1925 to 1946 all over the nation, but there was no case to equal the Scottsboro case, which became its *cause célèbre*. Mass organization was considered a significant aspect of legal defense, with community opinion and pressure developed to help balance the weighted scales of justice. Awakening latent indignation to the miscarriage of justice was to be Moore's major contribution.

When news of the arrests broke Moore immediately fired off a telegram to Governor Miller of Alabama and prepared a call for action to save the young men. The NAACP responded to the indictments of March 31 as well as the ILD and a long struggle ensued for the opportunity to represent the defendants in court. At stake in the dispute over custody of the defense was the difference in approach, with the NAACP condoning only the use of strict legal procedures and the ILD insisting upon mass demonstrations as an essential element of the defense. One of Moore's chief duties as vice-president of the ILD became promoting the Scottsboro campaign outside of the courtroom.

He organized mass demonstrations, prepared press releases and instructions on conducting campaigns for local ILD groups and other supportive organizations, and spoke at hundreds of rallies, meetings, and demonstrations. In connection with the protest at the White House on May 13, 1934, attended by some of the mothers of the defendants, he prepared a pamphlet, *Mr. President: Free the Scottsboro Boys* (see Chapter 7).

Moore went on four cross-country tours for the ILD, primarily in the North. On the first trip, he traveled alone from May to August 1931. The second trip was a combined Mooney-Scottsboro campaign projected to cover one hundred cities. The Mooney campaign had been mounted years earlier to free Thomas J. Mooney, a white Socialist sentenced to death for allegedly setting a bomb in San Francisco in 1916. When arrangements were made by the Mooney Molders' Defense Committee, directed by Mooney from his jail cell at San Quentin, California, for the ILD to represent him in 1932, he consented for his eighty-four-year-old mother to serve as a stellar attraction on the campaign trail. Mrs. Mary Mooney, referred to as "Mother Mooney," joined Moore in May of 1932 when he reached the West Coast, and they appeared in sixty cities from California to New York in three months. In anticipation of a European tour, Mooney wrote to a friend in Ireland, "Mother does not speak except for saying just a very few words—then a very brilliant member of the Colored Race, Richard Moore, who has been Mother's companion for the past several months along with another young Jewish girl comrade do the real talking on this case. Mother's presence is a drawing card."[58] The Department of Justice anticipated that Moore would also accompany Mother Mooney on the projected tour of Europe and was successful in frustrating his application for a passport in October.[59]

Mrs. Janie Patterson, mother of defendant Haywood Patterson, accompanied Moore on the third tour in May and June of 1933. On the fourth tour, commencing mid-November 1937, he took Roy Wright and Olen Montgomery, two of the Scottsboro Nine who had been freed in August 1937. While they were not forceful orators, their straightforward story, like that of Mother Mooney and Mrs. Patterson, was effective material that Moore could then "hammer home." Typical of the tour schedules, the itinerary called for appearances in forty-five cities covering twenty-three states in seventy-two days.[60] Without the advantage of the airplane, it was a grueling feat to traverse the northern states on one-night stands during the frigid months from November 15 to January 26.

Such tours were far from smooth operations. Frequently the police awaited Moore's appearance along with the sympathetic audience huddled in some fraternal or religious hall that would permit the use of its facilities by "Reds." On one occasion he had to be sneaked into Los Angeles by car and slipped into the hall just long enough to make his speech to avoid the "Red Squad." Wright and Montgomery would get apprehensive whenever the trail took a somewhat southern route. They would warn Moore, "We're going into the South now; don't talk all that stuff about mulattoes being the result of the rape of black women by white plantation owners."[61] But he would not let the geography alter his social message.

Moore has explained that the main objective was to gain support for the campaign in the form of telegrams and demonstrations, rather than simply to recruit members for the ILD. He viewed the tours as influential in the conduct of the Scottsboro cases, and as contributing to the ultimate release of all of the young men, as well as building the ILD and the Communist Party. Certainly the Communist Party in Harlem reached its zenith during

this period. In appraising the Scottsboro campaign at a meeting of the
National Conference of the ILD in Washington, D.C., in 1940, Moore
stated:

> The Scottsboro Case is one of the historic landmarks in the struggle of the
> American people and of the progressive forces throughout the world for
> justice, civil rights and democracy. In the present period, the Scottsboro Case
> has represented a pivotal point around which labor and progressive forces
> have rallied not only to save the lives of nine boys who were framed . . . but
> also against the whole system of lynching terror and the special oppression
> and persecution of the Negro people.[62]

By the mid-thirties the promise of the 1922 Theses on the Negro Question of the Fourth Comintern Congress had begun to fade. The depression
had brought intensified malaise and suffering to the Afro-American community and the Communists had rallied to assist families in gaining some
share of the meager home relief, housing, and jobs available to the broader
community. To strengthen their position, they battled not only the social
agencies, landlords, and owners of business, but the members of race-
oriented organizations referred to as "nationalists." Moore engaged in
these verbal forays but had not anticipated that the venom released upon
the nationalists would seep back to contaminate inner-Party relations.

In the campaigns designed to secure employment of Afro-Americans in
the completely white-dominated businesses in Harlem, the Party took the
position that the employment of blacks was not intended to affect white
workers. Moore argued that the unemployed in Harlem would neither
understand nor rally to campaigns that promoted the protection of white
workers. He also protested the assignment of young, inexperienced white
workers as section organizers in Harlem, insisting again that the Party was
not acting to engender the faith and respect of the Afro-American community.

The various dissatisfactions and disagreements within the Party may be
traced to the shifts in leadership and structure as well as to Party positions.
Mark Naison provides keen insight into the confusion and changes in the
Harlem section as a result of Comintern criticism of the American Party:

> [W]hen the Comintern criticized . . . the Party's low membership and their
> failure to discredit socialist leaders with whom they sought alliances, CPUSA
> leaders responded with an almost hysterical vigilance against unorthodox
> practices in the Party's local organizations. . . . In July, 1933, the Central
> Committee designated Harlem as a "national concentration point" of the
> Party, and appointed . . . James Ford, as special Harlem organizer. Within
> nine months of his arrival, Ford had pushed Harlem's pioneering black
> Communists, Richard B. Moore and Cyril Briggs, out of positions of in-
> fluence in the Harlem Party and had transformed it from a freewheeling
> agitational center into a model of political orthodoxy.
> Significantly, the Harlem Party's actions in the Scottsboro movement, its

most successful single project, provided the initial target for Central Committee dissatisfaction. . . . Harlem Communists had been so caught up in the enthusiasm of these protests, *Daily Worker* editor Clarence Hathaway wrote, that they had forgotten that the purpose of the united front was "to destroy the influence of the reformist leaders" and not "to make peace with them." . . . Party theoretician James Allen . . . reminded Harlem Communists that their goal was "to establish the unchallenged leadership of the Communist Party in the Scottsboro struggle," and not merely to organize the broadest mass movement. . . .

To Central Committee leaders, these derelictions from Party policy suggested that black Harlem Communists had become too responsive to the moods and feelings of Harlem's population. . . . The behavior of Harlem leaders during the Scottsboro upheaval—their willingness to make alliances with blacks of all backgrounds, and their encouragement of skeptical attitudes towards whites among the Party's black rank and file—all cast doubt on the Harlem Party's political reliability.[63]

Moore and Briggs certainly considered the appraisal of the Harlem work as incorrect. As Ford moved to implement the Central Committee's directives, he installed a group of inexperienced white Communists as administrators and focused upon waging a campaign against nationalist tendencies rather than white chauvinism. Clearly he perceived Briggs and Moore as a threat and did not trust them. They viewed his personality, ruthless style, and reliance upon the Central Committee as a mixture of opportunism and Uncle Tomism, hardly what they had in mind when they had sought increased Afro-American leadership.

In time they "constituted themselves as spokesmen of a 'left-opposition' within the Harlem Party, determined to resist any de-emphasis of the struggle against white chauvinism and any tendency to replace blacks with whites in key Party posts."[64] Ford determined that he would show them that even talented Afro-American Party veterans were not indispensable to the Harlem section and could be disciplined. He removed Briggs as editor of *The Harlem Liberator* in October 1933. The assignment as a reporter for *The Daily Worker* was intended to diminish his influence in Harlem.

Naison has pointed out that while "ideologically 'suspect' on the jobs issue, Moore was the Party's most effective black orator, and Ford felt compelled to make use of his talents to dramatize the Party's militant opposition to lynching and jim crow."[65] Nevertheless, at a meeting of the National Executive Board of the League of Struggle for Negro Rights in April 1934 Moore tendered his resignation as general secretary. Harry Haywood has indicated that he "was elected national secretary, relieving Richard B. Moore who was in ill health."[66] The three Scottsboro tours had taken their toll on Moore's health, but it was also his political health that was suffering.

The conflicts within the Party went beyond the confrontation with the nationalists on job campaigns and criticism of the conduct of the Scottsboro campaign and erupted into the media when Moore's former close associates in the ANLC, George Padmore and Herman Mackawain, withdrew from the Party. Padmore had been serving in Hamburg and Paris as secretary of the International Trade Union Committee of Negro Workers (the Red International of Labour Unions or Profintern's Negro Bureau) and editing its organ, *The Negro Worker*. His activities and writings had included vigorous support for the Scottsboro campaign along with exposés on conditions in the various colonies and agitation for trade union development in Africa, the Caribbean, and the United States.

Several months after Padmore was expelled in February 1934 by the International Control Commission of the Comintern for charges including "an incorrect attitude to the national question" and deviations "in the direction of Negro petty bourgeois nationalism," there was a deluge of articles in *The Daily Worker* and the Afro-American press. Padmore claimed that the Comintern had planned to reduce its anticolonial agitation "in order not to offend the British Foreign Office which has been bringing pressure to bear on Soviet diplomacy because of the tremendous indignation which our work has aroused among the Negro masses in Africa, the West Indies and other colonies against British imperialism."[67] The coinciding of his refutation, released in October 1935, with developments in the Ethiopian War gave rise to questions regarding the Communists' commitment. The continuation of the *RILU-NW* and its publication under the leadership of Otto Huiswoud from 1934 to 1938, contrary to Padmore's charges that the organization was being liquidated, did not seem to quell the perception that the victims of colonialism were being betrayed.

Mackawain, still functioning in the Harlem section, took the Party to task in August 1935 for suppressing internal dissent on the part of Harlem leadership during the Harlem jobs movement and protests in defense of Ethiopia, and waging a campaign of harassment against those who complained of the Soviet Union's duplicity in trading with fascist Italy.[68]

Moore was critical of the manner in which Padmore, Mackawain, and others expressed their opposition to current policies, but he certainly pondered the disputes being waged within the Party and the reaction in the Afro-American community. Later he could not help observe the difference between the responses of some Communists to political developments in Spain and in Ethiopia: "internationalists" joined the Lincoln Brigade but "nationalists" advocated the same support for Ethiopia.

By February 1935 the pressure for the alliance of antifascist forces had created another round of united-front approaches. The Harlem section's increased cooperative spirit toward noncommunist organizations did not cancel the criticism of Moore and Briggs by Hathaway, Allen, and Ford. In fact, the confirmation of the Party's position enunciated at the Eighth National Convention in April 1934, which emphasized the struggle against black nationalism rather than white chauvinism, and the abandonment of the self-determination position by the Central Committee in 1935 served as signals to Moore that the Party had already begun deemphasizing the Negro and colonial questions. He continued to function within the ranks as a disciplined worker but a defiant member.

Naison sums up the decline of Moore's and Briggs's influence:

> Both Briggs and Moore had lived in Harlem for over fifteen years, and had a following in the community based upon their uncompromising commitment of black liberation throughout the world and their considerable personal abilities. . . . [They] were agitators rather than administrators. . . . The Ford regime's new emphasis on administrative efficiency, Party discipline, and the struggle against black nationalism seemed to mark a movement away from the uncompromising militancy on racial issues that had first attracted them to the Party.[69]

During 1935 and 1936 Moore was assigned to Boston as field representative of the ILD. During that period the National Negro Congress was formed to replace the LSNR, and he attended as a delegate from Massachusetts. He served as a member of the National Executive Council and the General Resolutions Committee of the Congress.

As part of his organizational efforts in Boston he conducted campaigns against Mussolini's invasion of Ethiopia, including leading a demonstration at the Italian Consulate, gave lectures on Afro-American History, led a delegation that secured removal of two prejudiced textbooks from the Boston schools, and joined in initiating the "Night of Negro Music" as an annual feature of the Boston Pops Symphony Orchestra. He continued in his post as a vice-president of the ILD, but his role was far less influential than it had been early in the decade.

In 1937 he became ill again from exhaustion and the doctor prescribed rest and a regular, highly nutritious diet. He withdrew to a farm in Hillsboro, New Hampshire, for recovery before returning to New York, "looking like a sick man." In September the Scottsboro Defense Committee authorized him to establish a Harlem Scottsboro Defense Committee, a broad-based organization with Rev. Adam Clayton Powell, Jr., as chairman.[70] Moore served as secretary and later in the year he conducted the fourth cross-country Scottsboro tour.

The Scottsboro tours and the Boston assignment had been intended in part to negate his influence in the community as well as the Harlem section of the Party but had not successfully undermined his contacts with the community. Upon his return to New York he became involved in the formation of Caribbean organizations responding to the outbreaks of "disturbances" in several islands. As soon as he adjourned a meeting of the Harlem Scottsboro Defense Committee, he would dash to one sponsored by the West Indies Defense Committee. The question was, however, what Party assignment awaited him? Undaunted, Moore had an answer.

Throughout his association with the Party Moore had utilized Afro-American history in his oral and written appeals and stimulated its incorporation into workshops and lecture series. More recently he had begun to press the leadership to publish a series of pamphlets with popular appeal on significant Afro-Americans. The Party's interest in Afro-American history had long been demonstrated through pamphlets and articles prepared primarily by white writers. He believed he had been successful in projecting the first one on Frederick Douglass and had started a draft when he discovered there was no real support. Despite keen disappointment, he promoted the publication of a limited subscription edition of Douglass's autobiography, *The Life and Times of Frederick Douglass,* which had been out of print for forty years. He founded the Frederick Douglass Historical and Cultural League to provide an organizational base for reaching potential subscribers. In February 1940 a copartnership, The Pathway Press, was established as the vehicle for publication, with Moore as president, Angelo Herndon as secretary-treasurer, William Fitzgerald, and Cyril Philip. Subsequently George B. Murphy, Jr., acted as president, Philip as vice-president, Herndon as treasurer, and Moore as secretary.[71]

Moore edited the copy for printing, wrote the Editor's Note, prepared promotional material, and signed up hundreds of subscribers. Others also solicited subscribers but the project turned into a nightmare when Moore discerned that Herndon was engaged in the unauthorized use of the Press's minuscule funds and was trying to force him out of the business. Moore claims that after he had delivered the copy to the printer, changes were made in the Editor's Note, which all partners had agreed he was to write.

> When next seen by me after the printing, the Editor's Note had been ruthlessly changed and many of the explanatory notes badly mangled. The name of Richard B. Moore as editor had been surreptitiously removed and the signature "The Editors" substituted. . . .
>
> An unseemly legal conflict was avoided when the lawyers involved denied the demand of Angelo Herndon that all the remaining copies of the book be turned over to him. The decision was made that I should keep possession of the copies in the office and continue to promote the sale and distribution. The decision was made as well that with the completion of such distribution, the Pathway Press should no longer be continued. Plans for more and lower-priced reprints had to be abandoned.[72]

Moore had also pushed for the publication of a separate pamphlet of Douglass's 1876 oration delivered at the Unveiling of the Freedmen's Monument in memory of Abraham Lincoln, and had other republications in mind when it became clear that a Negro Publication Society of America, at the same address as the Pathway Press, had been formed with Angelo Herndon and Cyril Philip as two of the eight members of the board of directors. Without the inclusion of Moore the launching of this venture was tantamount to the establishment of a competing project to undermine the Pathway Press. Clearly the idea of an Afro-American series of publications was "in" but Moore was "out."

Evidently the agreement reached with legal assistance on May 10, 1941, referred to above, did not completely settle the manner in which finances were handled or the confusion growing out of two seemingly closely associated publishing companies. The release of the book in March had created greater pressure for payment of debts rather than a significant increase in revenues. The financial responsibility and pressure weighed so heavily on Moore that he finally resorted to preferring charges against Herndon in January 1942. In submitting charges to the Harlem section and the New York State Disciplines Committee of the Party, he called attention not only to Herndon's "repeated financial irregularities in connection with and including misappropriation of the funds and property of the Pathway Press" but to "acts to use the credit and the goodwill of the Pathway Press and the Pathway Press, Inc. for the development of a rival and competing organization, namely, the Negro Publication Society of America . . . after agreeing with the Directors and attorneys of the Pathway Press to liquidate the Negro Publication Society."[73]

The outcome of the charges is not known, but the more relevant fate of the publishing efforts is documented. Each group reprinted one book, and it was twenty years before out-of-print books by Afro-Americans came onto the market again.[74] Moore counted the two publications that the Pathway Press managed to release as accomplishments, but found the personal encounters a bitter pill. To Moore the machinations of Herndon seemed to be indicative of a destructive intent by others in the Party; the conflicts within the Pathway Press were a prelude to the bitterest pill of all—expulsion.

The precise charges leveled against Moore in 1942 by members of the Party have not been completely revealed. A list compiled from reports by Department of Justice informants includes: "frequent deviation from party program" or "party line," "extreme nationalist tendencies," "an independent thinker and difficult for leaders to dictate to."[75] George Schuyler reported that Moore and Briggs were expelled for their "Negro Nationalist way of thinking."[76] There may be a bit of truth in each comment. Moore's irritation with Party responses to his leadership in Harlem, the jobs campaign, the Ethiopian crisis, the program to publish out-of-print books by Afro-American authors, and his involvement in Caribbean organizations had been growing for eight years—since Ford's arrival. The issue described by Moore and members who were present at his expulsion, however, relates to Moore's persistent stand on the approach to Afro-American workers during the jobs campaign.

Abner W. Berry, an organizer for the Harlem section, later explained:

> He was expelled from the Party, and at that expulsion, I was the prosecutor. I think now wrongly, but at that time I was working [for] the Party. And what he had done was related to a problem that still exists. The problem was whether or not the white labor unions would fight for jobs for Negroes. Now

some said, "If you're fighting for jobs for Negroes, you can't stop short of a white worker being fired." Some said, "No, you have to fight for jobs for Negroes and for the white worker's job at the same time." Moore said, "We're just fighting for jobs for Negroes, and we can't be concerned whether a white worker is fired. We're just fighting for this job, right here." Well for that, we chased him out of the Party. The Party had already decided that we would fight for the right of Negroes for jobs, but would guarantee that white workers would not be fired. . . . It [Moore's] was a consistent approach. His approach, by the way, was not incorrect. I became the prosecutor and he was expelled for taking a divisive stand. . . . Later, I was very remorseful.[77]

It is impossible to gauge the trauma—the disappointment, hurt, bitterness, anger—and relief Moore might have experienced when the expulsion was announced. He took small comfort in the fact that he was not alone in receiving punishment for expressing his opinions. Many were expelled during this period, including Briggs, who wrote to his old friend Moore from California in 1947:

. . . have you returned to the Fold—been taken back? Or tried? I tried early last year and despite my very frank and blunt statement rejecting charges, the [Committee] was favorable to my application for *reinstatement*. The local Ford, however, did not like the idea. So that's that. It doesn't worry me. Nor influence my political beliefs one iota. I am reconciled to carrying on on the outside.[78]

Briggs returned to the fold. For Moore, there was no return, He took pleasure in reports that the Party was open to consideration for reinstatement; still he made no move to return.

Unlike others, he wrote no memoirs, confessions, or exposés of his years as a Communist. On one occasion he did admit that expulsion was the greatest thing the Party ever did for him. Except for a six-page memorandum regarding the Pathway Press, entitled "To Set the Record Straight," written primarily for his own file, brief comments in letters and articles, and guarded responses to interviews conducted by researchers three decades later, he kept his own counsel. In his words, he "closed the book."[79]

III

THE PAN-CARIBBEAN
MOVEMENT

Moore's break with the Communist Party created a challenge rather than a crisis. From a political perspective, he had lost an organizational base but not his voice or his ties to the Harlem community. Richard Wright's characterization of George Padmore's post-Comintern Pan-African work is applicable to Moore:

> HE CONTINUED HIS WORK ALONE, STRIVING TO ACHIEVE THROUGH HIS OWN INSTRUMENTALITIES THAT WHICH HE HAD WORKED FOR WHEN HE WAS IN THE COMINTERN HIERARCHY, THAT IS, FREEDOM FOR BLACK PEOPLE.

Wright also pointed out that the Afro-American, whether embracing Communism or Western democracy, seeks to use instruments owned and controlled by men of other races for his own ends. "He stands outside of those instruments and ideologies, he has to do so, for he is not allowed to blend with them in a natural, organic and healthy manner."[1]

Moore's continuous interest in the cause of Caribbean independence and self-determination had already been refueled in 1937, and there was no mystery or confusion regarding organizational direction or affiliations. The problem of personal finances required, however, more immediate initiative and imagination. At the age of forty-nine, operating elevators was unthinkable. A fifteen-year career as organizer for the Communist Party was certainly not very marketable. The solution was most fortunate and appropriate: a bookstore was the logical culmination of years of collecting and selling books. A small store, barely twelve feet wide, used by the *New York Times* as an advertising office, had been vacant for some time. The location, in the hub of the 125th Street business section between Seventh and Lenox Avenues, was ideal, and his friend Reginald Pierrepointe interceded with the agent of the building for Moore to rent the store.

With the financial backing of a close friend, Lodie Biggs, the Frederick Douglass Book Center was launched in 1942. Early stationery for the center carries the name of Cyril Briggs, "Promotion and Mail Order," in addition to Moore as "Manager" and Lodie Biggs as "Sales Representative," but there is no evidence that Cyril Briggs invested any money or was involved in the operation of the store. The initial stock was basically

Moore's personal collection. He operated the book center at 141 West 125th Street from 1942 until 1968, when all the buildings in the block were demolished for the construction of a new office building by the state of New York.[2]

Lodie Biggs became much more than a partner in the small business venture. Her small stature and warm walnut complexion, which conveyed a modest shyness and infectious smile, belied her ardent militancy. She had been a member of the Harlem section, a supporter of Moore, and had also waged a campaign with other Afro-American women against male chauvinism in the Party. His arguments on behalf of her cause had not enhanced his standing, nor had her unqualified support of Moore endeared her to Party leaders. She too was expelled.

At this critical time in Moore's life, Lodie provided not only comradeship based upon her philosophical compatibility and experiences in the Party, and support in his new business venture, but the warmth and devotion so absent during the years of existence in small, drab, dingy hotel rooms. On September 9, 1950, he and Lodie were married and began a new life enriched by family relationships and cultural explorations.[3] She preferred to address him as "Richard," which gradually replaced "Dick."

Lodie had grown up in Seattle, Washington, the daughter of a railroad fire tender who was a member of the IWW—an "old Wobbly," as she referred to him. She was a serious scientist by training and self-discipline and worked as a bacteriologist for the city of New York. She was about the same age as Moore but did not share his pride in revealing age or his joy in celebrating one's birthday. She was ageless—always young in spirit. Her interests were wide: science, medicine, socialism, music, ballet, gourmet cooking, but her interest in other people was her charm.

This was her first marriage, but she slipped into the role of grandmother with great aplomb and transformed Moore from the father who had managed only occasional visits to a Russian movie and a Chinese restaurant with his teenage daughter to a family patriarch. In time their small apartment in Brooklyn became virtually a museum of African, Afro-American, and Asian art pieces collected by Moore at auctions in the same manner he collected books. Grandchildren found few spaces in which to play amidst the books, artifacts, and plants, but they loved the never-ending designs and colors of the unique bric-a-brac and pictures, the delicious meals and goodies that emerged from the tiny corner that served as a kitchen, and the trips to museums, the ballet, and the ubiquitous Chinese restaurants.

The opening of the Frederick Douglass Book Center heralded a new life for Moore. Not only was he an entrepreneur in a small business and involved in family life, but he was liberated to pursue more extensively two interests that had always been paramount to him but had been relegated to side issues while he extolled the significance of class and economic oppression. The war and postwar period brought a resurgence of interest in Afro-American history and Caribbean political liberation. Moore was both a catalyst in that development and a beneficiary of the search for identity and nationhood.

The Center was an ideal vehicle for the propagation of African, Afro-American, and Caribbean history and literature. The store operated on a very slim margin and required almost daily stops at wholesale dealers and used bookstores to hunt for requested or anticipated orders. Practically all of his stock was carted to the store personally. He was hardly ever seen on 125th Street without appendages of brown paper packages neatly wrapped and carefully tied with cord to be untied and reused. His meager earnings did not inhibit the avid collector's eye from searching for unique volumes for which no request had been received. His desire to add to his personal library merged with his intent to create interest in little-known historical sources.

His collection grew, therefore, to include rare out-of-print volumes, and individuals from all over the United States and foreign nations sought to obtain books by visits to Harlem or by mail. Some of his early customers were servicemen who were eager to fill their isolated hours at Jim Crow Army camps by reading the new novels by Richard Wright, Chester Himes, Ann Petry, and Frank Yerby, but they were joined by others attracted to the less popular rare books.

Moore's interest and knowledge of Africa and his unique collection of books on Africa attracted many African students. His stock became enriched with African art objects obtained mostly from students who augmented their income by selling or trading articles from home. It was partially through these contacts that he became involved in a limited way with causes in support of African independence.

Moore not only collected and sold books, he read them. It was soon recognized that the Center was a resource for more than an occasional new book. In their quest for greater understanding of their past, members of community groups turned to Moore as a speaker on Afro-American history. By the sixties, when the tide of African, Afro-American, and Caribbean studies reached a tumultuous pitch, Moore was in constant demand. "The Origin and Meaning of Christmas," "African Religion Before Judaism and Christianity," "Early Man in Africa," "Zimbabwe or Rhodesia?" "Afro-Americans in Invention and Science," "The Anatomy of Slavery," "Human Rights and the Afro-American Experience," "Afro-Caribbean Leaders: Queen Mary, Marianna Maceo and Mary Seacole" are just a few examples of the topics upon which he expounded. Frequently a book display was also featured to demonstrate the range of books available for all age groups.

Moore became noted as an authority in the field and lectured in his vigorous style at colleges and universities such as Columbia University, Mills College, Nassau County Community College, State University of New York at Stony Brook, and the Immaculate Conception Seminary in Conception, Missouri, until 1976, when he was eighty-three years old. No matter what the topic or audience, he could find some example, quotation, or parallel in Frederick Douglass's life to inspire his listeners. He continually agitated for the inclusion of Douglass in the New York University Hall of Fame and the perservation of the Douglass home in Anacostia, Washington, D.C., as a historic monument.

In December 1958 Moore instituted Sunday afternoon lectures and book parties at his Moor's Gallery in the Apollo building and later at his expanded store at 23 East 125th Street or the YMCA. Most of the programs were conducted under the auspices of the Afro-American Institute, which he founded in 1969 and served as president until his death. While he was a key lecturer in the Institute series, he played the role of chairperson, provocateur, summarizer, or commentator while taking great pleasure in presenting notable scholars and authors such as Kofi Awooner, Wilfred Cartey, John Hendrik Clarke, Alice Childress, Elton Fax, Franklin W. Knight, and Elliott P. Skinner. It was the literary version of the People's Educational Forum.

During the late fifties articles by Moore began to appear in Afro-American and Caribbean magazines, newspapers, and organizational journals. His previous work had been largely limited to press releases and promotional material for radical organizations. The Communist Party, with no shortage of writers, had not needed to encourage his writing abilities. Rather, they had treated his great oratorical talent as the valuable asset to be utilized. When the captivating voice was transferred to prose during the forties, the hackneyed expressions of the Party lingo tended to hamper acceptance. It is fortunate that subsequent specific requests from editors, particularly John Hendrik Clarke, and officers of organizations elicited a more appropriate style and created the urgency to commit ideas and recount experiences in a written form. Thus a collection of essays on various issues and events emerged, resulting in a permanent record, unlike the fate of most of his speeches.

Moore's intent to write on topics of his own choice was realized only in a limited way and in an unexpected direction. As he pondered the development of racial prejudice, he became convinced that race was a concept devised by European exploiters and that racism had been carefully nurtured in human behavior. The trait that distinguishes humans from other species is the unique use of language for transmitting ideas and influencing behavior. To Moore the precious gift of language was being misused to demean some human beings, and he engaged in several campaigns to demonstrate how critically loaded words such as "Negro," "native," and "black" perpetuate negative images and responses.

This emphasis on semantics as a force for change produced several works that he published with the Afro-American Publishers or the Pathway Publishers. In each case the essay developed as a lecture or letter in response to situations which he had found irritating and illustrative. *The Name "Negro"—Its Origin and Evil Uses,* published in 1960 in hard and soft cover, was the best known and most often sought long after it was out of print (see chapter 10). Mary Frances Berry and John Blassingame consider this small volume to have been "one of the most significant attacks on the term."[4] At the time of his death Moore was working on a revision and another monograph, "Language: Some Uses and Misuses."[5]

The campaign launched to change the name "Negro" to "Afro-American" instead of "Black," as trumpeted by the Black Power Movement in 1964, was conducted by Moore and his associates through the Committee to Present the Truth About the Name "Negro" during the sixties and the Afro-American Institute during the seventies. Letters and notices were circulated to the press, organizations, and schools. Gradually "Afro-American," which had been in use at the turn of the century, moved into usage. One change that Moore was instrumental in effecting directly was the name of the Association for the Study of Negro Life and History, founded by Carter G. Woodson in 1916. He introduced resolutions for three years until the name Association for the Study of Afro-American Life and History was adopted in 1972. He was not successful in getting the name of the *Journal of Negro History* changed at the same time but would have continued to champion such a change had he lived to attend the annual conferences. There is also evidence that his campaign reached Africa. Jean Blackwell Hutson, former curator of the Schomburg Collection, has recounted how President Kwame Nkrumah shocked members of the board of the *Encyclopedia Africana* by instructing them at a meeting in Ghana after reading Moore's book that he did not want to see the word "Negro" used anywhere in the encyclopedia.[6]

Moore's deep interest and fifty-year involvement in promoting Afro-American history was matched by his concern for the Caribbean. His continuous study of Afro-American life was broad enough to encompass Africans in Africa and the Americas as well as Caribbean peoples wherever they were. As an activist he regarded his eclectic studies as formulations to be applied to the current scene. While Harlem had become home, his "scene" had never ceased to include the Caribbean, and it is in the cause for Caribbean nationhood that his writings and speeches best reflect his grasp of history and use of language.

His concentration on Caribbean liberation commenced prior to the opening of his Book Center as a response to historic events in the islands. Like the series of 1919 riots across the nation, the wave of riots extending in 1935 from St. Kitts to Trinidad, British Guiana, St. Vincent, and St. Lucia, then again in 1937 and 1938 from Trinidad to Barbados, British Guiana, St. Lucia, and Jamaica created a stir among the Caribbean community in New York. Reginald Pierrepointe, a journalist with *The Amsterdam News,* was so disturbed by the general situation and particularly the 14 killed, 44 wounded, and 453 arrested in his native Barbados that he promptly organized the West Indies Defense Committee to solicit relief aid for the victims. He had been in the United States since 1920 but had not really known Moore long before 1937. He involved Moore, Stanley Lowe, Walter Miller, Cyril M. Philip, Hope R. Stevens, James S. Watson, and others in initiating protests to the British government. They issued a statement demanding immediate cessation of the massacres and other repressive acts to every member of Parliament. Moore considered Pierrepointe quite clever to have called attention to the practice of working children in "cricket gangs" and beating them brutally with cowhide whips on the Belle and Mount plantations owned by E. C. Lascelles, the husband of King George V's sister.

The Moyne Commission was Britain's response to the riots and to the wave of protests that followed from organizations in the United States such as the West Indies Defense Committee and the Jamaica Progressive League (which sent Ethelred Brown to present a statement to the Moyne Commission and $2,000 in aid to Jamaica) and those in Great Britain such as Dr. Harold Moody's League of Coloured Peoples and George Padmore's International African Service Bureau.[7] In the Caribbean, however, there was another response. The riots gave birth to a new political climate; Afro-Caribbean leaders emerged and political and labor organizations were constituted.

On many occasions Hope Stevens has related with his usual wit, humor, and eloquence how the veteran politicians Pierrepointe and Moore hatched plans to send him, "an innocent" young lawyer, into the Caribbean fray. The many miles between the Caribbean and New York created a communications gap. While he had access to a wire service as a journalist, Pierrepointe hastened to take advantage of Stevens's projected visit to see his parents in Nevis following his admission to the bar in 1938. Nevis is four hundred miles from Barbados, but that was of little consequence to Moore and Pierrepointe. Stevens was pressed to extend his trip to establish better contact between the islands and the "awaymen," as Moore has referred to those in New York.[8]

In one account, Stevens has written:

> On a bright and cloudless morning in the Spring of 1938, I looked at Barbados for the first time, from the deck of a Canadian National Steamship tourist liner. . . . I had been charged with a mission by a group of Caribbean-American citizens in New York headed by a Barbadian-American Reginald Pierrepointe. . . . Pierrepointe had sent me to [Wynter A.] Crawford [editor of *The Barbados Observer*]. . . . Our day was spent in discussing the way in which the disturbances in the island had developed, their aftermath and the inquiry made by the Moyne Commission.
>
> In the course of the afternoon we were joined by Edwy Talma, a young solicitor. It was agreed that a discussion of suggestions for some kind of political action would be resumed when I came back on the return trip from British Guiana and Trinidad two weeks later. And so it was that on the evening of the return of my ship to Bridgetown a group of eight of us gathered around a large table in the dining room of a local soda water

manufacturer MARTINEAU and I was introduced as the representative of the Caribbean Community in New York. . . . Those present were Mr. Martineau, Wynter A. Crawford, Edwy Talma, Dr. Philip Payne, John Beckles, Christopher Brathwaite and Dr. Hugh Cummins, the last two then being members of the legislature.

During the course of this meeting it was made clear that no permanent political organization had been achieved following the recent upheavals. However, it was patent that a political climate had developed in the island and everyone agreed that the time was ripe for action aimed at crystallizing the widespread interest in the social and economic problems of the people.

Having informed the group of the desire of the islanders in the United States to see leadership arise in the islands behind which the American residents could rally, I proposed that a political party be formed by the seven persons present. I was asked to chair the meeting. By 2:00 A.M., we had written the constitution of the Barbados Labour Party and elected its officers, the Hon. Christopher Brathwaite being made first President.

The organizers wanted to have as the first Vice President a young lawyer . . . and Grantley Herbert Adams was elected in absentia to that office.[9]

The unexpected success of Stevens's mission greatly encouraged the New York contingent, and it was not long before Moore had another mission for him. The potential threat to the Caribbean by Hitler following the fall of France stimulated the United States to call a meeting of foreign ministers of nations in the Western hemisphere. In a chance meeting of Moore and Domingo on Lenox Avenue, Domingo mentioned his fears that the interests of the Caribbean peoples would not be represented at such a meeting. They both agreed that the West Indian community needed to seek expression there and that the vehicle should be a coordinating type of organization rather than one identified with a sole island, like the Jamaica Progressive League, which Domingo had helped organize in 1936. They quickly launched the West Indies National Emergency Committee in June 1940 with Domingo as president, Moore as vice-president, Herman P. Osborne of Trinidad as secretary, and Arthur E. King of British Guiana as treasurer, and sought the cooperation of officers of New York Caribbean organizations. Later the officers were expanded to include Dr. Charles A. Petioni, Mrs. Ivy Bailey-Essien, and T. E. Chalwell as vice-presidents, and the name changed to the West Indies National Council.[10]

"The Declaration of the Rights of the Caribbean Peoples to Self-Determination and Self-Government," largely the work of Moore, was drafted and Stevens was delegated to go to Havana to endeavor to secure adoption of the principles of the declaration (see chapter 11). The Jamaica Progressive League also prepared and forwarded a memorandum advocating dominion status for the people of the British West Indies. Cooperation was secured from the Council for Pan-American Democracy, which delegated Dr. Charles Obermeier to assist. When the committee officers ascertained that the proposed Act of Havana and the published address of the United States secretary of state, Cordell Hull, contained no recognition of the rights of the Caribbean people to self-determination, Moore prepared and dispatched the "Reply to Cordell Hull" (see chapter 11).

Stevens contacted various foreign ministers, conducted publicity including a radio broadcast, and secured the support of the foreign minister of Argentina, Leopoldo Melo, who took the lead in advocating self-determination in the proceedings. As a result, the Act of Havana was amended to include recognition of "the principle re-affirmed by the declaration that peoples of this continent have the right freely to determine their own destinies."[11]

While this collaboration between Moore and Domingo was in progress, they were giving the appearance of ardent opponents to some who did not fully understand their deep friendship and their ardor for forensic forays. Both were adept at debating and could argue either side of a question. But the series of debates they waged in 1940 had them arguing for positions they supported at the time, with the intent of opening significant questions for consideration. The circumstances surrounding the initial debate are not known, but it must have been a success. The debates became a popular program presented by different organizations. "Should British Colonial Negroes Support the British Empire in the Present War?" with Domingo arguing the affirmative and Moore the negative, was sponsored by the Caribbean Union on December 17, 1939, and the Pioneer Negroes of the World on April 21, 1940. According to Moore, he debated Domingo five times and won all the debates.

As the war progressed, Moore, Briggs, and Huiswoud found themselves on Domingo's side, favoring support for the Allies—a position contrary to their vehement stand against World War I. They began to appreciate that the war would aid their cause against British and Dutch colonialism but failed to anticipate that it would deal two of them a harsh blow. In a few short years Moore was left holding the Harlem fort virtually alone. In 1942, it was necessary to dispatch Hope Stevens a third time—this time to Suriname—to investigate the detention of their friend Otto Huiswoud.

Huiswoud had made many trips to the Caribbean islands including Jamaica, Trinidad, Haiti, Cuba, Curaçao, Barbados, and British and Dutch Guiana to make contact with labor leaders and report on conditions. The most publicized was his visit to Jamaica under the sponsorship of the ANLC in August 1929, when he challenged Garvey to a debate during the UNIA convention. His emphasis on class rather than race as the issue in the Caribbean was published, but no serious attention was given to his observations on federation. While Harry Haywood had accused him of "bourgeois liberalism" in reponse to his article "World Aspects of the Negro Question," in which he recommended "a broad movement for the fight of self-determination, giving proletarian leadership to the struggle for a 'Federated West Indies,' " the colonial governments had marked him as a revolutionary.

In January 1941, while en route from New York to his homeland,

Suriname, to recuperate from a serious kidney operation, his cabin was searched by Trinidadian authorities when the Dutch freighter docked in Port of Spain. The only piece of "subversive" literature found was Du Bois's book *The Negro*. The Dutch captain reported the search to the Port Police in Paramaribo and Huiswoud was arrested the next morning. He was interned at the Convent at Copieweg almost two years, without benefit of charges, trial, or representation.[12] It cannot be assumed that Stevens's inquiry was instrumental in gaining Huiswoud's release, but he was freed in October 1942 and remained in Suriname for the duration of the war. He chose not to return to the United States and settled in Amsterdam in 1947, where he focused his organizational efforts on behalf of the independence of Suriname. The collaboration between Moore and Huiswoud was thus broken, but not the bond that they shared in their mission to free the Caribbean and African nations.

One year after the launching of the West Indies National Council, Domingo made a trip to Jamaica, where he had previously relocated his family, and, like Huiswoud, was arrested on arrival. It did not seem to matter that he had not chosen Huiswoud's affiliation with the Communist Party. Intercepted letters from Domingo to Norman W. Manley, who had invited Domingo to work with him on organizational matters for the Peoples National Party, and Martin Luther Campbell, former militant associate in Harlem during the early twenties now residing in Jamaica, were cited by the governor of Jamaica as evidence of Domingo's intent "to impede the policy of the imperial and local governments in relation to the war effort," "excite opposition to the policy of the Imperial Government of allowing the United States to establish defense bases in Jamaica," and "foster among the Colonial population of Jamaica feelings of . . . racial animosity . . . by alleging the existence of such feelings among officers and men of the United States forces, likely to be stationed in Jamaica."[13] On June 18, 1941, Domingo was detained by the British in the Up-Park Internment Camp for twenty months, along with Alexander Bustamante and other political prisoners. Neither Huiswoud nor Domingo had become a United States citizen and under war powers they could be detained without due process by their colonial governments.

This gave the New York organization another cause and stimulated the link with George Padmore in London in order to exert pressure on the British. Several appeals were made for Domingo's release. Interestingly, members of the West Indies National Council cited Domingo's position during the Moore-Domingo debates as one proof of his loyalty to the British war effort. A huge rally was held July 14 under the auspices of the Council and the Jamaica Progressive League. Moore was one of the speakers, along with Walter White, Rev. Ethelred Brown, Pierrepointe, and others. Four years after his release Domingo was able to gain reentry to the United States and continue his advocacy of Caribbean independence, particularly on behalf of Jamaica.

The presence of Moore and a few other radicals in the Council suggested to some members of the community and the Department of Justice that the organization was a Communist front. Ironically part of Moore's difficulty with the Party had been the unstated accusation that "he had his own base" in his "nationalist bourgeois," i.e., West Indian, organizations. Moore was already in the process of being expelled from the Party when fear of identification with an organization perceived to be led by Communists caused dissension in the American West Indian Association on Caribbean Affairs. The Association was established in 1942 for the purpose of gaining representation of West Indians on the Anglo-American Caribbean Commission and the President's Caribbean Advisory Committee. Moore's organization, the West Indies National Council, also pressed for representation but recommended both individuals residing in the United States and those in the Caribbean, some of whom were viewed as "the most outstanding opposition leaders in the area in both the labor movement and political life." The Association became divided over the question of cooperating with the Council and coordinating the two organizations' appeals to the United States government. Moore was faced with the dilemma of being rejected by the Party for his own Caribbean agenda and by conservative Caribbean-Americans for his identification with Marxism. A. M. Wendell Malliet and Isaac Newton Braithwaite, who had known Moore for years (and would work with him in the future), were alleged to have resigned rather than belong to a group cooperating with the West Indies National Council.[14]

The dissension did not affect Moore's leadership, however, and the Council delegated him and Dr. Charles A. Petioni, who was president at the time, to lobby on behalf of Caribbean interests at the founding conference of the United Nations in San Francisco, April 25 through June 26, 1945. Prior to their departure Moore and Petioni participated in a Conference on Colonialism on April 6 in Harlem called by Dr. W. E. B. Du Bois. As early as 1941 Du Bois had conceived of assembling a group to prepare a presentation on "the cause of the Negro, not only of America but of the West Indies and Africa, at the next peace Conference."

Moore's presentation of the approach that the West Indies National Council would be projecting in San Francisco included a description of British control in the Caribbean that merited an intelligence report to the British government:

> Mr. Moore said that England, although small in area compared with other countries including the West Indies and British Guiana combined, wielded considerable influence in world affairs. Obviously size has nothing to do with ability to control. The West Indies were a shield for the continent of America and had played an important role in this war. They have been under the control of European powers for well nigh 300 years, and have contributed very largely to the amassing of great fortune by nationals of those European powers controlling them. . . .

The British Government talks about the cost to the British taxpayers of schemes for the Caribbean. The debt which the European powers owe to the Caribbean peoples does not begin to be repaid by these imperialistic opportunities. Moreover, these funds are not being spent as people want, but as determined for them. . . .

The amount of self government granted is negligible. The colonial office retains control over the destinies of these people, control which is inimical to their interest. . . .

It was a mis-statement to say that there was no problem of race. The British . . . since they are in the minority, found it politic not to obtrude the principle of race but to carry through a policy based on discrimination. You will see that they always divided colonies into 2 groups. . . . The whites went on to Dominion status, and the blacks and browns remained in a state of complete subjugation and utter exploitation.[15]

The NAACP was one of the few organizations invited by the State Department to serve as a consultant to the United States Delegation. They sent Walter White, Mary McLeod Bethune, and Du Bois, armed with the six-hundred-word statement "Colonialism, Peace, and the United Nations" on behalf of the NAACP, proposals on trusteeship concepts drawn up by Du Bois, and suggestions garnered from the deliberations of the Conference.[16] The fact that the West Indies National Council had not received consultant status did not dampen their determination to speak on behalf of their Caribbean brothers and sisters. Moore has explained that they felt particularly compelled to lobby in San Francisco, as they had in Havana at the Pan-American Foreign Ministers' Conference, because "we realized that the situation was such that the people could not speak for themselves. So we said we will have to do it for them. And we did."[17] Domingo took pains, however, to explain the presumption of the New York delegation in the Caribbean press.[18]

Moore prepared "An Appeal on Behalf of the Caribbean Peoples," which he and Petioni circulated among official delegates and other members of pressure groups (see chapter 11). They could not address the conference but participated in unofficial programs arranged by various organizations seeking to influence the critical charter of the world organization. When Petioni was not successful in obtaining a hearing to present the Appeal to the United Nations Conference on International Organization, Moore wrote to the secretary general, Alger Hiss:

This Council respectfully requests that consideration be given this Appeal. This is especially urgent in view of the powerful opposition evident in this Conference, even to the proposals made by China and the Soviet Union for the declaration of "eventual independence" as the object of proposed trusteeships for colonial people.

Freedom for the Caribbean peoples, as well as for the other 750,000,000 colonial peoples of America, Africa, Asia, is a prime requisite for world security and peace. Forthright guarantees for the independence of these peoples are necessary to fulfill the plain, simple, and just provisions of the Atlantic Charter, which were reaffirmed in the declaration of the United Nations and by the Yalta Conference.

Such reaffirmation and the implementation by this Conference are necessary to speed the defeat of the Japanese militarists and ensure victory over fascist slavery, terror, and war. The conflict in Syria and Lebanon warns of greater conflicts to come unless trusteeships, mandates, and all forms of imperialist rule are made to give way peacefully to independence of all subject peoples.

Will the statesmen of the United Nations not heed this warning and the plain lessons of history? Will you not keep faith with the millions living and dead who have endured great agonies and made heroic sacrifices to win freedom, security, and peace for all mankind? Will you not in this New World Charter "Proclaim liberty throughout all the land unto all the inhabitants thereof"?[19]

The brief reply from Hiss indicated that the purpose of the Conference was "to formulate the best possible charter . . . to maintain peace and security for all people of the world regardless of race, color, religion or sex. It will devote its energies and its labors exclusively to this task and it is not intended that the matter you mention will be the subject of action here."[20]

Petioni had to return to his practice, but Moore, as a representative of the Paragon Progressive Community Association and the Provisional Council of Dominated Nations in addition to the Council, stayed on contacting delegates and lobbyists, distributing copies of the Appeal and the letter to Hiss, cranking out letters and news releases, appearing on a broadcast, and speaking at meetings. The euphoria generated by the prospects of charting peace, and the cooperative exchange among representatives from diverse groups and geographic areas was exemplified by the Free India Meeting, sponsored by the United Races of America under the leadership of Hugh I. Macbeth from Los Angeles, and the program sponsored by The First Congressional Church and The American Anti-Prejudice Society on June 1. On these occasions Moore shared the platform with lobbyists such as Dr. Maneck K. Anklesaria, director of the United Press Service of India; Dr. Ramkrishna Shahu Modak, president of the Provisional World Council of Dominated Nations; Julio Pinto Gandia, secretary-general of the Nationalist Party of Puerto Rico; Raden Agoes Daroesman, president of the San Francisco Indonesian Association; and Kilsoo K. Haan of the Sino-Korean People's League.

Du Bois's pessimistic report to Arthur Spingarn stated, "Not a whisper against colonialism could be heard except from Molotov."[21] But Moore found an ally in Brigadier General Carlos P. Romulo of the Philippines, who made a stand to include independence as the goal of all colonial peoples. Moore was also encouraged by a telegram sent by the Secretary of the Interior Harold Ickes urging the American delegation to "come out strongly for independence for peoples under colonial and mandate administration. If this country failed to do so, it might well be regarded as a reversal of our traditional policy."[22]

Moore's persistence seems to have had some effect. Hugh Macbeth introduced Moore as "the gentleman who made the wonderful fight which inspired General Romulo of the Philippine delegation . . . to come out for all the people of the earth." Surely the second response from the secretary general was vastly improved. Bryant Mumford wrote to Moore for Hiss on June 23:

> The text of the chapter on trusteeship which the Commission has recom-
> mended for inclusion in the charter makes provision for the promotion of
> the political, economic, social, and educational advancement of the trust
> territories and their inhabitants and for their progressive development
> toward self-government. . . . I believe you will find that the policy stated
> provides opportunity for advancement to dependent peoples in accordance
> with their capabilities.[23]

Moore considered that the resulting section of the Charter of the United Nations, Article 76, Chapter XII, International Trusteeship, with the phrase "and their progressive development towards self-government or independence" might in time "prove to be a Magna Carta of freedom for all these peoples, provided adequate struggle is brought to bear for its implementation."[24] As a gesture of appreciation for the support given by particular delegations at the founding Conference, the Council in conjunction with the One World Association sponsored a banquet to honor Romulo, Molotov, and Mrs. Vajaya Lakshmi Pandit of India on December 6, 1946. Moore was one of the speakers.

When the sessions in San Francisco ended, Moore was still carrying the torch, giving speeches on the West Coast from Vancouver, Washington, to Los Angeles. It was not solely the demand for his appearances or his visit with his friend Cyril Briggs that delayed him; he did not have sufficient funds for the return trip. Council members were beginning to get annoyed with their stray delegate, but Petioni finally calmed them and a return ticket was obtained.

Moore has pointed out that it was often necessary to organize ad hoc committees to respond to certain developments. Such was the nature of the American Committee for West Indian Federation formed in 1947, the United Caribbean American Council in 1949, the Caribbean and Associated Advocates, and the Caribbean League of America, both active in 1957. The first group was organized by Augustine A. Austin, a Harlem realtor, upon an appeal from Caribbean political leaders to support the Second Caribbean Labour Congress. As chairperson, Austin's task was to raise $10,000 to underwrite the Congress, which he delivered personally. As secretary, Moore was charged to prepare a statement on federation.

The concept of federating some of the British colonies was far from new but had gained new impetus following the rise of local leadership during the postriot period. Moore had included a demand for federation in the resolutions prepared at the Brussels Congress Against Colonial Oppression and Imperialism in 1927, and his position along with that of his colleagues had been expressed by George Padmore, who was working with Moore in the ANLC at the time:

> The Federation of the British West Indies will undoubtedly make for the beginning of a nationalist movement. . . . Those in this country can be depended upon to play an important role in helping their countrymen to foster such a forward movement as the Federation of the Islands. Their group life in America has tended to unite them . . . for it is the first time in the history of these peoples that they have been brought together. . . . *The Negro Champion* . . . stands ready to give its full support to a militant movement among the islanders for the federation and the freedom of the West Indies.[25]

Otto Huiswoud had also reported the growing sentiment in favor of federation in the Caribbean in 1930, but sustained efforts by the Harlem contingent could not be mounted until there were sufficient developments in the Caribbean that could be supported. The issue was not simply whether to form a federation or which islands should be included. A basic question was, Which came first, independence or federation?

The "Memorandum on Federation and Self-Government" that Moore prepared for the Caribbean Labour Congress at Coke Hall in Kingston, Jamaica, September 2–9, 1947, took the position that there could be "no federation worthy of the name where there is no recognition or achievement of actual independence and sovereignty." The Kingston meeting was intended to serve as a caucus, affording an opportunity for some of the Afro-Caribbean leaders to iron out problems, resolve some of their insular differences, and present a more unified approach on federation at the conference called by the secretary of state for the colonies of Great Britain, Arthur Creech-Jones, for September 11–19 in Montego Bay. Moore and his colleagues wanted to strengthen the argument for a federation of independent nations rather than a structure within the crown colony. Prior to the conference in Kingston, Moore and a small group called upon the colonial attaché of the British Embassy, Ernest Sabben-Claire, in order to influence British acceptance of federation associated with independence and of financial support to rebuild the economy in the region. Their nineteen-page document addressed to the Congress included previous statements presented at the 1940 Pan-American Foreign Ministers' and the 1945 United Nations conferences, the record of the meeting with Mr. Sabben-Claire, and a Historical Summary and Political Analysis of Federation. It was presented in Kingston to influence the deliberations in Montego Bay (see chapter 11).

Moore's article "West Indies Federate for Nationhood," which appeared in *The Amsterdam News,* September 27, 1947, indicates the success of the Montego Bay conference toward federation but also reveals the opposition of the key leader of Jamaica, Alexander Bustamante, who refused to attend the Kingston meeting of the Caribbean Labour Congress. As Moore put it: "A great deal remains to be done if the Caribbean nation born at the Kingston Conference and swaddled at Montego Bay, is to live, grow strong and make its contribution to democracy in the Americas and the world at large."

Moore's vision of the role of independent Caribbean nations in the United Nations deliberations was jolted in September 1948, when Grantley H. Adams, who was serving as president of the Caribbean Labour Congress, accepted the invitation by the secretary of state for the colonies to serve as an alternate on the British delegation to the United Nations General Assembly. Moore was appalled by reports from Paris that Adams was a spokesman for Britain's stand against a resolution requiring controlling governments of non-self-governing areas to submit information on economic, social, and educational affairs to the United Nations. As secretary of the American Committee for West Indian Federation, he fired off press releases repudiating Adams's statement and charged:

> For a leader of the suffering colonial people in the Caribbean, elected to office on a program of complete self-government, to attack any power upholding the rights of colonial people to secure presentation of the truth about their miserable plight before the United Nations, is not only to sanction the attempted denial and betrayal of basic human rights of all oppressed peoples but also to exhibit such abysmal political ineptitude as would tend to deter and destroy all support for the struggle of the colonial peoples for their freedom.[26]

Moore's communication with Richard Hart, secretary of the Caribbean Labour Congress, evoked a similar response from Hart, who promptly placed Moore's letter and his own statement of repudiation in the next bulletin of the Congress.[27] Strong objections were also being circulated by African groups in Africa and London, declaring in one case that "Adams by his irresponsible and inspired utterances put into his ignoble mouth by his British masters has dealt a wicked blow to all suffering peoples."[28] Adams's allies were able, however, to counteract the charges against their leader by claiming that Hart had acted without sanction from the officers of the Congress. They also obtained a statement from Dudley Barrow in New York upholding Adams's position in an attempt to discredit Moore. Even though Wynter Crawford published the releases from New York and Africa in *The Barbados Observer,* he is convinced that the people of Barbados did not understand the import of Adams's role. In years to come, some who rallied to the defense of "their man in Paris" regretted having participated in the hero's welcome when Adams returned to Barbados. But at the time, Moore and his colleagues in New York were discovering that their recognition of Adams as the "West Indian darling of the Colonial Office" was not shared by many Adams followers in the Caribbean.[29]

In 1950 the New York group was called upon by Caribbean leaders to support the Caribbean Labour Congress slated to convene in April in Trinidad. The second drive to raise $10,000 faced the resistance of the McCarthy era. Some former supporters withdrew "because of the association of the United Caribbean American Council with progressive leaders and organizations militantly fighting against reaction in the country and for that reason branded by the current hysteria. . . ."[30] At a Caribbean-American Folk Festival on January 25, 1950, at which T. Albert Marryshow, vice-president of the Caribbean Labour Congress, was the guest speaker, Moore pledged his support for the forthcoming meeting of the Congress.[31] When the Trinidad conference was cancelled the Harlem contingent was relieved of the pressure to meet Richard Hart's urgent requests for financial assistance, but it is clear that Moore had attempted to sponsor appeals because of his conviction that the Congress was a unique force struggling to promote a militant and progressive labor policy, and the 1950 meeting significant as an effective expression of the will of the Caribbean people.

The Harlem Caribbean leaders did not only resort to ad hoc committees in order to press their position on independence and federation. On at least two occasions, A. M. Wendell Malliet arranged for presentations to British representatives in the United States and called upon Moore to assist as spokesman. In 1947, prior to the Montego Bay Conference, Moore made a statement clarifying the type of federation sought at a discussion held with Mr. Ernest Sabben-Claire, colonial attaché of the British Embassy, serving as representative of the British government on the Caribbean Commission. The delegation, which included V. P. Bourne-Vanneck of *The New York Age* and Augustine Austin in addition to Malliet and Moore, first presented six questions regarding the British government's position on federation and then countered Sabben-Claire's response with Moore's reply (see chapter 11). Their demands included a substantial sum to be provided by the British government to furnish necessary initial financing for a Caribbean Economic Plan for Rehabilitation.

In 1953 at a luncheon for Lord Listowel, arranged by Malliet at the Hotel Theresa in Harlem just prior to the London Conference on Federation, Moore made the main address, stressing again the significance of genuine federation (see chapter 11). He reminded the distinguished visitor that the Caribbean peoples for a considerable period had been executing actual administration and government except for the few topmost officials appointed by the British government, and that the majority were descendents of people brought from Africa, where they had governed themselves for centuries. He challenged the necessity for continuing "guardianship" and raised the question: "Who will guard the guardians; who will civilize the civilizers?"

Moore and his colleagues were critical of Caribbean leaders for not developing a specific economic Caribbean Plan, but they continued to press for British financial support for federation. When Britain denied the Caribbean request for two hundred million pounds, the Caribbean and Associated Advocates issued a supporting "Statement on British Secretary's Rejection of Federation Committee's Request For Financial Aid to Caribbean People" prepared by Moore in 1957, claiming that the sum requested was a small part of the wealth drawn from the area. He warned that:

> Unless an adequate Plan for Economic and Social Development is speedily achieved, along with the requisite financial underwriting, there will be no possibility whatsoever of a beneficial free Federation. There would then emerge only a forced fusion of existing indigence, hunger, squalor, misery, disease and death in an anachronistic, poverty-ridden, colonial danger zone, spread out along the vital approaches to the richest citadel in the broad domains of the Western World, whose watchwords are freedom and democracy.[32]

Federation became a reality January 3, 1958—joining the islands of Barbados, Jamaica, Trinidad and Tobago, the Leewards group (Antigua, Montserrat, and St. Kitts-Nevis-Anguilla) and the Windwards group (Dominica, Grenada, St. Lucia, and St. Vincent). Ceremonies were not limited to Trinidad, the new seat of government. New York also had its "Salute to The Federated West Indies" on April 22, sponsored by the Caribbean League of America along with other events marking the great occasion.

Federation proved, however, to be short-lived. To the bitter disappointment of the Harlem associates, the federation established was flawed as they had feared and became a fact of history when Jamaica withdrew in 1962. As the structure faltered, more articles appeared analyzing the insular direction of some of the leaders. Moore prepared several articles, creating quite a stir in the Caribbean press with reports of Grantley Adams's tactless derogatory remarks regarding Jamaicans and Trinidadians at a meeting in New York. In similar articles Domingo declared Adams unfit for his high office.[33]

The long years of collaboration between Moore and Domingo reached a turning point in 1956. To Moore's consternation Domingo reversed his commitment to federation and issued an essay, *British West Indian Federation—A Critique,* strongly disapproving the inclusion of Jamaica as "artificial and fraught with the possibility of disaster" because the island would have 38 percent of the seats in the Federal Parliament while it had 59 percent of the territory and 53 percent of the population. He delivered an unexpected and devastating blow when he claimed that "Leadership of New

York federationists is in the control of individuals from the eastern islands where the issue has been alive for generations. . . . They see in federation a source of borrowed strength and the means of easing population pressures . . . thereby effecting their own insular improvement and salvation." To avoid the possibility that Jamaica's independence might be delayed by federation, Domingo argued that "Any demand for both objectives to be obtained together invited failure and revealed a lack of elementary political sagacity."[34]

An unpublished essay, "Independent Caribbean Nationhood: Has It Been Achieved or Set Back?" expressed Moore's deep disappointment and dismay (see chapter 12). His response to his friend and others affirmed that his advocacy of Caribbean nationhood was unshaken. He never relented in his conviction that federation was essential for national survival and integrity.

In 1982 Hope Stevens at the fourth annual conference of the Barbadian-American Alliance in New York raised the question "Does the history of the Caribbean since 1959 suggest that the need for closer union is today more urgent than it has ever been?" In his affirmative answer, he reminded the audience:

> It was Moore's basic conviction that no federation of West Indian colonial units could succeed. Federation, he believed, and he supported this view with copious historical references, could only be achieved by the voluntary decision of free and independent states coming together for their mutual advantage. But he nevertheless supported every effort to end colonial control of the Caribbean units, hoping always that the freed Caribbean colonies would coalesce eventually into a true Federation of independent island states.[35]

It should be noted that the establishment of military bases in the Caribbean was a concern that Moore and his associates expressed on many occasions. Aside from the potential threat to the development of national sovereignty, they anticipated the introduction of an American brand of racism by United States military personnel as had occurred during the American occupation in Panama and Haiti. This fear of U.S. military bases, which had been a factor in Domingo's internment, extended well beyond the war period. In 1957 the issue flared up again and the Caribbean League of America demanded the return of the Chaguaramas site to the people of Trinidad.

Moore was also quite distressed when the British suspended the Constitution of British Guiana in 1953. He has stated that he drafted and presented a "Declaration and Appeal for Upholding the Democratic Rights of the People of British Guiana and of the Caribbean." The document, however, has not been located.

The purpose of the United Caribbean American Council, organized in 1949 with Austin as chairman (succeeded by Captain Hugh Mulzac) and Moore as secretary, was to counteract passage of legislation restricting immigration by the U.S. Congress. Protests against the Judd Bill were not only registered with United States legislators but also submitted to the British government. Austin and Moore called upon the British Embassy in March 1949 with the hope that the British would urge the United States to alter the restrictive policy toward British subjects. They also submitted a statement against the Judd Bill at the public hearing held by the Subcommittee of the United States Senate Committee on the Judiciary on July 20, 1949.

The Judd Bill was defeated, but the McCarran Act, which spawned the Committee to Act Against the McCarran and Walter Bills of 1952, with J. A. Rogers as chairman and Moore as secretary, was passed. The three-page document Moore prepared on that occasion, "Memorandum Submitted by the Committee to Act Against the McCarran and Walter Bills," was widely circulated but failed to convince the legislators that one hundred immigrants per year from Caribbean "colonies" was grossly disproportionate to quotas for other areas.

While the emphasis here is deliberately on Moore's role, it should be clear that he always worked with a group of interested fellow Caribbeans and Afro-Americans born in the United States, and that the support garnered for any particular cause involved a sizable group. The players changed slightly from time to time or from issue to issue, but the main objective was consistent: self-determination, independence, federation.

The appeals and statements cited in this account represent the tip of the iceberg. There were many other letters, documents, resolutions, petitions, and press releases that reflect the passion and extent of the strike for Caribbean independence levied from Harlem. Moore was but one of many fired by this cause. Reginald Pierrepointe (Barbados); W. A. Domingo, Rev. Ethelred Brown, A. M. Wendell Malliet, and J. A. Rogers (Jamaica); Atty. Hope R. Stevens (Nevis); Dr. Charles Petioni and Herman P. Osborne (Trinidad); Augustine A. Austin (Antigua); Atty. Joseph C. Morris (Guyana); and Dr. Gerald A. Spencer (St. Lucia) were just a few of the talented leaders from different islands, walks of life, and political persuasions engaged in the Pan-Caribbean movement. They were very capable, articulate writers and spokesmen whose story has yet to be told. Moore's record is traceable, to some extent, because they recognized his polemical and promotional talents and elected or selected him to act as spokesman and/or secretary. They could count on his keen command of both the spoken and written word no matter what the occasion.

Pierrepointe has stated that when ideas had to be put into writing Moore was the one who did it. When he came into a meeting he would bring drafts for approval. "Here and there there were changes and obviously those ideas were approved by whatever organization or committee. . . . Without a doubt, he wrote most of the documents."[36] Thus Moore's penchant for wording resolutions and appeals provided the Harlem group with a series of historic documents testifying to thirty years of protest utilizing every possible instrument within their limited command.

To achieve this record, there were hours and hours of talk, seemingly innocuous steam-venting, or recreational banter whenever the cronies congregated. Moore's book store was appropriately called a "center," for there were more arguments than books exchanged in the tiny quarters. Like Campbell's Tailor Shop, which Department of Justice informers frequented to overhear the political commentary of the radicals of 1920, Moore's shop became a center of dialogue on world affairs. On any evening one could find a small group intensely engaged in discussion, with Lodie perched on the single available stool acting as combination scorekeeper and amen corner or as referee when the debate became overheated. Out of these encounters and similar ones next door in King's shoe store grew decisions to form organizations and delegations—actions to implement the ideas honed through deliberation.

These "awaymen" dared to direct their appeals to all resources that might respond: world and regional bodies, United States legislators, British officials, and Caribbean labor and political leaders. They attempted to mold community opinion in the United States and the Caribbean. They presented Caribbean leaders such as T. Albert Marryshow of Grenada, Wynter Crawford and Grantley Adams of Barbados, Norman Manley and E. L. Allen of Jamaica, Victor Bryan of Trinidad, John Carter of British Guiana, and Albert A. Thorne of Barbados and British Guiana to New York audiences. They directed a barrage of releases at the local and Caribbean press. Articles by Domingo, for example, appeared quite regularly in Jamaican newspapers. Through Pierrepointe's West Indies News Service and other similar channels there was more communication between New York and the islands than between the various islands.

Paul Blanshard's 1944 report to the United States government on social and political forces in the Caribbean gives a clue as to how the stage was set for such dramatic activity centered in Harlem:

> There is no single city in the Caribbean area which serves as a racial capital of the region, and the various radical movements in the dependent territories have no central controlling group.
>
> In fact, the evidence indicates that they have very little contact with each other. Many of the most important Negro and West Indian leaders of labor and political organizations have never even met each other, and the newspapers of the various territories carry only meager allowances of news from other Caribbean centers.
>
> To some extent New York City supplies the deficiency as an intellectual capital for the Negro peoples of the hemisphere. . . .
>
> British West Indian Negroes gravitate to New York City, and have formed there a large Negro colony which serves as an important focus of West Indian thought. . . .
>
> In Harlem the West Indian Negro is subjected to a general and a special influence, the general pressure of the Negro community in favor of the improvement of racial status, and the special pressure of several West Indian

propaganda organizations which seek to mobilize all natives of the West Indies in favor of economic reform and the extension of self-government.[37]

Franklin Knight credits these West Indian expatriates of the Harlem Renaissance, particularly McKay, Garvey, Domingo, and Moore, "who were articulate, politically organized, and aware of the Caribbean position in world affairs" as giving "support to a more vigorous local press by contributing fiery letters and provocative articles, and [beginning] the literary shift away from the Eurocentric romanticism of the nineteenth century to a type of work focusing on Caribbean society and classes." But he also points out that there were factors that undermined the growth of a larger Caribbean nationalism.[38] Other scholars and leaders in the Caribbean have recognized the development of this "fragmented nationalism" among the Caribbean peoples and an impetus for a Pan-Caribbean movement from émigrés abroad.

One might wonder why the New York group deemed it necessary to expend their energies fueling the Caribbean press. Wynter A. Crawford, a member of the Barbados Assembly for twenty-six years and publisher of *The Barbados Observer* for forty-one years, confirmed not only that he received and printed information regularly supplied by Pierrepointe and Moore but that their organizations "really fomented the interests and efforts" in the Caribbean.[39] H. A. Vaughn, who served the Barbados government in many capacities including legislator, chief magistrate, and ambassador to the United Nations, has explained that pan–West Indian protests were not put forward by the early local leaders, not even Charles Duncan O'Neal, who had wide experiences in Britain and various islands.

> That was a point of view which would rather strike the others in the States more than it would strike those in the West Indies. . . . We had no sense of community. It was just separate and very distinct communities, each with its own peculiar history, in some cases with its own peculiar dialect, pursuing its own peculiar goals. . . . It seems to me that the one thing that inevitably caused those [in the United States] to rise together was the marked contrast between the suave and subtle but none-the-less degrading discrimination of the West Indies and the open, frank, brutal, uncompromising rule and method . . . in the United States. . . . The chaps who went to the United States from the West Indies had some sort of cohesion knocked into them and it forced them to stand up and confront something more brutal than anything you could dream up in the West Indies.

Vaughn concludes that the strong motivation and perspective for a Pan-Caribbean movement was due in large part to the resurgence of race consciousness in the United States, which gave rise to a political consciousness. This stimulus of race pride helped the émigrés realize that "the majority of the inhabitants of the West Indies were looked down upon, were held back, trampled upon because of their African ancestry. Therefore, they felt toward the West Indies as Du Bois, Walter White or Padmore felt toward Africa. 'These are our people. We have to be Pan-Caribbean.' "[40]

Gordon Lewis ties the absence of "any real Pan-Caribbean consciousness in the region" to "the anomalous decentralization" and isolation of each island produced by the controlling external relations of each particular island with its imperial owner rather than with its Caribbean neighbors.[41] Thus, it was essential for the Harlem advocates to maintain pressure on more than one front in order to elicit solidarity among the populace in the Caribbean as well as relief from the domination of the colonial powers.

The spate of activity as reflected by the documents prepared by Moore was directed primarily at the seats of power. When Moore was grounded by the loss of his passport, his role evolved as wielder of the pen rather than organizer in the Caribbean like Huiswoud and Domingo.[42] To maintain as broad a base of support as possible in Harlem and to strike the target at each opportunity, it was necessary to limit the strategies to realistic pressure upon government forces. Independence and federation were essential first steps before the Caribbean people could exert self-determination. Hence there are no appeals addressed to the Caribbean people or treatises describing the type of society that he hoped would develop following independence.

Yet from his Caribbean vantage point Gordon Lewis was able to discern that there was a vision beyond the transference of power from Britain to local leaders. In 1968 he wrote:

> For after 1938 the potentially revolutionary *élan vital* of the masses was anaesthetized by being canalized into institutions—trade unions, political parties, co-operative societies—controlled by the bourgeois groups. The leadership elements that resisted the process—whether because of a radical racial perspective, as with Garveyism, or because of a radical political perspective, as with individuals like Lennox Pierre and John La Rose in Trinidad and Richard Moore and Reginald Pierrepointe in Barbados—were either pushed aside or purged by the dominant right-wing forces.[43]

Attempts to influence opinion in the Caribbean were subtle and can only be discovered in rare comments such as Francis Mark's description of the forces of change following the 1938 riots. In *The History of the Barbados Workers' Union*, he stated: "Into the ferment, too, went a number of other factors— . . . the editorial policies of W. A. Crawford whose visit to the U.S.A. in 1938 resulted in his constant advocacy of trade union organization after his return."[44]

Surely the New York effort cannot be singled out as the major factor in the gaining of federation and the independence of some islands. There were significant developments in the islands as well as pressure from Caribbean expatriates in Britain. Indeed, the complex events associated with the course of the British Empire and World War II cannot be ignored.

The New York stalwarts were convinced, however, that their agitation played some part in hastening the day when they could participate in independence celebrations. They could also take pride in the fact that their agitation had been through their own organizations.

November 23, 1966, was a glorious day, when Moore set foot on Barbados soil again. Fifty-seven years had passed, but it was not just the return "home" that excited him. Witnessing the Union Jack being lowered and the new Barbados flag of blue and yellow with Neptune's trident hoisted over the Garrison Savannah on November 29 made his return truly momentous. In preparation for the grand celebration, the Barbados government had extended invitations to individuals viewed as having been helpful to the cause of independence. Moore's invitation was based upon his contribution to Caribbean independence and the field of Afro-American, African, and Caribbean history.[45] Moore and his wife, Pierre-pointe, Hope Stevens, and a few others from New York were guests of the government for the eight days of ceremonies.

Moore decided to share this significant moment in history with his family and took along his daughter, her husband, their three children, and his grandson's wife. The Moore-Turner enclave of eight participated enthusiastically in as many activities as the formal invitations permitted, then reluctantly separated for their return to New York. Moore and his wife remained for a month to explore and experience the island more fully. There were no relatives that he knew of to visit. He searched for his Stream Road homestead with the help of Bishop Reginald Barrow but could not locate any site that he could recognize. Barbados had changed and so had Richard B. Moore.

IV

THE "AWAYMAN" RETURNS
TO BARBADOS

The invitation from the government of Barbados to the Independence celebration inspired another change in Moore's life. While the dream of returning "home" is always retained by expatriates, Moore had never planned to leave New York. Errol Barrow has pointed out that Moore seemed to see Barbados very differently once he had visited there in 1966.[1] The fifty-year-old memory overlaid with reports emphasizing the difficult conditions in the islands had produced a tarnished image. The Barbados of 1966 cast a spell and Moore began to consider spending time there.

To Moore's family the announcement, which coincided with the Barbados trip, that New York State intended to comdemn all the buildings in the block where his store was located in order to construct a high-rise office building seemed like an appropriate signal for retirement. To the seventy-three-year-old collector the concept of retirement was anathema. He would consider only relocation of the store, despite illness and the decision to part with his collection.

For some time he had been considering the establishment of a library. He was fearful that his extensive collection, carefully assembled over half a century, might be dispersed like those of earlier Afro-American collectors, George Young and Rev. Charles D. Martin, rather than retained for the public's use like Arthur Schomburg's. Harlem already had the Schomburg and Howard University the Moorland-Spingarn Libraries. For a period the emerging nations of Africa seemed to be serious contenders for the library.

Moore's books and pamphlets could not be housed in one location and were distributed among the stock for sale at the store, in rented space in the Apollo building on 125th Street, and at his apartment in Brooklyn. The store was frequently closed because of illness or other business, and his friend, Reginald Pierrepointe, who feared that the valuable books might be destroyed by fire or vandalism, urged him to consider Barbados. Other Barbadian friends took up the argument in favor of Barbados, but it was Errol Barrow, the premier of Barbados (prime minister following Independence), who interceded directly with Moore and convinced him that Barbados was a suitable home for his collection.

Barrow negotiated an agreement by sending the chief archivist of Barbados, Michael J. Chandler, to appraise the collection and then obtained the consent of his cabinet and the financial support of the Lions Club of Barbados for the purchase and shipment of the books.[2] Barrow has described the negotiations:

> It started with one of my trips to New York discussing what he was going to do about the books. . . . Richard indicated to me that he was going to give up the business and that several universities were interested. Since Barbados was his birthplace, I thought they should be here and I started agitation with the cabinet. . . . If the Lions had not decided to come forward with the money, we would have found the money to buy them. Somebody at the University suggested the Lions . . . the first really national thing they would be doing for Barbados. So they came forward with the $30,000. It is just as simple as that.[3]

The price paid for the library does not reflect the true value of the collection. The books, pamphlets, and documents estimated by Chandler to total 15,000 volumes not only represented the investment of his lifetime earnings but was Moore's sole insurance for the future. He was satisfied with the agreement, however, because Barbados was to be the permanent home of his endeavors.

In his article "The Richard B. Moore Collection and Its Collector," W. Burghardt Turner explained other factors influencing Moore's decision:

> The placement of the Moore Collection at the Centre for Multi-Racial Studies at Cave Hill, Barbados, is the result of a deliberate decision on the part of Mr. Moore. Protection and use were the key factors. He wanted assurance that his collection which represented so many years of effort and sacrifice would be properly used and protected. He also wanted to be sure that students would have full access without danger of censorship or restriction. He feared this might not be the case if his collection fell under the control of a "pro-imperialist" or "pro-capitalist" institution such as one of the major predominantly "white" universities. He concluded that his collection could go only to an African University, a Caribbean country, the University of the West Indies, or one of the predominantly Afro-American colleges in the United States. . . . The housing of the library at the Centre at Cave Hill seemed to offer the best of all solutions to the Barbadian expatriate and political radical who had worked so long for Caribbean independence.
>
> His preference for the collection to go to Barbados was evidently quite clear to Mr. Chandler. . . . In a confidential letter to the ministry he wrote, "the owner (Mr. Moore) is very keen that the Library should come to Barbados, and it is unlikely, if it does not, that any other institution could purchase it at this price."[4]

Chandler considered the collection unique and as late as 1979 stated that there was not a library in the Caribbean to equal it.[5] While he reported to the Ministry of Education in 1965 that "it is impossible not to be enthusiastic about the prospect of acquiring the collection," he warned that the purchase should not be made unless funds were provided for the maintenance, development, and extension of the library on a permanent basis. He indicated that Moore would wish certain conditions to be observed: "The books should be preserved as a reference collection, but should be made available to the public. They should be suitably housed, and cared for by adequate specialized staff. The collection should be developed and extended to keep it up to date." Chandler went on to state: "It would be a denial of true scholarship and a breach of faith with Mr. Moore to allow the library to become a 'dead' collection. He regards it as an endowment to his native land, but not in mortmain."[6]

The significance of the conditions and considerations transmitted by Chandler has been heightened by the fact that the library, transferred and officially presented on December 30, 1971, has been closed ever since Sussex University discontinued the Centre for Multi-Racial Studies in 1973. Moore was distressed that the books were not available but felt helpless to intervene because the ownership and responsibility rested completely with the government of Barbados.[7] From time to time the fate of the collection is revived in administrative and legislative deliberations. An editorial in *The Nation* in April 1984 urged the reopening of the library:

> The books he had collected in a lifetime of service to his cause—the education of black people in their history and accomplishment—accompanied Richard Moore when he returned to his native land and are now the property of the Barbadian people. They have spent the last several years since their arrival lying fallow in a building near the Cave Hill Campus of the University of the West Indies while bureaucracy made up its mind about what should be done with them. That decision ought not to have been difficult since books are, by definition, to be read.[8]

Within four short years, from 1967 to 1971, Moore experienced several major readjustments. The shelves of the bookstore and his home library had been stripped for shipment of the collection to Barbados; his book center had been closed after a quarter of a century, relocated on a second floor much farther east on 125th Street, and then closed permanently after a few years; his plan for another visit to Barbados with Lodie had been abandoned; and Lodie had died. Her death in March 1971 was a serious blow, and he could no longer live in their apartment in Brooklyn. He moved to his daughter's home in Patchogue, Long Island, New York.

Despite his tragic loss, he made new plans for a stay in Barbados at the guest house operated by his friend from the days of the 1938 upheavals in Barbados, Wynter A. Crawford. A new pattern emerged of escaping the northern winter by going to Barbados in the fall and returning to Patchogue each spring. Bathing in the tropical sea and relaxing in the warm sun seemed to stimulate his "work" of lecturing, writing, and publishing, which he pursued vigorously wherever he was. While in Barbados he lectured at the Centre for Multi-Racial Studies, the Barbados Workers' Union, Erdiston College, and the Barbados Rediffusion broadcasts. In 1972 he took off from Barbados under the sponsorship of the Afro-

American Institute and with the assistance of Jill Sheppard, warden and organizing secretary of the Centre for Multi-Racial Studies, for a speaking tour of ten islands: St. Vincent, Grenada, Trinidad, St. Lucia, Dominica, Antigua, Montserrat, St. Thomas, Haiti, and Jamaica. His granddaughter, Sylvia, accompanied him to four islands and his daughter to four other islands, but he declared they came along for the ride, not because he needed any assistance.

He wrote articles for Barbados newspapers and magazines, including a review of a series of musical programs conducted at the Barbados Museum, and reacted to local events with letters to the editor. He was very careful to avoid political matters because he recognized that, with the coming of independence, Barbados no longer needed the voice of the "awayman." In fact, advice from "outsiders" was resented, so he kept his political views to himself.

While residing in Patchogue he filled requests for lectures from colleges and community groups, served as a curriculum consultant to the Uniondale School District, attended meetings of the Association for the Study of Afro-American Life and History, and organized the Pathway Publishers in order to print and distribute monographs on Afro-American and Afro-Caribbean affairs. *Caribs, "Cannibals," and Human Relations,* which he wrote following his trip to Antigua, where he saw a sign in the museum regarding cannibals (see chapter 10), and T. Albert Marryshow's *Cycles of Civilization,* written in 1917, were published in 1972 and 1973 respectively. The third publication was to have been a reprint of Frederick Douglass's "Lecture on Haiti," but it never went to press.

Amid these pursuits and orchestrating the business of the Afro-American Institute, he conceived of another trip "home." He was a great follower of the archeological investigations of Louis and Mary Leakey and wanted to see Olduvai Gorge in Tanzania. He attempted to organize a tour including Olduvai Gorge, Ethiopia, and Egypt. When that proved to be a rather complicated endeavor, he decided to attend the Second World Black and African Festival of Arts and Culture in Lagos, Nigeria. He had arranged for a friend to accompany him and was preparing a manuscript to deliver when a postponement was announced. By the time the festival commenced in January 1977 it seemed risky because of his health for him to attend.

He made one more plan for Africa. His daughter and family invited him to join them on a trip to Senegal in September 1977. He made reservations to share accommodations with his grandson Mitchell but became ill, and his place was taken by his other grandson, Richard. He took pleasure in his grandsons' memorable expedition but had to face the disappointment that he would never see Africa.

The second attack of cancer of the prostate, which occurred in August 1977 while he was in Barbados, did not have a good prognosis and he was hospitalized for four months. To the doctor's surprise Moore rallied with the help of the nursing staff and the presence of his family, especially that of his granddaughter, who insisted on spending a week at the hospital with him. When he began to assume the role of organizer on the ward, it was a sign that his recovery warranted a change to a nursing home. One year after his admission to St. Joseph Hospital, he entered Queen Elizabeth Hospital, where he died on August 18, 1978. After a brief ceremony during which J. Cameron Tudor delivered the eulogy, Moore was buried at Westbury Cemetery in the land of his birth.[9] The article on Moore by Mel Tapley that appeared in *The New York Amsterdam News* on September 23, 1978, concluded: "It is appropriate that the sign, 'Frederick Douglass Book Center,' although the center has long since gone and its proprietor has hung out a 'Closed' note for the last time, still hangs in Harlem." In 1984 it was still there.

To the German Catholic nun responsible for his care during his months in St. Joseph Hospital, Moore was an enigma. She pondered, worried about, and prayed for this man who insisted he had no religion yet expressed himself in Latin and biblical phrases. She knew he was really religious because it was obvious that he was a good man, a thoughtful man, a gentleman. Little did she imagine that his language could also be punctuated with vitriolic castigations against the oppressors he considered the real sinners. Nor could she comprehend why the philosophy of Marx had replaced that of Christ's followers. Nor could she appreciate that he had substituted a vision of a better way of life on earth for a vision of heaven, and that he feared a world of injustice, bigotry, and war for his grandchildren more than death. Despite her inability to know whence her patient came, her summation was right: he was good, thoughtful, and a gentle man as well as a gentleman. Those who knew him better would have added: But he was a fighter!

While he had lost the poem that McKay dedicated to him, another written by McKay in 1919, which he characterized as the "famous cry of passionate revolt," was always with him. It was the essence of the inspiration that he shared on hundreds of occasions, particularly the lines:

> If we must die, Oh let us nobly die,
> So that our precious blood may not be shed
> In vain; then even the monsters we defy
> Shall be constrained to honor us though dead!
> . . . .
> What though before us lies the open grave?
> Like men we'll face the murderous cowardly pack,
> Pressed to the wall, dying, but fighting back!

Like McKay, Domingo, Briggs, and Huiswoud, Moore had chosen his weapon to fight back: not swords, not guns, but words.

V

COLLECTING RICHARD B. MOORE'S SPEECHES AND WRITINGS

The hundreds of speeches that Richard B. Moore was asked to make, and the numerous articles he published and was invited to contribute to various newspapers, magazines, and journals would have amounted to a sizable collection. Despite his great productivity over five decades, none of his speeches and few of his writings were considered available. Scholars conducting research on the Harlem Renaissance, Afro-American radicals, Garvey, or activities among Afro-Caribbeans in New York sought information and materials from Moore and members of his family, but his publications were not compiled nor his personal papers organized or complete. The organizations with which he had been associated had not maintained archives. The history of those functioning prior to 1939 seemed relegated to the few notes prepared by the Works Progress Administration Writers' Program of New York City or the agents of the Justice Department, while facts about those of the subsequent thirty years were confined primarily to participants' memories. Errol Barrow was entirely accurate when he surmised: "The political organizations were of a vague character based upon oral expression, probably not making and retaining adequate records nor appreciating their historic role."[1]

The decision by his daughter and son-in-law to compile a collection of his works and prepare a biographical essay to place those expressions in context was based upon several considerations: (1) the dearth of information on radicals in Harlem and the highly biased accounts of the Cold War era (most of which had only fleeting references to Moore); (2) the demand for details on Moore's activities and his associates; and (3) his intent to publish a small collection of articles and issue a revised version of *The Name "Negro"—Its Origin and Evil Use*. The search for articles by and about Moore required dogged detective work because many of them had appeared in obscure or foreign publications. His papers, which were in the possession of the editors, were a valuable asset despite the limited scope and poor condition of many files. As family members the editors also had access to close friends and associates, many of whom were interviewed, and to interviews of Moore that had been conducted by one of the editors and five other scholars associated with universities. Pertinent archival records and newspapers were combed and records sought from the United States departments of Justice, State, Immigration, and Labor under the Freedom of Information Act.

It is ironic that some of the most vivid descriptions of Moore's speeches were found in the Department of Justice records. The actual speeches were elusive, however; most had vanished with the wind, especially the hundreds given extemporaneously. The true flavor and impact of his oratory, which depended upon the astute use of devices—modulations in tone, rising tempo and pitch of the voice, stress, clarity of enunciation—could not have been captured for the reader but certainly would have been of value for the record. Unfortunately, that opportunity did not present itself. Very few true speeches were identified compared to the number of prepared lectures. Over seventy written presentations were located, covering a range of lengthy polemical treatises, carefully researched, original historical monographs, mimeographed appeals, news releases and articles, fiery open letters, descriptive essays, book reviews, poetry, and unpublished manuscripts. There was even an "Exiles' Anthem" composed for the independence of Barbados. Correspondence was not considered for inclusion.

In order to arrive at a balanced selection, the editors determined that the items chosen for inclusion should (1) be representative of his perspective, (2) reveal events or activities of the period, (3) reflect the variety of his interests and concerns, (4) illustrate the various modes of expression and range of publications, (5) present a unique interpretation, (6) document responses of groups in Harlem to national or international issues, and (7) collectively represent various periods of his life. The themes that emerged are a reflection of his socialist development during the Harlem Renaissance, his reaction to distortions in African and Afro-American history, with its legacy of racism, and his commitment to Caribbean liberation. While the editors strove for a kind of balance in the collection, it should be noted that the content of Moore's writings is not in direct proportion to his activities. To fellow Harlemites, he was clearly associated with the movement for Afro-American identity and liberation through his lectures and the book center's emphasis on Afro-American and African history. Yet the assembly of his writings reveals his long-term agitation for Caribbean independence and nationhood. It is because of the preponderance of materials on the Caribbean and the fact that these documents have not been previously collected and printed that they occupy a major portion of the collection finally selected for publication.

The documents pertaining to the New York Caribbean organizations' thrust evolved in a chainlike fashion, with each document citing previous appeals. Deletions have been made to avoid some highly repetitious statements, but much duplication is retained because it is anticipated that the selections will be viewed independently. Copies of the originals will be available at the Schomburg Center for Research in Black Culture and the Barbados Department of Archives for reference.

Moore's style of writing was greatly influenced by his rhetorical devices, particularly the manipulation of phrasing, alliteration, emphasis, and repetition, and the inclusion of poetry and other quotations. In order to include a large selection of significant articles, elisions have been conservatively used to avoid redundancy and thereby conserve space. Five long selections (*The Name "Negro"—Its Origin and Evil Use, Caribs, "Cannibals," and Human Relations,* "A New Look at African History," "Du Bois and Pan-Africa," and "Independent Caribbean Nationhood") have passages omitted to render them more concise and appropriate for a collection. In all cases Moore's original ideas, expressions, and format have been retained. Rare insertions to accommodate grammar or continuity are clearly indicated. At the time of the formation of the Afroamerican Institute the spelling "Afroamerican" appeared in some of Moore's writings because it was the preference of the majority of the members of the Institute. "Afro-American" has been used consistently by the editors, however, because it was Moore's preferred usage.

The thirty-three selections have been grouped topically, using a chronological succession within each of the eight sections. The earliest article appeared in 1920, when Moore was twenty-six years old. While there is a progression throughout the decades, half of the works were produced during the sixties. This quantity may indicate Moore's productivity during his seventh decade but says more about his times. It was not until then that the tide began to overtake his long agitation for recognition of and response to the history, contributions, and plight of Africans, Afro-Americans, and the peoples of the Caribbean.

Moore's life and works were brought together in this volume not solely to supply missing information and give testimony to his contribution but, it is hoped, to encourage students of Afro-American and Caribbean history to complete the picture of the radical and Pan-Caribbean movements in Harlem, and to inspire the youth in whom he had placed much hope. For in 1974 Moore was quick to admit, "Much was achieved but the basic liberation of the people of African descent remains, in the main, unsolved."[2] Most assuredly, he would have said the same in 1988.

NOTES

I. From Barbados to Harlem

1. Interview of Bishop Reginald G. Barrow by editors, Barbados, August 22, 1978. The Barrow home was built for the father of Reginald Barrow, grandfather of Prime Minister Errol Barrow.

2. Interview of Richard B. Moore by W. Burghardt Turner, Patchogue, New York, November 30 and December 1, 1973. Information regarding Moore's background in Barbados and early years in New York is drawn largely from these interviews.

3. Ibid.

4. Interview of Alice T. Moore by editors, Barbados, October 17, 1978.

5. Ibid.; letter from Alice T. Moore to Joyce Turner, n.d.

6. Interview of Reginald Barrow.

7. Barbados Department of Archives, Will of Josephine Thorn Moore, RB 4, Book 93, p. 489.

8. U.S. Department of Commerce Bureau of the Census, *Thirteenth Census of the United States: 1910*, New York Enumeration District 600, Sheet 13B.

9. Interview by W. B. Turner.

10. Interview of Richard B. Moore by unidentified interviewer, June 1973.

11. Moore is not mentioned in the record on "Negro Tennis" compiled by the WPA Writers Program of New York City, but it confirms that the Ideal Tennis Club initiated the sport in Harlem with courts at 137th Street between Lenox and Seventh Avenues.

12. *The R. L. Polk Directory*, 1917–1918, lists the second firm as the Cosmo-Advocate Publishing Company, 2305 Seventh Avenue.

13. Jervis Anderson, *This Was Harlem* (New York: Farrar, Straus & Giroux, 1982), p. 100.

14. Constantine Francis Chassebeuf de Volney, *The Ruins: or A Survey of the Revolution of Empires*, translated from the French (London: Printed for J. Johnson, St. Paul's Church-Yard, 1792), pp. 252, 29.

15. *The Messenger*, July 1918, p. 8.

16. Ibid., September 1919, p. 27.

17. National Archives, Records of the Federal Bureau of Investigation, Record Group 65, OG 208369, September 11, 1920, p. 30.

18. *The African Times and Orient Review*, mid-October 1918, p. 31.

19. W. E. Burghardt Du Bois, *The Souls of Black Folk* (Chicago: A. C. McClurg, 1904), p. 13.

20. Claude McKay, "A Negro Poet," from *Pearson's Magazine*, September 1918, in *The Passion of Claude McKay*, ed. Wayne Cooper (New York: Schocken books, 1973), p. 48.

21. These sessions are not to be confused with the Sunday morning breakfast discussions at Randolph's home described by George Schuyler in his autobiography.

22. Interview by W. B. Turner.

23. Ibid.

24. *The New York Call*, August 28, 1921, p. 7.

25. Interview by W. B. Turner.

26. Ira De A. Reid, *The Negro Immigrant: His Background, Characteristics and Social Adjustment, 1899–1937* (New York: Columbia University Press, 1938), p. 146.

27. Philip S. Foner, *American Socialism and Black Americans* (Westport, Conn.: Greenwood Press, 1977), p. 279; Jervis Anderson, *A. Philip Randolph* (New York: Harcourt Brace Jovanovich, 1972), p. 94.

28. Interview by W. B. Turner.

29. Roi Ottley and William J. Weatherby, *The Negro in New York* (New York: New York Public Library and Oceana Publications, 1967), p. 226.

30. *The Emancipator*, March 13, 1920, p. 4.

31. *Revolutionary Radicalism. Report of the Joint Legislative Committee Investigating Seditious Activities, Filed April 24, 1920, in the Senate of the State of New York* (Albany, New York: J. B. Lyon, 1920), Part I, Vol. II, p. 2004. In *American Communism and Soviet Russia*, Theodore Draper states that *Revolutionary Radicalism* mistakenly listed the future communists Richard B. Moore and Cyril V. Briggs as contributing editors of *The Messenger*, but Draper had failed to cite the notation correctly. The Lusk Report reference was to Moore and Briggs as contributors to *The Emancipator*.

32. Richard B. Moore, "The Critics and Opponents of Marcus Garvey," in *Marcus Garvey and the Vision of Africa*, ed. John Hendrik Clarke (New York: Random House, 1974), p. 229.

33. Moore used the title *African Times and Orient Review*, but the year of distribution coincides with the later title.

34. National Archives, RG 65, OG 329359, August 14, 1920, August 30, 1920, and September 20, 1920; BS 198940-22, December 3, 1920.

35. National Archives, RG 65, OG 258421, June 11, 1920.

36. *The Emancipator*, March 27, 1920, p. 3.

37. National Archives, RG 65, OG 258421, March 26, 1920.

38. *The Crusader*, November 1918, p. 3.

39. Interview of Richard B. Moore by James C. Boyd, Patchogue, New York, September 2, 1974.

40. Interview by W. B. Turner.

41. *The Crusader*, November 1918, p. 3; *The Messenger*, September 1919, p. 4.

42. Arthur I. Waskow, *From Race Riot to Sit-In, 1919 and the 1960s* (Garden City, N.Y.: Anchor Books/Doubleday, 1967), p. 12.

43. Reid, *The Negro Immigrant*, pp. 159–60.

44. African Blood Brotherhood letterhead, Richard B. Moore Papers.

45. Interview of Richard B. Moore by Ernest Allen, Patchogue, New York, October 12, 1974.

46. "Race Catechism," in *Negro Year Book 1918–1919*, ed. Monroe Work (Tuskegee Institute, Alabama: The Negro Year Book Publishing Company, 1919), p. 100. No date is given for the original publication of the selection from *The Crusader*. Contrary to the claim by Theodore Vincent in *Voices of a Black Nation*, *The Crusader* of November 1918 did not include "Race Catechism."

47. Philip S. Foner, "Cyril V. Briggs: From African Blood Brotherhood to Communist Party," manuscript, presented at ASALH Convention, October 14, 1978 (courtesy of P. S. Foner.)

48. Harry Haywood, *Black Bolshevik* (Chicago: Liberator Press, 1978), p. 122; National Archives, RG 65, BS 202600-667-76, August 6, 1921.

49. National Archives, RG 65, OG 185161, March 1, 1920; OG 208369, October 20, 1920, p. 17.

50. It is impossible to know if Moore considered himself forever bound by the secret oath he took or a victim of memory lapse. He and Briggs were circumspect when queried in later years and may have enjoyed keeping researchers guessing.

51. *The Crusader*, July 1921, pp. 13–14.

52. National Archives, RG 65, BS 202600-2031-3, June 14, 1921. Evidence does not support assertions that Moore was a member of the United Communist Party in 1921.

53. The African Blood Brotherhood appears to predate the Communist Party. It could not have been organized as claimed by William Z. Foster in his *History of the*

Communist Party of the United States and could hardly be considered a Marxist organization at its inception.

54. Interview by unidentified interviewer.

55. Interview by E. Allen.

56. National Archives, Records of the Department of Justice Mail and Files Division, RG 60, #198940-283, letter, January 26, 1923.

57. Richard B. Moore, "Marcus Garvey: His Opposition," manuscript, presented at Afro-American Institute, December 6, 1970, Richard B. Moore Papers.

58. Ibid.; interview of Richard B. Moore by Wilfred D. Samuels, Patchogue, New York, November 17, 1974.

59. For Moore's account of Garvey's opposition, see his chapter, "The Critics and Opponents of Marcus Garvey," in *Garvey and the Vision of Africa*, ed. John Hendrik Clarke.

60. Announcement for African Blood Brotherhood meeting on January 11, 1925, Richard B. Moore Papers.

61. Robert L. Allen, *Reluctant Reformers* (Garden City, N.Y.: Anchor Books/Doubleday, 1975), p. 244.

62. Ethelred Brown, "The Harlem Unitarian Church," manuscript, September 11, 1949, Unitarian Universalist Association Archives, Boston, pp. 4–5.

63. Interview by W. B. Turner.

64. Ethelred Brown, letter to Rev. Walter R. Hunt, March 12, 1926, Unitarian Universalist Association Archives, Boston, p. 5.

65. Interview by W. B. Turner.

66. National Archives, Records of the Federal Bureau of Investigation, RG 65, BS 202600-667-76, August 6, 1921.

67. Foner, *American Socialism and Black Americans*, p. 205.

68. Moore told of the encounters with Algernon Lee and Julius Gerber on many occasions but did not specify who was present or the dates.

69. Foner, *American Socialism and Black Americans*, p. 357.

70. Ibid., p. 213. See Foner for an account of Harrison's effort.

71. *Revolutionary Radicalism*, pp. 1505–1507.

72. Jervis Anderson, *This Was Harlem*, p. 107.

73. Ibid., p. 186.

74. W. A. Domingo, "Gift of the Black Tropics," in *The New Negro*, ed. Alain Locke (New York: Albert and Charles Boni, 1925), pp. 346–49.

II. Radical Politics

1. Elinor Des Verney Sinnette, "Arthur Alfonso Schomburg, Black Bibliophile and Curator" (Ph.D. diss., School of Library Science, Columbia University, 1977), p. 72.

2. Letter from Hermie Dumont Huiswoud to Joyce Turner, March 28, 1983.

3. "Report on the Negro Question," *International Press Correspondence*, January 5, 1923, pp. 14–15.

4. Claude McKay, *The Negroes in America* (Port Washington, N.Y.: Kennikat Press, 1979), p. 88. McKay, a writer from Jamaica, worked as assistant editor for *The Liberator* with Max Eastman as editor. This publication is not to be confused with one of the same name issued by the American Negro Labor Congress.

5. Letter from Richard B. Moore to Arthur A. Schomburg, August 7, 1922, Arthur A. Schomburg Papers, Schomburg Center for Research in Black Culture, The New York Public Library, Astor, Lenox and Tilden Foundations.

6. Cooper, *The Passion of Claude McKay*, pp. 92–93.

7. McKay's bitterness was due in part to the American delegation's aloofness and divided position over the issue of the American Party's operation as an un-

derground or as a legal body. In addition, he was disappointed during his sojourn in Europe that his friends in the United States, including Moore, were not more responsive to his needs.

8. Jane Degras, ed., *The Communist International 1919–1943 Documents*, vol. I (New York: Oxford University Press, 1956), pp. 400–401.

9. McKay, *Negroes in America*, p. 38.

10. *The New York Amsterdam News*, December 6, 1922, p. 1; *The Messenger*, April 1923, p. 653.

11. FBI File #61-50-401, letter, July 2, 1923.

12. *The New York Amsterdam News*, August 8, 1923, p. 3; FBI File #61-50-422, "Negro Radical Activities," August 27, 1923; FBI File #61-50-477, "African Blood Brotherhood," November 19, 1923. Huiswoud's trip probably coincided with the Farmer-Labor Party Convention held in Chicago on July 3, 1923.

13. *The New York Amsterdam News*, August 29, 1923, p. 7; FBI File #61-50-420, "African Blood Brotherhood," August 28, 1923.

14. FBI File #61-50-433, "African Blood Brotherhood," September 13, 1923; FBI File #61-50-493, "African Blood Brotherhood," November 27, 1923.

15. *The Messenger*, September 1923, p. 819.

16. *The New York Amsterdam News*, January 10, 1923, p. 9; March 28, 1923, p. 1; June 27, 1923, p. 6; Foner, "Cyril V. Briggs," pp. 30–31. Arthur Preuss, ed., *A Dictionary of Secret and Other Societies* (St. Louis: B. Herder, 1924), pp. 4–5.

17. *The Messenger*, October 1923, p. 830.

18. Kelly Miller, from *The Negro Sanhedrin*, in *Black Nationalism in America*, ed. John H. Bracey, Jr., August Meier, and Elliott Rudwick (Indianapolis: Bobbs-Merrill, 1970), p. 349; Degras, *Communist International Documents*, vol. II, 1960, p. 97.

19. Huiswoud is identified as an ABB representative, but the second delegate is never named. The delegates of the Workers Party were Lovett Fort-Whiteman, Gordon O. Owens, P. Eugene Burton, Ethel Hall, and H. V. Phillips.

20. Interview by W. B. Turner.

21. Interview by J. Boyd.

22. *The Worker*, July 15, 1922, p. 2; August 5, 1922, p. 5. The August article was undoubtedly referring to Richard B. Moore, Grace Campbell, and Claude McKay. No further references could be found to the West Side Branch during this period. *The Negro Champion* article of September 8, 1928, describing Moore as the Workers Party candidate for Congress, gives the year 1919 for his affiliation with the Party. This date appears, however, to be too early; it is in conflict with documented activities of Moore in the Socialist Party as well as his statements.

23. Interview by W. B. Turner.

24. U.S. Immigration and Naturalization Service File #2270-52523, May 11, 1933; FBI File #100-109110-1, "Richard Benjamin Moore," May 28, 1942.

25. Interview by W. B. Turner.

26. Evidently Briggs did not attend, and Huiswoud, who had been listed in the call for the conference as a representative of the ABB, registered as a representative of the United Labor Council of New York City. No other references have been found to the Ethiopian Students' Alliance.

27. FBI File #61-5941-3, "American Negro Labor Congress," November 5, 1925.

28. Mark D. Naison, *Communists in Harlem during the Depression* (Urbana: University of Illinois Press, 1983), pp. 12–13.

29. Theodore Draper, *American Communism and Soviet Russia* (New York: Octagon Books, 1977), p. 205.

30. Haywood, *Black Bolshevik*, p. 145. The poem McKay dedicated to Moore was greatly prized but unfortunately lost.

31. "A Midsummer Chase of Reds," *The Literary Digest*, August 2, 1930, p. 7.

32. Interview by Allen; *The New York Amsterdam News*, October 6, 1926, p. 1.

33. Interview of Richard B. Moore by Elinor Des Verney Sinnette, New York, August 28, 1973 (courtesy of E. D. Sinnette).

34. *Das Flammenzeichen vom Palais Egmont. Offizielles Protokoll des Kongresses gegen koloniale Unterdrückung und Imperialismus, Brüssel, 10.–15. Februar 1927* (Berlin, 1927), p. 252; *The Negro World*, February 19, 1927, p. 2.

35. National Archives, Records of the Department of State, RG 59, 800.00B Anti-Imperialist League/2, June 24, 1927.

36. *The Daily Worker*, March 15, 1927, p. 3.

37. Imanuel Geiss, *The Pan-African Movement* (London: Methuen, 1974), p. 325.

38. According to Moore, Senghor was imprisoned by the French shortly afterward and died in prison in November.

39. Lovett Fort-Whiteman, "American Negro Labour Congress," *International Press Correspondence*, August 27, 1925, p. 983.

40. *The Liberator*, December 7, 1929, p. 1.

41. *The Daily Worker*, August 25, 1927, p. 1; August 30, 1927, p. 4. In "Du Bois and Pan Africa," Moore refers to the Fourth Pan-African Congress as the Fifth because he considered that the conference held in 1900 in London should be considered the first.

42. *The Liberator*, December 7, 1929, p. 1.

43. James R. Hooker, *Black Revolutionary* (New York: Praeger Publishers, 1970), pp. 8–9. According to Hermie Huiswoud, the name "George Padmore" was assumed by Malcolm Nurse when he consulted with her regarding a suitable pseudonym. She suggested "Padmore," after a Liberian minister, and Nurse responded, "By George, you've got it," whereupon she added "George" to "Padmore," which he liked and adopted.

44. "C. I. Resolution on Negro Question in U.S.A.," issued by the Political Secretariat, Communist International Moscow, USSR, October 26, 1928, in *The Daily Worker*, February 12, 1929, p. 3.

45. Draper, *American Communism*, p. 329; Degras, *Communist International Documents*, vol. III, 1965, p. 97. The statement by Fort-Whiteman is attributed to James Jackson, which was his pseudonym.

46. Interview of Harry Haywood by editors, New Brunswick, New Jersey, January 17, 1984.

47. Draper, *American Communism*, p. 345; Haywood, *Black Bolshevik*, p. 253; "Interview with Otto Hall," in *The Black Worker*, vol. VI ed. Philip S. Foner and Ronald L. Lewis (Philadelphia: Temple University Press, 1981), pp. 435–36.

48. *The Negro Champion*, March 23, 1929, p. 2; Naison, *Communists in Harlem*, p. 19.

49. U.S. Immigration and Naturalization Service File #2270-52523, letter, April 15, 1933; *The Negro Champion*, September 8, 1928, pp. 1, 5; *The Liberator*, June 7, 1930, p. 2.

50. *The Daily Worker*, September 16, 1929, pp. 1–2; September 18, 1929, p. 2.

51. *The Liberator*, April 5, 1930, p. 1; June 7, 1930, p. 3.

52. Mark D. Naison, "The Communist Party in Harlem: 1928–1936" (Ph.D. diss., Columbia University, 1976; Ann Arbor: University Microfilms International, 1982), p. 47.

53. Draper, *American Communism*, p. 346.

54. *Race Hatred on Trial*, issued by Communist Party U.S.A., n.d., p. 21; *The Communist Position on the Negro Question*, n.d., p. 35.

55. *Race Hatred on Trial*, pp. 27–29, 43, 37.

56. Ibid., p. 32.

57. Earl Browder, *Communism in the United States* (New York: International Publishers, 1935), p. 293.

58. National Archives, RG 59, 811.4016 Scottsboro/153-1/2, December 17, 1932.

59. Richard H. Frost, *The Mooney Case* (Stanford: Stanford University Press, 1968), p. 439; interview by W. B. Turner; National Archives, RG 59, 811.4016/147, October 18, 1932.

60. "Schedule for National Scottsboro Tour," Richard B. Moore Papers.

61. Interview by W. B. Turner.

62. William L. Patterson, *The Man Who Cried Genocide* (New York: International Publishers, 1971), p. 133.

63. Naison, *Communists in Harlem*, pp. 95–98.

64. Ibid., p. 102.

65. Ibid., p. 103.

66. Haywood, *Black Bolshevik*, p. 436. Haywood gives the year as 1932, but the change in leadership from Moore to Haywood was announced in *The Daily Worker* of April 26, 1934.

67. *Daily Worker*, April 25, 1934, p. 6; *The Negro Worker*, May 1934, p. 14; *The Crisis*, October 1945, pp. 302, 315.

68. Naison, *Communists in Harlem*, p. 174.

69. Ibid., p. 98.

70. Letter from Morris Shapiro to All Organizations and Friends of Justice for the Scottsboro Boys, September 10, 1937, Richard B. Moore Papers.

71. Pathway Press "Agreement of Co-Partnership," February 7, 1940, Richard B. Moore Papers.

72. Richard B. Moore, "To Set the Record Straight," n.d., Richard B. Moore Papers.

73. "Charges Preferred Against Angelo Herndon," January 8, 1942, Richard B. Moore Papers.

74. The reprint issued by the Negro Publication Society of America was *The Kidnapped and the Ransomed*, by Kate E. R. Pickard.

75. FBI File #100-109110-1, "Richard Benjamin Moore," May 28, 1942; #10-109110-3, "Richard Benjamin Moore," December 6, 1944; #100-109110, "Richard Benjamin Moore," March 20, 1956.

76. *The Pittsburgh Courier*, November 7, 1942, p. 1.

77. Interview of Abner Berry by Mark Naison, New York, July 5, 1977 (courtesy of M. Naison).

78. Letter from Cyril V. Briggs to Richard B. Moore, January 26, 1947 (postmark), Richard B. Moore Papers.

79. In a letter to Reginald Barrow on September 4, 1969, Moore wrote regarding Harold Cruse's *The Crisis of the Negro Intellectual:* "Cruse sought to solve his own crisis by purveying a 'Crisis of Negro Intellectuals.' When he condemns and decries every one but himself, it becomes apparent to thinkers that he seeks deliberately to derogate everyone else in order thereby himself to shine. What he has written about me is mainly false; reflection soon shows that he is guessing and surmising and has no basic knowledge of what he projects, for instance, he states that he really doesn't know whether I *left* or was *expelled* from the Communist party. As a matter of fact, he has no proof that I ever joined or became 'bitter' about any experience with this party."

III. The Pan-Caribbean Movement

1. Richard Wright, "Foreward," George Padmore, *Pan-Africanism or Communism* (Garden City, N.Y.: Anchor Books/Doubleday, 1972), pp. xxiii–xxiv.

2. Robert Hill states in *The Marcus Garvey and Universal Negro Improvement Association Papers*, vol. I, that Briggs and Moore opened the bookstore, but Reginald Pierrepointe has confirmed that Briggs was not involved in the financing or operation of the store.

3. Moore's estranged wife, whom he had never divorced, died in 1946.

4. Mary Frances Berry and John Blassingame, *Long Memory—The Black Experience in America* (New York: Oxford University Press, 1982), p. 393.

5. Moore had rushed to have the latter published in Barbados in preparation for the Second World Black and African Festival of Arts and Culture held in Lagos, Nigeria, but he was not satisfied with the proofs. The project was never completed.

6. Richard B. Moore Memorial Program, New York, November 9, 1978.

7. Ken Post, *Arise Ye Starvelings* (The Hague: Nijhoff, 1978), p. 321.

8. The term "awaymen" was used in Harlem but seems to be unfamiliar in the Caribbean.

9. Richard B. Moore and Hope R. Stevens, "Some Contributions of Barbadians Abroad," *Salute to Barbados Independence*, November 30, 1966, pp. 56, 58. Stevens was notified after he returned to New York that the name of the Party had been changed to the Barbados Progressive League to avoid a radical connotation. Later it was changed back to the original name. Wynter Crawford, who invited the group to meet with Stevens, has indicated that John Beckles was not present and that Dr. Arleigh Scott attended but did not participate in susequent meetings.

10. Interview by unidentified interviewer.

11. American Committee for West Indian Federation, "Memorandum on Federation and Self-Government of the West Indies Addressed to the Caribbean Labour Congress," September 2–9, 1947, Appendix I, p. 2, Richard B. Moore Papers.

12. Letter from Hermie Huiswoud (Amsterdam) to Nationale Voorlichtings Dienst, N.V.D. (Suriname), November 20, 1985.

13. *The Case of Domingo* (Kingston, Jamaica: People's National Party, 1941); National Archives, R.G. 59, 800.20211 Domingo W.A./12 PS/TL, February 24, 1943.

14. Paul Blanshard, "Social and Political Forces in Dependent Areas of the Caribbean," U.S. Section, Anglo-American Caribbean Commission, Department of State, December 1944, pp. 413–17 (courtesy of Robert Hill).

15. Public Record Office, London, CO28/336/7, "Notes of a speech made by Mr. Moore at a Conference on Colonial Problems held in April, 1945, by the National Association for the Advancement of Colonial Peoples" *(sic)*, July 23, 1949 (courtesy of Anthony Phillips).

16. Herbert Aptheker, ed., *The Correspondence of W. E. B. Du Bois*, vol. III (Amherst, Mass.: University of Massachusetts Press, 1978), p. 8. The text of the NAACP Statement can be found in Aptheker, ed., *A Documentary History of the Negro People in the United States 1933–1945* (Secaucus, N.J.: The Citadel Press, 1974).

17. Interview by unidentified interviewer.

18. *Public Opinion*, Jamaica, March 10, 1945, p. 3; April 9, 1945, p. 3.

19. Letter from Richard B. Moore to Alger Hiss, May 25, 1945, Richard B. Moore Papers.

20. Letter from Alger Hiss to Richard B. Moore, June 1, 1945, Richard B. Moore Papers.

21. Aptheker, *Correspondence of Du Bois*, p. 14.

22. West Indian National Council, news release, June 13, 1945, Richard B. Moore Papers.

23. Letter from Bryant Mumford to Richard B. Moore, June 23, 1945, Richard B. Moore Papers.

24. American Committee for West Indian Federation, "Memorandum on Federation," p. 5.

25. *The Negro Champion,* August 8, 1928, p. 12.

26. Manuscript, n.d., Richard B. Moore Papers.

27. Letter from Richard Hart to Richard B. Moore, October 19, 1948, Richard B. Moore Papers; *Caribbean Labour Congress Monthly Bulletin,* September–October 1948 (courtesy of Richard Hart).

28. F. A. Hoyos, *Grantley Adams and the Social Revolution* (London: Macmillan, 1974), p. 140.

29. Interview of Reginald St. Aubyn Pierrepointe by editors, New York, May 24, 1984; Interview of Wynter Algernon Crawford by editors, Barbados, April 7, 1984; Gordon K. Lewis, *The Growth of the Modern West Indies* (New York: Modern Reader Paperbacks, 1968), p. 248.

30. Confidential memorandum, "Importance of the Campaign to Support the Caribbean Labour Congress convening in Trinidad, B.W.I. April, 1950," n.d., Richard B. Moore Papers.

31. *The Beacon,* Barbados, February 11, 1950, p. 8.

32. Caribbean and Associated Advocates, "Statement on British Secretary's Rejection of Federation Committee's Request for Financial Aid to Caribbean People," May 31, 1957, pp. 4–5, Richard B. Moore Papers.

33. Sir John Mordecai, *The West Indies—The Federal Negotiations* (Evanston: Northwestern University Presss, 1968), p. 187.

34. W. A. Domingo, "British West Indian Federation—A Critique," in *The Aftermath of Sovereignty,* ed. David Lowenthal and Lambros Comitas (Garden City, N.Y.: Anchor Books/Doubleday, 1973), pp. 174–75, 178.

35. *Sunday Advocate-News,* Barbados, March 21, 1982, p. 18.

36. Interview of Reginald Pierrepointe by editors, New York, January 8, 1983.

37. Blanshard, "Social and Political Forces," pp. 400–402.

38. Franklin W. Knight, *The Caribbean* (New York: Oxford University Press, 1978), pp. 178, 188.

39. Interview of Crawford.

40. Interview of Hon. Hilton A. Vaughn by editors, Barbados, May 23, 1983.

41. Gordon K. Lewis, "The Caribbean: Colonization and Culture," *Studies on the Left* 1. no. 4 (1961): 26.

42. Agents of the Department of Justice obtained Moore's passport from his wife during an interview with her in 1931 without his knowledge. At the time, The Bureau of Naturalization of the Department of Labor was trying to determine whether he was a Communist prior to naturalization but "developed no evidence of communistic beliefs or activities on Mr. Moore's part prior to his naturalization on September 11, 1924, which would serve as a basis for cancellation action."

43. Lewis, *Growth of the Modern West Indies,* p. 397.

44. Francis Mark, *The History of the Barbados Workers' Union* (Barbados: Barbados Workers' Union, n.d.), pp. 81–82.

45. Interview of Hon. Errol W. Barrow by editors, Barbados, May 18, 1983.

IV. The "Awayman" Returns to Barbados

1. Interview of Errol Barrow.

2. Michael Chandler, "Richard B. Moore Collection," report to the Barbados Permanent Secretary, Ministry of Education, August 9, 1965, Richard B. Moore Papers. The report included the following description:

The whole collection has been stated to be near 5,000 books. After my examination, I estimate that the total number of volumes is more than 15,000 in addition to the numerous pamphlets and periodicals. . . . [T]he scope of Mr. Moore's collection is very wide. Basically he is concerned with the history of African peoples from their earliest days, their cultures and civilizations, their emigrations to and influences on Europe and Americas, slavery, emancipation, race relations, and the biography of persons of African descent. In extension of these fields he has material on mythology, religion, comparative religion and Christian criticism, the history of the Jews, and of the Inquisition, the history of science, sexual customs, the indigenous races of the Americas, U.S. history, colonialism and imperialism, world affairs (especially between the World Wars), and Russian and Chinese politics, Communism, etc. There is no doubt that this is a very remarkable private collection. . . .

3. Interview of Errol Barrow.
4. W. Burghardt Turner, "The Richard B. Moore Collection and its Collector," *Caribbean Studies* (April 1975): 135–45.
5. Interview of Michael J. Chandler by editors, Barbados, December 1, 1979.
6. Chandler, "Richard B. Moore Collection," p. 2.
7. Inquiries since Moore's death have met with assurances that the library is maintained under favorable environmental conditions and has been placed under the Ministry of Information and Culture for incorporation in the master plan for an expanded public library. The expansion requires a capital expenditure and no date has been established for the project.
8. *The Nation*, Barbados, April 11, 1984, p. 4.
9. The eulogy was published in the *Advocate-News*, Barbados, August 23, 1978, *The Nation*, Barbados, August 23, 1978, and *Caribbean Studies*, April–July 1979.

V. Collecting Richard B. Moore's Speeches and Writings

1. Interview of Errol Barrow.
2. Interview by Samuels.

Young converts of the Christian Mission, Barbados, c. 1908. *Left to right, top row:* Edwin Clarke, Cheltenham Smith, Clement Clarke, Lewis Braithwaite, Marcus Jordan; *bottom row:* Edgar Phillips, Henry Nurse, Annie Coope, Richard B. Moore.

Richard B. Moore, New York City, c. 1919

Kathleen Ursula James, c. 1919. She and Richard B. Moore were married on June 24, 1919, in New York City.

Richard B. Moore, New York City, c. 1930. *(Photo courtesy of the Schomburg Center for Research in Black Culture, The New York Public Library, Astor, Lenox and Tilden Foundations.)*

Mothers of the Scottsboro boys appeal to the White House, May 13, 1934. Four of them are pictured with Ruby Bates, one of the women allegedly attacked. *Left to right:* Ida Norris, Janie Patterson, Ruby Bates, Mamie Williams, Viola Montgomery, and Richard B. Moore. *(Photo courtesy of the Schomburg Center for Research in Black Culture, The New York Public Library, Astor, Lenox and Tilden Foundations.)*

111

Richard B. Moore, New York
City, c. 1935

Otto Eduard Huiswoud, 1936

Wilfred Adolphus Domingo
(date unknown)

Domingo-Moore Debate, April 21, 1940, New York City. *Left to right:* W. A. Domingo, J. A. Rogers, Richard B. Moore, George Weston (in background).

Richard B. Moore at Domingo-Moore
Debate, April 21, 1940, New York City

The United Nations Conference on International Organization, San Francisco, California, May 1945. *Left to right:*
Brigadier General Carlos P. Romulo, chairman of the Philippine delegation; Richard B. Moore, vice-president of the
West Indies National Council; Dr. Maneck K. Ankesaria,
director, United Press Service of India.

Book party for Benjamin Quarles, sponsored by Frederick Douglass Cultural Society, July 15, 1949, New York City. *Center*, Professor Benjamin Quarles, autographing copy of *Frederick Douglass; right*, Richard B. Moore; *second from left*, Lodie Biggs. (*Photo by A. Hansen.*)

Cricket match on Caribbean Freedom Day, July 31, 1949, sponsored by the United Caribbean American Council, New York City. *Top row, left*, Capt. Hugh Mulzac; *second from right*, Richard B. Moore; *right*, Augustine A. Austin; *bottom row, left*, William Chase; *second from left*, Hope R. Stevens; *center*, Waddell Cruze of Jamaica; *second from right*, Harri Hollis. (*Photo by A. Hansen.*)

Bishop Reginald G. Barrow and Richard B. Moore at the Frederick
Douglass Book Center, c. 1955. (*Photo by Geraldo Guirty.*)

Richard B. Moore at home,
Brooklyn, New York, c. 1958

Lodie Biggs Moore at home, Brooklyn, New York, c. 1958. She and Richard B. Moore were married on September 9, 1950.

Richard B. Moore reviewing L. S. B. Leakey's *The Progress and Evolution of Man in Africa*, New York City, c. 1962. (*Photo by Art Williams.*)

Hope R. Stevens and Richard B. Moore at book review, New York City, c. 1962. (*Photo by Art Williams.*)

Richard B. Moore Seventieth Birthday Testimonial Dinner, September 17, 1963, New York City. *Left to right:* Hope R. Stevens, Richard B. Moore, and Lodie B. Moore.

Reception given by Barbados Tourist and Development Boards, January 20, 1966, New York City. Hon. Errol Walton Barrow (premier of Barbados and prime minister following independence) and Richard B. Moore marking agreement regarding transfer of Richard B. Moore Library to Barbados. (*Photo by Gilbert Pictorial Enterprise.*)

Richard B. Moore Seventy-seventh Birthday Luncheon, September 27, 1970, New York City. *Left to right:* John H. Clarke; Hon. Branford Taitt, consul general of Barbados; Richard B. Moore; Charles B. Rangel; Percy Sutton; Keith E. Baird.

Richard B. Moore, September 1972, Patchogue, New York.
(*Photo by Mitch Turner.*)

Association for the Study of Afro-American Life and History Annual Convention, October 1973, New York City. Richard B. Moore speaking on resolution to change name of organization. (*Photo by David McAdams.*)

II.

Speeches and Writings
Edited by W. Burghardt Turner
and Joyce Moore Turner

VI

THE CARIBBEAN VIEWED FROM HARLEM

The essay "Caribbean Unity and Freedom," which serves as an introduction to the writings of Richard Benjamin Moore, highlights his consistent concern for Caribbean liberation as well as his leadership in the Harlem-based Pan-Caribbean organizations. It is both historical and autobiographical— characteristic of much of his later writing—and provides a key to analyzing his polemical skill as well as the rest of his activities during his most productive years. The organizations referred to were largely his vehicles and the documents, his work (see chapter 11). The brief overview of significant events in the development of the Caribbean sets the necessary backdrop for the divisiveness that the New York group had to contend with and try to overcome. Written four years before his homeland achieved independence, this article was as much an appeal to leaders in the Caribbean as it was a history lesson for the reading public. It seems important now, almost a quarter of a century later, to bring this message to the attention of the present and future leaders of the Caribbean. It reveals the pitfalls and booby traps that ensnared previous endeavors and may help the region to avoid the necessity of repeating the mistakes of the past.

CARIBBEAN UNITY AND FREEDOM

Freedomways, Third Quarter, 1964, pp. 295–311.

To explore the possibilities of Caribbean unity and freedom, it seems necessary to consider the historical heritage of the people. It would thus be realized that for centuries disunity and slavery have disfigured the natural beauty of this area. Present difficulties appear then to stem largely from the conflict inherent in an order set up by adventurers, sea rovers, traders, plantation owners, and imperial rulers. Evidently the legacy of the Caribbean past still weighs like a mountain upon the living present.

When Christopher Columbus and his band of adventurers set foot on an island of the Caribbean on October 12, 1492, there intruded the vanguard of a powerful and dominating force which brought division and enslavement into these "isles of the blest." That fateful entry, despite the direful events which followed, has been hailed rather effusively by an Hispanic historian as the greatest event since the advent of Christ.

The idyllic and evergreen Caribbean islands were described as a virtual paradise by Columbus in his *First Letter:*

> I found many islands inhabited by men without number. . . . All these islands are very beautiful . . . and full of a variety of trees stretching up to the stars; . . . some of them were blossoming, some were bearing fruit; . . . the nightingale and various other birds without number were singing. . . . There are also excellent pine trees, vast plains and meadows, a variety of birds, a variety of honey, and a variety of metals excepting iron.

Today nearly five centuries later the Caribbean becomes more and more the paradise and preserve of tourists, settlers, and investors from Europe and the United States. In contrast, the stark conditions of poverty-stricken, slum-dwelling native Caribbeans have been expressed by the exclamation of Francisco, the sage of Puerto Rico, who declared to the writer Albert Balink: "My Paradise is Hell."

From the Bahamas southwest of Florida where Columbus landed, the Caribbean islands stretch in an arc down to Trinidad just above the northern coast of South America. Due south from Barbados, most easterly of the islands, lies Guiana on the mainland. Historically and culturally, Guiana is an integral part of the Caribbean, as also is English-speaking Honduras in Central America. In the broad shining expanse of the Caribbean Sea, the largest islands are Puerto Rico, that occupied by the Dominican Republic and Haiti, Jamaica, and Cuba.

This whole area was misnamed "the Indies" by Columbus, since from his reading of the *Travels of Marco Polo,* he erroneously imagined that he had reached the Indies of Asia and was soon to find the gold of Cipango and Cathay. To end the ensuing confusion, these islands were later called the "West Indies," and the true Indies then qualified the "East Indies." Through social lag, the compounding of ignorance, or subservience to colonial rulers, the misnomer "West Indies" is still often used, instead of the accurate and euphonious native name Caribbean.

Christopher Columbus, whose first name we are told means "Christbearer," introduced disastrous division and lethal slavery. From the very first he observed ominously that the indigenous people "would make good servants." Soon Columbus began the division of the native people into "inoffensive Indians," later called Arawaks and Tainos, and "savage Caribs." The Caribs were then branded by Columbus as "cannibals." But this was only a pretext for a horrible slave traffic which would exchange native human beings for cattle from Spain!

To the Spanish sovereigns Columbus sought to justify this nefarious slave traffic by urging this necessary to "the welfare of the souls of the said cannibals." But this canard of "cannibalism" has been directly refuted by the statement of the Spanish conquistador, Juan de Castellanos, who in his *Elegies* declared that the Caribs were so branded "not because they ate human flesh but because they staunchly defended their homes."

War against the indigenous people was soon accompanied by conflict among the conquerors. The insurrection led by Roldan against the rule of Columbus issued in a compromise which gave rise to the slave system of "repartimientos" or divisions. The land was thus parcelled out among the European colonists in great estates, along with the indigenous people living on these lands which had been their own ancestral domains.

Driven mercilessly by the Spanish conquerors in the gold bearing mines and rivers and on the plantations, the indigenous Caribbean people were simultaneously mowed down with firearms and torn to pieces by ravenous dogs. After just fifty years, in 1542, the humane priest, Bartolomé de las Casas, in his *Very Brief Account of the Destruction of the Indies* pointed mournfully to the more than two thousand leagues in the Caribbean which had been completely depopulated "by the infernal deeds and tyranny of the Christians."

African Slave Trade

To replenish the labor force, the Spanish colonizers brought in African slaves beginning as early as 1501. These Africans, it was said, "soon fled to the Indians and taught them bad manners." Resistance to slavery was called "bad manners" by the slavedrivers. Risings of African slaves on sugar plantations were recorded from the year 1518; a rebellion is noted which started at the sugar mill of Columbus in 1522. The "troubles" in San Juan, Puerto Rico, during 1532 were charged to the Wolofs or Berberisci. An uprising of African slaves distressed the colonizers in 1548 at San Pedro in Honduras. Such facts belie the oft-repeated affirmation of "the happy contented slave."

The Spanish empire made exclusive claim to all this hemisphere, except Brazil which fell to the Portuguese, either by first conquest or through the donation of the Pope. Challenging this claim, the British, French, Dutch and Danish powers intrigued and pushed their way into the Caribbean. Illegal forerunners of these powers were English slavetraders like John Hawkins and privateers such as Francis Drake, who sailed in such piously named ships as the *Jesus of Lubeck* and the *Grace of God*. Both of these plundering marauders were duly knighted by Elizabeth I, which gracious Queen shared handsomely in their vast and bloody spoils. Other notorious pirates were the Welshman, Henry Morgan, the French buccaneers Le Grand and L'Ollonois, the Dutch Brasiliano, the unidentified Mansvelt.

Privateers, pirates and buccaneers of all the chief European nations infested the Caribbean Sea. Their chief but by no means sole prey was the Spanish galleon, laden with wealth in gold and silver plate, jewels and pearls, and cities like Porto Bello and Nombre de Dios in Panama where fabulous treasures were stored for transportation to Spain. It was, perhaps, from observing the gory seizure of such loot, erstwhile violently extracted by the Spanish from the indigenous creators and rightful possessors, that the transplanted Africans in the Caribbean coined the proverb "tief from tief mek God laff."

No laughing matter though were the terrible crimes of arson, murder, and torture frequently committed by these freebooters. In *The Buccaneers of America*, Esquemelling has recorded this monstrous deed:

> L'Ollonois grew outrageously passionate; insomuch that he drew his cutlass, and with it cut open the breast of one of those poor Spaniards, and pulling out his heart with his sacrilegious hands, began to bite and gnaw with his teeth like a ravenous wolf, saying to the rest: I will serve you all alike if you show me not another way.

The treaty of 1670 between Great Britain and Spain signalled the end of buccaneering from Jamaica. The treaty of Ryswick between Spain and France in 1697 stopped filibustering from Hispaniola, Tortuga, and other centers. Pirates now became merchants, or "gentleman planters," and like Henry Morgan and Jean Baptiste Du Casse, were transformed into knighted, decorated, and highly honored governors. This pattern of rewarding dubious deeds and services rendered with knighthood and courtly distinction seems to have persisted down through the centuries, in broad outline if not in specific detail.

Britain and France, at the beginning of their overt colonial careers in the Caribbean, jointly seized the island of St. Christopher or St. Kitts about 1625. Under the pretext that they were friendly to the Spanish, the native inhabitants were set upon by these newcomers during the night. Their leaders were killed and the remaining "Caribbees" driven from their land. Colonies were then established there by the British and French usurpers who divided the island between them. Captian Burney, in his *History of the Buccaneers of America* has commented:

> Thus in usurpation and barbarity was founded the first colony of the British and French governments in the West Indies; which colony was the parent of our African slave trade.

Such mutual accommodation and collusion of empires did not last long. For conflict over the lion's share is inherent in the very nature of empire. War and bloodshed were thus renewed and became endemic in the Caribbean. As the fortunes of war and diplomacy rose and fell, St. Christopher was shifted forth and back. St. Lucia changed hands within a short period at least seven times, Dominica fifteen times, Tobago no less than twenty. Unusual in being held without interruption by the British was Barbados, and this anomaly of history came to be a source of strange and precious pride among colonial subjects who boasted themselves to be "little Englanders."

This phase of Caribbean history is illumined by Captain Burney's further observation:

> In the history of so much robbery and outrage the rapacity shown in some instances by the European governments in their West Indian transactions, and by governors of their appointment; appears in a worse light than that of the buccaneers, from whom, being professed rascals, nothing better was to be expected.

To carry forward the exploitation of the colonies, African slaves were brought in by the thousands. The frightful mortality on the Caribbean plantations required constant importation of slaves. Africa was therefore denuded of millions of her people and thus, despite the great mortality, Africans became the great majority of the population in most Caribbean colonies.

Resistance to slavery and escape to the mountains gave rise to the Maroons, who were hunted furiously by armies equipped with ferocious dogs. Nevertheless, the Maroons by their ingenious camouflage and military prowess succeeded in winning two notable victories. The British were forced to sign a treaty with Captains Cudjoe, Accompong, Johnny, Cuffee, and Quaco, recognizing the independence of the Maroons in Jamaica in 1738. Likewise, in 1777 the Dutch were finally compelled to defer to the invincibility and sovereignty of the Maroons of Suriname who had fought valiantly under leaders like Araby, Adoe, Zam Zam, Boston, Quaco, Baron, Joli Coeur, Bonny, and Cujo. The Maroons established themselves in the hinterland of Guiana where they survived by utilizing many cultural techniques of their African ancestors.

Growth of Colonial Pyramid

The glittering, golden pyramid of empire in the Caribbean reached its apex near the close of the eighteenth century. Spain still held on to Cuba, San Domingo, and Puerto Rico. Britain had seized the lion's share including Bermuda, the Bahamas, Anegada, Tortola, Virgin Gorda and other Virgin Islands, Anguilla, Barbuda, St. Kitts, Nevis, Redonda, Montserrat, Antigua, St. Vincent, Barbados, Grenada, Tobago, Trinidad, Jamaica, and Honduras. The Netherlands dominated Saba, St. Eustatius, Bonaire, Curaçao, Aruba, shared the island of St. Martin with France, and possessed the colonies of Suriname, Berbice, and Essequibo on the South American mainland. Denmark ruled St. Thomas, St. John, and St. Croix among the

Virgins. France controlled Guadeloupe, Martinique, St. Lucia, Cayenne in Guiana, and the greatest prize of that period, St. Domingue, now Haiti.

At the top of this colonial pyramid the European governors and high officials, plantation overlords, and wealthy merchants disported themselves in affluence and prodigality. Below them in lesser style but grand pretension, were the petit blancs, or little whites, managers, bookkeepers, small storekeepers. Next came the *gens de coleur* or people of color, free in a limited sense, wealthy and educated, but deprived of most political and human rights. Supporting this vast social structure with their unrequited toil, sweat, tears, and blood were hundreds of thousands of slaves derived from Africa.

The African slaves were driven to long and arduous toil with cowhide whips and the dreaded "cat o' nine tails." Excruciating torture was imposed upon slaves suspected of any insubordination. In Barbados slaves were even thrown into tayches or vats of hot, boiling, sugar-cane juice. A house of punishment was maintained in Jamaica where slaves, while being beaten were forced to cling to a bar suspended over a moving treadmill. To fall into this was to be horribly mangled to death. In Dutch Guiana men and women were stretched upon the rack and their bones smashed with iron bars. In his book *Caribbean Sea of the New World,* German Arciniegas has recorded the general treatment of the slaves:

> The Negroes of this "Paris of the Antilles" were publicly whipped in the streets, salt and lemon juice being put on the wounds to prevent gangrene from setting in. To punish a cook who let a cake in the oven burn, the mistress would go to the kitchen and say: "Throw that nigger in the stove!" ... In the country the slightest disobedience was punished by burial alive; the culprit's head was left exposed, molasses was poured over it, and the ants finished the job.

The Haitian historian, J. N. Leger in *Haiti: Her History and Her Detractors* has cited some of these horrible atrocities from Baron de Vastey's account, "The Colonial System Disclosed." Well-nigh incredible, but vouched for, was the pouring of boiling wax, on the order of a plantation owner, into the ears of his own slave daughter; a slave forced to eat his own roasted ears; the tongues of slaves cut out to render them dumb servants; iron masks forced upon the faces of slaves who were then left to die. The account is quoted from Rabau by Benito Sylvain of slaves "sawed between two boards. I stop; my pen cannot describe such frightful scenes."

Contrary to the general impression, the investment of capital did not ensure protection to the chattel slaves. There was no protection at all when it became profitable to work a slave to death in seven years and replace him with a new purchase.

The wealth acquired from the monstrous slave trade and from the toil and produce of the slaves in the Caribbean was immense. From this primary accumulation of capital the commerce and industry of Europe expanded prodigiously. Dr. Eric Williams in *The Negro in the Caribbean* has given the following significant account:

> Tremendous wealth was produced from an unstable economy based on a single crop, which combined the vices of feudalism and capitalism with the virtues of neither. Liverpool in England, Nantes in France, Rhode Island in America, prospered on the slave trade. London and Bristol, Bordeaux and Marseilles, Cadiz and Seville, Lisbon and New England, all waxed fat on the profits of the trade in the tropical produce raised by the Negro slave. . . . The tiniest British sugar island was considered more valuable than the thirteen mainland colonies combined. French Guadeloupe, with a population today of a mere 300,000, was once deemed more precious than Canada, and the Dutch cheerfully surrendered what is today New York State for a strip of the Guiana territory. . . .
>
> As Mr. Winston Churchill declared four years ago: "Our possession of the West Indies, like that of India, . . . gave us the strength, the support, but especially the capital, the wealth, at a time when no other European nation possessed such a reserve, which enabled us to come through the great struggles of the Napoleonic Wars, . . . but also to lay the foundation of that commercial and financial leadership which . . . enabled us to make our great position in the world."

Similarly, German Arciniegas in *Caribbean Sea of the New World* has recounted the great vital value of African slave labor to France:

> But Haiti was the source that gave life to Marseilles, Bordeaux, Nantes. Fifteen hundred ships a year called at its ports, many more than at Marseilles. Twenty-four thousand seamen were employed on the seven hundred and fifty ships engaged exclusively in trade with Haiti. In Bordeaux there were sixteen factories refining sugar from the island; the sugar was imported, brandy was exported, and a hundred small industries had sprung up in connection with the distilleries. The merchants of Nantes had £50,000,000 ($200,000,000) invested in the island. The cocoa of Haiti supplied France with all its chocolate, and in addition to the cocoa, the island exported seventy-three million pounds of coffee and six million pounds of cotton. All this was produced by slave labor.

In French St. Domingue in that fateful year of 1791, there were some 40,000 Europeans and Creoles, 28,000 people of varied African and European ancestry, and 500,000 slaves of African descent. The European and Creole overlords were in open rebellion against the principles of the French Revolution of 1789, and rebuffed official representatives of the Revolutionary Assembly of France. The decree of this body, affirming political rights for the free people of color, was spurned by the slaveholding oligarchy. The last desperate blow struck by men of color to secure these rights was defeated and their leaders Oge and Chavannes were monstrously broken on the wheel. But this rising was the prelude to the epoch-making revolution soon to follow.

Watching the conflicts of royalist and republicans, and of the free men of color against the ruling European slaveholders, the great majority of African slaves smarted under their frightful oppression. All former slave risings in St. Domingue had been ferociously crushed; the leader of the most formidable plot, Mackandal, had been seized and horribly burned alive. The ferocity of the planters had reached new heights when Le Jeune attempted by the most monstrous means of torture to wring a confession of poisoning from two slave women on his plantation.

By night slaves gathered and pondered upon their plight, while performing rites called Vodun or Voodoo, which were based on some aspects of an ancestral African religion. The hymn of liberty which Mackandal had often sung with them was chanted now with new resolve: "Throw down the pictures of the god of the whites who has so often caused us to weep; listen to the voice of liberty which speaks in the hearts of us all."

To the rhythmic beat of the drums in an ever rising crescendo, the slaves of African origin intoned in increasing unison:

> Eh! Eh! Bomba! Heu! Heu!
> Canda, bafii te!
> Canga, moune de leó
> Canga, do ki la!
> Canga, do ki la!
> Canga, li!

C. L. R. James, author of *The Black Jacobins,* has interpreted this in English: "We swear to destroy the whites and all that they possess; let us die rather than fail to keep this vow."

On the night of August 22, 1791, like the tropical tornado which raged, the slaves of St. Domingue rose, determined to break the chains of chattel slavery. Their first leaders Boukmann and Jean François were soon succeeded by Toussaint Louverture, who had made full use of the opportunity to learn to read, who had pondered upon the historical and political writings of Abbé Raynal, and who had studied military memoirs and manuals.

Role of Toussaint Louverture

Marshalling an army and skillfully deploying his forces, Toussaint succeeded in defeating the greatly superior forces of France and Spain and the army sent by the British. Through adroit political measures, including the election of French deputies to representative offices in France, as well as by his military victories, Toussaint made himself master of the entire island. In 1801 Toussaint Louverture administered the island under a constitution that made him Governor-General for life with power to choose his successor. By a thorough reorganization of the economy, this revolutionary genius achieved a new prosperity for all the people.

But Napoleon set out to reconquer St. Domingue as the nucleus for a grandiose French empire in the Americas based upon chattel slavery. A vast and powerfully equipped army was despatched to the island under the command of Napoleon's brother-in-law Leclerc. Still significant now are the secret instructions of Napoleon which craftily applied the master strategy of empire: "divide and rule."

> No. 18. You should give particular attention to the caste of coloured people. Put them in a position to develop their natural prejudices on a wide scale, and give them the opportunity to rule over the blacks, and by these means you will secure the submission of both.

Toussaint fought heroically against the French invading army and inflicted many heavy blows. But at a low ebb in the conflict, his most trusted generals, Dessalines, Christophe, and even his own nephew, went over to the French army. General Brunet, carrying out Leclerc's foul plan, invited Toussaint to a conference, and after Toussaint appeared he was treacherously seized, transported to France, and imprisoned in the fortress of Joux where he died of hunger and cold on April 7, 1803.

As the great liberator was being forced aboard the ship which was to take him from his native soil, he declared prophetically: "The tree of liberty which I have planted, you will never be able to uproot." His seizure evoked a broad rising of the people, and the generals who had defected, realizing that a similar fate awaited them, resumed leadership in the revolutionary armies. The military struggle which followed, aided by the ravages of yellow fever among the French forces, finally achieved victory for the first successful revolution of chattel slaves in history.

National independence was declared at the very spot where Toussaint had been seized and the new nation was launched on January 1, 1804. Appropriately, the slavemasters' designations "St. Domingue" and "San Domingo" were cast off, and the indigenous Caribbean name *Haiti,* which means land of mountains, was adopted. The Haitian Revolution sounded the death knell of the infamous slave trade, opened the way for the abolition of chattel slavery throughout the hemisphere, and gave impetus to the struggle for the independence of all the peoples of South and Central America. Though hardly remembered today, it was the financial, military, and other assistance, twice rendered by President Alexandre Pétion of Haiti to the forces led by Commodore Aury and the liberator Simón Bolívar, which contributed decisively to the success of the liberation movements of Latin America.

A direct result of Napoleon's defeat in Haiti was his agreement to the Louisiana Purchase of 1803. This secured to the United States all the vast region of Louisiana, Kansas and Nebraska, Iowa and Wyoming, Montana and the Dakotas, most of Colorado and Minnesota, and all of Washington and Oregon. A significant contribution had earlier been made by a volunteer force of 800 Haitians of African descent, who in 1778 at Savannah, Georgia, saved the day by their valiant charge which rescued the retreating American army from annihilation.

In Haiti the revolution finally abolished the plantation system, and the land was divided into small peasant holdings. But this plantation economy was maintained intact in all the Caribbean colonies. Emancipation from chattel slavery thus left the great majority of the people landless, and therefore compelled to toil on the estates at wages far below a decent human subsistence level. As these workers began to secure small plots of land, they left the plantations. The planters then brought in some Chinese, Japanese and still more Indian indentured laborers, to work on the estates. Thus were sown more seeds of dissension and disunity which today bear frightful fruit.

Throughout the Caribbean region during this period there developed middle classes, composed chiefly of African and European ancestry, small land owners, traders, artisans, clerks, doctors, lawyers, and juridical and administrative officials. With but few exceptions these were oriented by their European training towards the ideas and system of imperial overlordship. These Caribbean colonials came even to speak of the metropolitan countries as "home." Of unusual importance for the understanding sought in this survey is the fact keenly observed by Dr. Eric Williams in *The Negro in the Caribbean:* "they remain profoundly ignorant of the neighboring islands, each group basking in its special isolation."

The Morant Bay rebellion of 1865 in Jamaica caused panic in the ruling oligarchy of planters and merchants. People of African descent were slaughtered indiscriminately by the hundreds. The martyr George William Gordon, who had in no wise participated in the rebellion, was hanged by Governor Eyre because he championed the rights of the downtrodden people. Rather than permit the possibility of united political action or any participation in government whatever by the people, the Jamaican ruling clique connived with the British government to reimpose direct Crown Colony government. Any development towards democratic rule was thus deliberately set back. Save for Barbados, where the planters took the astute counsel of Sir Conrad Reeves, and thus maintained certain legislative powers, retrogression towards unmitigated colonial despotism was imposed on the whole Caribbean region.

Independent Haiti was of course excepted from this direct political bondage. But the fledgling Haitian nation had for thirty-four years to resist the diplomatic and naval endeavors of France to regain suzerainty. Under threat of force Haiti had to pay France an "indemnity" of twelve million dollars. Gunboat diplomacy and bombardment drained Haiti's slender resources steadily. The occupation of Haiti by the United States marines from 1915 to 1934 converted Haiti into the special colonial preserve of

American financiers such as the National City Bank and the Haitian-American Sugar Company. One of the baneful effects of this occupation was the re-establishment of color caste division with the encouragement of "colored people" to occupy chief positions and rule over the peasantry of African origin.

Movement toward Unity

The people of the Caribbean elsewhere began slowly to emerge from this colonial "slough of despond." Significant strivings toward unity and freedom appeared with the development of an organized labor movement and political efforts for federation and independence, under the outstanding leadership of Captain A. A. Cipriani of Trinidad and the journalist T. Albert Marryshow of Grenada. The Dominican Federation Conference held in 1932 marked the first broadly representative and signal, if halting, steps toward a united, inclusive, independent Caribbean Nation.

Expressive of the common consciousness and developing unity among the impoverished and suffering people were the risings during 1937–1938, widespread throughout the Caribbean area. Lacking unifying leadership on an overall scale, this upsurge was ruthlessly repressed by the British and colonial governments through mass shootings and arrests of hundreds of people. Support for the defense of the victimized Caribbean workers was organized in New York by the West Indies Defense Committee in which Reginald Pierrepointe played an active role. Labor movements developed rapidly; the topmost leadership being assumed by the middle class whose narrow and insular colonial mode of thought has already been noted. Nevertheless, the strivings toward unity of the working people led to a significant attempt at overall unification. The first Caribbean Labour Conference was held in Barbados during 1945. A noteworthy statement of this Conference was the declaration: "Caribbean Labour demands federation with self-government, not without it."

After the fall of the Netherlands to Hitler's army on May 10, 1940, the danger became acute that the French-ruled Caribbean would fall into the hands of the fascist monsters. As a counter move President Roosevelt engineered the exchange with Britain of bases in the Caribbean for fifty over-age destroyers. But this deal was carried out without any consultation with the Caribbean people. Chaguaramas in Trinidad and other bases still remain a denial of their sovereign rights, even though in the age of atomic missiles such bases actually provide no defense, but are rather a source of danger to the Caribbean people.

The United States had earlier joined the ranks of the empires dominating the Caribbean by intervening in the Spanish-American War in 1898. With the blowing up of the *Maine* and the jingoist incitements of the American press, Cuba and Puerto Rico were converted into virtual colonies by the United States. In 1917 the Virgin Islands were purchased from Denmark, ruled by U.S. naval forces, and still remain dominated colonies.

The divisive and repressive tactics, noted by Carleton Beals in *The Crime of Cuba*, were employed in all these Caribbean colonies: "In appointments the white Creoles were favored and social barriers set up." The comment of Professor Miguel Araunuz, also cited by Beals, was revealing and remained pointed down to very recent times:

> In those days we thought America came to make us free; now we know you came to win Cuba for yourselves. All the island belongs to you Americans—ninety percent of its cultivable area is owned or leased to you. Our people are bowed beneath a tyranny as bad as that of Butcher Weyler. And Havana, lovely old Havana, is gone forever, your wealthy tourists have made it a saloon and brothel and gambling house. . . .

Pertinent for the understanding here sought are the following statements of two great Caribbean liberators, the Cuban patriots General Antonio Maceo and the intellectual José Martí. When a friend attempted to incite him against another less pigmented leader, Maceo rejoined: "My sword can never compete with that of General Máximo Gómez." Shot down by Spanish soldiers, his throat pierced by a machete, Antonio Maceo's last words were: "Long Live Cuba!" His great compatriot, José Martí, who also died while heroically fighting for independence, declared prophetically:

> The Antilles freed will save the independence of our America and the honor, already tainted and wounded, of Anglo-Saxon America.

Efforts in defense of the Caribbean people, put forward chiefly by Caribbean Americans and their Afro-American friends in New York, culminated in the Declaration of Rights of the Caribbean People to Self-Determination and Self-Government presented to the Pan American Foreign Ministers' Conference at Havana in 1940. As a direct result of this intervention, the statement of the Havana Conference was amended to include specific recognition of basic rights to the Caribbean people. An Appeal to the United Nations Conference on Behalf of the Caribbean People was registered at the founding of the United Nations in San Francisco in 1945 by the West Indies National Council of New York. Attorney Hope R. Stevens was delegated and worked to secure support in the Havana Conference for the principles of the Declaration. Dr. Charles A. Petioni and the author were delegated to present this Appeal.

Responding to the appeal of Caribbean leaders for support to the Second Caribbean Labour Conference, the sum of $10,000 was raised and transmitted by the real estate broker Augustine A. Austin. A Memorandum on Federation and Self-Government, drafted by the present writer, was sent in support of the avowed aim of the Caribbean leaders to achieve a federated and independent Caribbean Nation. Broadly representative of various areas, the Second Caribbean Labour Conference convened in Coke Hall, Kingston, Jamaica, in September 1947. The following primary resolution and basic declaration was unanimously adopted:

> The Conference is convinced that the development of West Indian nationhood, the evolution of our cultural standards, the expansion and stability of our economy . . . can best and most fully be secured by the Federation of the Territories concerned.
>
> That the Federal Constitution must provide for Responsible Government equivalent to Dominion Status.

Attempt at Federation

Despite all counsel, warnings, and entreaties, the chief political Caribbean leaders, together with their British imperial tutors, then launched the ill-planned and ill-fated West Indies Federation on April 22, 1958. But this was a federation in name only, lacking all the essential elements of true nationhood: independence, a common customs union, free movement of the people, basic economic integration and planning, and the elimination of costly unit imperial governors and duplicating administrative apparatus. Besides, no basic education of the people on the issues involved was ever conducted; no Economic Plan for the entire Caribbean was outlined. No adequate initial provision of essential capital was secured, as partial and due restitution by the British imperial financiers, who for centuries had drained vast wealth from the toil and misery of the Caribbean people.

The disastrous result is now a matter of history. The secession of Jamaica, followed by the withdrawal of Trinidad and Tobago, spelled the doom of the abortive "federation." A new light was thereby thrown on the earlier statement of the Prime Minister, Sir Grantley Herbert Adams, who had absolved Britain of any responsibility and blamed the people "if the West Indies Federation is not further along." Likewise, the true nature became transparent of the confident assurance given by the outstanding Caribbean political figure of that period, the Hon. Norman Washington Manley, Q.C., "that within five years or less the West Indies will achieve independence." Illumined also was the message and supplication of Sir Alexander Bustamante: "Creation of Federation bold step for W.I. people but most unfortunate it must start on wooden leg . . . No Money . . . So we are praying. . . ."

Those of use who by enforced economic exile, or through some enlightening experience, have managed to overcome narrow insularity, petty provincialism, purblind prejudice, and smug satisfaction, ought to exercise care lest we stir the ever smouldering embers of disastrous discord. This, then, is hardly the time to identify personalities responsible for the miserable, petty demagogy, strange intellectual weakness, cupidity, insularity, and titled ineptitude, unexplained insistence upon unitary association as yet unrealized, self-centered leadership and opportunist opposition, which even now hinders the fruition of a genuine Eastern Caribbean Federation as a step forward. Let us then simply say now that all the chief Caribbean political leaders of that period together bear responsibility, in varying degrees, for the miserable debacle and the distressing setback of the Caribbean liberation movement.

It is pointless and in the end disastrous to bring forward easy excuses. "Too much water separates us," but much more water separates vastly more islands in united Indonesia. "The people weren't ready," but the people were not adequately informed. "The conditions were not propitious," but conditions of extreme poverty have rendered the Caribbean area ripe for change. However, favorable conditions do not automatically produce change. A conscious, devoted, and able leadership is needed to take advantage of favorable conditions.

From the foregoing historical survey it becomes evident that the possibilities of Caribbean unity depend upon the ability to overcome this crippling heritage of varied division and manifold slavery, as the indispensable condition for freedom. This task has become more difficult, even as the realization of independence, because of the stiffened attitudes of the imperial powers. Recently General De Gaulle, of Free France fame, flatly refused to consider the demand voiced by Aimé Césaire for an independent Martinique. Britain holds desperately to the status quo out of deference to powerful imperial forces in the United States. The Bay of Pigs invasion of Cuba has now been followed by the deepening crisis in Guiana.

The government democratically elected by the people of Guiana is now being overthrown with the reimposition of direct imperial rule by Britain. The former ruler of the seas is today increasingly seen as a junior ally of the United States. How tragic it is that it has been possible to incite bloody conflict between groups suffering the same common oppression, through arousing racist hostility between Guianese of Indian and those of African origin! Who that thinks can fail to consider the significance of a certain meeting between New York financiers and a Guianese leader of African descent? Whence and why the funds funnelled by complaisant American trade union leaders into Guiana? What had all this to do with the subsequent disorders and present dire events?

Clear and challenging is the urgent necessity of overcoming the virus of fratricidal division and mental enslavement which is all too dominant still in the Caribbean body politic. It may well be that we may have to look to the presently emerging generation for the leadership that will strive to realize that unity which is essential to the achievement of an all inclusive, consciously welded, economically viable, and truly significant independent Caribbean Nation.

In *The Destiny of the West Indies*, as envisioned by the Jamaican-born

journalist, A. M. Wendell Malliet, in New York during 1928, the searching
question was put forth, which has become even more urgent today:

> Is there no West Indian who is patriotic enough to take his stand, as it were
> under the inspiration of Massini, Italian patriot, and declare, "I swear to
> dedicate myself wholly and forever to strive to constitute the British West
> Indies one united group, nominally free and independent, enjoying full
> dominion status as the large self-governing nations within the British Com-
> monwealth of Nations, and possessing in abundance the means wherewith to
> satisfy the spiritual, moral, cultural and material needs of its inhabitants"?

Extending to the still broader horizon of the all inclusive Caribbean and
even beyond to the great mother Africa, is the call of the stirring and
appealing lines written in 1939 by Aimé Césaire of Martinique in his
famous poem *Cahier d'un retour au pays natal* (Statement of a Return to My
Native Country):

> for it is not true that the work of man
>   is finished
> that man has nothing more to do in the
>   world but be a parasite in the world
> that all we now need is to keep in step
>   with the world
> but the work of man is only just beginning
>   and it remains to man to conquer all
>   the violence entrenched in the recesses
>   of his passion
> and no race possesses the monopoly of beauty,
>   of intelligence, of force, and there
>   is a place for all at the rendevous
>   of victory . . .

George Lamming of Barbados is one of the able group of writers developed in the Caribbean recently, but mostly forced to go abroad to seek
opportunity, like hosts of other native Caribbeans who have gone forth to
Panama, the United States, Canada, and Britain. In "The Pleasures of
Exile," written for the *Tamarack Review* of June 1960, George Lamming
noted that "colonialism is the very base of the West Indian's cultural
awareness." But Lamming himself expressed a new and opposite awareness when he asked, "Why, then, wasn't the British West Indies a sovereign
state ten years ago? Why isn't it a sovereign state today?" With insistence
this writer then properly called upon the political leaders of the Caribbean
to get on with the work of unification and liberation.

While supervising livestock on the Breda plantation in St. Domingue,
Toussaint Louverture read, pondered upon, and finally answered the call
put by history and expressed by Abbé Raynal: "A courageous chief only is

wanted. Where is he? Where is he? He will appear, doubt it not, he will come forth and raise the standard of liberty."

As Toussaint Louverture responded and ably fulfilled the mission required by his time, may we not hope that there will now arise those who will meet the demands of our day and provide the dedicated leadership so greatly needed by the oppressed Caribbean people? So may it be:

> That the rages of the ages shall be cancelled
> Consciousness the will informing till it fashion all things fair.

VII

EARLY HARLEM AGITATION

Richard B. Moore's reputation and influence rested mainly on his extraordinary skill as an orator. During his early years as a radical, particularly during the 1920s, he was a nightly visitor to the street corners of Harlem, where his tall, lean figure could be seen precariously perched on a stepladder, haranguing an audience. Unfortunately, the few fragments preserved are in reports by informers for the Department of Justice and are not adequate for inclusion. His first-known written statement appeared in the first issue of The Emancipator, *a newspaper started in 1920 with W. A. Domingo. "Bogalusa" is the only piece identified as written by Moore during his socialist years. This powerful polemic, written in a stilted, oratorical style filled with biblical reference, was inspired by the labor disturbances in Bogalusa, Louisiana, in which several white workers were killed while protecting and defending a black worker. It clearly demonstrates the influence of Bouck White's* The Call of the Carpenter, *which helped pave his path from Christian dogma to socialism.*

Other contemporary articles in this section indicate his activities and interests while he was involved with the Communist Party. As a delegate of the American Negro Labor Congress to the organizing Congress of the League Against Imperialism in Brussels, he served as secretary of the committee on the Negro question and was largely responsible for the drafting of the resolution that was adopted. A translation of his introductory statement from the official proceedings of the Congress and the English version of the resolution, which he delivered to W. E. B. Du Bois for publication in The Crisis, *follow. "An Open Letter to Mr. A. Philip Randolph" exposes not only the problems confronting Afro-American workers and the great breach separating Afro-American leaders but also the sharp animosities generally within the labor movement. Moore and Randolph had worked together as socialists but ten years later Moore's stand "against the misleadership of the prejudiced labor aristocrats of the A. F. of L." was frequently in bitter opposition to that of his former comrades. Randolph's response to Moore's challenge was, "I am not going to debate with anybody about the Brotherhood."*

As organizer and president of the Harlem Tenant's League, Moore wrote the editorial "Housing and the Negro Masses," which appeared in The Negro Champion *and* The Daily Worker. *It is interesting to note that*

Moore's original statement regarding the necessary struggle for "the salva-
tion of the race" was changed to "the salvation of the black and white
workers" in the Daily Worker *version. The reprint in* The Daily Worker
also carried an excerpt of his statement on housing at the New York State
Legislature hearing. "Problems and Struggles of the Negro Workers" is a
succinct analysis of the special concerns of the Afro-American, which Moore
was constantly striving to clarify for his white comrades. The second part of
the article, published a day later, dealt with racial prejudice as an ideology
of capitalist imperialism. His most important and exhausting assignment
was to help manage the Scottsboro campaign. The thirty-page pamphlet
from which excerpts have been selected typifies the material he prepared
during the campaign.

BOGALUSA

The Emancipator, March 13, 1920, p. 4.

Strange is the name and stranger still the deed which will cause it to live
on in the memory of countless workers—black and white. Strange, indeed,
and well nigh incredible, yet grand and heroic is the eventful happening
which will lift this rude lumber town of Louisiana out of obscurity into
historic prominence. As strange and as grand as that great undertaking
which stamped the name of Harper's Ferry upon the page of history and
immortalized its hero, John Brown of Osawatomie.

And we dare hope that the sacrifice of Bogalusa holds as great significance for the 15,000,000 black freedmen (?) and for their white fellow-
citizens (?) as held the sacrifice of Harper's Ferry for the chattel slaves of
the South and the free laborers of the North.

Not without ground do we hope, either. For it is a matter of history that
though John Brown perished at the hands of the slave owners whose power
he had assailed, not many years elapsed before the victorious Union Army
marched in triumph through the slave confederacy singing exultantly:
"John Brown's body lies a'mouldering in the grave, but his soul goes
marching on." If history repeat itself, as we are assured it does, and if it be
true that "the blood of the martyrs is the seed of the church," then may we
confidently hope that the night of wage slavery with all its gruesome horror
is at last to yield place to the dawn of a better day for all who toil, black and
white alike.

Williams, Gaines, Bouchillon, O'Rourke, Dechus, these are names that
should now be on the lips and hearts of all workers the world over.

Through the ministrations of toil and suffering, these attained unto great heights of fellowship, service, and sacrifice. Driven by the pressure of a direful and iniquitous system of oppression, the soulless, merciless, capitalist profit-system, they came to a consciousness of common woe; then yearned together for a common weal; and learned devotion to a common cause. Arrogant race pride and resentful hatred, both were consumed in the crucible of bitter experience through which these passed. Thus they came to labor together in their Labor Union, as men and equals, as comrades and brothers, for the protection and advancement of the cause of labor. Together they braved the assaults of their enemy the tyrannous lumber trust; together they defied the wrath of the slave-loving, Negro-baiting South. Together they faced the crucial test, shoulder to shoulder, black and white. Yes, these white Southern workers dared defend their black comrades against the fury of the blood-thirsty mob. They might have saved themselves by yielding up Dechus, but they would not; they stuck by him, saved him, and for this they paid the great price. O'Rourke is seriously wounded; the others are dead.

Williams, Gaines, and Bouchillon have given their lives. O'Rourke imperilled his life, in the cause of true freedom. Not for white labor, not for black labor (though they died defending a Negro), nor yet for any race or nation, did they make the supreme sacrifice, but for Labor, that great universal fraternity of striving, suffering human-kind which though despoiled, despised, and rejected, alone holds promise for the emancipation of the race. Well might Labor—black, white or yellow—honor the memory of their great sacrifice. Well might Labor glory in, and glorying follow, their splendid example of loyalty, courage, and heroism. Of these noble, courageous, class-conscious workers, martyrs of today, let us say with Byron:

> "They never fail who die
> In a great cause; the block may soak their gore;
> Their heads may sodden in the sun; their limbs
> Be strung to city gates and castle walls—
> But still their spirit walks abroad. Though years
> Elapse and others share as dark a doom,
> They but augment the deep and weeping thoughts
> Which overpower all others, and conduct
> The world at last to freedom!"

The Carpenters again lead the way to freedom. They follow in the footsteps of that greatest Labor Leader, the Carpenter of Nazareth. Two thousand years ago, he called to the workers: "Come unto me, all ye that labor and are heavy laden," forsaking his work-bench to pursue his holy mission "to preach deliverance to the slaves." Even while laying the axe to the root of that dire despotism that had overshadowed mankind with a deep darkness and despair, he was crucified for "stirring up the people." But his Spirit they could not crucify. Though the oppressors have diligently sought to compass this, brazenly using his name as a cloak for their tyrannous greed, and subtly perverting his uprising words of deliverance into a religion of submission, an establishment of organized plunder and oppression; yet have they failed. His Spirit is still abroad crusading against the Mammonism of today—the Capitalist-Imperialism that plagues and scourges the toiling, dying masses of humanity—even as on the hills of Judea he inveighed against the Mammonism of Imperial Rome with fiery indignation and revolt.

That Spirit was incarnate in the Carpenters of Bogalusa. It is incarnate in the militant class-conscious proletariat of the world. It is even now moving in the deep unrest and divine discontent which like the surging ocean compasses the system of Mammonism the world around today. It is moving to destroy its vicious antithesis, the spirit of grab and crush embodied in the World System of Capitalism which breeds strife, within the races and between the races; war, within the nations and between the nations; evil, pestilence, and all manner of ill: Lynchings, pogroms, massacres, disease, destruction, death.

The Cross conquers the Eagle. The Manger overthrows the Empire. The Spirit of the Carpenter is moving, we say, to the destruction of this Monster which is impoverishing and embruting mankind. Let those who are bloated with wealth and drunk with power, whose yoke is heavy and grievous to be borne, beware, for the Day of the People is at hand, the prophecy of her who gave birth to the Carpenter moves on to its fruition. Is even now to be fulfilled, that sublimest ode of human aspiration, the Prayer of Woman, the Battle Cry of Man, the thunderous, revolutionary Magnificat:

> "He hath showed strength with his arm;
> He hath scattered the proud in the imagination of their hearts.
> He hath put down the mighty from their seats.
> And exalted them of low degree.
> He hath filled the hungry with good things;
> And the rich he hath sent empty away."

Then shall subject peoples, races, classes achieve their freedom. Then and thus. Then shall Ethiopia stretch forth her hand to God. Then shall "Afric's chains be burst and Freedom rule the rescued land." Then shall the emancipated workers—black, white, yellow—possess the Kingdom which is at hand, the Kingdom of Man, of Comradeship, of a just Social Order upon the Earth—the Co-operative Commonwealth—the Great Commune of Peace and Plenty for All Mankind.

Then, then only, and not until then!

STATEMENT AT THE CONGRESS OF THE LEAGUE AGAINST IMPERIALISM AND FOR NATIONAL INDEPENDENCE, BRUSSELS, FEBRUARY 1927

Proceedings of the Congress (Berlin, 1927), pp. 126–30; *The Crisis,* July 1927, pp. 165–66.

Introduction of Resolution on the Negro Question

The delegate of the "American Negro Labor Congress" and the "Universal Negro Improvement Association," Richard B. Moore (USA) explained:

Since time is short and the most important historical facts concerning the condition of the Negro peoples have been summarized in the resolution which will be presented, I shall ask for only two minutes of your attention. I would like to discuss some important aspects of imperialism.

We have to realize that the fight against imperialism is first of all an incessant struggle against imperialistic ideology. We must fight fascism, the Ku-Klux-Klan, chauvinism and the doctrine of the supremacy of the white race. As long as the European workers are poisoned with these abominable ideas, it is impossible to free the world of the oppression of imperialism. Therefore it is our task to show the workers that they will no longer occupy a privileged position in their mother countries. Soon their standard of living will be lowered to the level of the most suppressed colonial workers. This can only be prevented by uniting with these people in a common struggle against a common enemy.

There is a lot to be learned from our oppressors. Mister Lothrop Stoddard, the main advocate in the United States of the theory of the supremacy of the white race, has published two books. These books demonstrate clearly the imperialistic oppressors' views concerning the workers in the mother country and in the colonial countries. In his book *The Rising Tide of Colour,* Mr. Stoddard attempts to prove that the struggle for the liberation of the colonial peoples poses a threat to civilization; in *The Revolt Against Civilisation* he attempts to prove that organized labor movements (unions, socialism, bolshevism) also threaten civilization. However, it is clear to us that civilization is endangered by the monstrosity of world imperialism which is mauling all people in its deadly claws. Therefore, it is our duty, to unite the European workers with the workers in the colonies for a common fight against this monster.

The imperialists are concocting a new world war, a terrible war in which race will fight against race. If they should succeed, we will face a general devastation which will be far worse than that of the last World War. The masses of the people will have to pay for this war with suffering and death. It is therefore our duty to prevent such a terrible event which would indeed destroy civilization. We must conquer the minds and hearts of the workers and the people. We must organize them for the struggle against militarism and imperialism, and for the final battle for world liberation.

Today the Negro is despised and suppressed. Even in the most progressive groups of the labor movement we are treated as inferiors. But I remind you that the Negro had a decisive role in the Civil War which abolished slavery. The British workers played an important role as well. Although almost starving, the cotton workers of Manchester organized protests under the leadership of John Bright and Karl Marx. These protest meetings prevented Lord Palmerston from intervention in the South. This is a laudable example of unity and solidarity. We must work harder to organize the Negro masses. It is conceivable that the despised Negro peoples will be instrumental in tipping the scale of freedom in favor of the oppressed classes against the imperialistic oppressors in the event of a war between the oppressed and the exploiters.

And now I shall propose the following resolution for the benefit of the oppressed Negro peoples in the world.

Common Resolution on the Negro Question

For five hundred years the Negro Peoples of the World have been the victims of a most terrible and ruthless oppression. The institution of the slave trade, as a consequence of the commercial revolution and expansion of Europe, was the beginning of a regime of terror and robbery that is one of the most horrible in the history of mankind. As a result of this traffic, Africa lost a hundred million of her people. Four out of every five of these were killed in the bloody business of capture and transport, the survivors being consigned to a most cruel slavery in the New World.

The immense wealth derived from this gruesome trade was the foundation of the wealth and development of European merchants and states. But the development of the African peoples was thereby abruptly arrested and their civilization, which in many areas had reached a high state of advancement, was almost completely destroyed. These peoples henceforward were declared to be heathen and savage, an inferior race, ordained by the Christian God to be slaves of the superior Europeans, without any rights that a white man is bound to respect. And a bitter and hostile prejudice arose against the Negro race which has dominated the feeling of almost all Europeans towards them, causing them to be subjected to numerous unequal, degrading and pernicious proscriptions.

The abolition of chattel slavery freed the Negro peoples only from the thralldom of being legally held as personal property; the enslavement, exploitation and extermination of these peoples continue until the present moment. The process of subjugation was greatly accelerated by the mad scramble of European Powers for African territory between 1880 and 1890. This was due to the desire that financial capital had to put its reserves into the production of raw material, far from those areas of the industries of transformation which had just begun to develop in Europe. Afterwards, for the sake of its own development, industrial capitalism is joined to financial capitalism in the colonial robbery. By force and fraud the independent African states were subjected, their lands and possessions almost all forcibly expropriated and distributed among European corporations and persons, and their peoples driven by a most brutal and inhuman system to produce immense wealth for their oppressors. Virulent diseases were introduced among the people and devastation can be realized from the fact that despite the great virility and fecundity of the African peoples, Africa is now the least populous of the continents of the world.

Thus were the blessings of Christianity and civilization brought to the Africans. So that today in that vast continent of 11,500,000 square miles only two small states, Abyssinia and Liberia, are accounted independent. The former is now menaced by the Anglo-Italian pact, and the latter with its customs and constabulary in the hands of American officials, and a great concession granted to a Wall Street corporation, can no longer be considered free. The expropriation of the lands and extermination of the people proceeds grimly in Kenya and the Sudan, a suitable reward from the imperialists to the Africans whom they sacrificed in the great World War which was heralded as a war "to make the world safe for democracy and for the rights of weaker peoples."

Similarly the Union of South Africa has recently enacted a Color Bar Bill which prohibits the native from working with machinery and from employment in the civil services which adds new burdens to these people already oppressed by Pass Laws, Hut Taxes and the like, and who are herded into miserable reservations and compounds and terribly exploited on the farms and in the mines. Everywhere also in Africa, excepting a small area on the West Coast where the lands and customs of the natives have been maintained by them, there exists a rigorous repression of the people under the yoke of foreign imperialists. The productivity of this area which is 8 times greater than that of neighboring areas of European owned plantations, is an irrefutable proof of the utterly wanton and vicious nature of this system of modern slavery.

In the United States, the 12 million "Negroes" though guaranteed equal rights under the Constitution, are denied full and equal participation in the life of the nation. This oppression is greatest in the Southern states where the spirit of chattel slavery still predominates. Segregation, disfranchisement, legal injustice, debt and convict slavery, and lynching and mob violence degrade and crush these peoples. This vicious system of suppression operates to reduce this race to an inferior servile caste, exploited and abused by all other classes of society.

Haiti, established by Toussaint Louverture and his fellow-slaves by the first successful slave revolution in history, is now crushed and subjugated by the marines of that very power which proclaimed "the war for democ-

racy." More than 3,000 Haitians have been murdered and large numbers
are enslaved for the building of military roads under the corvée system.
They have been despoiled of their lands and liberties, and imprisonment
and torture is the lot of all who dare to speak for their freedom. In the
Caribbean colonies, the Negro peoples are subjected under varying forms
of imperialist rule. Limited franchise and oppressive plantation systems
reduce these masses to a permanent condition of serfdom and penury. In
Latin America, Negroes suffer no special suppression. The cordial relations resulting from the social and political equality in the races in these
countries prove that there is no inherent antagonism between them.

For the Republic of Haiti, Cuba, Santo Domingo and for the peoples of
Porto Rico and the Virgin Islands, we must demand complete political and
economic independence and the immediate withdrawal of all imperialist
troups. For the other Caribbean colonies, we must likewise demand and
obtain self-government. The Confederation of the British West Indies
should be achieved and the Union of all these peoples accomplished.

For the emancipation of the Negro peoples of the world, we must wage a
resolute and unyielding struggle to achieve:

1. Complete freedom of the peoples of Africa and of African origin;
2. Complete equality between the Negro race and all other races;
3. Control of the land and governments of Africa by the Africans;
4. Immediate abolition of all compulsory labor and unjust taxation;
5. Immediate abolition of all racial restrictions, social, political and economic;
6. Immediate abolition of military conscription and recruiting;
7. Freedom of movement within Africa and elsewhere;
8. Freedom of speech, press and assembly;
9. The right of education in all branches;
10. The right to organize trade unions.

To accomplish these ends we must prosecute the following measures:

1. The organization of the economic and political power of the people:
   (a) Unionization of Negro workers
   (b) Organization of co-operatives
2. Organization and co-ordination of the Negro liberation movements;
3. Prosecution of the fight against imperialist ideology: Chauvinism,
fascism, kukluxism, and race prejudice;
4. Admission of the workers of all races into all unions on the basis of
equality;
5. Unity with all other suppressed peoples and classes for the fight
against world imperialism.

AN OPEN LETTER TO MR. A. PHILIP RANDOLPH, GENERAL ORGANIZER OF THE BROTHERHOOD OF SLEEPING CAR PORTERS

The Negro Champion 1, no. 14 (August 8, 1928): 11.

July 31, 1928

Dear Mr. Randolph:

You have time and again declared that the fight of the Pullman Porters is not only their struggle, but the concern of the entire Negro race, since it is the basic struggle for the economic well-being of the Negro Race. In this you are entirely correct, and it is because we realize the importance of this struggle for the oppressed Negro masses and for the exploited workers that we are addressing you this open letter.

It is our duty to declare to you that the policy which you have followed, and in which you still persist, is a policy which can only bring disaster and ruin to the cause of the Porters and Maids. This policy of trailing behind the labor aristocrats who betray the interest of the workers, who follow a policy of co-operation with the employers, of refusal to strike, and of narrow craft segregation, has been proved to be a policy which weakens and divides the workers, which surrenders their interests to the bosses who exploit them.

That you have completely fallen for this ruinous policy was proved by your "postponement" of the strike at the instance of Wm. Green of the American Federation of Labor, and by your further statement that the strike orders now in the hands of the Regional Supervisors will only be opened "after the consultation of the Pullman Porters' leaders with Mr. Green."

Now we submit, Mr. Randolph, that Mr. Green did not organize the Pullman Porters; that his very failure to do so is evidence of his lack of interest in these workers. We submit that the Porters Union was organized because the Porters themselves rebelled against the miserable wage and the inhuman treatment to which they were subjected by the Pullman Company. And we say that to turn the organization of the Porters, built up by their sacrifice and struggle, into the hands of this misleader of labor, is to doom this organization to defeat.

It is now over seven weeks since the strike was "postponed." Immediately we issued a statement warning against the danger which threatened these workers from this backdown. We clearly warned against the misleadership of the prejudiced aristocrats of the A.F.L. and the narrow craft monopolists of the railroad brotherhoods. We called for a united front with the progressive rank and file of these unions, to overthrow the isolation of the Porters and to strengthen their union. We called for a new policy of militant struggle against the oppressive Pullman Company and against the agents of these oppressors in the labor movement. We demanded action to save the Porters Union, to strengthen the position of the Porters and Maids whose livelihood and status are at stake.

The Bulletin which you issued, explaining why the strike was postponed, clearly shows your subservience to Mr. Green. You say: "Gossip about Mr. Green being insincere is the veriest nonsense and silliest tommy-rot which could only emanate from crack-brained fanatics and low-grade morons." This abuse does not answer the criticisms of your mistaken policy, nor does it whitewash the known record of Mr. Green, as a labor misleader who consistently refuses to lead the workers in active struggle for the improvement of their conditions but who on the contrary aids the employers in schemes, plans and moves for binding the workers more securely to their lot of oppression and exploitation.

In this Bulletin, you further betray your complete failure to understand what strike strategy really is, what is really necessary to bring the oppressors of labor to book. You say: "We have done almost as much damage to the company by threatening a strike as we would have done by striking." Perhaps this is what you wished to do; but seriously, Mr. Randolph, do you think that the Pullman Company has been in the least disturbed by an empty threat of strike which failed to materialize? No indeed! One does not need to be a labor expert to know that the Pullman Company has merely used that threat to perfect a strike machinery, which it can now use to damaging effect against the Porters. And this very fact, that you did not have the courage to go through with the strike, means only one thing for the company, that you lack the power and the spirit actually to strike.

But the Porters had the courage and the spirit. According to your own statement, "85 percent of the men would not only have walked off but would have prevented others from walking on." And you revealed that you were not at all prepared for this when you stated: "I myself was amazed at the spirit of the men for the strike."

Why should you be amazed, Mr. Randolph? When you yourself issued a call to action in which you declared to the Porters: "The war is on! We must fearlessly face the fight to the finish for freedom. Our task now is to stand firm, steadfast and immovable, and prepare to go on with the fight TO THE FINISH, regardless of cost. Now, men, this is the time for ACTION, MORE ACTION, and STILL MORE ACTION."

The men responded like men to this appeal. They were "weighed in the balance and not found wanting." But you were not prepared for action. You were not ready to lead the men forward into the struggle, into the action, which was absolutely necessary to protect their interests.

You could have further declared, Mr. Randolph, "We are certain that we could win the strike alone, without the co-operation of any other labor organization." Now this is rather doubtful, but it is remotely possible. The question which it raises, which you will have to answer if you can, is: "Why did you then 'postpone' the strike? Why did you, then, submit to Mr. Green's 'advice?' Why do you still trail meekly and supinely behind the American Federation of Labor?" Obviously there is no need for this if you are assured that you are sufficiently powerful to win your struggle without their aid.

Moreover, Mr. Randolph, are you blind to what is happening under your very eyes in the labor movement? Do you not see that Wm. Green, John L. Lewis, etc. have aided the employers in wrecking the United Mine Workers of America, in defeating the strike of the miners of Pennsylvania and Ohio, thousands of whom are Negro workers? Do you not see that this same reactionary officialdom is playing the role of betrayal in the strike of the textile workers of New Bedford? And are you not aware of the complete disaster brought to the workers of the Interborough Rapid Transit Company by these very labor misleaders?

A.F. of L. officialdom took control of the worker's strike. They assumed the leadership of the old union, of the Consolidated Traction Workers Union. What did they do? They ditched the former leaders who had built up the union and they dallied around with Mayor Walker and the Tammany Hall politicians and completely betrayed the struggle of these workers. Their union was smashed, their strike defeated, and their interests completely betrayed into the hands of the Interborough. Today the company union of the Interborough flourishes and the condition of the workers of this company is miserable indeed.

Should not this be a warning to the Porters? Should not this keep them from giving over the leadership and control of their union, which they have sacrificed to build up, into the hands of these same labor betrayers and union-wreckers?

This struggle of the Porters is too important a matter to be passed over lightly. It is too significant a struggle for all the oppressed Negro workers against their exploiters to permit its weakening by mistaken policies or its betrayal by treacherous labor misleaders.

And so we must insist, Mr. Randolph, that this matter be openly threshed out in order that a correct policy and an efficient and courageous leadership, shall be assured these struggling workers, who are groaning under the burden of capitalist exploitation. We must ask you to debate this question with us. We feel that this is a duty which we cannot escape. We will meet you at any time and at any place that you will mention to discuss this question which is so vital to the economic well-being of the Negro masses. We will maintain that the present policy of the leadership of the Porters' union of non-strike, of co-operation with the employers, and of trailing behind the prejudiced and treacherous labor aristocrats, is a policy which threatens destruction and defeat of this great movement for the advancement of the Negro workers.

We trust that you will accept this invitation to debate in the spirit in which it is made, the spirit of sincere devotion to the cause of the workers, and we await your reply.

Yours for militant struggle in the interest of the workers,

AMERICAN NEGRO LABOR CONGRESS,
Richard B. Moore, National Organizer

HOUSING AND THE NEGRO MASSES

The Negro Champion, September 8, 1928, p. 8.

One of the most vital problems which the Negro masses face is the problem of Housing. How very vital, in fact, how actually menacing this problem now is, will be realized when it is known that the record of the death rate in cities shows that Negro children are dying from two to eight times faster than the children of other races. This frightful mortality, this slaughter of the innocents, is due directly to the terrible housing conditions imposed upon the Negro masses under the present oppressive system which is based upon RENT, INTEREST, and PROFIT.

Rent profiteering, overcrowding, unsanitary and beastly conditions are at their worst in the segregated districts where Negroes are compelled to live. Unable to move out of these miserable Ghettoes, the Negro masses are forced to pay the most exorbitant and outrageous rents for houses in every state of dilapidation and lack of sanitation. They are the prey of the greedy landlords and grasping capitalists who literally suck the life blood out of them.

Exploited at the point of production where they are paid the lowest wages for the most taxing and menial labor, Negro workers are set upon at the point of consumption by rent hogs and landlord sharks who take advantage of their segregated situation to gouge and bleed them to death. Terrible indeed is the plight of our people caught in the meshes of this vicious and lethal system of profit-making and rent-gouging. Impoverishment, degradation, disease and death—this is the terrible toll which we are forced to pay under this evil system which yields ill-gotten gain and blood-money to a few capitalist and landlord parasites.

It is a fact worthy of special note and full of great significance that Negro landlords and real estate agents are ready participants in and active supporters of this system which pauperizes, degrades, and crushes the masses of the Negro race. It is an undeniable and weighty fact that Negro landlords and agents are no more considerate of the purse, safety, health and lives of Negro tenants than white landlords.

Indeed, it is to be observed that Negro real estate agents have been a very active class in increasing rent. They are exceedingly active and skillful in the business of persuading landlords to put in colored tenants at *doubled* rentals. What does it matter to them what these tenants do or how they live in order to pay these oppressive rents? What does it matter to these Negro agents whether black babies live or die? Only one thing matters with them as with all landlords and capitalists of whatever race, and that is—PROFIT.

The higher the rent, the greater the commission, the larger the gain. And again, the less coal burned, the fewer repairs made, the greater the profit. So rents are raised, steam heat and hot water are hardly to be obtained, and repairs and sanitation are neglected by black as well as by white landlords and agents. With results for the masses of our people that are terrible to contemplate. Destitution, degeneration, disease, and death, these are the tragic results.

When measures are introduced for the protection of tenants or for the improvement of housing conditions, such as the extension of the Emergency Rent Laws and the Dwellings Law Bill which were brought before the New York legislature this year, it is to be noted that black and white landlords are united in the fight to defeat them. They line up together to kill laws which would help to abolish firetraps and disease breeding slums and which would improve standards of safety and health in the homes of the masses. They fight as one to erase from the statute books laws which afford tenants and workers some protection against "unjust, unreasonable, and oppressive rents." The Negro landlords and agents protect their class interests, their profits, not the interests of the oppressed Negro masses who are being driven to the wall.

It is the workers and tenants organizations that are found fighting for the protection of the masses of our people. The AMERICAN NEGRO LABOR CONGRESS sent telegrams to the governor and legislature of New York State and HARLEM TENANTS LEAGUE sent resolutions and delegates along with the representatives of other tenants leagues, labor bodies and social agencies to fight for these measures for the protection of the welfare and lives of the masses of the people.

The lesson of this situation is plain and pointed. It is clear before our eyes. The fight to reduce high rents and to clean up the housing conditions which menace the health and survival of the Negro race will have to be waged against the bitter opposition of both black and white landlords who fatten upon these vile and murderous conditions. The Negro tenants and workers, united with the tenants and workers of other races, will have to carry on this necessary struggle for the salvation of the race.

They must build strong tenants leagues and powerful labor unions as their essential and effective instruments for this vital struggle. They must organize politically to defeat the parties of the capitalists and the landlords, the Republican and Democratic parties. They must build and support the party of the workers, farmers, and tenants which fights militantly against the system of rent profiteering and capitalist exploitation.

Only thus can this vital problem of Housing be solved. Only thus will we be able to meet and master this deadly menace to the welfare, safety, and survival of the oppressed Negro race.

STATEMENT ON HOUSING BEFORE THE NEW YORK STATE LEGISLATURE

The Daily Worker, September 17, 1928, p. 6.

(*The Daily Worker* Editor's Note: One of the most militant fighters for the protection of the tenants and workers in that struggle [over the Dwellings Law Bill] was the candidate of our Party, Richard B. Moore, who as president of the Harlem Tenants' League, appeared at all the hearings at Albany. We quote in part from one of his speeches exposing before the legislature the oppressive housing conditions.)

If the legislature were conversant with the terrible housing conditions now existing, and if it were moved by considerations for the health and welfare of the people, it would pass this bill forthwith. The dreadful conditions among the masses will be realized from the pathetic fact that we have mothers appearing in court with children whose fingers and cheeks have been eaten by rats because rapacious landlords refuse to make repairs. The issue which this legislature is now called upon to decide, the issue now squarely before it, is whether the richest state of the richest country in the world cannot find enough resources, cannot provide a housing code which will provide sufficient light and air and which will compel standards for the protection of the health and lives of its citizens.

The landlords have raised the cry of confiscation. It must be answered that millions of dollars of slave property were confiscated in order to abolish chattel slavery. But the issue is not now confiscation. We have not yet come to that again. There is not a single confiscatory provision in this Dwellings Law Bill which requires only the barest minimum standards for health and safety. As a matter of fact, this bill does not begin to require what is really necessary for the protection of the masses. Against this false cry of confiscation, we raise the true cry of murder, for the lethal conditions under which the masses of people are now compelled to live amount to murder. To the gentleman who quoted from the decalogue, "Thou shalt not steal," we reply, that there is another commandment which is still more binding, "Thou shalt not kill."

I ask this legislature not to be overawed by this display of the landlords who have packed this hearing. The millions of the people demand the passage of this law. They are the fewer here for the reason that even now at this hour they are toiling and sweating and grinding to produce the profits and rents which these oppressors squeeze out of them. But these workers are watching to see whether this legislature will sacrifice the health and lives of its citizens to the greed of oppressive profiteers. They will judge and act accordingly.

PROBLEMS AND STRUGGLES OF THE NEGRO WORKERS

The Daily Worker, June 6, 1929, p. 6.

One of the most challenging social problems of America is the problem of the oppressed Negro race. The 12 million descendants of the Africans who were brought to America as slaves are still victims of a rigid and brutal system of social caste oppression which holds them as an inferior servile class at the bottom of capitalist society, exploited, degraded, and persecuted by the white imperialist master class and by prejudiced whites of all classes. The general emancipation from chattel slavery which resulted from the Civil War and which was accomplished by the Thirteenth Amendment to the Constitution in 1865, just 63 years ago, freed the Negroes only from the thralldom of being bought and sold as personal property. The counter-revolution of the slave-holders was successful in establishing new forms of slavery and social subjection consonant with the capitalist system of wage-slavery. Black codes, vagrancy laws, peonage, systems of debt and convict slavery, disfranchisement, legal discrimination and oppression, segregation, social ostracism, lynching and mob violence—these are the brutal means by which the Negro masses are mercilessly exploited, abused and repressed. From this repression and the struggle of these masses against it, there arises a prejudiced antagonism and hostility between the races which permeates the whole social life of America and which flares forth at its worst in terrible and bloody race conflicts. In every phase of life, in industry, in politics, in school, press and church, even in the labor movement itself, this prejudice appears in a very open and definite way.

This menacing situation of exploitation, prejudice and conflict exists throughout the world wherever capitalist imperalism dominates. It is at its worst in the southern states of the United States and in the Union of South Africa. In the colonies, in Africa and in the West Indies, it is a powerful and tremendous social force. Within the so-called "home countries" of Europe it exists though not to the same degree as in the colonies. It is almost absent in France where the declining man-power of this imperialist power dictates a policy of better treatment for the Negro. There is only one country in the world today where the Negro is treated as a social equal in every sense of the word, where he is welcomed as comrade and an honored brother—that is in the Union of Socialist Soviet Republics where the system of capitalist imperialism has been abolished, where the workers and farmers have established their own class government, and where a Communist society is being consciously constructed.

The same social forces which created the labor problem, precipitated the race problem. The development of the commercial and industrial capitalist profit-system, not only expropriated the European masses from the land, and brought into being a class of laborers possessing only their labor-power and exploited by the owners of capital. It caused also the expansion of European capitalists and freebooters into Africa, Asia and America and the plunder, enslavement and proscription of the aboriginal races of these continents. As Marx graphically puts it: "The discovery of gold and silver in America, the extirpation, enslavement and entombment in mines of the aboriginal population, the beginning of the conquest and looting of the East Indies, the turning of Africa into a warren for the commercial hunting of black skins, signalized the rosy dawn of the capitalist era of production." (*Capital*, Vol. I, p. 775). "The colonial system ripened, like a hot-house, trade and navigation. The colonies secured a market for the budding manufactures, and through the monopoly of the market, an increased accumulation. The treasures captured outside Europe by undisguised looting, enslavement, and murder, floated back to the mother country and were there turned into capital." (Ibid., p. 778) . . .

When the further development of the system of capitalist wage slavery demanded the abolition of chattel slavery, this was accomplished ruthlessly by the capitalists against the opposition of the slave-holders. While the capitalist exploiters proclaimed "liberty and equality" for the black slaves, they carefully and deliberately maintained the system of racial caste oppression under new forms as a necessary part of their system for the exploitation of the labor-power of the black masses and for the division of the white workers against the Negro workers in order to secure the exploitation and degradation of the entire working class, and the supremacy of their own tyrannous class rule.

With the development of capitalism into its final stage, imperialism, the race problem becomes still more acute. Africa is partitioned among the European imperialist powers and the African peoples are subjugated and exploited. They are ruthlessly expropriated from the land especially from those areas which the Europeans regard as suitable for themselves and are enslaved under compulsory labor systems, hut taxes, pass laws and the like. They are mercilessly driven to death in the gold, diamond and metal mines, and on the rubber, cocoa and cotton farms of the states. They are compelled to do the most taxing and disagreeable manual labor and are prevented in certain sections from doing any skilled work whatsoever. They are segregated, abused, ostracized and massacred. The imperialist powers tighten their grip upon the Negro peoples of Haiti, the West Indies, South and Central America.

The condition of the Negro masses in America grows steadily worse as the racial caste system spreads more and more into the North and West, becoming daily more deeply intrenched in the life of the nation. Large sections of the white workers of Europe, America and Africa are bribed with a share of the imperialist spoils drawn out of the toil and degradation of the Negro masses, and are filled with white imperialist prejudice against these workers. The social development of the system of racial caste oppression clearly proves that it is rooted in the economic exploitation of the capitalist imperialist class system. Race oppression is a form of capitalist imperialist class oppression. The Negro problem is basically a labor problem. The labor problem is organically bound up with the Negro problem. The Negro problem cannot be solved save through the solution of the labor problem. The labor problem cannot be solved unless the race problem is solved.

MR. PRESIDENT: FREE THE SCOTTSBORO BOYS (Excerpts)

Pamphlet, International Labor Defense, New York, 1934.

The President is "Not In!"

On Mothers' Day, May 13th, [1934,] the mothers of five of the Scottsboro boys [Mrs. Janie Patterson, Mrs. Ida Norris, Mrs. Mamie Williams, Mrs. Josephine Powell, and Mrs. Viola Montgomery], accompanied by a delegation of 30 prominent people, went to Washington to request President Roosevelt's intervention in the case. The President had been adequately informed ahead of time of the intended visit. Nevertheless, he deliberately chose to spend the day cruising about on the Potomac River, even keeping away from the Mothers' Day Banquet arranged on that day for his mother.

The delegation arrived at the appointed time and was informed by the White House attendants and the police that the President was out for the day. They were curtly told that there was no one left who could be handed the letter which these mothers had brought to the President. Even the White House usher was away!

The heartbroken mothers stated they would come again the next day. When the delegation returned the following morning it received an equally hostile reception. "Only the mothers and their spokesman are permitted within the gates," declared the captain of the guards. The whole delegation of representative Negro and white women was forced to wait outside. The police forbade the reporters to take any statements from members of the delegation. They even prohibited pictures being taken of the delegates facing the White House!

After the five mothers and Richard B. Moore of the I.L.D.—their spokesman—had been allowed within the sacred portals of the White House, they were not permitted to see the President. He was "too busy on important matters" to spend a few minutes on the Scottsboro frame-up—a dastardly attempt to burn alive nine innocent Negro boys—denounced in an avalanche of world-wide protest, exposed by Horton, the trial Judge himself, as a case based on flimsy manufactured "evidence."

The mothers and their spokesman were met by the President's secretary. One of them grudgingly took the letter they had brought; impatiently listened to their pleas. President Roosevelt completely avoided receiving the delegation. He remained hidden behind barred doors and formal legal technicalities in order to cover up the approval of the administration and its direct participation not only in the atrocious Scottsboro frame-up, but in the whole reign of terror against the Negro people. . . .

Scottsboro Mothers' Plea

The Scottsboro mothers' plea that President Roosevelt refused even to receive, is a heart-rending document:

"Mr. Franklin Delano Roosevelt
President of the United States
Mr. President:

"This day has been set aside as Mothers' Day. Therefore, we come to you as mothers suffering the greatest pain, because our innocent sons are made to endure the most terrible tortures. Though guilty of no crime, the State of Alabama holds them in dark and terrible cells, and tortures them with the electric chair staring them in the face.

"It is now three years that our sons have been forcibly torn from us. Our boys were framed on a terrible charge of which they are innocent. We know that Judge Horton in granting a new trial to Haywood Patterson said that the evidence is in favor of the boys. Yet, the rulers of Alabama keep them locked in dark dungeons.

"What can be the reason for such a crime against our boys when they have been proven innocent? It is the prejudice and oppression against the Negro people. We know that Negroes were not allowed to sit on the jury which gave the death penalty to our innocent sons.

"Mr. President, we ask you to act in behalf of our sons. We ask that you, as the chief executive of this country, as one who is supposed to take an interest in the welfare of the people of this country and to see that justice is done to all alike, speak out against the murderous persecution of our children.

"Your word, Mr. President, would have great weight throughout the land. Millions of people in America and other countries have already raised their voices in protest against this terrible wrong. Men and women in high places all over the world have spoken for the freedom of our boys, because the evidence shows our boys to be innocent. Ruby Bates, southern white girl, who in fear of her life, was forced to speak against our sons, has now honestly told the whole truth proving the innocence of our boys. Will you not, as President of the United States, speak and dc everything in your power to free our wronged and tortured sons?

"With anxious hearts we await your reply and shall watch the press for your public statement.

Earnestly,
THE SCOTTSBORO MOTHERS"

Excerpts from Statement to President Roosevelt On the Scottsboro Case

History of the Case

"The history of this case, extending now over three years, is the stark record of a ruthless ruling-class conspiracy to carry through the hideous, wholesale lynch massacre of nine innocent, unemployed Negro boys. Thrust into starvation by the capitalist crisis, these boys set out to look for jobs (two of them being ill, to seek medical attention), only to find themselves in the clutches of official lynch torturers, faced with the electric chair and the constant menace of savage mob lynching.

"The significant circumstances and events of this outrageous frame-up are too many to enumerate in this statement, but a few must be mentioned. The legal lynch orgy at Scottsboro when eight of these boys were railroaded to the electric chair in 72 hours, to the sadistic gloating of a deliberately organized lynch mob of 8,000 which surrounded and jammed into the court-room. The terrorizing of witnesses and defense attorneys at the Decatur trial; organized lynch mobs actually started from Scottsboro and Huntsville and were turned back only when Judge Horton declared from the bench that the mobs would be met with bullets.

"Highly important is the brazen denial of the right of Negroes to serve on the jury, though numerous Negroes took the witness stand in the terrorist atmosphere of the Decatur court and proved their qualifications. The violent appeals to chauvinism, prejudice and race hatred by the prosecuting officials and Attorney-General Knight. 'Free that "nigger" and every white man will tremble for his daughter tonight. We have built an Anglo-Saxon civilization and we mean to maintain it.' The burning of the house of the witness Lewis, a Negro worker, in Chattanooga, following upon the Decatur trial; the threats of Ku Klux Klansmen against him and his subsequent death from 'mysterious' poisoning.

"Still further demonstrative of the true nature and ruling class origin of this lynch frame-up are the following unmistakable manoeuvres. The introduction of Judge Callahan, a reputed Ku Klux Klansman, into the case, after Judge Horton rendered his decision reversing Haywood Patterson's conviction, because of the too rank nature of the frame-up and the pressure of international mass protest. The subsequent railroading of Haywood Patterson and Clarence Norris under his openly biased direction at the second Decatur trial.

No "Miscarriage of Justice"

"Flagrant and indicative is the forging of the names of Negroes to the Jackson County jury roll and the despicable manoeuvres of Judge Callahan, acting in collusion with Attorney-General Knight, in connection with the delaying of the trial transcript, granting extensions of time and reversing these a few days before the time for appeal would expire in order to deprive these boys even of the right of appeal. (See Brief to the Alabama Supreme Court, pages 51–62; 137–142).

"In addition, there is the refusal during these more than three years to give a trial before a juvenile court to Roy Wright, who was 14 years old at the time of the Scottsboro trial when a mistrial was declared in his case. The similar refusal in the case of Eugene Williams who was 13 years old when framed-up, despite the decision of the Alabama Supreme Court ordering such a trial. The denial of the right of bail to all these boys and their torture and several attempts at further frame-ups in the jail. All these events and deeds prove conclusively that the Scottsboro case is no ordinary 'criminal' case, no accidental 'miscarriage of justice.' . . .

"A National Emergency"

"You, Mr. President, have declared a national emergency under which you found the power to intervene in all states to close and re-organize the banks, thus protecting the swollen fortunes of the bankers. You have secured the power to organize a special federal force to operate in all states to protect the rich and their children against kidnapping.

"You have inaugurated the N.R.A. and have found the power to enforce this program in all states, to limit the production of cotton, etc. and to enforce discriminatory differential labor codes in the southern states. But you declare through your secretary to the anguished mothers who came with bleeding hearts to petition for the release of their innocent, tortured boys: 'The Scottsboro case is the business of the state of Alabama and not the business of the President.'

"Can the millions of oppressed Negro people and suppressed white toilers believe that you can do nothing to stop the frightful wholesale legal lynch massacre of the nine innocent Scottsboro boys? Can they hold the impossible idea that you are impotent to enforce the democratic rights plainly written in the U.S. Constitution? Can they imagine in the face of your sweeping powers and action under the N.R.A., etc. that you are powerless to do anything whatever to stop the rapidly increasing production of lynchings, legal lynch massacres, and murderous fascist attacks with which the rich ruling-class exploiters and their governmental agents ruthlessly attempt to crush the Negro and white toilers into starvation and slavery under this very N.R.A.?

Free the Scottsboro Boys!

"In the name of hundreds of thousands of members of our organization and affiliated bodies, and in the name of millions of toilers, and other people in the United States and throughout the world, who support the struggle for the freedom of the nine innocent Scottsboro boys, we protest vehemently against this statement of yours to the Scottsboro mothers. This statement gives direct aid and support to the Alabama ruling-class lynch terrorists in their attempt to burn the Scottsboro boys and also to the fascist suppressors of the Negro people and the entire working class throughout the whole country, and indeed, throughout the world.

"We protest further against your refusal to receive and to hear the Scottsboro mothers and their entire delegation and against the humiliating and hostile treatment accorded them. We protest also against your similar action toward the delegation of 5,000 Negro and white workers and other people who marched to Washington on May 8 last year with a petition signed by hundreds of thousands, demanding the freedom of the Scottsboro boys and the adoption of the Bill of Civil Rights for Negroes, presented by them for the enforcement of the thirteenth, fourteenth and fifteenth amendments to the Constitution.

"Your action in these and other instances compel us to recall the following statement among the catalog of oppressive acts set forth in the Declaration of Independence as the occasion and the necessity for the revolution of 1776. 'In every stage of these Oppressions, We have Petitioned for Redress in most humble terms. Our repeated Petitions have been answered only by repeated injury.'

"We demand that you act as chief executive of the United States government to secure the immediate, unconditional and safe release of the nine, innocent Scottsboro boys. We demand that you act to enforce all the democratic rights of the Negro people and the working class enumerated in the Constitution. We demand full equal rights, economic, political and social, for Negroes, and the right of self-determination for the Negro people in the Black Belt of the South. We further demand the release of Angelo Herndon, Tom Mooney, and all victims of class oppression. We demand that you take steps to stop the lynching and oppression of the Negro people, the murder of striking workers, and the increasing brutal attacks upon the masses of impoverished and unemployed workers and poor farmers and their organizations."

INTERNATIONAL LABOR DEFENSE
William L. Patterson
National Secretary

Richard B. Moore
Spokesman of the Scottsboro Mothers Delegation

VIII

HARLEM AND PAN-AFRICAN POLITICS

The retrospective essays in this section are illustrative of the period of Moore's collaboration with John Hendrik Clarke. "Africa Conscious Harlem," which appeared in Freedomways *and was later reprinted in several publications, is his most frequently quoted writing. "Du Bois and Pan-Africa" reflects his admiration for W. E. B. Du Bois and the Pan-African Movement. This tribute is a far cry from the period when the young, militant "New Negroes" referred to Du Bois as a "mis-leader." While Moore draws no analogy between the Pan-African and Pan-Caribbean movements, one should bear in mind that he was involved during the second half of his life in a similar cause seeking to organize Americans to oppose colonial rule and agitate on behalf of peoples who were not politically free to speak for themselves. These articles, along with his chapter "The Critics and Opponents of Marcus Garvey," in Clarke's* Marcus Garvey and the Vision of Africa, *which was not included here because of its length, represent the view of a deeply involved participant looking back and giving a clear and articulate analysis of events of an earlier era.*

AFRICA CONSCIOUS HARLEM

Freedomways, Summer 1963, pp. 315–34

Consciousness of Africa, if not coeval, certainly existed very early in the development of the Afro-American community in Harlem. This consciousness grew almost as rapidly as the community itself expanded. From the few occupants of two houses on 134th Street west of Fifth Avenue in 1900, this unique community had grown by 1920 into a city within the City of New York. Embracing many thousands, this Harlem enclave then reached from 127th Street on the south to 145th Street on the north and from Fifth to Eighth Avenues. Now some 300,000 people of African descent reach

161

down below 110th Street and up into the Washington Heights area, spread almost from the East to the Hudson Rivers.

Harlem's main thoroughfare in 1920 was 135th Street between Lenox and Seventh Avenues, with an almost solid block of houses and stores on its north side owned by St. Philip's Protestant Episcopal Church. In one of these stores, number 135 to be exact, sharing space with the weekly *New York News*, George Young conducted the first Afro-American book shop in Harlem. A pullman porter who had made good use of his travels through the country to assemble a fine collection of Africana and Afro-Americana, Young also endeavored to supply such literature to his people.

In Young's Book Exchange, known then as *The Mecca of Literature Pertaining to Colored People*, there was to be seen what would seem to many, even today, an astonishing array of material treating with Africa and her dispersed descendents. In this small establishment during 1921, a visitor would have seen several copies of the compact book by Dr. W. E. B. Du Bois, which bore the all too current title *The Negro*, though this was chiefly devoted to Africa. Alongside would be seen *From Superman to Man* by J. A. Rogers, which exposed racism and pointed to the ancient history and culture of the African peoples.

On the shelves at Young's there reposed histories written by Afro-Americans such as George W. Williams' *History of the Negro Race in America*. These generally followed the pattern set by William Wells Brown in *The Black Man, His Antecedents, His Genius, and His Achievements* and *The Rising Son*, which began with an account of the African background. *A Social History of the American Negro* by Prof. Benjamin Brawley of Howard University, then just published, also included an entire chapter on Liberia.

Books by African authors included the older *Letters of Ignatius Sancho* and the *Life of Olaudah Equiano* or *Gustavus Vassa*. Beside these were more recent treatises: Dusé Mohamed, *In the Land of the Pharaohs;* Sol T. Plaatje, *Native Life in South Africa;* Casely Hayford, *Ethiopia Unbound, Gold Coast Native Institutions,* and *The Truth About the West African Land Question;* Dr. James Africanus B. Horton, *West African Countries and Peoples and A Vindication of the African Race;* John Mensah Sarbah, *Fanti Customary Laws;* Bishop Samuel Adjai Crowther, *Journal of an Expedition Up the Niger and Tshadda Rivers.*

Numerous books by European and Euro-American authors included important references to Africans by Abolitionists such as Granville Sharp, Thomas Clarkson, Wilson Armistead, Abbé Gregoire, Anthony Benezet, Mrs. Lydia Maria Child, and Charles Sumner. Beside these were accounts of explorers, travelers, missionaries, and investigators—Mungo Park, Livingstone, Moffat, Bruce, Speke, Baker du Chaillu, Reclus, Barth, Schweinfurth, Caillie, Du Bois, Burton, Crawford, Talbot, Ellis, Cardinall, Duff Macdonald, Bleek and Lloyd, Pitt-Rivers.

Specially emphasized were Frobenius, *Voice of Africa;* Ratzel, *History of Mankind;* Mary Kingsley, *West African Studies;* Flora L. Shaw (Lady Lugard),

A Tropical Dependency; Dennett, *At the Back of the Black Man's Mind;* Morel, *Red Rubber* and *The Black Man's Burden.* George Young's signed personal copy of this last, purchased from his widow, is still among the highly prized books in my collection. As a special indulgence to those who evinced great interest, Young would exhibit such rare, old, large tomes as Ludolph's *History of Ethiopia* and Ogilby's *Africa.*

Expressing the consciousness of Africa already existing among Afro-Americans, there were revealing volumes like *The African Abroad* by Prof. William H. Ferris, and *Negro Culture in West Africa* by George W. Ellis which recorded the alphabet and script invented by a genius of the Vai-speaking peoples. There, too, was the masterful work of the Haitian scholar Anténor Firmin, *De l'égalité des races humaines,* which marshalled evidence of early African culture and its significant contribution to Europe and the world in a crushing refutation of the racist theories of inequality propounded by Gobineau.

Though written in 1886, the challenging book *Liberia: The Americo-African Republic* by T. McCants Stewart urged Afro-Americans to "put their own ships upon the sea. . . . We must have our own vessels carrying our African workers, our civilization, and our wares back to the 'Fatherland,' and bringing back its riches." This exhortation concluded with the confident vision of a great "Americo-African Republic," extending "into the Soudan, throughout the Niger and into the Congo; and under a mighty African ruler, there will arise a stable and powerful Government of Africans, for Africans, and by Africans, which shall be an inestimable blessing to all mankind."

Likewise far-visioned were the writings of Alexander Crummell: *The Future of Africa* and *Africa and America.* This last contained his classic essay on *The Relations and Duties of Free Colored Men in America to Africa,* originally published in 1861. This dedicated thinker affirmed "a natural call upon the children of Africa in foreign lands, to come and participate in the opening treasures of the land of their fathers."

Further indicative of this consciousness of African provenience and common heritage were typical writings by scholars native to the African motherland, the Caribbean areas, and the American mainland. Pointed to with particular pride by George Young would be such books as the *History of the Yorubas* by Rev. Samuel Johnson, *Glimpses of the Ages* by Theophilus E. Samuel Scholes, *The Lone Star of Liberia* by F. A. Durham, and especially *African Life and Customs* and *Christianity, Islam and the Negro Race* by Edward Wilmot Blyden.

That this consciousness of Africa was active and widespread was perhaps significantly shown in the reprinting and distribution by George Young in 1920 of *The Aims and Methods of a Liberal Education for Africans,* the Inaugural Address delivered by Edward Wilmot Blyden, LL.D., President of Liberia College, January 5, 1881. Nor was this interest in Africa a new thing. For despite ruthless repression under the chattel slave system, the transplanted Africans could never be reduced to total cultural blankness.

Early Ties to Africa

Consciousness of their ancestral homeland has thus been historically evident from the first arrivals when some of these Africans, brought as slaves into the Americas, killed themselves believing that they would thereby return to Africa. Awareness of their heritage of culture and dignity continued during the colonial period and the early days of this republic. The name *African* was then preferred and used instead of the slavemasters' degrading epithet "negro." Witness thus The Free African Society, founded in Philadelphia in 1787 by Richard Allen and Absalom Jones. This was the forerunner of the African Protestant Episcopal Church of St. Thomas and also of the African Methodist Episcopal Church. Note also the African Lodge of Prince Hall Masons in Boston; the African Methodist Episcopal Zion Church, African Society for Mutual Aid, African Grove Playhouse in New York, and many so named throughout the country.

As early as 1788 an organized body of Afro-Americans in Newport, R.I., which included Paul Cuffe who was soon to make history in this respect, wrote to the Free African Society of Philadelphia proposing a plan for emigration to Africa.* In 1811 Paul Cuffe sailed in his own ship to Sierra Leone to investigate the feasibility of founding a settlement there. In 1815 at his own expense amounting to some $4,000, Captain Paul Cuffe, consummating twenty years of thought and effort, sailed forth again to Sierra Leone, this time commanding the good ship *Traveler* with 38 Afro-American emigrants abroad, which included several whom he had boldly rescued from slavery along the Atlantic seaboard.

Paul Cuffe's achievement gave impetus to the founding of the American Colonization Society in 1817. But this body was dominated by slaveholders with the object of getting rid of free Afro-Americans whose very presence and example encouraged the slaves to seek freedom. Hence the American Colonization Society was powerfully opposed by free-spirited Afro-Americans and their Abolitionist allies.

Nevertheless, several Afro-American leaders took advantage of the operation of the American Colonization Society to foster self-government in Africa through the founding of Liberia. Outstanding among these were Daniel Coker, Elijah Johnson, Lott Cary, Colin Teague, John B. Russwurm, Hilary Teague, and Joseph Jenkins Roberts who was elected first president of Liberia in 1848. By this time the population of Liberia included some 3,000 persons of African descent who had emigrated from the United States of America and the Caribbean.

*Editors' note: Apparently Moore relied upon Benjamin Brawley's *A Social History of the American Negro.*

The distinguished Afro-American scholar, Rev. Alexander Crummell, after graduating from Cambridge University in 1853, spent 20 years teaching and laboring in Africa. Commissioned by a convention of Afro-Americans held in Chatham, Canada West, in 1858, Martin R. Delany led an expedition into what is now Nigeria and published his *Official Report of the Niger Valley Exploring Party* in 1861. This mission had even signed a treaty with African rulers at Abeokuta which authorized a projected settlement, but this project lapsed after the outbreak of the Civil War in the U.S.A. The other commissioner of this expedition, Professor Robert Campbell, published his report in *A Pilgrimage to My Motherland*.

After the Civil War and Reconstruction, interest was revived in African settlement as a great exodus began from the south, due to the wholesale massacre of some 40,000 Afro-Americans by such terrorist organizations as the Ku Klux Klan. This reign of terror reached monstrous proportions after the withdrawal of federal troops from the south. A new movement for migration to Africa was fostered jointly by Afro-American Baptists and Methodists; Bishop H. M. Turner played a leading part in this endeavor. Organizations were established in several states, notably the Liberian Exodus and Joint Stock Company in North Carolina and the Freedmen's Emigration Aid Society in South Carolina. This last acquired the ship *Azor* for $7,000 and this ship actually carried 274 emigrants to Africa on one of its trips, despite the efforts of prejudiced European Americans to impose outrageous costs and to hinder its operation. The *Azor* was soon stolen and sold in Liverpool; the attempts to recover it failed when the U.S. Circuit Court refused even to entertain the suit brought to this end.

About 1881 a descendant of Paul Cuffe, Captain Harry Dean, sailed to Africa commanding his ship the *Pedro Gorino* with the object "to rehabilitate Africa and found an Ethiopian Empire as the world has never seen." Another expedition took 197 emigrants from Savannah, Georgia to Liberia. "Chief Sam" of Kansas launched a movement to sail ships and build a state in Africa but this movement failed to achieve its goals.

Role of Speakers and Press

This tradition was known in Harlem and interest in Africa was constantly stimulated by the generally well-informed outdoor speakers of the twenties. Free lance advocates such as William Bridges, Strathcona R. Williams, Alexander Rahming, Edgar M. Grey, Arthur Reid, and the Basuto "Prince" Mokete M. Manoede held forth constantly on African history and stressed unity with the African people.

Militant socialists like Chandler Owen, A. Philip Randolph, Rev. George Frazier Miller, Grace P. Campbell, Anna Brown, Elizabeth Hendrickson, Frank Poree, Otto Huiswoud, W. A. Domingo, Tom Potter, Frank D. Crosswaith, Rudolph Smith, Herman S. Whaley, John Patterson, Victor C.

Gaspar, Ramsay, Ross D. Brown, and the writer of this account—all steadily emphasized the liberation of the oppressed African and other colonial peoples as a vital aim of their world view. Above all Hubert H. Harrison gave forth from his encyclopedic store, a wealth of knowledge of African history and culture which brought this consciousness to a very great height.

A vigorous press which circulated widely in Harlem also intensified this consciousness of Africa. Notable among these journals were *The Amsterdam News* while edited by Cyril V. Briggs, the *Crisis* magazine under Dr. Du Bois, the *Challenge* of William Bridges, the radical *Messenger* magazine projected by Chandler Owen and A. Philip Randolph, the *African Times and Orient Review*, published by Dusé Mohamed in London, imported by John E. Bruce, and distributed by this writer, the *Crusader* magazine edited by Cyril V. Briggs as the organ of the African Blood Brotherhood, the powerful *Voice* of the Liberty League of Afro-Americans then being led by Hubert H. Harrison. Later the *Emancipator* conducted chiefly by W. A. Domingo and this writer, warned against the weaknesses of the Garvey movement, while striving for an end to colonialist subjugation and all forms of oppression.

Vibrant echoes too had reached Harlem of the Pan African Conference, organized in London during 1900 by Henry Sylvester Williams, a barrister-at-law born in Trinidad of African ancestry. This Conference elected as general chairman Bishop Alexander Walters of the African Methodist Episcopal Zion Church and Dr. W. E. B. Du Bois chairman of the Committee on Address to the World. Stimulating news had come also of the Second Pan-African Conference organized by Dr. Du Bois and held in Paris early in 1919, following the significant though unsuccessful attempts made independently by William Monroe Trotter and Dr. Du Bois to present the case of the oppressed peoples of African descent before the Versailles Peace Conference in 1918.

Several distinguished visitors to Harlem contributed greatly to this ever growing consciousness of Africa, among them F. E. M. Hercules, a native of Trinidad and founder of an organization seeking to unify all the descendants of Africa everywhere. Dr. J. Edmeston Barnes, born in Barbados, came directly from London with a similar program calling also for the rejection of the disrespectful and denigrating name "Negro," which he condemned as "a bastard political colloquialism." Likewise, Albert Thorne of Barbados and Guiana projected the ideas of his African Colonial Enterprise which was designed to embrace all peoples of African origin.

Arrival of Marcus Garvey

Harlem had thus become considerably Africa conscious and this consciousness was soon to build the movement which was carried to great heights of mass emotion, widespread projection, and stupendous endeavor by the skillful propagandist and promoter, Marcus Garvey. When Garvey arrived from Jamaica in 1916, Harlem was emerging as the vanguard and focal point, "the cultural capital," of ten million Afro-Americans and to some extent also of other peoples of African origin in the Western Hemisphere. The demand for labor, due to the first World War, rapidly augmented the growth of Harlem, as thousands poured in from the south, the Caribbean, and Central America.

Harlem then seethed with a great ferment, bitterly resenting oppression and discrimination, particularly the treatment meted out to its crack Fifteenth Regiment. Harlem reacted vigorously also against the brutal lynchings then growing throughout the country, and especially against the frightful wholesale massacre in East St. Louis in July 1917. Some 10,000 of Harlem's citizens marched down Fifth Avenue carrying placards in the Silent Protest Parade led by the National Association for the Advancement of Colored People. The hanging of 13 Afro-American soldiers following the Houston affair, when they had retaliated against wanton attack by prejudiced southerners, stirred mounting anger, frustration, and despair.

Marcus Garvey saw the opportunity to harness this upsurge against oppression and to direct the existing consciousness of Africa into a specific organized movement under his leadership. Realizing the deep-seated if unconscious desire of the disinherited people of African origin for equal or similar status to that of others in every phase of human thought and endeavor, Garvey projected various means and enterprises which appealed to and afforded expression of this basic human desire.

After a poor initial meeting at St. Mark's Hall and some outdoor attempts, Marcus Garvey secured his first favorable public response when introduced by Hubert H. Harrison, leader of the Liberty League of Afro-Americans, at a huge meeting at Bethel A.M.E. Church. Following several abortive attempts, Garvey finally launched the reorganized New York Division of the Universal Negro Improvement Association and African Communities League. With the publication of the *Negro World* in January 1918, carrying sections in French and Spanish as well as in English, the movement spread through the United States and abroad.

The founder of the *Negro World* was astute enough to secure the editorial services of Professor William H. Ferris, graduate of Yale University and well versed in African lore, of the able and erudite Hubert H. Harrison, and of such skillful writers as W. A. Domingo, Eric Walrond, and Hudson C. Pryce. Dusé Mohamed, the Sudanese Egyptian nationalist who had formerly employed Garvey in London, and from whom Garvey had derived the slogan, "Africa for the Africans," also worked for a time on the *Negro World*. Contributors like John E. Bruce (Grit), William Pickens, T. Thomas Fortune, Anselmo Jackson, and Hodge Kirnon presented various aspects of the ancient history, noteworthy achievements, and the current aspirations of people of African origin.

The convention held in August 1920 in Liberty Hall, the dramatic, colorful, and impressive parade, costumes, and pageantry, and the mammoth meeting at Madison Square Garden, established the Garvey movement as a powerful international force. Stirring hymns with African themes, especially the U.N.I.A. anthem composed by Rabbi Arnold J. Ford of Barbados, were rendered by choral groups and massed bands. Thousands joined the U.N.I.A., the African Legion, the Black Cross Nurses, and later the African Orthodox Church. Enthusiastic supporters poured their savings into the enterprises started by Garvey, the restaurant, hotel, grocery, millinery, tailoring and dressmaking establishment, publishing concern, and finally the Black Star Line, and the Negro Factories Corporation.

Estimate of Garvey

It is difficult and perhaps somewhat hazardous to attempt an objective estimate of the Garvey movement, yet this is necessary if we are to learn from its lessons and to apply them wisely in our present endeavors. To the present writer it appears that the founder and leader of the U.N.I.A. demonstrated two powerful drives which were basically opposed to each other. One was clearly the progressive tendency which projected "the redemption of Africa" and the "Declaration of Rights of the Negro People of the World." The other was obviously reactionary in its Napoleonic urge for personal power and empire, with the inevitable accompaniment of racial exclusiveness and hostility. This latter tendency was evident when Garvey declared, on taking the title of Provisional President of Africa in 1920, "The signal honor of being Provisional President of Africa is mine. . . . It is like asking Napoleon to take the world."

Unfortunately, Marcus Garvey veered evermore toward the more extreme forms of empire building, unlimited individual control, and unrestrained racism. At length these destructive forces were allowed to overshadow and outweigh the constructive, pristine ideas of African nationalism, liberation, and independence. Stridently advocating "racial purity," Garvey came at length to agree openly with the worst enemies of the Afro-American people—the white supremacist leaders of the Anglo-Saxon clubs and even of the murderous Ku Klux Klan—in declaring America to be "a white man's country."

Besides, the constant attacks which Marcus Garvey made upon people of both African and European ancestry, whom he derisively called "the hybrids of the Negro race," did not conduce to the unifying of all people of African descent, who, regardless of varying shades of color and other physical characteristics, were compelled to suffer similar oppression whether as colonial subjects or as oppressed minority groups. Likewise, Garvey's condemnation of the principal leaders and organizations who were striving for human rights and equal citizenship status for the Afro-

American minority groups in this country, was bound to arouse opposition and internal strife.

Finally, the open condemnation of Liberian officials by Marcus Garvey, his severe reprisals against several of his chief associates, his poor choice of certain officers, and the inept conduct of the business enterprises which he controlled, left the movement wide open to the disastrous blows of those who began to fear its growing power. Following his conviction and imprisonment on February 8, 1925, upon a charge of using the mails to defraud in connection with the sale of Black Star Line stock, the Garvey movement split into wrangling factions, and despite efforts to revive it only a few splinter groups remained. Nevertheless, the Garvey movement did heighten and spread the consciousness of African origin and identity among the various peoples of African descent on a wider scale than ever before. This was its definite and positive contribution.

Harlem Literary Renaissance

Developing almost parallel with the Garvey movement was what has come to be known as the Harlem Literary Renaissance. A number of creative writers of poetry, fiction, essays, and criticism then emerged: Claude McKay, Langston Hughes, Countee Cullen, Jean Toomer, Eric Walrond, Rudolph Fisher, Wallace Thurman, Nella Larsen, Zora Neale Hurston, James Weldon Johnson, Jessie Fauset, Georgia Douglas Johnson, Lucian B. Watkins, Walter White, and others.

This literary movement was no Minerva sprung full-fledged from the head of Jove, for while its immediate inspiration lay in the surrounding social conditions, its roots, too, went back through earlier Afro-American writers to the bards of ancient Africa. Alain Locke in his preface to *The New Negro* which proclaimed this movement in 1925, noted "the approach to maturity" and the role of *Crisis,* under the leadership of Dr. Du Bois, and *Opportunity,* edited by Charles S. Johnson, in fostering this movement by publishing many of the works of these budding authors. Locke further observed two constructive channels: "One is the advance-guard of the African peoples in their contact with Twentieth Century civilization; the other, the sense of a vision of rehabilitating the race in world esteem. . . ."

How these Harlem avant-garde writers felt, expressed, and stimulated consciousness of Africa may be observed in a few typical outpourings. In the sonnet *Africa* published in *Harlem Shadows,* the Caribbean born poet Claude McKay extolled:

> The sun sought thy dim bed and brought forth light,
> The sciences were sucklings at thy breast;
> When all the world was young in pregnant night
> Thy slaves toiled at thy monumental best.
> Thou ancient treasure-land, thou modern prize,
> New peoples marvel at thy pyramids!

The rather pessimistic note on which this sonnet ended still persisted in *Outcast* when McKay lamented the ancestral motherland in a mood of wistful nostalgia:

> For the dim regions whence my fathers came
> My spirit, bondaged by the body, longs
> Words felt, but never heard, my lips would frame;
> My soul would sing forgotten jungle songs.

In *Enslaved* the poet broods over his people

> For weary centuries despised, oppressed,
> Enslaved and lynched, denied a human place
> In the great life line of the Christian West;
> And in the Black Land disinherited,
> Robbed in the ancient country of its birth; . . .

At length this searing consciousness gave rise to that famous cry of passionate revolt in *If We Must Die*—

> What though before us lies the open grave?
> Like men we'll face the murderous, cowardly pack,
> Pressed to the wall, dying, but fighting back!

And in *Exhortation: Summer, 1919*, Claude McKay turns toward the future confidently with this clarion call:

> From the deep primeval forests where the crouch-
>   ing leopard's lurking,
> Lift your heavy-lidded eyes, Ethiopia! awake!
> . . . .
> For the big earth groans in travail for the strong,
>   new world in making—
> O my brothers, dreaming for long centuries,
> Wake from sleeping: to the East turn, turn your eyes!

Similarly, in *The Negro Speaks of Rivers* in his first published volume *The Weary Blues,* Langston Hughes sang profoundly:

> I've known rivers:
> I've known rivers ancient as the world and older than the
>   flow of human blood in human veins.
>
> My soul has grown deep like the rivers.
>
> I bathed in the Euphrates when dawns were young.
> I built my hut near the Congo and it lulled me to sleep.
> I looked upon the Nile and raised pyramids above it. . . .

Langston Hughes further expressed his retrospective identification with Africa:

> We should have a land of trees
> Bowed down with chattering parrots
> Brilliant as the day,
> And not this land where birds are gray.

Again, in the poem *Georgia Dusk* included in *Cane*, Jean Toomer, while etching the toilers in southern cane-field and saw mill, recalls the ancestors from the long-past life of dignity and freedom in Africa:

> Meanwhile, the men, with vestiges of pomp,
> Race memories of king and caravan,
> High priests, an ostrich and a ju-ju man,
> Go singing through the footpaths of the swamp.

Countee Cullen mused long and lyrically in the poem *Heritage* which is outstanding in the book *Color:*

> What is Africa to me:
> Copper sun or scarlet sea,
> Jungle star or jungle track,
> Strong bronzed men, or regal black
> Women from whose loins I sprang
> When the birds of Eden sang?
> *One three centuries removed*
> *From the scenes his fathers loved,*
> *Spicy grove, cinnamon tree,*
> *What is Africa to me?*

Plaintively pondering his "high-priced conversion" to Christianity and humility, the poet needs must transmute this experience in terms consonant with his deeper ancestral self:

> Lord, I fashion dark gods, too,
> Daring even to give You
> Dark despairing features where,
> Crowned with dark rebellious hair,
> Patience wavers just so much as
> Mortal grief compels, while touches
> Quick and hot, of anger, rise
> To smitten cheek and weary eyes.
> Lord forgive me if my need
> Sometimes shapes a human creed.

The sense of dignity and power derived from Africa led this poet to an anguished effort to restrain with reason from a premature revolt against intolerable oppression:

> *All day long and all night through,*
> *One thing only must I do:*

Quench my pride and cool my blood,
Lest I perish in the flood,
Lest a hidden ember set
Timber that I thought was wet
Burning like the dryest flax,
Melting like the merest wax,
Lest the grave restore its dead.
Not yet has my heart or head
In the least way realized
They and I are civilized.

Finally, Lucian B. Watkins looked with serene confidence to Africa exulting in his *Star of Ethiopia:*

Out in the Night thou art the sun
Toward which thy soul-charmed children run,
　The faith-high height whereon they see
　The glory of their Day To Be—
The peace at last when all is done.

Following the failure of the Garvey movement, consciousness of Africa was bolstered in Harlem by the campaign of the American Negro Labor Congress for the liberation of the colonial peoples of Africa and Asia. Representing this body, the present writer went as a delegate to the Congress Against Imperialism held in Brussels in 1927. As the forerunner of the Asian-African Conference held at Bandung in April 1955, the Brussels Congress was recalled and noted by President Sukarno of Indonesia in his opening address: "At that Conference many distinguished delegates who are present here today met each other and found new strength in their fight for independence."

The Commission on the African Peoples of the World elected at the Brussels Congress Against Imperialism included the brilliant Senegalese leaders Lamine Senghor, who unfortunately died shortly afterward in a French jail, and Garan Kouyatte who was shot by the Nazis during their occupation of Paris in 1940. Other outstanding members of this Commission were Mr. Makonnen of Ethiopia, J. T. Gumede, vice president of the African National Congress of South Africa, and J. A. La Guma, secretary of the South African Non-European Trade Union Federation. The writer of this present summary served as secretary of the Commission.

The resolution prepared by the Commission and adopted by the Brussels Congress Against Imperialism, called for the complete liberation of the African peoples, the restoration of their lands, and several other measures including the establishment of a University at Addis Ababa for the training of candidates for leadership in the trade union, cultural, and liberation movements of the oppressed African peoples.

Reaction to Mussolini's Aggression in Ethiopia

A new wave of consciousness spread through Harlem as the people reacted strongly against Mussolini's fascist, military aggression against Ethiopia in October 1935. Organizations were set up to mobilize support; the executive director of the International Council of Friends of Ethiopia, Dr. Willis N. Huggins, was commissioned to deliver an appeal on behalf of Ethiopia to the League of Nations in Geneva, Switzerland. Arden Bryan, president of the Nationalist Negro Movement, sent petitions to the League and protests to the British Foreign Office and the U.S. State Department against their failure to aid Ethiopia.

When invading Italian airplanes monstrously rained down deadly yperite gas on the Ethiopian people, huge protest meetings were organized. The Ethiopian Pacific Movement, from a gigantic rally at Rockland Palace, forwarded protests and also sent telegrams to Asian, African, Australian, Central and South American nations, appealing for action in defense of Ethiopia. Several organizations joined in the United Aid to Ethiopia with Rev. Wm. Lloyd Imes, chairman, Cyril M. Philip, secretary, and Dr. P. M. H. Savory, treasurer.

The officers just named were sent as a delegation to seek to influence the First Congress of the International Peace Campaign, which met at Brussels early in September 1936, to take action in support of Ethiopia. The delegation interviewed Emperor Haile Selassie in London, and requested him to send a representative to cooperate in the work here. Dr. Malaku E. Bayen, cousin and personal physician to the Emperor, was appointed and was greeted with acclaim at a great meeting at Rockland Palace. Meanwhile funds were raised and medical supplies sent through the Medical Aid to Ethiopia, of which body, Dr. Arnold W. Donawa was chairman and Dr. J. J. Jones, secretary.

The Ethiopian World Federation, then organized in Harlem, spread through the country, the Caribbean, and elsewhere. *The Voice of Ethiopia* published news from the Ethioplian front and further stimulated the campaign of resistance. J. A. Carrington and Dr. R. C. Hunt published the pamphlet *Yperite and Ethiopia*, with the full text of *Emperor Haile Selassie's Memorable and Immortal Speech at Geneva*, along with pictures of victims of the horrible yperite gas, so called because this gas was first used at Ypres in Belgium. Volunteers generally could not secure passports to go to join in the military defense of Ethiopia, however, the Afro-American aviator, Colonel John C. Robinson, known as the "Brown Condor," executed many heroic missions in that ravaged land. The *Pittsburgh Courier,* then directed by Robert L. Vann, sent J. A. Rogers as a war correspondent who on his return published the booklet *The Real Facts of Ethiopia.*

After the Italian invaders were driven out of Ethiopia in 1941, this intense fraternal consciousness in Harlem subsided into a residual sense of unity with all African peoples. But when Egypt was invaded in October 1956 by Israel followed by Britain and France, and ruthless massacre and destruction descended upon the people of Port Said, Suez, Alexandria, and Cairo, Harlem reacted with a rally organization by the Asian-African Drums and demonstrated its solidarity with President Nasser and the stricken people of Egypt. Harlem rejoiced when the note sent by Premier Khrushchev of the Soviet Union, demanding that withdrawal of the invading forces begin within 24 hours, led to the timely evacuation of these aggressors.

Harlem Rallies to African Freedom

Consciousness of Africa mounted again as more and more African nations regained their independence. The inhuman atrocities of the French colonialists against the Algerian people, who were struggling valiantly for their independence, aroused widespread sympathy and fraternal support among the people of Harlem. Active consciousness reached its zenith when the Congo was betrayed and dismembered and its dedicated leaders, especially the Prime Minister Patrice Lumumba, were foully and brutally done to death. Harlem boiled with fierce resentment against the failure of the United Nations to support the government of the Congo Republic and to prevent the murder of its Prime Minister and other officials.

This white hot indignation among the people of Harlem gave rise to the outburst in the visitors' gallery of the United Nations on February 15, 1961. Reactionary forces loudly denounced this protest upsurge and pseudo-liberals like Max Lerner in his *New York Post* column presumed to lecture and to condemn the protesting Afro-American people while excusing the Belgian and other colonialist seceders and murderers. An open letter exposing Max Lerner's hypocritical and racist attack, was addressed by this writer to him and to the editor and owner of the *New York Post*. But this answer to Lerner's diatribe has never been published or even acknowledged by them.

Harlem remains today quite conscious of its African heritage and basic kinship. This consciousness is by no means limited to the various groups which call themselves "nationalists," and who are quite vocal but actually contribute little or no substantial, direct support to the African liberation movements. *Yet such effective support is vitally needed at this very moment in the present critical and decisive struggle now being waged for the liberation of the peoples of Central and South Africa.*

The limits of this article preclude more detail here. It should be stated, however, that these "nationalist" groups are as yet unable to unite among themselves, due largely, it appears, to self-centered power drives and competition for leadership. The tendency persists among them, unfortunately, to oppose other organizations which have the largest following of the Afro-American people and to condemn these leaders caustically and constantly. Obviously, this hinders rather than helps to achieve essential *united action* either in support of the African liberation movements or to further the struggle for civil liberties and human rights here in the U.S.A.

Returning to the main currents of Harlem life, it is fitting to recognize the chief intellectual forces which have heightened consciousness of Africa since the 1930's. Outstanding is the Schomburg Collection of literature on Africa and people of African descent, brought together during a lifetime by Arthur A. Schomburg and established as a special reference library by the New York Public Library. The development of this institution has been carried forward by Mrs. Catherine Latimer and by the present genial curator, Mrs. Jean Blackwell Hutson. The Countee Cullen Branch, under the supervision of Mrs. Dorothy R. Homer, displays and features books on Africa for general circulation. Stimulating study classes were led by Dr. Willis N. Huggins and of special note were the several profound and scholarly lecture series given by Prof. William Leo Hansberry.

Significant also has been the activity of the Association for the Study of Negro Life and History, founded by Carter G. Woodson. This dedicated scholar published many volumes treating of Africa, notably his own *The Negro in Our History*, with its opening chapter emphasizing our African heritage, and the *African Background Outlined*. Among other widely read books were those by Dr. W. E. B. Du Bois, *Black Folk Then and Now* and the *World and Africa;* the writings of J. A. Rogers, *World's Great Men of Color, Sex and Race*, and *Africa's Gift to America;* Dr. Willis N. Huggins and John G. Jackson, *Guide to African History* and *Introduction to African Civilizations;* George G. M. James, *Stolen Legacy;* J. G. de Graft-Johnson, *African Glory;* Jomo Kenyatta, *Facing Mount Kenya;* Elton Fax, *West African Vignettes;* the writings of George Padmore, concluding with *Pan-Africanism and Communism;* and those of Dr. Kwame Nkrumah, *Ghana* and *I Speak for Freedom*. Making their contribution have been the works of the English author Basil Davidson, *Old Africa Rediscovered* and *Black Mother*, as well as that of the German writer Janheinz Jahn, *Mantu: An Outline of Neo-African Culture*.

Quite encouraging is the fact that today, in the main stream of life and thought in Harlem, interest as well as identification with Africa grows apace. In homes, more books on African life and development are seen and read. This concurs with the increasing sale of African literature in Harlem bookshops; the trend in the Frederick Douglass Book Center has been markedly away from general fiction and toward the history and culture of peoples of African origin. Among fraternal societies and clubs, in church and school, libraries and lecture hall, more programs than ever before are being presented on various aspects of African life and liberation.

To mention a few indications: A program for African diplomats organized by Sudia Masoud, secretary of the African-Asian Drums, began at the

Prince Hall Masons' Auditorium and concluded with a dinner at the Hotel
Theresa. The Seventh-Day Adventist Church presented several repre-
sentatives of African states. The Afro-Arts Cultural Center, Simon Bly, Jr,
Executive director, in cooperation with Dr. Charles M. Schapp, Assistant
Superintendent of District Schools, has conducted In-Service courses on
Africa for teachers for several years. Along with its work to emphasize the
names *African* and *Afro-American* as fitting and honorable designations, the
Committee to Present The Truth About The Name "Negro" has con-
ducted and plans more lecture series on *The History and Culture of African
Peoples.*

In Unity Lies Strength

Still more significant was the American Negro Leadership Conference
held last November at Arden House in Harriman, New York. For this
involved the principal Afro-American organizations active or represented
in Harlem and the country—the N.A.A.C.P., C.O.R.E., Brotherhood of
Sleeping Car Porters, National Council of Negro Women, National Urban
League, the Southern Christian Leadership Conference, and the American
Society for African Culture. It has been alleged that these leaders suddenly
evinced a new interest in Africa, but even in that case this interest definitely
reflects the rising consciousness of Africa among the vast majority of the
members and supporters of these organizations.

In any case such expressed concern for the African peoples should be
welcomed and encouraged by all who are sincerely devoted to African
liberation. If any of these Afro-American leaders exhibit wariness or weakness, then those who honestly and wholeheartedly seek to aid Africa
should, in order to infuse greater clarity and strength, indicate what they
consider these weaknesses to be. Thoughtful supporters of African unity
and progress must, therefore, regret the ill-advised, intemperate, and
harmful attack made in the article entitled *Negro Stooges Bid For Africans
Challenged,* which stands out offensively in the January 1963 issue of *Voice
of Africa.*

When the leaders in the American Negro Leadership Conference are
challenged on the ground that "they had the audacity to make attempts to
move ahead of the African nationalists in America," this statement admits
motivation from selfish considerations on the part of those who make this
challenge. It is also obviously feared that these Conference leaders might
get ahead in securing diplomatic posts or other prized considerations.
Branding these Conference leaders as "opportunists," after making such a
charge, will be logically regarded as an unconscious confession of competition in opportunism. Again, to affirm that "these organizations represent
American colonialism, imperialism, and exploitation," is patently to go
beyond the bounds of truth.

Moreover, such a statement is destructive of unity and must offend and repel the hundreds of thousands of members of the organizations in this Conference who are rallying to the cause of African freedom and progress. Thinking people, too, must pause to question the strange self-praise projected in this article by self-styled "Ghana patriots," who are not known to have given up their United States citizenship or to have been accorded citizenship by the government of Ghana. Likewise deplorable is the unwarranted use of the good name of Osagyefo of Ghana in these divisive proceedings which tend only to separate the Afro-American leaders and people from the African statesmen and their peoples.

But utterly reprehensible is the disruptive campaign being waged by George S. Schuyler and his accomplices in mind-twisting which has rendered aid and comfort to the Belgian and other neo-colonialist oppressors in the Congo Republic and to the Portuguese imperialist butchers of the peoples of Angola and Mozambique.

Completely disproving the false and venomous general accusations made by George S. Schuyler *et al.* in the *N.Y. Courier* against African statesmen, of indifference and hostility against Afro-American people, was the reported reaction of African Foreign Ministers at the Conference of African States held in Addis Ababa, Ethiopia. *The New York Times* of May 19th published their special correspondent's report that the Foreign Minister of Nigeria rose "to denounce racial discrimination in South Africa and the United States." This report also states, "American observers have been dismayed to hear Alabama linked with South Africa in attacks on apartheid inside and outside the conference hall," and further that "American correspondents approaching members of delegations frequently hear the question, 'What's the latest news from Birmingham?' "

The Ethiopian *Herald,* which is the official publication of the Ministry of Information, is quoted as having commented:

> What happened in Birmingham last week shows the United States in its true light. To be black is still a crime. . . . The colored American must fight hard for freedom rather than waste time and much needed energy bellyaching about Communism. The United States version of 'civilized apartheid' must be fought.

Acting on behalf of the 30 African nations assembled in this Conference at Addis Ababa, Prime Minister Milton Obote of Uganda sent a letter to President Kennedy of the U.S.A. which condemned the "most inhuman treatment" perpetrated upon Afro-Americans at Birmingham, Alabama, and which further stated:

> Nothing is more paradoxical than that these events should take place in the United States at a time when that country is anxious to project its image before the world as the archetype of democracy and champion of freedom.

At a news conference held on May 23rd, as reported in the *New York Times,* Prime Minister Obote recognized that those "who had been doused with blasts of water from fire hoses in Birmingham were 'our kith and kin,' " and declared further that, the eyes of the world were "concentrated on events in Alabama and it is the duty of the free world, and more so of countries that hold themselves up as leaders of the free world, to see that all their citizens, regardless of color, are free."

It may be predicted confidently, despite the malicious efforts of a few venal slanderers, that consciousness of Africa will continue to grow in Harlem and among Afro-Americans generally. An even more vigorous and healthy development of this consciousness will come when it is more fully realized that rationally no conflict really or properly exists between vital interests in our African heritage and the liberation of the African peoples and deep and active devotion to the cause of human rights and equal citizenship status here in the U.S.A. For the same social forces which spawned colonialist subjugation in Africa and other areas are the identical forces responsible for brutal enslavement and racist oppression in the Americas and elsewhere.

Freedom and the full development of the human personality, therefore, require independence for the African peoples as well as full citizenship rights with equal status and opportunity for the minority people of African descent wherever they now exist. The same inherent self-respect and will to be free, which led Paul Cuffe to wage a successful struggle for the vote and equal citizenship rights in Massachusetts, immediately after the American Revolution of 1776, also led this great pioneer leader to promote self-determination through migration and the development of Sierra Leone in Africa. An enlightened awareness of African lore and liberty is, and will continue to be, the inevitable expression of the indomitable will to self-knowledge, self-determination, self-realization, and self-development on parity with all mankind.

DU BOIS AND PAN-AFRICA

Freedomways, First Quarter 1965, pp. 166–87.

> Do ba-na co-ba, ge-ne me, ge-ne me!
> Do ba-na co-ba, ge-ne me, ge-ne me!
> Ben d' nu-li, nu-li, nu-li, nu-li, ben d' le.

So sang the great-grandmother of William Edward Burghardt Du Bois who in his autobiography *Dusk of Dawn* wrote wistfully: "With Africa I had only one direct cultural connection and that was the African melody which my great-grandmother Violet used to sing." This melody had been set down by the talented author in his classic book *The Souls of Black Folk* in the final chapter "The Sorrow Songs"—"these weird old songs in which the soul of the black slave spoke to man."

The song which his maternal ancestor had crooned to the child between her knees was passed on through generations thus: "The child sang it to his children, and they to their children's children, and so two hundred years it has traveled down to us and we sing it to our children, knowing as little as our fathers what the words may mean, but knowing well the meaning of its music."

What had caused this African song to possess uncommon significance is also recorded in that great and revealing book *The Souls of Black Folk* where the youthful seer Du Bois at the very outset spoke "Of Our Spiritual Strivings." There inimitably and touchingly portrayed is the descent of the veil of prejudice and proscription, the result of that system of slavery and segregation which cruelly shut out people of African descent from full participation in the mainstream of life and culture in these United States of America.

It is precisely the recoil from this system of prejudice which directly thrust the Afro-American back to the quest for his ancestral culture and history. Something of this evidently affected the grandfather of Du Bois on his paternal side. For his grandfather, Alexander Du Bois, who had been brought from the Bahamas in the Caribbean to Connecticut in the U.S.A., has been characterized by his illustrious grandson as a "rebel, bitter at his lot in life, resentful at being classed as a Negro and yet implacable in his attitude toward whites."

Unlike Alexander Hamilton, Alexander Du Bois allied himself through marriage with the people of African descent in America. Apparently it was his rebellious spirit which led him to migrate to Haiti some time after that nation had achieved independence as a result of the Revolution of 1791–1804. There in that free and sunny Caribbean island, where Toussaint Louverture and his comrades in arms had routed the French colonial slavemasters, Alexander's son, Alfred I. Du Bois, the father of W. E. B. Du Bois, was born in 1825.

Shortly thereafter the Du Bois family returned to the United States where they lived in Connecticut and then in Massachusetts. In the little town of Great Barrington, Massachusetts, three years after the close of the Civil War, on February 23, 1868, a child was born who was to become one of the greatest men of letters, history, and social science of America and one of the most conscious and resolute champions of the people of Africa and their dispersed descendants.

However, it is not by physical or "racial" heredity, but by cultural processes, that African consciousness is passed on from one generation to another. This Du Bois himself clearly understood and wrote accordingly:

"My African racial feeling was then purely a matter of my own later learning; my recoil from the assumptions of the whites; my experience in the South at Fisk. But it was none the less real and a large determinant of my life and character. I felt myself African by 'race' and by that token was African and an integral member of the group of dark Americans who were called Negroes."

This background of the Pan-Africanism of W. E. B. Du Bois is essential to a clear understanding of his role. It seems necessary then to explore this somewhat further. Noting how the concept of "race" had become more and more devoid of "exact definition and understanding," Dr. Du Bois explained further while discussing "The Concept of Race" in *Dusk of Dawn* as follows:

> Since then the concept of race has so changed and presented so much of contradiction that as I face Africa I ask myself: what is it between us that constitutes a tie which I can feel better than I can explain? Africa is of course my fatherland. Yet neither my father nor my father's father ever saw Africa or cared over-much for it. My mother's folk were closer and yet their direct connection, in culture and race, became tenuous; still, my tie to Africa is strong. On this vast continent were born and lived a large portion of my direct ancestors going back a thousand years or more.
>
> But one thing is sure and that is the fact that since the fifteenth century these ancestors of mine and their other descendants have had a common history; have suffered a common disaster and have one long memory. The actual ties of heritage between the individuals of this group, vary with the ancestors that they have in common and many others: Europeans and Semites, perhaps Mongolians, certainly Indians. But the physical bond is least and the badge of color relatively unimportant save as a badge; the real essence of this kinship is its social heritage of slavery; the discrimination and insult; and this heritage binds together not simply the children of Africa, but extends through yellow Asia and into the South Seas. It is this unity that draws me to Africa.

A better understanding should thus be reached of why and how Dr. Du Bois achieved the prophetic world vision which encompassed his idea of Pan-Africa. At the turn of the century the doctor declared: "The problem of the Twentieth Century is the problem of the colorline—the relation of the darker to the lighter races of men in Asia and Africa, in America and the islands of the sea."

What had given rise to the problem of the color-line was later stated, as he saw it, by Dr. Du Bois in *Dusk of Dawn*. After surveying the events of that period, the social scientist had reached this conclusion: "That history may be epitomized in one word—Empire; the domination of white Europe over black Africa and yellow Asia, through political power build on the economic control of labor, income and ideas. The echo of this industrial imperialism in America was the expulsion of black men from American democracy, their subjection to caste control and wage slavery."

With such insight and awareness W. E. B. Du Bois, then Professor of Economics and History at Atlanta University, was thus prepared to participate in the First Pan-African conference where he began his prominent and continuing role in this great endeavor. The call for this Conference was issued by Henry Sylvester Williams, a barrister at law from Trinidad who had made fraternal and fruitful contacts with African students and leaders in London. Thus was the idea born of a Pan-African Conference which would "bring into closer touch with each other the peoples of African descent throughout the world."

To Bishop Alexander Walters of the African Methodist Episcopal Zion Church, president of this First Pan-African Conference, we are indebted for a summary of its proceedings. Among the thirty-two delegates who assembled in London at Westminster Hall on July 23–25, 1900, there were four representatives of African peoples: the Emperor of Ethiopia, Menelik II, delegated his Aide-de-Camp, M. Benito Sylvain of Haiti; the Republic of Liberia sent its former Attorney General, Hon. F. S. R. Johnson; from Sierra Leone came Councillor G. W. Dove; and from Ghana, then "Gold Coast," came the barrister at law, A. F. Ribero, Esq.

A fair representation of Afro-Americans at this important initial Pan-African gathering consisted of eleven delegates, including four women, all prominent in professional and public activity. Some thirteen delegates had come from the Caribbean either directly or indirectly as sojourners in England and Scotland. The famous Afro-English composer S. Coleridge Taylor participated; attending also were the director of the Fisk Jubilee Singers, J. F. Loudin and his wife, then resident in England though hailing originally from the United States. Rev. Henry Box Brown of fugitive slave fame represented the community in Lower Canada.

Welcomed and its delegates feted by the Lord Bishop of London Dr. Creighton, this First Pan-African Conference adopted and presented a Memorial to the British Government. This Memorial protested against "acts of injustice directed against Her Majesty's subjects in South Africa and other parts of her dominions." A reply was sent to the Secretary H. Sylvester Williams assuring the Pan-African Conference that "Her Majesty's Government will not overlook the interests and welfare of the native races." It is distressing and challenging to note that today, after sixty-four years, such horrendous injustices still persist in apartheid South Africa and are even intensified.

As Chairman of the Committee on Address to the Nations of the World, Professor W. E. B. Du Bois, submitted the Address which included the following significant pronouncement: "In any case the modern world must needs remember that in this age, when the ends of the world are being brought so near together, the millions of black men in Africa, America and the islands of the sea, not to speak of the myriads elsewhere, are bound to have great influence upon the world in the future, by reason of sheer numbers and physical contact."

Duly adopted by the First Pan-African Conference, this Address was "sent to the sovereigns in whose realms are subjects of African descent." The appeal was made among others that the peoples of Africa should not be "sacrificed to the greed of gold, their liberties taken away," etc.; that the British nation should accord "the rights of responsible government to the Black Colonies of Africa and the West Indies"; that Afro-Americans should be granted "the right of franchise, security of person and property." Similar appeals were also made to the German Empire, the French Republic and the Congo Free State.

The Address to the Nations of the World then concluded with the following general appeal and call to action:

> Let the Nations of the World respect the integrity and independence of the free Negro states of Abyssinia [properly Ethiopia], Liberia, Hayti, etc. and let the inhabitants of these States, the independent tribes of Africa, the Negroes [people of African descent] of the West Indies and America, and the black subjects of all Nations take courage, strive ceaselessly, and fight bravely, that they may prove to the world their incontestable right to be counted among the great brotherhood of mankind.

Ironically enough this First Pan-African Conference was almost forgotten. Because of the minuscule difference in the designating terms *Conference* and *Congress,* or perhaps due to the frailty of the human mind however great, this historic first international body which pointed specifically to the unifying and liberating of all people of African origin and descent, was not even counted along with the subsequent "Pan-African Congresses."

From the vantage point of the present, however, it would now appear appropriate to recognize all these bodies as Pan-African Congresses, and to number them inclusively, beginning with this first epoch-making Congress of 1900. This has already been recognized by Colin Legum in *Pan-Africanism.* It appears that Dr. Du Bois himself moved in this direction when in writing of "The Pan-African Movement" he stated: "This meeting attracted attention, put the word 'Pan-African' in the dictionaries for the first time."

It should now be clear that whether in motivation, conception, or composition, all these Pan-African Congresses have alike expressed the same basic purpose. That aim has been stated by Dr. Du Bois in *Dusk of Dawn,* namely, to achieve "such world organization of black men as would oppose a united front to European aggression. . . . Out of this there might come, not race war and opposition, but broader cooperation with the white rulers of the world, and a chance for peaceful and accelerated development of black folk."

Growth of Pan-Africanism

While tracing the specific background and development of W. E. B. Du Bois in the Pan-African endeavor, there should be observed some other important aspects of the unfoldment of this great idea. For though mirrored in the mind of the individual, Pan-Africanism was and is a widespread social force. The Pan-African idea grew directly out of reaction against colonialist domination and racist oppression. Its roots, therefore, like its branches, are not single but manifold.

Whence the observation made by Colin Legum in his study *Pan-Africanism:* "It developed through what Dr. Shepperson described as 'a complicated Atlantic triangle of influences' between the New World, Europe and Africa." This might be viewed as the counterpart of that earlier triangle of traffic across the Atlantic which involved the exchange of New England rum, African slaves, and Caribbean molasses. Our limits here preclude any extended treatment of all these widespread influences or these manifold Pan-African roots. Nevertheless, some indication of these seems necessary and appropriate.

As might be expected, it was in Haiti, where the bonds of chattel slavery and colonialist subjugation were first burst asunder in the Western Hemisphere, that the Pan-African idea began to germinate. Foreshadowed even earlier, the cultural aspect of Pan-Africanism was still more definitely expressed in the epochal work of Antenor Firmin, *De l'égalité des races humaines*, 1885, later in Hannibal Price's *De la réhabilitation de la race noire*, 1900, and still later in the *Ainsi parla l'oncle* of Jean Price-Mars, 1928. Even later still the Haitian poet Jacques Roumain avowed overtly and poignantly, "Africa I have kept your memory. Africa you are in me."

George Padmore, who also made an outstanding contribution in keeping alive and developing the Pan-African Movement, has pointed in his book *Pan-Africanism or Communism?* to several of these roots in the various Back-to-Africa movements. . . .

It was in Liberia that there grew to maturity Edward Wilmot Blyden, the man who appears to have been the earliest forthright advocate of the "African personality," and champion of independent nationhood, African continental unity, and cultural Pan-Africanism. An able scholar, educator, and statesman, Dr. Blyden's ancestors had been brought as slaves, either from Ghana or Togo, to St. Thomas in the Virgin Islands of the Caribbean. Migrating to the United States and failing to find the educational opportunity which he sought, Blyden sailed back to Africa specifically to Liberia in 1850.

Dr. Blyden's Inaugural Address as President of Liberia College in 1881 bespoke the great change then beginning in Africa. Among many deep insights and sage counsels, Dr. Blyden declared: "We must not suppose that the Anglo-Saxon methods are final. . . . We must study our brethren in the interior, who know better than we do the laws of growth for the race." Though Blyden often spoke in terms then current of "the Negro race," he took a firm stand "against perpetuating race antagonism." In the conclusion of his address the educator and stateman underscored the necessity for successful efforts to build up a nation, to wrest from Nature her secrets, to lead the van of progress in this country, and to regenerate a continent.

Closely associated with Dr. Blyden in the furtherance of these ideas was the scholarly and genteel Alexander Crummell. Following years of shocking and direful mistreatment at the hands of his Christian Euro-American brethren and bishops, and after unfolding in the more amicable and cultured climate of Cambridge University in England, the Reverend Dr. Crummell went voluntarily to Africa—Sierra Leone and Liberia. There from 1853 to 1873 Alexander Crummell labored earnestly for the regeneration of Africa. His views classically expressed in *Africa and America* were far-seeing and germinal for Pan-Africa.

Similar ideas were approached by Dr. James Africanus Horton of Sierra Leone in 1865 and again during 1868 in *A Vindication of the African Race*. These ideas of Pan-African unity and regeneration blossomed as the Twentieth Century dawned. African themselves had been deeply stirred by the defeat of the imperialist Italian invaders of Ethiopia by the armies of Menelik II at Adowa in 1896. In the following year Sudanese officers rose to wrest Uganda from British rule. From Barbados and Guiana that same year there burgeoned the African Colonial Enterprise, projected by Albert Thorne for the settlement of Afro-Caribbeans in Central Africa. From Trinidad too there came F. E. M. Hercules building an organization to unite all people of African descent. During 1898 the confrontation of French and British imperialist armies at Fashoda in the Eastern Sudan barely missed setting off a European war, but led to the rise of a new militant Egyptian nationalism.

In West Africa during 1895 there had erupted the protest of some 5,000 people at Lagos, Nigeria against a proposed house and land tax. This struggle against British domination was carried forward rigorously from 1908–1948 by Herbert Macaulay, father of Nigerian nationalism. A revolt flared up likewise during 1898 in the Sierra Leone Protectorate against poll tax and corporal punishment. John Mensah Sarbah, Jacob Wilson Sey, and other leaders organized the Aborigines Rights Protection Society in 1897 in the "Gold Coast," now Ghana. Another barrister and able nationalist leader Joseph Casely Hayford prepared a successful protest against legislation which threatened to alienate African lands to the British Crown. Kings and chiefs of the Western Province also petitioned for the right to participate in legislation. Progressing in Pan-Africanism, the far-seeing Casely Hayford inspired the West African National Congress in 1920 which united peoples of four colonial areas: Gambia, Sierra Leone, Gold Coast—now Ghana— and Nigeria.

In South Africa and later in Central Africa indigenous Africans had broken away from the segregated Christian Church and formed Ethiopian and Zionist Churches of their own. Nationalist to a degree, these Ethiopian Churches sought contact with the African Methodist Episcopal Church of the U.S.A. and Bishop H. M. Turner toured Africa in 1898 to affiliate these churches. Like the Rev. Charles S. Morris of the National Baptist Convention, Bishop Turner was said to be filled with a compelling sense of the mission of Afro-Americans "to redeem their unhappy brethren in Africa."

Notable indeed was the project of the AFRICAN CHRISTIAN UNION launched by the British missionary Joseph Booth, first in Natal during 1896 and a year later in Malawi, then "Nyasaland." This followed on a trip to the United States where Booth made contact with Afro-American leaders among whom it is said was Dr. W. E. B. Du Bois. Set forth in twenty-one points was the striking plan for an organization which possessed the principal features that marked the movement launched by Marcus Garvey in Harlem over twenty years later, including the chief conjuring slogan AFRICA FOR THE AFRICAN! In fact Booth wrote to his daughter on April 9, 1897 rather prophetically: "There are many signs that a great work will spring from this side of the ocean also. I am lecturing on 'Africa for the Africans.'"

In the booklet *Africa for the Africans,* published in Baltimore, Maryland, during 1897, Joseph Booth stated his ideas fully. These involved securing capital for Industrial Missions; demanding equal rights for people of African origin; seeking the participation of "every man, woman and child of the African race," especially those in the United States and the Caribbean; developing agricultural, manufacturing, and mining enterprises as well as means of transport; Back to Africa repatriation and training of Africans in modern techniques; guiding labor toward upliftment and commonwealth; calling upon Europeans to return lands to the Africans; publishing literature in the interest of the African "race," and pursuing the policy of Africa For The African and hastening a united African Christian Nation!

But the African Christian Union foundered on the rock of distrust of Europeans, which had resulted from the bitter experience of Africans with European conquest, plunder, forced labor, imperialist subjection, and denial of human dignity. The horrible Boer wars against the Zulus and the depredations of Cecil Rhodes and other chartered companies in various areas had well nigh convinced all Africans that Bishop Colenso, friend and advisor of the Zulu king Cetewayo, "was the last of the race of true white man friends," and that "there was no white man living who was a safe guide for the African people." . . .

At the opening of this century then, even as Professor W. E. B. Du Bois penned the historic Address to the Nations of the First Pan-African Congress, indigenous Africans throughout the continent, and people of African descent in the Caribbean and on the American mainland, were stirring with the sentiment of nationalist and freedom-loving resistance against European colonialist aggression, degradation and domination. But though efforts were made toward permanent organization, the Pan-African Movement subsided following the return of its founder H. Sylvester Williams to Trinidad where some time later he died.

Nevertheless, knowledge and consciousness of Africa were ever more widely spread by Dr. Du Bois and other scholars. Outstanding among these was Dr. Carter G. Woodson. . . . Historical scholars like Dr. William Leo Hansberry and Dr. Rayford W. Logan of Howard University, and Dr. Horace Mann Bond of Lincoln University, advanced African studies and the training of African students, among them the now famous Dr. Nnamdi Azikiwe, President of Nigeria, and Dr. Kwame Nkrumah, President of Ghana.

However, during the decade 1918–1928 the idea of "African redemption" and the "unity of the Negro race" was spread as never before directly and widely to the millions by Marcus Garvey through the Universal Negro Improvement Association and African Communities League and through the newspaper the *Negro World*. . . . [In London] Garvey worked with the famous Egyptian nationalist of Sudanese descent Dusé Mohamed. From this African scholar who edited the *African Times and Orient Review,* Garvey derived many of his ideas of African nationalism and the electrifying slogan *Africa for the Africans!*

Writing of this two-year stay in England as "the most decisive period in Garvey's life," Robert Hughes Brisbane, Jr. in "Some New Light on the Garvey Movement" reveals the following: "Garvey heard such slogans as "India for the Indians" and "Asia for the Asiatics" (Asians is the non-abusive and proper term). He became interested in the condition of the African Negro as a result of discussions with the followers of Chilembwe of Nyasaland and Kimbangu of the Congo." . . .

[Concerning the difference between the Back to Africa and Pan-African movements, outstanding writers have made] the observations which follow. The first has been made by Shepperson and Price in *Independent African:* "Du Bois and Garvey though they were political opponents with fundamental disagreements on tactics, were, in reality, working for the same end: to raise the status of the Negro, materially and spiritually, in his own eyes, and in the eyes of the world at large." The second has been set down by George Padmore in *Pan-Africanism or Communism?* thus: "Pan-Africanism differed from Garveyism in that it was never conceived as a Back to Africa Movement, but rather as a dynamic philosophy and guide to action for Africans in Africa who were laying the foundations of national liberation organizations." The third and final observation is that made by Dr. Kwame Nkrumah, President of Ghana, on April 7, 1960 at the Positive Conference for Peace and Security in Africa: "When I speak of Africa for Africans, this should be interpreted in the light of my emphatic declaration that I do not believe in racialism and colonialism. The concept 'Africa for

Africans' does not mean that other races are excluded from it. No. It only means that Africans, who naturally are the majority in Africa, shall and must govern themselves in their own countries. The fight is for the future of humanity, and it is a most important fight."

At the end of the First World War, W. E. B. Du Bois determined to revive the Pan-African Movement. Accordingly he maneuvered to get to Paris as a press correspondent in order to make a representation to the Allied Peace Conference which met in nearby Versailles. A similar effort at representation was made by William Monroe Trotter of the National Equal Rights League and editor of the *Boston Guardian*. Denied a passport by the U.S. government, Trotter had to disguise himself as a cook on a ship to get to France.

Both Dr. Du Bois and editor Trotter were given the cold shoulder by that august international body convened to realize the great Wilsonian slogan "Make the World Safe for Democracy"—for which thousands of men of African origin and descent had fought and died. Nevertheless, the publicity secured in the press about their representations by Du Bois and by Trotter caused much concern among the Allied rulers. For while Woodrow Wilson at the Peace Conference appeared before the world as the champion of the right of self-determination, neither this spokesman of democracy, nor any of the European colonialist powers, had the slightest idea of according that selfsame right to their colonized subjects in Africa or elsewhere.

Second Pan-African Conference

Outwitting the great opposition which he encountered, Dr. Du Bois succeeded in reviving the Pan-African Movement and in holding a Second Conference in Paris, February 19–21, 1919. This Dr. Du Bois was able to accomplish through the aid of M. Blaise Diagne, African deputy from Senegal and Commissaire-Général for the recruitment of African troops. While Secretary Polk of the U.S. Government was giving assurance that no such assembly would be held, the Pan-African Congress was already in session.

The account later given by Dr. Du Bois himself is most fitting here:

> This Congress represented Africa partially. Of the fifty-seven delegates from fifteen countries, nine were African countries with twelve delegates. The other delegates came from the United States which sent sixteen, and the West Indies with twenty-one. Most of these delegates did not come to France for this meeting, but happened to be residing there, mainly for reasons connected with the war. America and all the colonial powers refused to issue special visas.
>
> The Congress specifically asked that the German colonies be turned over to an international organization instead of being handled by various colonial powers. Out of this idea came the Mandates Commission.

It will be seen by comparison with the First Pan-African Congress of 1900 that there was an increase of representation at this Paris Congress of 1919. African representation was still smaller than that of Afro-Americans, while that from the Caribbean still predominated. Resolutions adopted called for a Code of Laws for the international protection for Africans, for the establishment of a Bureau to oversee the application of such laws for the welfare of the African people, and for the future government of Africans in accordance with principles stated more in detail in respect to Land, Capital, Labor, Education, and the State.

Seeking to build a permanent Pan-African organization, Dr. Du Bois arranged for the Third Pan-African Congress which met in three sessions in London, August 28–29, in Brussels, August 31–September 2, 1921, and in Paris, September 4–5, 1921. Total representation doubled with the largest representation this time, forty-one from Africa, twenty-four from people of African descent living in Europe, and seven from the Caribbean.

The considerable drop in Caribbean representation was attributed by Dr. Du Bois to the hindering influence of the Garvey organization; likewise he felt that certain opposition also arose from being confounded with the Garvey movement and from a bald statement in the Brussels *Neptune* which falsely declared that the organizers of the Pan-African Congress were "said in the United States (to) have received remuneration from Moscow (Bolsheviki)."

Resolutions adopted in London, which contained a statement critical of the colonial regime in the Congo, were bitterly opposed in Belgium and an innocuous substitute stressing goodwill and investigation was declared adopted by M. Diagne, despite the opposition of a clear majority. Resolutions also affirmed equality of races to be "the founding stone of world and human advancement" and continued: "And of all the various criteria of which masses of men in the past have been prejudged, that of the color of the skin and the texture of the hair is surely the most adventitious and idiotic." Eight specific demands in the interest of African peoples were then particularized.

Third Pan-African Conference

This Third Pan-African Congress sent a Committee headed by W. E. B. Du Bois to interview the officials of the League of Nations. A petition filed by this committee was published as an official document of the League of Nations. However when M. Dantes Bellegarde of Haiti in the Assembly of the League of Nations condemned the ruthless bombing and massacre in May 1922 of the African Bondelschwartz of South-West Africa, which had been approved by Jan Christian Smuts, the Haitian statesman M. Bellegarde was recalled by the United States forces which then controlled Haiti. This plea of M. Bellegarde has been recognized, nevertheless, as "a courageous and impassioned appeal that even now stands as one of the models of eloquence in the Assemblies of the League."

At the Third Convention of the Universal Negro Improvement Association in 1922, Marcus Garvey appointed a delegation led by George O. Mark of Sierra Leone as chairman and J. Adam of Haiti as secretary to present a petition to the League of Nations. This petition asked that the former German colonies be placed under the control of the U.N.I.A. Through the cooperation of the representative of Persia—now Iran—the petition was presented to the League during October 1922. The next year when the chairman returned to press this appeal, he was denied even an audience under a new rule which required such petitions to be presented through the imperial governments. A similar petition to the League of Nations was forwarded by Arden Bryan of Barbados, former Commissioner of the U.N.I.A., during 1923. Efforts to enlist the offices of the British government for transmission as required were unavailing when the British Ambassador replied that his government could not support the petition.

The attempt again made to form a permanent Pan-African organization was unsuccessful when the young secretary who taught school in Paris sought to bring in profit-making schemes and delayed the calling of the next Pan-African Congress. With inadequate preparation, therefore, the Fourth Pan-African Congress met in 1923 rather weakly in London and somewhat better attended in Lisbon due to the participation there of the Liga Africana. Specific demands were set forth in eight cardinal points and the statement concluded: "In fine, we ask in all the world, that black folk be treated as men. We can see no other road to Peace and Progress. What more paradoxical figure today fronts the world than the official head of a great South African state striving blindly to build Peace and Goodwill in Europe by standing on the necks and hearts of millions of black Africans?"

Strivings toward Pan-Africa was stimulated by the meeting of delegates of African descent at the Brussels Congress of the League Against Imperialism during February 1927. Its Commission on the African Peoples of the World included the dedicated Garan Kouyatte who was slain by the Nazis while they occupied Paris; the brilliant Senegalese leader Lamine Senghor who was martyred shortly after this Congress in a Paris jail; the Vice President of the African National Congress of South Africa, J. T. Gumede, whose gift book, still among my most prized treasures, is inscribed "with the best wishes for the success of our common struggle for a better day;" the Secretary of the South African Non-European Federation, J. A. La Guma; the Ethiopian representative Mr. Makonnen; and the present writer who acted as secretary of this Commission and drafted its resolution.

This Resolution on the Negro Question was adopted by the entire Congress of the League Against Imperialism. It recounted in summary the centuries old colonialist and racist oppression of peoples of African descent, called for their complete freedom and independence, and set forth specific demands in nine major points. Readily recognized by Dr. W. E. B. Du Bois as "a strong set of resolutions," an abstract was published by him in the *Crisis* magazine of July 1927. The Pan-African program thus gained the fraternal endorsement of hundreds of influential delegates from Europe and Asia. Several of these Asian leaders such as Prime Minister Jawaharlal Nehru of India, and President Sukarno of Indonesia, were to assemble again in the historic Asian-African Conference at Bandung, Indonesia, during April 1955.

Fifth Pan-African Conference

An effort to hold a Pan-African Congress in the Caribbean during 1925 was frustrated by exorbitant travel rates and the opposition of colonial powers. But during August 21–24, 1927, the Fifth Pan-African Congress met in New York with two hundred eight delegates from twenty-two states of the American Union and ten other countries. African representatives came from Ghana, then "Gold Coast," and from Sierra Leone, and Nigeria. The Resolution stressed six points, the chief being "The development of Africa for the Africans and not merely for the profit of the Europeans." The people of the West Indies were urged "to begin an earnest movement for the federation of the islands." Recognizing that "the narrow confines of the modern world entwine our interests with those of other peoples," the Resolution concluded thus:

> We desire to see freedom and real national independence in Egypt, in China and in India. We demand the cessation of the interference of the United States in the affairs of Central and South America.
> We thank the Soviet Government of Russia for its liberal attitude toward the colored races and for the help which it has extended to them from time to time.
> We urge the white workers of the world to realize that no program of labor uplift can be successfully carried through in Europe or America so long as colored labor is exploited and enslaved and deprived of all political power.

The writer well remembers this Pan-African Congress and the participation of a forthright group of young radicals including Otto E. Huiswoud of Guiana, dominated by the Dutch, and F. Eugene Corbie of British colonized Trinidad.

The ensuing effort to hold a Pan-African Congress in Africa itself at Tunis was nullified by the final refusal of the French government to allow such an assemblage on African soil, and also by the setting in of the economic depression in the Western World.

Sixth Pan-African Congress

The Pan-African idea thus remained dormant until the assembling, largely through labor union representatives, of the Sixth Pan-African Congress, October 15–21, 1945, in the Chorlton Town Hall at Manchester, headquarters of the recently formed Pan-African Federation. Chiefly responsible for this Congress was the secretary of the Federation, the dedicated George Padmore, who like the initiator of the First Pan-African Congress of 1900, H. Sylvester Williams, hailed originally from Trinidad. Ably supporting Padmore was the devoted chairman of the Federation Dr. Peter Milliard, who came from Guiana held as a colony under British rule.

A preliminary conference elected as joint political secretaries to prepare this Pan-African Congress George Padmore and Kwame Nkrumah, while Jomo Kenyatta was elected assistant secretary. A powerful but unheeded Open Letter was sent by this Secretariat to Prime Minister Attlee, who as leader of the British Labor Party had just taken office in England.

Elected to preside over the first, as over most of the other sessions of this Sixth Pan-African Congress at Manchester, Dr. W. E. B. Du Bois was hailed as "Father" of Pan-Africanism by George Padmore, designated chairman of the Platform Committee, and unanimously elected International President of the Pan-African Congress. The distinguished doctor now settled graciously into the role of elder statesman and "Grand Old Man of Pan-Africanism." Unquestionably all these tributes were well deserved, since W. E. B. Du Bois had rendered long and vital service in keeping alive and nurturing the Pan-African idea which was now developing into a new and higher stage.

The Pan-African Movement was indeed maturing with the emergence and participation of such African leaders as Kwame Nkrumah of Ghana, Jomo Kenyatta of Kenya, Ja-Ja Wachuku and O. Awolowo of Nigeria, Hastings K. Banda of Malawi, the Ghanian historian J. C. De Graft Johnson, and the South African writer Peter Abrahams. Impressive and moving was the participation of Gershon Nishie-Nikoi who represented 300,000 cocoa farmers of Ghana and Nigeria, and who though bearing a petition, had been refused an audience by Secretary Hall of the British Labor Party, then in power.

Significant also at this Manchester Pan-African Congress was the attendance of J. S. Annan of the African Railway Employees Union, of A. Soyemi Coker of the Trades Union Congress and Magnus Williams of the National Council of Nigeria and the Cameroons who also represented Dr. Nnamdi Azikiwe. Important too was the appearance of I. T. A. Wallace Johnson of the Sierra Leone Trade Union Congress, E. Garba-Jahumpa of the Gambia Trades Union, I. Yatu of the Young Baganda, S. Rahinda of Tanganyika, Marko Hlubi of the South African National Congress, and many others.

Broadly representative of all the people—workers, farmers, students, civic leaders, and intellectuals—the Sixth Manchester Pan-African Congress of 1945 brought together some ninety-four regular delegates, twenty-six from Africa, thirty-three from the Caribbean, and thirty-five domiciled in Great Britain. Unlisted among the delegates, perhaps because *sui generis*, was the eminent Pan-Africanist Dr. William Edward Burghardt Du Bois who seemed the sole participant from the United States. Among eleven fraternal delegates and observers were representatives from Somali, Cyprus, India, Ceylon, the Women's International League, Common Wealth, the Independent Labor Party, and the Negro Welfare Association.

The keynote of that epoch-making Manchester Pan-African Congress of 1945 was struck in its Declaration to the Colonial Workers, Farmers, and Intellectuals: "We affirm the right of all Colonial Peoples to control their own destiny. All colonies must be free from foreign imperialist control, whether political or economic." A new note of militancy was there expressed: "We say to the peoples of the Colonies that they must fight for these ends by all means at their disposal." A new spirit of urgency was explicit in the projection of "A PROGRAM OF ACTION."

Comprehensive resolutions were adopted treating of West Africa; the Congo and North Africa; East Africa; the Union of South Africa; The Protectorates of Bechuanaland, Basutoland, and Swaziland; the West Indies; Special Supplementary Resolutions presented by the delegation of the Universal Negro Improvement Association of Jamaica; also resolutions on Ethiopia, Liberia, Haiti; an additional resolution on Ethiopia; on Colored Seamen in Great Britain; and a resolution to the U.N.O. on South West Africa.

A Memorandum to the United Nations Organizations was presented through its Secretariat by Dr. Du Bois as International President of the Pan-African Congress. This Resolution urged as "just, proper, and necessary that provision be made for the participation of designated representatives of the African colonial peoples . . . to the maximum extent possible under the present Charter of the United Nations." This petition was supported by some thirty-five of the most powerful organizations of Africans and people of African descent in the United States, the Caribbean, and Britain. Broadly representative, organizations included civic, religious, fraternal, professional, press, labor, women's, student, and youth bodies.

The program of ideas and action achieved at the Sixth Manchester Pan-African Congress has been summarized by Colin Legum in *Pan-Africanism* in nine chief points which must be still further compressed here: 1. "Africa for the Africans." 2. United States of Africa. 3. African renaissance of morale and culture. 4. African nationalism totally transcending tribalism and narrowness. 5. African regeneration of economic enterprise. 6. Government on the principle "one man one vote." 7. Non-violent *Positive Action* unless met by forcible repression. 8. Solidarity of African and oppressed peoples everywhere. 9. Positive neutrality in power politics but "neutral in nothing that affects African interests."

Thence to Africa itself and to the various national liberation movements growing there was this program and the political drive of Pan-Africanism then transferred, while phases of its cultural propagation were still carried on in Europe and the Americas. Noteworthy among these ongoing phases of cultural Pan-Africa are the Conferences of Black Writers and Artists, the publication of books and the journal *Présence Africaine* edited by Alioune Diop in Paris since November 1947, and the development of the Society of African Culture in Paris followed by the associated American Society of African Culture.

With the final breakthrough of the Egyptian Revolution led by Colonel Gamal Abdel Nasser and with the independence of Ghana in 1957 under the leadership of Dr. Kwame Nkrumah, Pan-Africanism was in flower in its natural habitat. For there soon followed the First Conference of Independent African States in Accra, April 15–22, 1958. Thence proceeding through the various All African Peoples Conferences at Accra, 1958; Tunis, 1960; Cairo, 1961; and Governmental Conferences at Conakry, 1959; Sanniquelli, 1959; the Second Conference of Independent African States at Addis Ababa, 1960; Brazzaville, 1961; Casablanca, 1961; Monrovia, 1961; not without difficulties and setbacks but finally achieving mature stature at the Addis Ababa Summit Conference May 22–25, 1963, Pan-Africa loomed through the Organization of African Unity as a powerful political continental force and an international factor of prime magnitude. This Organization was further consolidated at the Conference in Cairo, during 1964.

The Manchester Congress of 1945 thus marked a milestone in the development of the Pan-African Movement. President Nnamdi Azikiwe of the Republic of Nigeria in his Goodwill Message for the republication in 1963 of the *History of the Pan-African Congress* observed that this 1945 Congress "marked the turning point in Pan-Africanism from a passive to an active stage." In the ninety-fifth year of his life, Dr. Du Bois wrote: "It carries messages which must not die, but should be passed on to aid Mankind and to inspire the darker races of Man to see themselves of one blood with all human beings. . . . For that was a decisive year in determining the freedom of Africa."

The President of Kenya, Jomo Kenyatta, welcomed the reprint of the report of the 1945 Manchester Pan-African Congress and declared: "The Congress was a landmark in the history of the African peoples' struggle for unity and freedom." Mrs. George Padmore in her Goodwill Message said of this decisive Pan-African Congress: "Its resolutions and resulting programmes inspired the leaders who participated in its deliberations to carry forward their endeavours in their native territories."

The Osagyefo Dr. Kwame Nkrumah, President of Ghana, in his Message revealed: "At Manchester, we knew that we were speaking for all Africa, expressing the deepest desires and determination of a mighty continent to be wholly free. The desire was very emphatically reiterated in Addis Ababa where the heads of state and Government of 32 Independent African States representing 250 million Africans, witnessed probably the most important turning point in the political and economic history of any continent."

Hearing the report in his ninety-sixth and last year of this Addis Ababa Conference from his wife Shirley Graham Du Bois, the doctor could well visualize that great meeting of Heads of African States and conceive its historical promise for a completely free, independent, and united Africa in the not too distant future. Thereafter, as the veteran spokesman for Pan-African liberation and champion of human rights relaxed his grasp upon the pen, or turned reluctantly from his dictation for the *Encyclopedia Africana,* as he prepared to lay himself down and to mingle his dust with the dust of his ancestral African forebears, he might well have heard the vibrant song which Union soldiers sang as they marched against the strongholds of the southern slaveholding oligarchy:

> John Brown's body lies a mould'rin' in the grave, . . .
> But his soul goes marching on.

For William Edward Burghardt Du Bois must have felt the certainty at the last that the struggle for freedom, which he had so ably waged, would be carried forward to final victory by ever more and stronger hands. So it does in truth go forward, as signalized on the occasion of the recent achievement of independence by the people of Zambia, in the words of the African poet A. C. Jordan:

> So Africa's hungry children shall survive
> And gain new strength to build a brighter world,
> Untrammell'd by the wiles of endless strife
> Created by the ravenous kings of gold.

IX

AFRO-AMERICAN HISTORY

One of the fruits of the civil rights struggle and the rise of "black" awareness was the massive surge of interest in African and Afro-American history. Moore had been promoting such studies, however, long before the 1960s. The contribution of the African to the development of the American nation was a popular theme in his lectures and his writings. The 1941 essay "The Negro in Freedom's Wars" was remarkably similar to his last formal lecture, "Bicentennial Reflections," given in 1975 at Nassau Community College in Garden City, New York, even though he did not have access to the earlier piece. Throughout Moore's life Frederick Douglass remained one of his favorite topics. The two articles on Douglass and "Afro-Americans and the Third Party Movement" reflect his attention to the many aspects of Douglass's life. "Afro-Americans and Radical Politics," a continuation of the telecast on the Third Party Movement, gives an insider's view of the politics and organizations of the 1920s and 1930s in Harlem.

THE FREDERICK DOUGLASS CENTENARY

The Crisis, March 1941, pp. 80, 90–91.

The hundredth anniversary now approaches of one of the most significant events in the history of the Negro people and of the American nation. It is the Centenary of the First Public Appearance of Frederick Douglass on the Abolition Platform at the Anti-Slavery Convention held in Nantucket, Massachusetts, August 11, 1841.

With never a day's schooling, only three years removed from the darkness of a chattel bondage, and facing imminent danger of recapture and return to the hell of slavery, the fugitive slave stood forth to address the Convention. Soon his misgivings and embarrassment were forgotten as the tale of the wrongs and sufferings of the slaves flowed from his heart and lips. His earnest and eloquent appeal for freedom moved the Abolitionists as never before against the crime of slavery and history leaped forward with a giant stride in its irresistible march towards emancipation.

This event is not noted by the historians or heralded by the publicists who distort history and interpret events for the greater glory of the oppressors of mankind. These purblind and prejudiced "savants" would bury in the limbo of forgetfulness this signal development in the progressive evolution of the Negro people and of the people of the United States. Diligent in the service of reaction, they must maintain the Negro only as "hewers of wood and drawers of water" in the fiction they fabricate for history as a means of ensuring this status of servitude and super-exploitation in life.

Happily for us, for posterity, and for the cause of freedom, the perverters of history have not wholly succeeded in erasing this great event from the shining scroll of history. Research yet recovers precious portions of the true and glowing record bequeathed to us from the heroic past for the enlightenment and inspiration of the present and the future. Several of the noble contemporaries of the great Negro abolitionist, liberator, and statesman have fittingly described the auspicious beginning of his great mission and have adequately appraised its profound historic significance.

The founder of the militant, moral-suasion, Abolitionist movement, William Lloyd Garrison, wrote thus in his Preface to the *Narrative* of Frederick Douglass: "Fortunate, most fortunate occurrence! Fortunate for the millions of his manacled brethren, yet panting for deliverance from their awful thralldom! Fortunate for the cause of Negro emancipation! And of universal liberty! Fortunate for the land of his birth, which he has already done so much to save and bless! . . . I shall never forget his first speech at the convention—the extraordinary emotion it excited in my mind—the powerful impression it created upon a crowded auditory, completely taken by surprise. . . . I think I never hated slavery so intensely, as at that moment; certainly my perception of the enormous outrage which is inflicted by it, on the godlike nature of its victims, was rendered far more clear than ever. There stood one in physical proportion and stature commanding and exact—in intellect richly endowed—in natural eloquence a prodigy. . . . As soon as he had taken his seat, filled with hope and admiration, I rose and declared that Patrick Henry, of revolutionary frame, never made a speech more eloquent in the cause of liberty, than the one we had just listened to from the lips of that hunted fugitive. So I believed at that time—such is my belief now."

A foremost leader of the political Anti-Slavery movement, Henry Wilson, has evaluated this event in the *Rise and Fall of the Slave Power*: "But in 1841 a champion arose in the person of Frederick Douglass who was destined to play an important part in the great drama then in progress. In him not only did the colored race but manhood itself find a worthy representative and advocate. . . . His life is in itself an epic which finds few to equal it in the realms of either romance or reality.

"In the conflict for freedom of speech and the right of free discussion Abolitionists had achieved a victory. . . . They had conquered a peace; but their opponents were determined it should be the peace of the grave. . . . Anti-slavery measures had lost much of their zest and potency; meetings became less numerously attended, and, consequently, less frequent; organizations, losing their effectiveness, began to die out. Something was necessary to revive and re-animate the drooping spirits and the languid movements of the cause and its friends. It was then, at this opportune moment . . . the young fugitive appeared upon the stage. He seemed like a messenger from the dark land of slavery itself; as if in his person his race had found a fitting advocate; as if through his lips their long pent-up wrongs and wishes had found a voice. No wonder that Nantucket meeting was greatly moved."

The importance of this great event looms even larger as we view in retrospect today the historic role of Frederick Douglass and its real relation to the vital events of his age. For the Abolition struggle was the core around which the whole history of the United States revolved for at least half a century. Its successful consummation in the emancipation of the chattel slaves was the crowning achievement of the greatest epoch of our past history. And the record clearly attests that the role of the despised and downtrodden slave class, of its many heroic leaders, and of its best representative and foremost political leader, Frederick Douglass, was unique, essential, and decisive in that sublime and glorious historic achievement.

Since it has become the fashion of the dominant and decadent reactionaries of our day to deride emancipation in a thousand different ways, it is necessary to mark its progressive character and beneficent consequence. Emancipation broke the yoke of barbarous chattel slavery from the limbs and minds of four million Negroes. It freed labor, the farmers, and all other classes from the degrading fetters of the monstrous, reactionary Slave Power. The entire American nation was thereby enabled to achieve the most rapid progress in every sphere of life, economic, political, cultural, and social, and to make the greatest advance towards the realization of unity, security, peace, and democracy. Let those who can deny the profound, progressive, liberating, world-historic consequence of that achievement.

The extraordinary role of Frederick Douglass in this achievement of emancipation and the magnitude and consequence of his life-work should ever be adequately appreciated and must never be obscured or forgotten. A summary view of the record reveals his eloquent and prodigious labors in arousing the people of the North and West to struggle against slavery and in mobilizing vital support for the cause of Abolition in Ireland, Scotland, England, and other countries. His establishment and conduct of the *North Star* furnished an influential organ and a significant demonstration for the capacity of the Negro slaves for freedom and accomplishment in the highest spheres of human endeavor. His pioneer labors for the

education and elevation of his people, in industry as in every sphere of
life, and his courageous struggle against discrimination, segregation,
disfranchisement, and lynch violence were of vital importance in the preservation and extension of civil liberties and democratic rights for all
Americans.

A leader of breadth, vision, and full stature, Douglass worked as occasion
offered with all the outstanding leaders of the Abolition struggle. A con-
ductor of the Underground Railroad, he aided John Brown, Harriet Tubman, Sojourner Truth, and countless others in their great work for freedom. Employing every possible opportunity, he neglected no means and
early realized the importance of the ballot to further the cause of Abolition.
As the crisis developed, he labored with statesmanship and effectiveness to
marshal and unite the people for resistance to the aggression of the Slave
Power and for the election of Lincoln.

During the Civil War Frederick Douglass rose to towering heights of
statesmanship and performed a most important and decisive role. Criticizing the attempted compromises and inadequate measures of Lincoln and
the Republican administration, he mobilized the people of the loyal states
to press the government forward to "make the war an abolition war" and to
"employ the arm of the Negro." When the government yielded to this
supreme historical necessity, Douglass issued his historic appeal: "Men of
Color, To Arms!" Protesting the discrimination practiced against the Negro soldiers who volunteered chiefly at his bidding, Douglass stopped
recruiting until assured by Lincoln himself of improvement in the treatment of the Negro troops whose valiant arms insured victory and the
progress of the Republic in peace and freedom.

Frederick Douglass carried forward his great leadership in the struggle
for enfranchisement and in the staunch fight against the reaction which
instituted with a saturnalia of violence a new slavery, proscription and
lynch terror. Appointed to high public office—Marshal of the District of
Columbia, Recorder of Deeds, Minister to Haiti—Douglass proved himself
the incorruptible and loyal champion of his people and of true democracy.
With rare consistency he labored early and long for equal rights and the
vote for women, for the rights of all minorities, and for freedom and
independence for oppressed peoples.

A pioneer champion of labor, he pointed the way to the organization and
unity of all working people and to their complete emancipation. Like
Lincoln and the truly great Americans of that day, Douglass fearlessly
opposed the slaveholders' war against Mexico as an unjust war of plunder
and empire. With profound insight he clearly perceived the essential distinction between wars of empire and war for the liberation of the oppressed. Frederick Douglass strove with basic consistency and extraordinary effectiveness throughout his long, eventful, and noble career
for peace, progress, security, democracy, and a better life for all.

THE NEGRO IN FREEDOM'S WARS

The Fraternal Outlook, August 1941, pp. 6–7, 23.

Almost a century before the Pilgrim fathers landed on these shores, the Negro had appeared on the stage of American history and had begun the battle for democracy. In 1526 a revolt of Negro slaves for freedom put an end to the colony which had been established by Ayllon. This appears to be the first great blow struck for democracy in the area that is now the United States of America. It was the first of hundreds of slave insurrections which occurred down to and during the Civil War of 1861–1865.

In the revolutionary struggle which wrested independence from the British Empire and which opened the era of emerging democracy not only for America but for the world, the Negro was the first to shed his blood. Leading what has been described as "a motley rabble of saucy boys, Negroes and mulattoes, Irish Teagues, and outlandish Jack Tars," Crispus Attucks braved the fire of mercenary British redcoats and was the first to fall in what is known to history as the Boston Massacre. "From that moment," said Daniel Webster, "we may date the severance of the British Empire."

It was a Negro, Peter Salem, at the Battle of Bunker Hill on the 17th of June, 1775, who rallied the American forces by the shot which laid Major Pitcairn low. This action of Peter Salem was symbolic of the chief part played by Negroes who, despite the continued existence of chattel slavery throughout the Thirteen Colonies and the waverings of some of the founding fathers of the Republic in respect to their enlistment, pressed into the Revolutionary Army to the number of over 5,000 freemen and slaves who thereby gained their emancipation. In numerous instances these Negro soldiers distinguished themselves for fortitude and bravery as at the battle of Red Bank in Connecticut when they repulsed three ferocious assaults made by the British and prevented the enemy from turning the flank of the American army. The Black Legion of San Domingo saved the day at the siege of Savannah in 1779. This Legion, composed of 800 Haitians who volunteered with the French forces to aid the Americans, successfully charged the British and saved the retreating American army by what has been appraised as "the most brilliant feat of the day."

In the War of 1812 when the British attempted to re-enslave the American people, the Negro was again found fighting valiantly. They fought with Perry on Lake Erie. The prejudice which Captain Perry showed at first was sharply rebuked by Commodore Chauncey who wrote, "I have yet to learn that the color of the skin, or the cut and trimmings of the coat, can affect a man's qualifications or usefulness. I have nearly fifty blacks on board of this ship and many of them are among my best men." Even the

Niles Weekly Register, the mouthpiece of the southern slaveocracy, declared, "When America has such tars she has little to fear from the tyrants of the ocean." At the battle of New Orleans 3,300 Negro soldiers helped to win the victory over the British invaders.

No less significant is the contribution of Negroes—slaves, fugitives, freemen—in the historic conflict against the barbarous, anti-democratic system of chattel slavery. The numerous heroic slave revolts, the daring flight of thousands to the North which led to the establishment of the vast Underground Railroad, their unceasing fight for civil liberties and democratic rights, their most effective role in arousing the people of the North and West to action against the encroachments of the Slave Power, the eloquent, able and heroic leadership of truly great figures like David Walker, Gabriel Prosser, Nat Turner, Denmark Vesey, Samuel R. Ward, Frederick Douglass, Sojourner Truth and Harriet Tubman—these demonstrate the vital role of the Negro in the anti-slavery and Abolition movement, in that great struggle for democracy which was the central core of American history for at least half a century.

But it was in the Civil War, that most critical conflict of our past history when democracy in America was threatened with complete destruction by the southern Slave Power, that Negroes performed the decisive role to the end "that government of the people, by the people and for the people, shall not perish from the earth." While thousands of Negro slaves flocked to the Union armies from which they were at first repulsed and returned to slavery, their great Abolitionist leader, Frederick Douglass, aroused the people of the North to press the government to "make the war an abolition war" and to "employ the arm of the Negro."

When this policy was finally adopted by Lincoln, Douglass issued his historic appeal: "Men of Color, To Arms!" Two hundred thousand brave black soldiers volunteered to crush slavery, to save the Union, and to fight for democracy. Nevertheless, they were subjected to such discrimination that Douglass found it imperative to stop recruiting until assured by Lincoln himself of measures to end this shameful discrimination. Negro soldiers fought in 213 battles and over seventy thousand were killed or wounded. "Now it is in part to the aid of the Negro in freedom," wrote the historian George Bancroft, "that the country owes its success in its movement of regeneration—that the world of mankind owes the continuance of the United States as the example of a Republic."

In these wars of liberation which were genuine struggles for democracy, black Americans unstintingly gave the last full measure of devotion. But following the leadership of Frederick Douglass and other truly great Americans like Lincoln, Garrison, Lowell and Whittier, they opposed the war against Mexico in 1846–1848 as an unjust war of plunder and empire instigated by slaveholders.

The experiences of the Negro people during and following the first World War have convinced them that all the fine words about a "war to make the world safe for democracy" did not guarantee elementary human rights or justice to them or ensure a truly democratic way of life to the peoples of the world. While fighting heroically on the battlefields of France and Flanders, black Americans were maligned as social inferiors and savages; they were humiliated and victimized by segregation, discrimination, and racial hostility; here at home they were subjected to proscription and peonage, to horrible lynchings and to mass massacres in East St. Louis, Tulsa, Chicago, and in Washington, the capital of our nation.

Today the Negro people are ready to struggle to establish the "four freedoms" and to destroy Hitlerism. At the same time they are aghast at the first official pronouncement of a President that segregation in the armed forces is "a policy which has proved satisfactory." For colored Americans know from bitter experience that segregation means degradation and a foul black-out of democracy which is beneficial only to slave-drivers, lynchers, and fascists. And history attests that the true democratic and beneficial policy was followed in the Revolutionary Army at the battle of Bunker Hill. "They took their place not in a separate corps, but in the ranks with the white man." (Bancroft's *History of the United States*, Vol. XII, p. 421.)

Still Negroes see themselves practically shut out of the air force and barred from the marines and from the navy save as messmen. The searing memory of the court-marshal, imprisonment, and discharge of Negro messmen from the U.S. Navy, solely because of their protest against discrimination and abuse, is yet fresh in their minds. Discrimination in the army and the recent lynching of Private Hall within the territory of Fort Benning, Georgia, convince the Negro people that the democratic way of life must be defended not only by the fight to defeat Hitlerism in Europe but also by the struggle to abolish fascist practices in our own country and to uproot the vicious counterpart in America of monstrous Nazi racism.

The perfidious and monstrous attack of the Nazi hordes upon the peace-loving peoples of the Soviet Union makes it clear to every thinking Negro, as to all other rational human beings, that victory for the Nazis means bloody conquest and frightful enslavement for all the rest of mankind. The Negro peoples everywhere are thereby menaced with the most savage persecution and ruthless extermination. Hence, with the exception of a few venal and treacherous misleaders and a small number deluded by these, the Negro people are now solidly for the rendering of all aid immediately to the peoples of the Soviet Union, Britain, and China who are now battling heroically in the most crucial conflict of all time for the liberties of all mankind.

At the same time, my people feel deep down that the defense of democracy also demands the most vigorous struggle here in America to abolish the poll tax and disfranchisement, to wipe out discrimination and segregation, to end lynching and mob violence, to preserve and extend civil liberties, to protect the rights of minorities, to abolish debt slavery and to gain equality in employment and social security, to assure the rights of labor and decent working and living conditions.

But let none dare to question the genuine patriotism of Negro Americans or their readiness to fight against the menace of Hitlerism. To all save the reactionary appeasers of fascism who make of patriotism a cloak for robbery and oppression, this very insistence upon the fulfillment of democratic principles is itself proof of the Negro's devotion to democracy and his resolute anti-fascist zeal.

Defense of the democratic way of life requires also the present forthright recognition of all democratic rights, including the rights of self-government and self-determination for the peoples of the West Indies and Africa, for our Latin American neighbors and for all oppressed colonial and semi-colonial peoples. The release of W. A. Domingo in Jamaica, Luiz Carlos Prestes in Brazil, Albizu Campos and Earl Browder in our own land, and other leaders of labor and the people now languishing in concentration camps and jails in the Americas, and of such leaders of the oppressed colonial peoples as Nehru and Bose in India—this is absolutely essential to the sincere prosecution of the struggle to preserve democracy.

The International Workers Order plays an increasingly important role in the struggle for democracy for the oppressed Negro people. For the Negro question is the acid test of democracy in America and democracy can never be assured to any worker or to any member of a minority group until it is fully assured to fifteen million black Americans. The significant contribution which the Negro people have made and are making to the progressive development of American democracy, culture, and life, shows them to be a vital force for the upbuilding and advancement of the Order. The election of Louise Thompson as a National Vice-President of the IWO is evidence of the growing recognition of this important fact.

The Order fully supports the struggle against lynching, the Anti-Poll Tax campaign now being conducted, the campaigns against discrimination and for jobs. The Plan for Plenty and the low-cost insurance and health programs are of specific significance to the Negro people.

The activity of the Order in the organization of the Ford workers and in promoting unity of black and white workers, the organization of Negro tenants in Sheepshead Bay, the support to the National Negro Congress especially in the recent bus strike in Harlem, the cracking of Jim Crow policies in two leading Chicago Hotels during its national basketball tourney—all demonstrate how effective the Order can be in the furtherance of real democracy in American life.

In bringing forward the cultural contributions of the Negro people, the Order is rendering a signal service. The publication of Langston Hughes' book of poems, *A New Song*, the promotion of his play *Don't You Want To Be Free?* by the IWO, the historic IWO pageant *The Negro in American Life*, and the Order's presentation of Paul Robeson—these are milestones in the cultural development of America. The new program for the development of a cultural center in Harlem is a great step forward and should stimulate similar activity in other cities. The resolute carrying forward of such activities of the Order will increasingly bring the Negro people into its ranks and will foster that unity of the people regardless of race, religion, nationality, or color which is the indispensable condition for the defeat of fascism and the preservation and extension of democracy in this crucial hour.

FREDERICK DOUGLASS AND EMANCIPATION

Liberator, February 1963, pp. 6–9.

"The first of January, 1863, was a memorable day in the progress of American liberty and civilization." So wrote the militant ex-slave who had become the great spokesman, orator, abolitionist, journalist, champion, and liberator of his people in that unique and revealing autobiography: *The Life and Times of Frederick Douglass.*

A great historic turning point was reached and passed on that day one hundred years ago when Abraham Lincoln, president of the United States of America and commander-in-chief of the armed forces of the Republic, issued the justly famous Emancipation Proclamation.

Couched in cautious constitutional language and plainly proclaiming its origin in military necessity, reflecting also the lack of power to enforce the immediate liberation of the majority of the slaves then held behind rebel Confederate lines, and even excluding at the moment slaves within the wavering border states, the Emancipation Proclamation, nevertheless, arrayed the power of the Federal Government finally, decisively, and irrevocably against the monstrous system of chattel slavery and decreed its deliberate and definite doom.

Awaiting this proclamation on the evening of that historic day, on the platform of Tremont Temple in Boston, was none other than Frederick Douglass, the outstanding leader and dedicated representative of the slaves and of the partially free but still oppressed Afro-American people.

This scene was not without poetic fitness, since it was in Boston some thirty-three years before that William Lloyd Garrison had boldly unfurled the flag of "immediate and unconditional emancipation." Boston had witnessed many memorable battles against pro-slavery bigots, yet it had remained in the forefront of the struggle to liberate the slaves.

"At last," Douglass later wrote about this assembly of some 3,000 persons which awaited the Emancipation Proclamation, "when patience was well-nigh exhausted, and suspense was becoming agony, a man (I think it was Judge Russell) with hasty step advanced through the crowd, and with a face fairly illumined with the news he bore, exclaimed in tones that thrilled all hearts, 'It is coming! It is on the wires!' " The overjoyed assembly broke into rapturous acclamation and repaired at midnight to the Twelfth Baptist Church there to continue the grand celebration until near daybreak.

Such was the nature, as described by Douglass, of that "worthy celebration of the first step on the part of the nation in its departure from the thraldom of ages." Similar celebrations were held by Afro-Americans during the entire ensuing month throughout the North. Frederick Douglass travelled as far West as Chicago addressing these fitting observances of what he has called "a day for poetry and song."

With these celebrations now recalled before our minds, we may well consider whether there have been commensurate observances organized by us of the recent Hundredth Anniversary of the Emancipation Proclamation. For the lessons of the past are necessary to prepare a people to meet the challenge of the present and the immediate future ahead. Have these lessons been resumed and spread abroad for the enlightenment and inspiration of the people, especially our youth today? Are these lessons being applied in the struggle now in progress?

A disturbing commentary on the present situation is the deplorable fact that very little indeed has been heard of the illustrious name and historic role of the Great Emancipator—Frederick Douglass. Yet none other contributed in greater measure toward the great consummation of freedom from the searing shackles of blighting chattel bondage than this self-taught, fugitive, and indomitable ex-slave.

Without detracting from any other abolitionist or anti-slavery figure, it is true and proper to say that when Frederick Douglass escaped from slavery in 1838, and three years later joined the ranks of the abolitionist fighters, a new dimension was thereby added to this movement. No longer was this simply a voice *for* the slaves; it now projected as well the voice *of* the slaves, speaking through the powerful, convincing, and compelling words of their most conscious, discerning, and devoted representative.

Through the long and arduous years up to the issuance of the Emancipation Proclamation, Douglass had labored and fought for the abolition of chattel slavery and for full human rights and citizenship status for his people. Lecturing and travelling at first for the Massachusetts Anti-Slavery Society, the self-emancipated slave had to face and circumvent or overcome indifference, prejudice, and hostility. In Pendleton, Indiana, Douglass was beaten unconscious and left for dead on the field by a brutal mob.

While there was much encouragement, aid, and good fellowship in the ranks of the Abolitionist movement, Douglass also encountered efforts on the part of some of the chief leaders to restrict him to the bare recital of his experience as a slave. "Give us the facts," said Collins, "we will take care of the philosophy." "Tell your story, Frederick," Garrison and others would urge.

But he who had early questioned "Why am I a slave?", who had striven to learn to read and to write despite the slaveholders' law and all obstacles, who had forcibly resisted the slave-breaker Covey, and who had torn himself from the grip of slavery, was not thus to be held back. "I was now reading and thinking," Douglass later informed us, "It did not entirely satisfy me to narrate wrongs; I felt like denouncing them. . . . Besides, I was growing and needed room. . . . These excellent friends were actuated by the best of motives and were not altogether wrong in their advice; and still I must speak just the word that seemed to me the word to be spoken by me."

Thus early did Douglass develop and display those sterling qualities of leadership which were to elevate him continuously and to ennoble his long and great career. His able denunciations of slavery soon made it necessary for him to write his *Narrative* in 1845, and this led to his successful tour of England, Scotland, Ireland, and Wales. In turn this led to the purchase of his manumission by English anti-slavery friends who also provided financial assistance for his project to establish a newspaper as the mouthpiece of his people.

When on his return to "the land of bondage," Garrison opposed the founding of "another anti-slavery paper," Frederick Douglass retired from Lynn, Mass. to Rochester, N.Y., where he launched the *North Star* in 1847. Changing the name to *Frederick Douglass' Paper* and with the help of friends, notably the Englishwoman Julia Griffiths, Douglass succeeded "to keep my Anti-Slavery banner steadily flying during all the conflict from the autumn of 1847 till the Union of the States was assured and Emancipation was a fact accomplished."

Active in defending and aiding others to freedom, this militant fugitive slave made his house in Rochester a chief station of the Underground Railroad, working with Harriet Tubman, Sojourner Truth, and other courageous anti-slavery workers. Douglass fearlessly counselled armed resistance to recapture when the Fugitive Slave Law was enacted in 1850. In his own home he gave refuge and later safe conduct to the three heroic Afro-American fighters, who, led by Parker at Christiana, Penn., had shot dead the pursuing slaveholder Gorsuch, wounded his son, and driven off the "officers of the law."

Yet Douglass always counselled his people to work and earn money, to learn trades, to practice temperance and thrift, and to develop business enterprise. An early advocate of industrial education (not however like Booker T. Washington in opposition to or instead of higher education) Frederick Douglass planned to establish a Manual Labor School. But this had to be abandoned when the necessary funds could not be raised.

Another aspect of his extraordinary capacity for leadership was demonstrated when Douglass, following a prolonged debate with another ex-slave leader, Samuel Ringgold Ward, abandoned the Garrisonian view of the constitutionality of slavery. From that moment Douglass realized that moral suasion alone was insufficient to overthrow slavery, and thus devoted himself to political action as the prime necessity as well. Hence, while he aided John Brown, Douglass did not join in the raid on Harper's Ferry.

Hunted nevertheless in that connection by United States marshals for the State of Virginia, Douglass escaped through Canada to Britain. There he renewed his Anti-Slavery work and laid the basis for the *Slave's Appeal to Great Britain* which he issued later in 1862. This appeal gave needed additional force to the great efforts made by John Bright and Karl Marx to keep Britain from intervening in the American Civil War on the side of the Confederate southern slave states.

Frederick Douglass now rose to the height of his career as statesman without portfolio. Through profound political analysis and sagacious foresight, Douglass resolutely pressed for the policy which Lincoln's administration finally adopted. While the Garrisonians mistakenly avowed the policy: "Let the erring sisters depart in peace," Douglass was convinced and "spoke as I believed, all over the North, that the mission of the war was the liberation of the slave, as well as the salvation of the Union."

"Hence, from the first," Douglass wrote in his *Life and Times*, "I reproached the North that they fought the rebels with only one hand, when they might strike effectually with two—that they fought with their soft white hand, while they kept their black iron hand chained and helpless behind them—that they fought the effect, while they protected the cause, and that the Union cause would never prosper till the war assumed an Anti-Slavery attitude, and the Negro was enlisted on the loyal side."

When Lincoln finally realized the necessity and adopted the policy pressed by Douglass: "Free the slaves and arm the blacks," Douglass issued on March 2, 1863, his historic call: "Men of Color, To Arms!" But when in August it became apparent that the heroic Afro-American soldiers were being discriminated against by the Government in pay, promotion, fatigue duty, and retaliatory protective measures, Frederick Douglass resigned from recruiting in an open letter to Major Stearns.

Urged by Stearns, Douglass took his protest directly to Lincoln at the White House who promised remedial measures, whereupon Douglass resumed recruiting. Some 200,000 brave black soldiers enlisted voluntarily and fought heroically in some of the bloodiest battles of the Civil War, bringing victory to the Union army as the decisive force.

Do we hereby seek to divest Abraham Lincoln of the title "Great Emancipator"? Not in the least. For if Douglass, as the best representative of the slaves and of Afro-American freemen, merited this encomium, so also did Lincoln as the chief political representative of the great majority of the European American people. True, Abraham Lincoln was slow in coming to his great decision to use the executive power to strike down the vile system of slavery; he was driven by events, moved by considerations of political expediency and military necessity, and pressured by Douglass and others. Yet Lincoln finally accomplished as an "act of justice" what no president before him had even considered, namely, the issuance of the proclamation which began the emancipation of four million human chattel slaves, and which was completed constitutionally when the Thirteenth Amendment was ratified on December 18, 1865.

The role of Abraham Lincoln as a great emancipator has been carefully weighed and evaluated by Frederick Douglass in the *Oration at the Unveiling of the Freedmen's Monument to Lincoln in Washington, D.C. on April 14, 1876.* This role was shared by several, such as Frederick Douglass, Harriet Tubman, John Brown, William Lloyd Garrison, Wendell Phillips, Charles Sumner, and Thaddeus Stevens.

This honored role of emancipator must be recognized as due also to the chief Abolitionists of Great Britain and other countries, and to him who was, perhaps, the greatest of them all—Toussaint Louverture, the incomparable leader of the Haitian Revolution of 1791–1804. For as Douglass has indicated, it was this first successful slave revolution in history which first called a halt to the infamous slave traffic and opened the glorious epoch of emancipation and national liberation of people of African descent.

After the Civil War and through the Reconstruction period, Douglass continued to lead the struggle for civil rights, the vote, and full manhood status. This may be followed in his *Life and Times* and in *Frederick Douglass* by Benjamin Quarles. Space permits now only the barest mention of his leading role in the National Convention of Colored Men which met in Syracuse, N.Y. on October 4, 1864, pursuant to a Call which declared that events "demand of us to be united in council, labor and faith." Might we not begin to prepare now—leaders, organizations, and people—for a Mammoth United Convention to be held on the hundredth anniversary of that date?

Mention must certainly be made of the breadth of Douglass's sympathies and views, and his support of all valid struggles of his time for human liberation and improvement: temperance, woman's rights, the labor movement, freedom for all oppressed nations and peoples. A consistent opponent of imperial subjugation, Douglass opposed the Mexican War of 1848 and gave staunch support to the struggle for the independence of Cuba in the early 1870's.

Mistaken, however, in his support of annexation of Santo Domingo as a state in 1871. Douglass was swayed by the thought that the abolition of slavery by the United States ought necessarily to lead to a more enlightened and liberal foreign policy. Appointed Minister to Haiti in 1889, Douglass administered his office as an upholder of American democratic pronouncements, and would not lend himself to any designs upon Haitian interests or sovereignty.

The high esteem in which Frederick Douglass was held by the Haitian government and people was shown when he was appointed Haitian Commissioner at the World's Columbian Exposition at Chicago in 1893. Following the death of Frederick Douglass on February 20, 1895, the Haitian government contributed the largest amount of the fund raised by J. W. Thompson to erect a monument to Douglass in Rochester, N.Y.

Significantly, while in England, Frederick Douglass recognized as "the greatest hindrance to the adoption of Abolition principles . . . the low estate everywhere in that country (U.S.A.) placed upon the Negro as a man; . . . The grand thing to be done, therefore, was to change this estimation. . . ." With our knowledge today of the vicious effect of smear lables, to change this estimation requires changing the name "Negro," the evil stigma which grew out of slavery and still brands all those so called for oppression and ultimate destruction.

As we move into the second century after emancipation from chattel slavery, determined to complete the work of liberation, enfranchisement, and the achievement of unsullied human dignity, an essential part of our struggle is the insistence upon a good name, properly connected with land, history, and culture—Afro-American.

Facing the future with firm resolve and heads erect, we may well say with the poet, Paul Laurence Dunbar, who had personal knowledge of the generosity and grandeur of the great humanist and liberator:

> Oh, Douglass, thou hast passed
> beyond the shore,
> But still thy voice is ringing o'er
> the gale!
> Thou'st taught thy race how high
> her hopes may soar,
> And bade her seek the heights,
> nor faint, nor fail.

AFRO-AMERICANS AND THIRD PARTY MOVEMENTS

WCBS-TV broadcast, Black Heritage Series, March 18, 1969. Manuscript, Richard B. Moore Papers.

The domination of "race" in politics clearly contradicts the democratic principles affirmed in the Declaration of Independence and the Constitution of the United States. The essence of these democratic principles was succinctly stated by Abraham Lincoln in his Reply to Senator Douglas at Peoria, Illinois, on October 16, 1854, thus: "No man is good enough to rule another man without that other man's consent. I say this is the leading principle,—the sheet-anchor of American republicanism." In like manner,

Frederick Douglass, the fugitive slave who became a statesman, pointed to "the elective franchise as the one great power by which all civil rights are obtained, enjoyed, and maintained under our form of government."

"Race" distinction in politics and disfranchisement based thereon constitute a harmful legacy from the "peculiar institution" of chattel slavery. The slave was not allowed to vote, since as a human personality the slave was considered to be nothing. But according to a compromise written into the United States Constitution at the behest of slave-holders, the slave was counted as three-fifths of a person in the appointment of Congressional Representatives of the slave-holding states.

As a result of petition and pressure, some free Afro-Americans were early accorded the right to vote; the action of the Afro-American builder and navigator, Paul Cuffe, and his brothers in Massachusetts was a significant instance of such successful struggle. In New York, however, discriminatory tests for residence and property qualifications imposed during 1821, had brought about the disfranchisement of most Afro-American citizens.

Despite such political discrimination, the fugitive slave Abolitionist leader, Frederick Douglass, became convinced of the necessity of political action in order to put an end to the chattel slave system. Accordingly, Frederick Douglass participated in the Free Soil Convention held in Buffalo, New York, in 1848. Attending this Convention also were several other militant Afro-American leaders of that period: Samuel Ringgold Ward, Henry Highland Garnet, Charles L. Remond, and Henry Bibb. All except Remond, who was born free in Salem, Massachusetts of an immigrant Afro-Caribbean father, had risked their lives to escape from slavery into the North where they then took active and leading roles in the movement to abolish the chattel slave system.

The Convention and founding of the Free Soil Party was deemed necessary to advance anti-slavery political organization, since the Liberty Party which had existed from 1840 no longer appeared capable of further growth or forward movement. Assessing the Free Soil Party in retrospect, Frederick Douglass wrote in his *Life and Times:* "It was a powerful link in the chain of events by which the slave system has been abolished, the slave emancipated, and the country saved from dismemberment."

Both major parties of that period, the Whig Party and the Democratic Party, were wholly committed to the maintenance of chattel slavery. Hence a third party appeared to be the only means of effective political action toward the abolition of the chattel slave system. In its turn, however, the Free Soil Party had to give way to the broader Republican Party which presented a national ticket in 1856 with John C. Frémont as its candidate for President. Frémont then carried eleven states and polled 1,341,264 votes. Four years later on a platform of resistance to the extension of slavery and with Abraham Lincoln as its standard-bearer, the Republican Party was elected into office. The Republican Party was thus transformed into a major party, while the Whig Party soon disappeared from the political scene. Through his paper and on the public platform Frederick Douglass greatly aided the election of Abraham Lincoln.

When the Southern states seceded and unleashed the Civil War in 1861, Frederick Douglass urged upon the North: "Make the war an abolition war! Free the slaves and arm the blacks!" But time and events were needed to bring Lincoln and his cabinet to realize that it was indeed a matter of stern military necessity to adopt this policy in order to win the war and save the Union.

After victory was brought to the Union armies through the decisive fighting force of some 200,000 Afro-American soldiers, Frederick Douglass and other free-spirited leaders urged and demanded that the vote and all other democratic rights be assured to the Afro-Americans who had begun to emerge from the prison-house of bondage.

In pursuance of such enfranchisement Frederick Douglass, together with George T. Downing, led a delegation in 1866 to President Andrew Johnson who had become chief executive of the nation after the woeful assassination of Abraham Lincoln. This delegation also addressed the Senate, urging the defeat of a proposed measure which would have made it optional whether any state or states should or should not accord the vote to Afro-American citizens. In opposition to this measure which would have opened the way to disfranchisement, Douglass, Downing and other members of this delegation, pressed upon Republican legislators "the wisdom and duty of impartial suffrage."

Later in 1866 Douglass was elected by his fellow-citizens of Rochester, New York, as their delegate to the National Loyalists' Convention which met in Philadelphia composed chiefly of Republicans. Refusing the request of certain fearful and prejudice-ridden Republicans that he stay out of this Convention, Douglass duly attended. Together with Theodore Tilton, Anna E. Dickinson, and others, Douglass succeeded in causing this Convention to declare for enfranchisement of the Afro-American freedmen.

But the enfranchisement of Afro-Americans in the South, during the first phase of the Reconstruction period after the Civil War, was partial and short-lived. By fraud and farce Afro-American citizens were deprived of the right to vote and to hold public office, as indeed of well nigh all other democratic rights. The terrorist reaction of the former rebel slave-holders triumphed through secret and violent organizations such as the Ku Klux Klan and the White Camelias. The Thirteenth, Fourteenth, and Fifteenth Amendments to the Constitution failed utterly to guarantee freedom, the right to vote, and other democratic rights. The essential content of this Reconstruction period was summed up by Frederick Douglass thus: "The old master was offended to find the Negro, whom he lately possessed the right to enslave and flog to toil, casting a ballot equal to his own, and resorted to all sorts of measures, violence, and crime to dispossess him of this point of equality."

The so-called "gentlemen's agreement," concluded at the Wormley Hotel in Washington, D.C., determined that the uncontested seating of Rutherford B. Hayes as President should be followed by the withdrawal of federal forces from the South. This deal signalized the abandonment by the powerful financial and industrial interests of the North of their erstwhile Afro-American allies to the tender mercies of the former slave-driving, confederate, "white supremacists" of the South.

By the year 1889 this process of disfranchisement and suppression was well-nigh complete. Let it be noted, nevertheless, that the flouting of the human rights and basic interests of Afro-American citizens by both major parties has inclined many Afro-Americans to look hopefully and to give considerable support to third party movements.

During the rise in the 1880's of the Peoples' or Populist Party, a third party movement mainly of poorer white farmers of the West and South, it appeared for a time that these Euro-American farmers would ally themselves with the Afro-American freedmen to secure a measure of political power, in order to protect their economic interests. Faced with a sharp drop in the price of their chief product, cotton, and at the same time with increased costs for railroad transportation and manufactured goods, these farmers were forced to borrow from banks at high interest rates and to mortgage their farms which were then often lost through foreclosures. Alliance with labor forces led to the projection of a national ticket by the Peoples' Party in 1892. The Populist candidate James B. Weaver polled over a million votes and carried six states west of the Mississippi. As a consequence, however, the Republican Party lost the election.

The Fusion of Populists with Republicans in 1894 led to the control of the state legislature of North Carolina. Many of these Republicans were Afro-Americans and numerous Afro-American magistrates were appointed by the Fusion legislature. In local areas the Fusion forces opened office to Afro-American deputy sheriffs, to several policemen in Wilmington, to policemen and eldermen in New Bern, and to a collector of the Port of Wilmington. These Fusion forces in North Carolina also achieved the election to the House of Representatives in 1896 of George H. White, the last Afro-American Congressman of that period.

But the Populist Party soon succumbed to the narrow and fatal notion that it was being hampered by the "Negro" question, and that it could itself wield the balance of power in the South if Afro-Americans were completely shut out of politics. The Populists then joined in the drive for "white supremacy." The decline and collapse of the Populist Party followed rapidly.

The Populist leader Tom Watson of Georgia, who had previously taken a forthright stand against race-prejudice, discrimination, disfranchisement, and lynching, now joined in degrading Afro-American citizens and in the open advocacy of all the oppressive measures which he had formerly denounced as reactionary. Now himself thoroughly reactionary, Watson bracketed Catholics, Socialists, and Jews with Negroes in his catalogue of hate.

With this abandonment of democratic principles and adoption of racist repression on the part of the leadership of the Populist Party, the last, best opportunity of those dreadful decades was tragically lost. Racism had destroyed for a long time the possibility of uniting American citizens of whatever color to work together in the rebuilding of society on a human and equitable basis, rewarding alike to citizens of African origin as well as to those of European derivation.

The third party movement led by Theodore Roosevelt launched the Progressive Party in 1912. Catering to the demand growing among the people for regulation and control of the big financial and industrial interests, Theodore Roosevelt advocated reforms, which seemed to promise some betterment to the farmers, small businessmen, and workingmen. Theodore Roosevelt had succeeded to the presidency in 1901 following upon the slaying of McKinley. But Roosevelt had done nothing effective as president to enforce the constitutional right of Afro-Americans to vote in the South, hence their considerable voting power remained largely nullified.

Besides, the summary action taken by Theodore Roosevelt as president in the Brownsville, Texas, affair, had caused many Afro-Americans throughout the country to doubt his fairness and dependability. For Roosevelt dishonorably discharged an entire battalion of Afro-American soldiers of the Twenty-fifth Regiment, following the involvement of a few of these soldiers in a shooting foray with prejudiced white supremacists in that town. Moreover, Roosevelt encouraged the building of the Progressive Party as a lily-white organization in the South.

The Democratic candidate for president in 1908, Woodrow Wilson, adopted most of the "progressive" measures advocated by Theodore Roosevelt. In a letter to Bishop Alexander Walters, Woodrow Wilson declared his "earnest wish to see justice done the colored people in every matter and not mere grudging justice, but justice executed with liberality and cordial good feeling." This campaign promise caused even the keen Dr. W. E. B. Du Bois to resign from the Socialist Party and to urge the election of Wilson in the *Crisis* magazine. As the sequel showed, Wilson's pre-election pledge was utterly false, since such prejudicial practices as segregation and discrimination were intensified against Afro-American federal employees under his administration. But such false promises served their purpose in garnering the votes which elected Woodrow Wilson president and defeated Theodore Roosevelt. The Bull Moose Progressive Party, lacking the spoils of patronage, soon passed out of existence when Teddy Roosevelt advised his followers to return to the Republican Party.

Another third party of similar liberal and progressive type was formed in 1924 and nominated Senator Robert M. La Follette for the presidency. Called the Conference for Political Action, but popularly known as the

Farmer-Labor Party, this party represented a coalition of farmer groups, workers' organizations, dissatisfied liberals, radicals from both major parties, and some socialists. Based chiefly upon the insurgent farmers of the West, this third party was unable to affect the political situation of the Afro-Americans in the South. Despite some support of Afro-Americans in the North and West, the Farmer-Labor Party polled 4.8 million votes, but carried only the state of Wisconsin.

This brings us now to third party movements which have advocated fundamental changes in the economic and social structure. In the latter half of the nineteenth century, socialist workers' organizations developed among German-American workers in New York. The International Workingmen's Association was formed in 1867, as a section of the First International of which Karl Marx was a prominent leader. Karl Marx and John Bright had organized great meetings of workers and middle-class people respectively, which prevented the British Prime Minister from intervening on the side of the Southern slave-holding Confederates. Such actions followed upon appeals made by Afro-American leaders, such as Frederick Douglass' Appeal to the People of Great Britain. Despite great suffering from unemployment due to a shortage of raw cotton for the textile factories, the English workingmen opposed any support from their government to the Southern slave-holders. Replying to the Address of the Workingmen of Worcester, England, President Lincoln acknowledged their "decisive utterances on this question as an instance of sublime Christian heroism which has not been surpassed in any age or in any country."

The first political party known to advocate socialist ideas in the United States was the Social Party of New York and Vicinity. Its platform in 1868 presented two planks of direct interest to Afro-Americans: the demand for the repeal of all discriminatory laws, and the requirements that all citizens be eligible for public office. The Social Party was soon disbanded to make way for the Labor Reform Party backed by the National Labor Union. Significant in this period was the nomination in 1872, by a section of the International Workingmen's Association on a national ticket, of the Afro-American leader Frederick Douglass as candidate for the Vice-President as the running-mate of Victoria Woodhull for President. Because of factional conflict, this ticket was not brought before the voters in the ensuing election. An important precedent had been set nevertheless, by the nomination of an Afro-American for the office next to the highest in the nation.

Socialist organizations soon developed in various cities. Many of these suffered disagreements and splits while striving for unity but were successful at times. Out of the uniting of certain of these groups, the Socialist Labor Party emerged in 1877 and has continued to function until now. Disdaining all partial improvement in the lot of the people as reformist, the Socialist Labor Party concentrated almost wholly upon propaganda for the total reconstruction of society. As a result this party has never influenced any considerable section of workers, nor concerned itself with any specific measures to ameliorate the lot of the particularly disadvantaged Afro-American people.

At the beginning of this century, a group withdrew from the Socialist Labor Party and sought unification with the Social Democratic Party. In July 1901 these and other socialist groups, except followers of the Socialist Labor Party, founded the Socialist Party of America. After settling the moot question of immediate versus ultimate demands by deciding to adopt both, the fledgling socialist body was thrown into sharp debate over a proposed resolution of sympathy with "the Negro race." A chief leader Morris Hillquit objected to "singling out the Negro race especially." A supporter of the resolution spelt out the discrimination, disfranchisement, and lynching which Afro-Americans especially suffered. A resolution was finally adopted which expressed kinship with "our Negro fellow-workers" and invited them to join the new party.

No positive or direct action was taken, however, by the Socialist Party against the oppression imposed upon the Afro-American people. On the contrary, a leading socialist, Victor Berger of Milwaukee, wrote in the *Social Democratic Herald* of May 31, 1902, that "negroes and mulattoes constitute a lower race." An editorial of this paper also branded "Negroes" as "inferior depraved degenerates." In contrast to this vicious racism, nevertheless, the outstanding standard-bearer of the Socialist Party, Eugene V. Debs, repeatedly denounced "race" prejudice and refused to speak to segregated audiences.

Yet dedicated as Debs was to human freedom, he did not recognize the need for special measures against the oppression of Afro-Americans. Debs thus declared that only socialism would solve such problems as discrimination and lynching. Not until World War I did the Socialist Party take any official stand against "race" discrimination. In 1902 Debs polled 917,999 votes, the highest number cast up to that time for the Socialist Party.

A firmer position against racist discrimination was taken by the Industrial Workers of the World which was founded in 1905. Though not a political party, the I.W.W. as it was popularly known, embraced political action, being allied for a time with the Socialist Party. In the South as well as the North and West, the I.W.W. strove to organize Afro-American workers, and insisted upon their right to equal status with all other workers, despite prevailing prejudice and laws imposing segregation. According to Ben Fletcher, an Afro-American officer of the I.W.W., out of a million membership cards issued during its most active period, some 100,000 were accorded to Afro-American workers. Regarding this as a direct class question, the I.W.W. therefore mounted no specific campaigns against racist attacks upon the Afro-American people.

Further consideration will be given to Third Party Movements in an ensuing presentation on "Afro-Americans and Radical Politics."

AFRO-AMERICANS AND RADICAL POLITICS

WCBS-TV broadcast, Black Heritage Series, March 19, 1969. Manuscript, Richard B. Moore Papers.

The term "radical," as qualifying "politics," has been too often misunderstood to mean a horrible and violent extremism, or an extremist who menaces everything good and decent in human life, and therefore a dangerous "ism" or creature who ought to be put out of the way by any and every force possible. As here used, however, the term "radical" means simply its original signification, i.e. "of or pertaining to the root," as derived from the Latin *radix* meaning root. Hence "radical" here refers to a program, or an advocate of a program, which proposes basic change in the economic, social, and political order.

A "radical" in relation to chattel slavery, for example, was one who advocated, not partial measures to limit the slaveholders' punishment, or to require an increase in the food and clothing of the slave, but who demanded abolition of the system of chattel slavery and its replacement by another system such as the free wage labor system.

In respect to the system of capitalism or the private ownership of the basic economic and productive forces of society and their operation for the profit of the owners, a "radical" is one who advocates the replacement of the capitalist system by a socialist order of society, which is generally held to mean the common ownership and management by the people of the socially necessary means of production and their operation for human use rather than for private profit.

In this sense, then, the *Messenger* magazine and the group of Afro-American socialists, who conducted and supported it in Harlem, were properly called "radical." Indeed, in its prospectus of 1917 the *Messenger* declared itself "the only magazine of Scientific Radicalism in the world published by Negroes." Its basic position was set forth in an editorial entitled "The Cause and Remedy for Race Riots" which stated:

> Revolution must come. By that we mean a complete change in the organization of society. Just as absence of industrial democracy is productive of riots and race clashes, so the introduction of industrial democracy will be the longest step toward removing that cause. When no profits are to be made from race friction, no one will longer be interested in stirring up race prejudice. The quickest way to stop a thing or to destroy an institution is to destroy the profitableness of that institution. The capitalist system must go and its going must be hastened by the workers themselves.

"Radical politics," then, has to do with the thorough-going nature of the ends sought and the means used to achieve these basic ends. . . .

In Harlem from about 1917 on a branch of the Socialist Party, the 21st Assembly District, composed almost wholly of Afro-Americans, functioned vigorously. Prior to this there had been such able, eloquent, and singular pioneer Afro-American advocates of Socialism as Helen Holman and Hubert H. Harrison.

Hubert H. Harrison, who had come from the Virgin Islands, was a man of exceptional intellect and wide knowledge. Studies in economics and sociology had led him to socialism and he soon became a leader in the socialist movement. Along with Elizabeth Gurley Flynn, Bill Haywood, and Morris Hillquit, Harrison was active in organizing silk workers in Patterson, N.J., and he was an instructor at the Modern School. But becoming dissatisfied with some of the socialists' attitude on the "race" question, Harrison left them for the Harlem scene. From 1917 on Harrison conducted a "university outdoors," speaking evening after evening on various subjects, particularly aspects of "race" in its world context and the history and achievements of people of African origin and descent everywhere.

Hubert Harrison organized the Liberty League of Afro-Americans and published *The Voice* as the organ of this movement. More than any other man of his time, he inspired and educated the masses of Afro-Americans then flocking into Harlem. It was Harrison, too, who gave Marcus Garvey his first significant introduction to the people of Harlem at the Liberty League mass meeting held in Bethel A.M.E. Church. In the foreword to his booklet *When Africa Awakes*, Harrison later spoke with truth of the period before Garvey "when the foundations were laid."

While Hubert Harrison moved more and more toward the position of "race first," a score of young, militant, and studious Afro-Americans were actively propagating Socialism, while at the same time examining its philosophy and possible practical application for the removal of the ills which they suffered along with their people. These youthful Afro-American seekers after knowledge and power studied diligently together on Sunday mornings *The Communist Manifesto, Socialism Utopian and Scientific,* and other writings of Marx and Engels. Through the People's Educational Forum on Sunday afternoons, they discussed events, inviting as speakers Afro-American intellectuals like Dr. W. E. B. Du Bois, anthropologists like Franz Boas, and Socialist spokesmen like Algernon Lee.

From the street corners of Harlem these youthful Afro-American socialists spoke out against the wrongs inflicted upon their people and pointed to socialism as a means for the complete liberation of all oppressed mankind. They sought, though with only partial success, to apply Socialist theory as a method of social analysis to the Afro-American situation and to that of oppressed colonial peoples in Africa, the Caribbean, and elsewhere. Often the question would be put as they were about to begin their meetings: "What shall we expound tonight, straight Socialism or Negro-ology?" Obviously, socialism had not yet been extended to a thorough analysis and comprehension of the special situation of the Afro-American people.

A dedicated and courageous group, these Afro-American socialists were seeking human status and full freedom. Only occasionally did leaders like Chandler Owen and A. Philip Randolph appear at these street meetings; these well-known socialists were more occupied with the editing of the *Messenger* magazine. The roster of the regular street speakers included W. A. Domingo, Otto E. Huiswoud, Rudolph Smith, Frank Poree, Anna Jones, Elizabeth Hendrickson, Frank R. Crosswaith, Herman Whaley, John Patterson, Victor C. Gaspar, Thomas Potter, Ramsay, and the present speaker.

In a vigorous campaign during 1918 around the candidacies of Rev. George Frazier Miller for Congress and Grace P. Campbell* for the State Assembly, the Socialist street speakers won 25 per cent of the Harlem vote. Rev. George Frazier Miller was a highly cultured yet socially conscious Protestant Episcopal minister of the caliber of his distinguished predecessor Alexander Crummell. Grace P. Campbell was a humanitarian social worker who maintained, largely from her own earnings, a needed home for deserted young mothers. The nomination of the first Afro-American candidate for Congress, since the post-Reconstruction period, on a radical party ticket, was significant in establishing a precedent which was to be carried to success with the election of Adam Clayton Powell, Jr. Similarly the nomination of an Afro-American for Borough President of New York City, on a radical party ticket, paved the way to the nomination on the major party tickets of such candidates, and led to the election of Hulan E. Jack and other Afro-American notables who have followed in that high office.

Seeking to discover whether the Socialist Party would furnish any significant force for the organization of their victimized people, the Afro-American socialists asked the Euro-American socialist leader Algernon Lee at a session of their Harlem Forum: "What program does the Socialist Party have for organizing the Afro-Americans, especially in the South?" Algernon Lee answered that the Socialist Party was the party of the proletariat, that by proletariat Marx meant the workers in industry, that the Socialist Party did not have enough forces to carry through this primary task and therefore had no forces to organize the Negroes. Though such organization was needed, said Lee, it would have to be done by some other bodies or by the Negroes themselves.

Algernon Lee was therefore soundly condemned for his doctrinaire position by the militant Afro-American socialists. The disciplinary attempt which followed by the Socialist Party District Committee further served to convince most of the Afro-American activists in the Harlem branch that the Socialist Party, as then controlled, had little or nothing to contribute to the solution of the situation of racist oppression in America, and, accordingly, these withdrew from the Socialist Party. The few who remained were apparently swayed by the prospect of getting some support in leadership

*Editors' note: Grace Campbell was a candidate in 1920.

careers from the Socialist Party or such organizations as followed its leadership.

But before the curtain thus came down on this activity under the aegis of
the Socialist Party, the Afro-American militants had played a not in-
considerable role. They had thus gained the attention of the *Crisis* magazine, organ of the N.A.A.C.P., which in an article of March, 1920, noted:
"For the first time in the Negro's history, he has a Left Wing or Radical
Group."

A significant radical action was the challenging of a court injunction
which prohibited the Colored Motion Picture Operators Union from activity to secure employment for its members in the Lafayette Theater in
Harlem. Though the arrest of the spokesman for the right to employment
and free speech was upheld by another court, the presence of the people
became such that this Jim Crow exclusion was soon ended and Afro-
American motion picture operators began to be employed.

A radical publication, and an influential force while it appeared, was the
Emancipator, edited and promoted by W. A. Domingo and Richard B.
Moore. Challenging editorials written by Cyril V. Briggs appeared in the
Amsterdam News during 1918. Soon thereafter Cyril V. Briggs launched the
Crusader magazine as the organ of the African Blood Brotherhood. These
activities together gave rise to a cultural and social climate which caused
Harlem to be known as "The Mecca of the New Negro." The movements
which soon followed were nurtured in this cultural climate and militant
temper which had been developed by the Harlem radicals and socialists.

Seldom recognized or understood, this relation of the preceding radicals
to the Universal Negro Improvement Association has been noted by a
well-known statesman and critic. Secretary of the National Association for
the Advancement of Colored People during this period, James Weldon
Johnson set down his considered conclusion in the book, *Black Manhattan,*
published in 1930 as follows:

> The Harlem radicals failed to bring about a correlation of the forces they
> had called into action, to have those forces work through a practical medium
> to a definite objective; but they did much to prepare the ground for a man
> who could and did do that, a man who was one of the most remarkable and
> picturesque figures that have appeared on the American scene—Marcus
> Garvey.

In the case of the Harlem Literary Renaissance it is obvious that the first
to appear to herald this renaissance was Claude McKay. This Afro-
Jamaican poet wrote in reaction to the monstrous lynchings of the American scene the famous impassioned sonnet "If We Must Die" which he
concluded:

> Like men we'll face the murderous cowardly pack,
> Pressed to the wall, dying, but fighting back!

Later, in response to the Russian Revolution, McKay wrote in "Exhortation: Summer 1919" the following clarion call:

> In the East the clouds grow crimson with the new
> dawn that is breaking,
> And its golden glory fills the Western skies.
> . . . .
> O my brothers, dreaming for long centuries,
> Wake from sleeping; to the East turn, turn
> your eyes!

The poet Claude McKay was, for a time, one of the editors of the radical *Masses* magazine to which journal he contributed a bitter retaliation against the "race" discrimination to which he had been subjected on going to see a play then being shown in Greenwich Village, entitled appropriately enough, "He Who Gets Slapped." McKay accepted an invitation and attended the Fourth Congress of the Communist International as an observer in Moscow during 1922.

That Fourth Congress was attended as an accredited delegate by the first known Afro-American communist in the United States, Otto E. Huiswoud. A migrant from Dutch Guiana, whence also came Jan E. Matzeliger, the inventor of the lasting machine which revolutionized the shoe industry of America, Huiswoud had gone over from the Socialist Party into the more militant Communist Party.

Another Afro-American, who after leaving the Socialist Party later joined the Communist Party, was Lovett Fort-Whiteman. After returning from a trip to Moscow, Fort-Whiteman became National Organizer of the American Negro Labor Congress founded in 1925. But Fort-Whiteman was Bohemian, wearing Russian shirts and boots, and appearing far removed from the workers whom he was expected to organize.

Afro-American militants were slowly attracted to the Communist Party where they constantly pressed for struggle against "race" prejudice, organization of Afro-American workers beginning on the basis of their immediate needs, and for representation on the executive bodies of the Communist Party and of workers' organizations generally.

Meanwhile, Afro-American Communists especially Harry Haywood, while studying in Moscow, and in conjunction with some Russian and other Communists, recognized the semi-colonial features of the condition of Afro-Americans. They moved on further to the position that "Negroes" in the southern United States constituted an oppressed nation, that "Negroes" were concentrated and formed a majority of the population in the Black Belt of the South, and that therefore it was necessary to recognize the right of self-determination for the "Negroes" as a nation in the South. At first rather considerably resisted, this position was in time adopted as the official position of the Communist Party. The League of Struggle for Negro Rights was organized during 1930, on the basis of recognition of this right of self-determination, with Harry Haywood as Secretary. In his book *Negro Liberation* published in 1948, Haywood gave a full statement of his position. But this was somewhat in the nature of a swan song, since the Black Belt was by then far gone in the process of disappearing due to the mass migrations of Afro-Americans to the North and West.

Progress was to come, however, from another direction. The arrest, trial, and sentencing to death of nine Afro-American youths at Scottsboro, Alabama, was met by the development of able legal defense and powerful mass protest. This case was thus connected into an international symbol of struggle against racist persecution and oppression.

Time permits here only a very brief statement. Suffice it to say that as Vice President of the International Labor Defense, the present speaker was connected with the Scottsboro case from its beginning until the last of these youths was released. During this time it was my duty to make four nationwide speaking tours to promote the mass protest deemed essential, and to take a delegation of their mothers to the White House to call for action on the part of President Roosevelt. But there should be recalled here a meeting held at the Civic Club in New York when William Pickens of the N.A.A.C.P. launched a sharp attack against the I.L.D. and the Communists whom he charged with seeking to sacrifice the Scottsboro youths to the Communist cause. Pickens had formerly praised the I.L.D. and the *Daily Worker* for having acted in their defense "more speedily and effectively than all other agencies put together." But being reprimanded by the top leadership of the N.A.A.C.P., Pickens had become an inveterate opponent of the I.L.D. On the contrary Dr. W. E. B. Du Bois called for "stressing our points of agreement rather than those of disagreement." This sage counsel had to be followed at the end when it was necessary to form the Joint Scottsboro Defense Committee with Dr. Alan Chalmers as a leading figure, with Roy Wilkins as a delegate from the N.A.A.C.P. and Anna Damon and myself as representatives of the I.L.D. A powerful force had been added to the Scottsboro defense when William L. Patterson succeeded J. Louis Engdahl as President of the I.L.D. Patterson in the tradition of the abolitionist Wendell Phillips had turned the key in his law office and had gone out to defend the Afro-American victims of racist oppression. This freedom-inspired course was followed by Benjamin J. Davis, Jr. who aided in the defense of the Scottsboro youths and Angelo Herndon, and who later became the first Afro-American Communist in the New York City Council.

As a result of the Scottsboro campaign and the work among the unemployed, the Communist Party attracted numerous Afro-Americans to its support and into its ranks. James W. Ford was elected to the Central Committee of the Communist Party and as its candidate for Vice President in the election campaign of 1932. Ford was a close follower of Robert Minor and then of Earl Browder. This was unwittingly expressed when James W. Ford, at an affair held in Harlem to mark the publication of his book, *The Negro and the Democratic Front*, distressed the Afro-American militants by declaring his dependence upon the Central Committee of the Party and how lost he felt when temporarily placed out of touch with this Committee. With the dropping of the right of self-determination by Earl Browder and the liquidation of work among Afro-Americans in the South, all of which was known to Ford but not revealed to the party generally, the Communist Party began to decline. Despite the efforts of such Afro-American leaders as Pettis Perry, Claudia Jones, and Henry Winston, who were persecuted and jailed in the reactionary McCarthy and Smith Act period, the repression served to reduce and to limit the activity of the Communist Party. The conclusion seems inescapable that so long as racist oppression persists, so long will the more militant Afro-Americans turn to radical parties seeking a solution to the oppressive conditions to which they are subjected.

X

RACISM AND IMPERIALISM

Richard B. Moore had a great concern for semantics and the precise use of words. In his oratory he was keenly aware of the power of words and usually began lectures and articles with clarification of terms. He frequently spoke and wrote passionately against the misuse of words like Negro, black, race, West Indian, savage, and even civilization. As part of his long battle against the concept of race, he organized the Committee to Tell the Truth About the Name "Negro." Out of that effort came a series of lectures that he published as a small book, The Name "Negro"—Its Origin and Evil Use. *It appeared at a critical period when the Afro-American community was in the throes of a search for identity and forcefully debating the inappropriateness of designations such as "Negro" and "Black." Both the cloth and paperback editions were sold quickly and remained out of print despite the many requests for the book. In the final years of his life Moore was in the process of revising it, with the assistance of the present editors. A concise version edited by Joyce Moore Turner follows. She points out, however, that every word in this abbreviated version was written by Moore. It has been shortened for brevity and clarity. None of the original thought has been lost. Moore was convinced that the myth of race emerged as a justification for colonialism, slavery, and oppression. This view runs through all of these lectures, articles, and book reviews.*

The lecture "A New Look at African History" was written before the general academic recognition and acknowledgment of the legitimacy of African history as a field of study. In the introduction Moore not only attacks the systematic use of derogatory terms and false images of a "Dark Continent," but he proposes a unique classification of periods of African history devoid of a Eurocentric perspective. In Caribs, "Cannibals" and Human Relations, *he again places quotation marks around what he considered to be an odious term. This polemic was provoked by a casual visit to the museum at Nelson's Dockyard in Antigua, where he saw a plaque describing the cannibalism attributed to the Caribs. He vigorously rejected the allegation. Since 1973 several other scholars have arrived independently at the same conclusion. In these articles Moore not only traces the genesis of the concept of race and colonialism but also heralds the end of colonialism with the "Passing of Churchill and Empire."*

THE NAME "NEGRO"—ITS ORIGIN AND EVIL USE

Afroamerican Publishers, New York, 1960.

At the outset I think it would be best if I state how I became convinced that a change in this name "Negro" was necessary. I had discussed this matter time and again with several people, because opposition to the name "Negro" has never ceased among people of African descent in this country. This name has never been fully accepted.

I recall some years back—I think it was in the 1920's—when Dr. J. Edmeston Barnes, who had recently come from London, delivered a lecture at the People's Educational Forum then held in the Lafayette Hall in New York City. In the course of his remarks Dr. Barnes said: "The name 'Negro' is a bastard political colloquialism which ought to be rejected."

At the time I thought Dr. Barnes was going rather beyond the requirements of the situation. I thought then, as some still do, unfortunately, that the important thing is the condition, and we had better channel all our energies toward improving our condition, and then the name would automatically take care of itself, because it would then reflect the condition. But I subsequently discovered that view to be very superficial, since that view leaves out of account the working of the human mind through association of ideas: so that when a name which has been connected with images and other associations in the human mind arises in consciousness, it immediately calls forth reactions with which the name is associated.

This association of ideas has been used by cunning oppressors for evil and murderous ends. A practical understanding of this may be gained by considering the pointed axiom: "Give a dog a bad name and you won't need to do the killing; just shout 'mad dog!' and others will kill it surely."

Yet unheedingly for a while I went my way fighting for the freedom of the Scottsboro boys, for civil rights, for social insurance, for all these immediate things, and later striving to spread knowledge of the history and culture of people of African origin and their relations with other peoples of the world through the Frederick Douglass Book Center. Then about the year 1948 I was invited to speak on a program of a so-called "Negro History Week." The speaker before me was a librarian whose subject was "The Negro Woman." She began by referring to a ship—a slave ship—which it is recorded, had landed at a port near Jamestown, Virginia, and twenty "negars" had emerged from the fetid hold of the slave ship. This, if you please, was the origin and the beginning of the history of "The Negro Woman."

Quite obviously this made an impact upon me which was unforgettable. What! thought I, does our history begin with this emergence from the stinking hold of a slave ship? O, no, I decided; this will have to be changed. When I was introduced to speak next, I said: "I am very sorry that I cannot speak to you any more on 'Negro' history, because what I have just heard about the beginning of this so-called 'Negro' history convinces me that we have to make a radical change here. Our history goes back into antiquity, into the very earliest development of the broad and highly structured human cultures of Egypt and Ethiopia and other areas of Africa. My subject then, will be, 'The Role Of Africans In World History.' " From that day to this I have never used this word 'Negro' except as a necessary quotation, and we hope that it will not be necessary even to quote this offensive term much longer.

Let us look back into history, then, and strive to discover the origin of this term "Negro." If you look at the unabridged edition of the *Oxford Dictionary,* you will be shown that the origin of the word "Negro," as far as is known in the English language, is in 1555. Nevertheless, that is not the beginning of the term because the English were not the first transgressors in this respect. The English adopted the word from the Spanish. The Spanish may have gotten it from the Portuguese; it isn't yet quite clear.

Here, parenthetically, I must say that some of us have the idea that history is something recorded correctly, and all you need to do is to go to the proper source, and there you will find the correct answer. This is not so, because history has frequently been written by not too honest people. History has often been written by mercenary scribes to cover up the aggression, plunder, and annexation perpetrated by their feudal or financial overlords. History often reflects the biases of conquerors and rulers and the prejudices of national controversy and of interested disparagement. Because of these biases, it is not so easy to discover the truth.

Frequently, too, primary documents and original narratives have been lost, sometimes carelessly laid aside and even deliberately destroyed it would seem, such as the original chronicle of the Portuguese exploits in Africa written by Cerveira. Mention of this early account was made by the Portuguese historian Joao de Barros who began publishing the *Decades of Asia* in 1552. From the study of "The Age of Discovery" contributed by E. J. Payne, Fellow of University College, Oxford, to the first volume of the *Cambridge Modern History,* 1902, revealing insights are given into this distortion of history by the following statement.

> The economic character of the Iffante's [Prince Henry] enterprise was felt, even in his lifetime, to be so little in accordance with the character which history demands for its heroes, that a contemporary chronicle in the Guinea expeditions, compiled by one Cerveira, is known to have been suppressed, and replaced by the garbled work of Zurara, whose object it was to write the Iffante's panegyric as a great soldier and eminent Christian, and as the patriotic founder of the Greater Portugal which posterity would never cease to associate with his name. As the enterprise assumed larger proportions, the pretence that the negro was captured and shipped to Portugal for the salvation of his soul was abandoned. Even more valuable for commercial purposes, than negro slaves, were the gold and ivory in which the tribes

south of the Gambia River abounded. The Portuguese, who were now expert slave raiders, found that the reward of their enterprise was best secured by disposing of their prey to the chiefs of other tribes, who were ready to give gold and ivory in exchange.

Nevertheless, so far as I have been able to penetrate the mazes of distortion and hypocrisy, it appears to be the Spanish or Portuguese who coined this term "negro" as an adjective meaning black. This seems to have been its first use.

However, the first use of the word "negro" as a noun or name in relation to African people is to be traced back to the period after 1441, when the Portuguese explorers went down the African coast until they reached below the Senegal river. They had referred to the people above that river as Moors or Azenegues. But when they saw the people south of the Senegal, who were of much darker hue and whose weapons were much less powerful than their crossbows and firearms, the Portuguese perceived the possibility of easy conquest and a lucrative slave trade. Thus they began to enslave the African people.

In such a chronicle as that of Azurara, or Zurara, we learn how these slaves were captured, how these good Christian Portuguese knights went ashore burning homes and capturing the people. They took them back to Portugal, and on a significant occasion, presented these captives to Prince Henry, the "Infante" as they called him, the leader of these expeditions. He came into the field riding a charger, and they made a division of the enslaved Africans. Even this official Portuguese chronicler Azurara was compelled to note the fact that the common people of Portugal, who had been given a holiday and brought from various areas to witness this new sight, were moved to tears when they saw the brutal partition and separation of mothers from children and the like.

It was in the development of this infamous, iniquitous, and inhuman slave traffic that the term "negro" was foisted as a noun, as a designation, as a name, upon those who were unfortunate enough to be caught in the clutches of the slave traders. This is the origin of the term "negro." Its origin is vile and infamous. It began in indignity. It began in immorality, and the consciousness and the dignity of man must now rise and dispense with it forever.

If you consult a book like the *Voyages of Cadamosto,* an Italian navigator who took service under Prince Henry of Portugal in these expeditions, you will observe that the book begins by referring to "the land of the Blacks of lower Ethiopia." This narrative was written some time after 1463 and first published in Vicenza in 1507. The English translation by G. R. Crone was published by the Hakluyt Society, London, 1937.

The Europeans knew very little about Africa in those days. As a matter of fact, Prince Henry was able to begin these explorations down the coast of Africa, because he had been instructed by Moors as to the nature of the terrain. The Portuguese, the Spanish, the Italians—indeed the Europeans generally—had received the elements of culture, along with most of the basic, scientific ideas and technical processes which were so significant for European development, from Moorish and Saracen scientists and from Jewish scholars who were intermediaries, which made it possible for them to lose sight of land and navigate on the high seas.

Because of their ignorance of the African continent and peoples at that time, European writers used the term Ethiopian for African. You will observe on some old maps that the name Ethiopian Sea is placed all the way over around the bend of West Africa, even down at the south of Africa. However, as the narrative proceeds, this record of Cadamosto shifts from the terms Blacks or Ethiopians to "negroes" and "negress." This was done as soon as the translator reached the account of the area from which the first slaves had been taken by the Portuguese. Similarly, in the Chronicle of Azurara, as soon as the area south of the Senegal river has been reached, where the modern slave trade was begun by the Portuguese, the designation of the native Africans is changed from Moors or Azenegues to "negros," which was later transposed into English as "negroes."

This *Chronicle of the Discovery and Conquest of Guinea* by Gomes Eannes Azurara states, in the subscript of the oldest manuscript which has come down to us, that it was completed in 1453. The first English translation, made by Beazley and Prestage, was printed for the Hakluyt Society in two volumes, the first of these in 1896. On page 99 of this volume, the first use in this text of the name "negroes" appears in the description of how Dinnis Fernandes Diaz "passed the land of the Moors and arrived in the land of the blacks, that is called Guinea."

> But when the negroes saw that those in the ship were men, they made haste to flee . . . but because our men had a better opportunity than before, they captured four of them, and these were the first to be taken by Christians in their own land. . . .

From this it appears that the term "negros," as a *name for slaves*, was already in use in Portuguese by the year 1453. Translations and reprints must be checked back to the earliest source materials. Due care must also be taken to distinguish the name "negros" as *applied to slaves*, and the term "negros" *simply meaning blacks*. For the same word "negros" was used for both meanings in Portuguese and Spanish, whereas in English "negroes" was generally used for *slaves*, and "blacks" for *simple color designation*.

The usage in the Catalan Atlas or map, dated 1375, is obviously that of "negros" *simply meaning blacks*. The reference there to Musa Mali as "fenyor de los negros de Guineua" is correctly translated "lord of the blacks of Guinea." The accuracy of this translation is confirmed when it is considered that the author of this map, the Jewish cartographer Abraham Cresques, could derive his knowledge of this kingdom of Mali only from the Moors, even if it were secured through some intermediary. For at that time only the Moors went thither over the caravan routes through the Sahara desert. All that area, including the Mali Empire, part of which was later called Guinea, was then known to the Moors in the Arabic language as *Bilad es Sudan,* which properly translated into English is "Land of the Blacks."

If Azurara's Chronicle was completed in 1453 as stated, then it is certain that the terms "negro" and "negros" were in use in Portugal by that date of 1453. Other statements in this Chronicle, cited hereinafter, also point to the use of the term "negros" even as early as 1443. This term "negros" was then used with a new and specific meaning as a name or designation particularly applied to African slaves. These slaves had been captured and brought to Portugal from the land of Guinea, below the Sahara and south of the Senegal river.

From that period onward, this name "negros" was connected to and loaded with vicious and degrading notions of class, "race," and color prejudice. In this way the black color and other physical features of African slaves were identified in the minds of the people generally with ugliness, repulsion, and baseness. By this name "negros," African slaves were thereby branded as bestial and savage, innately inferior, fit by nature only for slavery, and indeed ordained by God himself for perpetual slavery.

The course of the biblical patriarch Noah was accordingly interpreted for this evil purpose by Christian ministers of the gospel of glad tidings and "good will toward men." This curse was declared to be the true and undeniable word of God who had thereby condemned the Africans, said to be the sons of Ham, to perpetual slavery to the Europeans, conveniently held to be the sons of Japheth, and to Asian people, similarly deemed to be the sons of Shem.

Recounting how some of the first Moorish slaves, taken by Antam Gonsalves, were exchanged in 1442 for black slaves, Azurara pointedly declared these to be:

> slaves, in accordance with ancient custom, which I believe to have been because of the curse which, after the Deluge, Noah laid upon his son Cain, cursing him in this way: that his race should be subject to all the other races of the world. And from his race these blacks are descended.

Again, in describing the first considerable group of African slaves brought into Portugal in 1443, Azurara wrote discriminatingly debasing the "negro" slaves on account of color in the following words.

> Amongst them were some white enough, fair to look upon, and well proportioned, others were less white like mulattoes, others again were so black as Ethiops, and so ugly, both in features and in body, as almost to appear (to those who saw them) the images of a lower hemisphere [hell!].

Furthermore, in the edition of Azurara's Chronicle, translated by Bernard Miall, and published in London, 1936, on page 173, still more slanderous statements were resorted to in order to degrade the Africans, then enslaved and labelled "negros."

> I say perdition of their souls, because they were pagans without the light or flame of the holy faith, and of their bodies, because they lived like beasts without any of the customs of rational creatures, since they did not even know what were bread and wine, nor garments of cloth, nor life in the shelter of a home, and worse was their ignorance which deprived them of all knowledge of good, and permitted them only a life of brutish idleness.

As the immense profits to be derived from the slave traffic came to be realized, this shameful trade in human beings increased by leaps and bounds. From that most comprehensive and thorough study of slavery, *History of Slavery from the Most Remote Times to Our Day,* written by the Cuban scholar José Antonio Saco—unfortunately never translated into English—we learn how the companies of Lagos and Arguim were formed, "and after 1448 these two companies traded exclusively with all points of the African coast then discovered."

Soon thousands of African slaves were being brought into Portugal, since these companies "before 1460 already imported into that country annually seven or eight hundred Negroes." Large numbers were early sold into Spain and concentrated in such cities as Salamanca and Seville. So numerous had these Africans become in Seville by 1474, that the Spanish monarchs Ferdinand and Isabella issued a mandate appointing Juan de Valladolid, known as "el conde negro" or the Black Count as "our judge and mayoral of the same Negroes, freedmen and freedwomen."

From this account it may be seen that already the name "negro" had been identified with "slave" and that the annalist Zuñiga made reference to "this captive and despised color." By this time then the term "negro" as a noun, as a name, as a designation for the enslaved Africans, had been very well established. Arising out of these slave mores and customs, this name "negro" was fixed by designing slave masters in the minds of the people generally with vileness and bestiality and loaded with the scorn and hostility which the master has almost always held for the slave.

This development of language according to the requirements of the slave system has been aptly explained by Fernando Ortiz, Professor of Ethnography of the University of Havana, in his enlightening book *The Illusion of Races.* (Again it is to be deplored that this outstanding book has not been translated and thus made available to English-speaking peoples.)

> With the word "race" it happened as with the word "Negro," which was extended through Europe and America from Portugal and Spain by the traders in African slaves since the fifteenth century. Before that time there had been used in several European languages, including those of Iberia, the respective words indicative of dark color of pigmentation in order to designate black slaves, *blacks* in English and *noirs* in French. When the trade

spread, there prevailed in these lands other words derived from the Hispano-Portuguese *negro,* such as *nigger* in English and *negre* in French, and all these words had a contemptuous meaning as related to slavery. Even today in the French language a distinction is made between the words *noir* and *negre;* as in English *black* is differentiated from *nigger* and from *negro.*

Here it is necessary to heed the warning given by Saco in relation to the beginning of the modern slave trade by the Portuguese in the fifteenth century.

But we must guard ourselves against believing, as some illustrious historians erroneously think, that it was then that slavery, which had already been abolished, was reborn in Europe, for any such idea has been completely refuted by what I have said in Book III. . . . There I proved that this institution continued into the Middle Ages and later times in some nations of Europe and that the Saracenic domination of the Iberian peninsula (from 711 to 1492) along with the mercantile relations which were established between it and Africa, brought black slaves in abundance to Spain and Portugal many centuries before the Portuguese discoveries on the west coast of Africa. What was done then was to give a great impulse to the commerce in black slaves in those two nations, and to open direct traffic with the African countries recently discovered, without the necessity of the caravans which previously took them to Barbary.

More light has also been shed on this earlier slavery by Professor Ortiz.

In the Middle Ages and even at the beginning of the modern era, there was no people who did not frequently suffer the enslavement of its sons. Thus the blacks who were taken from the lands below the Sahara and the blacks of Mauretania, Barbary, and Egypt, like the whites of the Baltic and of the Caucasus and all the pigments of Asia and of Slavonia, even to the quince-colored Guanches, later, the Indians of the New World. Thus there have been slaves those who were pagans and Jews as well as Christians and Moslems.

How this earlier slave trade prepared the way for the later modern European development is important. This further development of the use of distinguishing physical characteristics like color, to project prejudice of "race" will be better realized when this following quotation from *The Illusion of Races* is now considered.

In the trade of slaves they proceeded as in the sale of horses, by endeavoring to establish in every detail the color, height, and the other bodily conditions of the beast, according to whether destined to the shaft, to be ridden, to war, or to the coach of luxury. The Oriental merchants, Moors, Turks, Arabs, and Hebrews, who in Ibiza, Venice, Barbary, Egypt, Constantinople, and Arabia dealt in the traffic of slaves who were so diverse, classified them according to their "race," employing the Semitic word *ras,* which indicates "head" or "origin," that is to say, their genetic antecedents.

When the modern European slave trade developed beginning with the events of 1441, the character of slavery soon changed into the production of commodities by chattels for the world market. For the explorations in Africa were rapidly followed by the rounding of the Cape of Good Hope in 1488 and the discovery of the sea route to India and the rich lands of spices in Asia.

With this enslavement and domination of African and Asian peoples there was thus precipitated the new and deadly poison of racism, with the accompanying notions of "white supremacy" and "natural superiority" of the European people, who were supposedly destined by God and nature to rule over and to exploit all other peoples.

Such is the clear import of the following declaration written in the year 1505 in the *Esmeraldo de Situ Orbis* by Duarte Pacheco Pereira. A Portuguese navigator and commander of slave-raiding expeditions, Pacheco was said to have been "associated with Diogo d'Azumbuja in the founding of the castle of St. George of the Mine" on the west coast of Africa, and later with the Albuquerques leading in the assault upon and domination of the people of India.

Falsely attributing his notions to Pliny, since there is no such parallel passage to be found in the writings of this Latin author, Pacheco thus boasted:

> Pliny in the first chapter of the third book of his *Natural History* says that Europe, being more excellent than all the other parts of the world, produces conquering races and that its position and foundation are more stable than the rest. Owing to its excellence some writers considered it to be not a third but a half of the whole earth; nor may we doubt that in cities, towns, walled fortresses and other stately and beautiful buildings Europe excels Asia and Africa, as also in her larger and better fleets, which are better armed and equipped than those of any other region; nor can the inhabitants of Asia and Africa deny that Europe possesses great abundance of arms and skill in them and much artillery, besides the most excellent scholars of all the world in every science, and that in many other respects it excels all the rest of the world.

Shortly before this time in 1492 Cristóbal Colón, who is known to the English-speaking peoples as Christopher Columbus, found the way to this hemisphere. The ensuing enslavement of the indigenous people in Hispaniola was quickly followed by the introduction of African slaves in 1501, first from Spain only and then direct from the continent of Africa. Two years later, the governor Ovando stopped the bringing in of enslaved Africans, "because they fled to the Indians and taught them bad manners" (rebellion against slavery). But three years later in 1506 when it was held that "the work of one Negro was worth more than that of four Indians," this ban was lifted and the importation of African slaves proceeded apace.

Many royal decrees and other laws were issued in respect to "negros" and "mulatos"; meanwhile these names developed still further the indignities and hostile feelings which inevitably grew along with the spreading slave system. Professor Ortiz furnishes additional enlightenment in the following statement.

> In the colonial countries the word "Negro" had a specific meaning beyond the simple connotation of color or skin. The expression "he is a Negro" was equivalent to saying "he is a slave." Since almost all the slaves in certain countries and epochs were "Negroes," "Negro" came to be synonymous with slave; just as in other geographical and historical situations . . . "Slav" was the synonym for slave. . . .
>
> When the flexibility of the vocabularies permitted it, there was applied restrictedly one word (*negro, negre, nigger,* etc.) for the slave, and another (*noir, black,* etc.) remained for the racial indication. Where this cannot be done as in Castilian, the word "negro" was in spite of everything commonly understood as the synonym for slave, particularly in colloquial language, when that came to be marked with a certain contemptuous and disagreeable tone. So degrading among the Hispanic peoples, not excepting Spain itself, were the words *negro* and *mulato,* that their use became limited to slaves, because they implicitly signified slavery or social vileness. . . . Thus the free black person was called *moreno* and the slave *negro,* in the same way that it was necessary to say *pardo* to the free mixed person of color and *mulato* to the person of mixed ancestry who was subjected to servitude. . . . To this very day anyone who wishes to insult "people of color," will always use the words *negro,* in place of *moreno,* and *mulato* in place of *pardo.*

What is the purpose of this word "Negro"? When you say this word is objectionable, some reach for a quotation from Shakespeare—"A rose by any other name would smell as sweet." A fine statement but taken completely out of context and miserably misapplied. Straight to the point indeed were the same author's apt and prescient lines in *Othello, The Moor of Venice* which treat directly on the significance of a name.

> Good name in man and woman, dear my lord,
> Is the immediate jewel of their souls.
> Who steals my purse steals trash; 'tis something, nothing;
> 'Twas mine, 'tis his, and has been slave to thousands;
> But he that filches from me my good name
> Robs me of that which not enriches him
> And makes me poor indeed.

The important thing about a name is the impression which it makes in the minds of others and the reactions which it invokes through the operation of the association of ideas. The purpose of the name "Negro" was to mark this people by virtue of their color for a special condition of oppression, degradation, exploitation, and annihilation. Has the term changed so much in all this time? To be sure, we no longer have chattel slavery, at least not the type the modern Europeans initiated. That has been abolished as a result of struggle, but we still have various kinds of oppression.

The record of history makes it abundantly clear that after the abolition of chattel slavery, the attempt was ruthlessly made to keep the freemen down at the bottom of society, still chained to the most laborious and menial tasks. In order to accomplish and to maintain this mode of oppression, the emancipated people were identified by their color and branded by the names "negro," "negress," "nigger," and the like for discrimination, segregation, and social ostracism.

Indeed, this campaign of caricature, ridicule, scorn, vilification, and debasement went even to the lengths of exciting gruesome lynchings and horrible massacres. Extermination and annihilation of people of African origin were openly incited, without any legal prohibition or governmental restraint, by such venomous writers as Hinton Rowan Helper in the book *Nojoque* published in 1867, who branded the "negro" in one chapter as "An Inferior Fellow Done For" and in another demanded "Removals—Banishments—Expulsions—Exterminations."

As a result of such monstrous incitements, over 40,000 Afro-American citizens were massacred during the Reconstruction period in the South by the Ku Klux Klan, the White Camelias, and such terrorist gangs. Many European-American citizens, who endeavored to uphold democratic rights for all, were also brutally murdered during this period of frightful reaction in the South from 1865 to 1876.

As late as 1905, the American Book and Bible House at St. Louis, Mo., published the book of Charles Carroll entitled "The Negro A Beast"—"but created with articulate speech and hands, that he may be of service to his master—the White man." Through poison pen and vicious picture, such as the *Birth of a Nation,* which is still being shown despite protest, the stereotype or image has been built up in the public mind of the "Negro," as at best a creature retarded by nature with the mentality of a child, and at worst a savage, bestial monster, who must be kept at bay while forced to labor for his "superiors," and who is ultimately to be destroyed. *This name "Negro," with all its vicious associations must therefore certainly be abolished.*

In the United States and the Caribbean, we have different forms of oppression. In the Caribbean the overwhelming majority of the population is of African descent and these people are still being denied their unalienable rights of self-determination and self-government. So the name "Negro" is being foisted upon them too. This offensive name is thus being spread through the Caribbean. When I was raised in the Caribbean, nobody considered this name "Negro" as being a fit name for him.

For those who say: "what is important is economic status; if you improve your economic status, you won't have to worry about your name!" I would state that you will have an extremely hard time improving your economic status if you do not change your name. To be sure, we need to improve our economic status, but who will ever begin to struggle to improve his or her economic status who has not within the driving force of human self-respect? If you are willing to accept the slave master's vile appellation "negro," you are also willing to accept segregated slums at double rentals and all the disabilities that go with tenth-class citizenship. The term "Negro" was coined for helots, for hewers of wood and drawers of water who were held to be incapable of anything else. Have we forgotten Carlyle's ruthless dictum—"the 'negro' is useful to God's creation only as servant"?

I thank whatever gods there be for a mother who, in my formative years, instructed me in this glorious, vital and important understanding of self-respect. Said she to me over and over again: "My son, you are a person of worth. You do nothing that a person of worth would be ashamed of. You conduct yourself with respect, as a person of worth, and you command respect of others."

This is the ancient and honorable teaching which has come down to us from the sages of Egypt, in particular Amenemope, and before him Ptah-hotep and others who gave the same wise and essential counsel. At the top of our letter-head, therefore, we have inscribed one of these quotations: "See to it that thou be respected of men."

In Africa there are many peoples who are still being oppressed by the vicious system of colonial conquest and domination. Out of this system came the predication of names such as "native," "munt," "Kaffir," and the like with all the contempt and degradation which go with them inevitably.

If there were any doubt, then what has happened in relation to the gruesome events in South Africa ought to clarify any murky misunderstanding that might exist. Consider those horrible massacres, beginning at Sharpeville, of hundreds of Africans, even mothers with babies on their backs, being shot down in the back by those illustrious examples of Christian Apartheid. It should then be clear how these loaded names "native," "Kaffir," "negro," are used to excite and to store up hate and hostility in prejudiced minds, which are then easily incited to perpetuate such inhuman, bloodcurdling, and murderous deeds.

What did we see in the general press of the United States? Newspaper after newspaper, magazines, and radio commentators likewise, writing and speaking about the "Negroes" of South Africa and frequently palliating and excusing these atrocious crimes committed against the indigenous African people in the bestial and monstrous Hitler technique. Such callous extenuation reached down even to the lowest depths when the correspondent for *Life* magazine, Gene Farmer, in the issue of April 11, 1960, retailed and spread a disgusting, lying, and lethal canard about savage Africans wildly infuriated with drink who pulled a white Christian nun from an automobile and ate her even before she died!

Not so long ago, however, Mr. Alan Paton contributed an article to *The New York Times* published in its Magazine Section of April 10. This enlightening statement, entitled "As Blind As Samson Was," revealed the pathological mindset of the ruthless rulers of the Union of South Africa.

Indeed it called to mind the fitting observation of the Greeks: "Whom the gods would destroy they first make mad."

Mr. Paton exemplifies the fact that not all Europeans think and feel as imperious slave masters and oppressors. On the contrary, some have been and are among the most stalwart fighters against such injustice and oppression. Mr. Paton writes and acts as one of these. The apartheid oppressors in South Africa not only arrested African leaders, but they also jailed a number of European leaders who had been standing up for the rights of the African people.

Explaining the attitude of the present apartheid minority ruler of the Union of South Africa, who, although a relatively recent immigrant from Holland, actually called himself the "Afrikaner," the "man of Africa," Mr. Paton revealed the following: "He even refuses to grant the black Africans the use of the word 'African'. The black African used to be a 'kaffir,' today he is a 'native' or a 'Bantu'."

Doubtless, Mr. Paton used the adjective "black" in order to identify the indigenous inhabitants of South Africa. But it must be pointed out here that this is a loose term which cannot be wholly separated from its racist overtones.

Observe that the apartheid usage dictates that "native" be written with a common "n." Clearly then the term "native" is a contemptuous name, and it carries with it ignominy, derogation, and hostility. Do you ever see *The New York Times* or any of these institutions of journalism referring to the European as a "native," or to American "natives," except when they mean the indigenous people of this country whom they have well nigh wiped out? In reference to themselves though, they are not "natives." The word "native" is proper for them only as an adjective, never as a noun or name. Nevertheless, they seem to think that the name "native" is proper for Africans and other indigenous people who are thus considered fit to be ruled, exploited, displaced, and even exterminated. See how the apartheid monsters are even now degenerating the good name Bantu which is African. They are associating it with ignominy and degradation.

Mr. Paton continued: "But he like the Afrikaner wants to be called a 'man of Africa.'" I submit now that the people of Africa, whose ancestors have inhabited this land from time immemorial, are the Africans. It is now altogether clear that the use of the term "Negro," like that of "native" and "Kaffir" and the like, is for the purpose of marking out the people for oppression, degradation, and destruction.

I wish to point out also that Africans generally resent the term "Negro." There are as many variations of color in Africa as there are in Europe or Asia, and yet the people of these two continents are always described as Europeans or Asians, or according to their nationality. The use of the term "Negro" in relation to Africans is an attempt to categorize and disparage them on the basis of American color prejudice.

Through the years, Afro-Americans have been uneasy about the name.

Many have rejected it. The names of early organizations of people of African descent in this country speak for themselves. The Free African Society was instituted in Philadelphia by Richard Allen and Absalom Jones in 1787. Shortly thereafter the African Methodist Church was founded by the former in 1790 and the First (Episcopal) African Church of St. Thomas was established by the latter in 1794.

The African Lodge of Masons was set up by Prince Hall, whose *Address to the Lodge* in 1797 speaks of African and Ethiopian but never "Negro." The militant and powerful *Appeal* of David Walker, published in Boston in the year 1829, was addressed to the *Colored Citizens of the World* . . . but in particular to those of the United States of America.

The early poet Phillis Wheatley, who had been brought from Africa to Boston, wrote in 1772 of Africa and Ethiop, only once falling into the use of the name "Negroes." Obviously, however, this use was due to her Christian teaching and to the dominant American slave mores as the following pathetic appeal clearly shows.

> Remember, Christians, Negroes black as Cain
> May be refined, and join the angelic train.

However, the slave poet of North Carolina, George M. Horton, never mentioned this name of proscription in *The Hope of Liberty* which was published in 1829.

Likewise conscious and forthright in this respect were the *Sentiments of the People of Color* which were printed as an Appendix to the *Thoughts on African Colonization* written by a founder of the modern Abolitionist Movement, William Lloyd Garrison. Beginning with the resolution of the "people of color" of Philadelphia in 1817, the statements adopted by such people in New York, Boston, Baltimore, Washington, Brooklyn, Hartford, Middletown, New Haven, Nantucket, Pittsburgh, Wilmington, Harrisburg, Rochester, Providence, Trenton, Lyme, Lewistown, and New Bedford—all evidently show how widespread and total was the rejection of the use of the offensive name "Negro."

Lydia Maria Child's *Appeal in Favor of that Class of Americans Called Africans,* published in 1833, demonstrates a similar and growing consciousness among some of the most informed of the European-American Abolitionists.

William C. Nell's book, which is the first, shall we say, formal account of the contributions of Afro-Americans, is entitled *Colored Patriots Of The American Revolution.* Throughout this book the term "colored" is emphasized; the name "negro" appears only in quotations or in a very few places under the obvious direct influence of other authors.

The first magazine published by persons of African descent in America was called *The Anglo-African Magazine.* For a long time, subsequently, there was a *Colored American Magazine* which eschewed the name "Negro."

However, the term "colored" is too vague and cannot now be accepted as a proper designation.

The first comprehensive account of our journalistic enterprise was written by I. Garland Penn and entitled *The Afro-American Press*. William Monroe Trotter, editor of *The Guardian* and one of the great champions of human rights in these United States, banished the word "Negro" from the columns of his newspaper. Likewise, *The Chicago Defender* while under the editorial supervision of its founder, Robert S. Abbott, disdained the use of this epithet. Father Divine in the *New Day* has spoken and written against this term "Negro."

Significant and weighty is the record of the numerous National Conventions held by American citizens of African origin, from 1830 until 1892 when their names regrettably began to change. Never were these Conventions called "Negro." Seldom was this odious word used in speeches in these assemblies. Instinctively and consciously, the name denoting slave status and "free" inferiority was not applied to themselves in the Addresses which they made to the nation and to the world.

Consult *A Documentary History of the Negro People in the United States* by Herbert Aptheker and read past the bold titles and headings inserted by the editor which parade the misnomer "Negro." Look into the official documents! You will read references to their organizations as "Colored Men," "People of Color," and so on—but no "Negro"! A striking example of this baneful tendency to read present harmful terms back into history is seen in the insertion of "Negro," first with brackets later even without, in the very title of the National Labor Union of 1870.

It would be well to mark the total absence of the degrading name "Negro" from the choice and fitly phrased wording of what is perhaps the most significant document of this entire period. The Call To Arms To Fight For Emancipation, which was made by the great Abolitionist leader Frederick Douglass, was particularly addressed: MEN OF COLOR, TO ARMS!

But by 1892 a backward trend was rising. The policy of "accommodation" to the requirements of reactionary oppressors was being shrewdly put over upon our people. The first self-styled *Negro* Conference was called by Booker T. Washington in 1892. The use of this name of indignity—Negro—was a symptom of the developing sickness of opportunism and of the increasing acceptance of inferior social and political status. This acceptance of a lower place for our people at the botton of American society was unblushingly proclaimed by Booker T. Washington in his notorious "separate as the fingers" speech, delivered at the Atlanta Exposition in 1895.

As this spirit of acceptance of the bottom place possessed more of our people, the degrading name "Negro" became more common. But for a time it appeared that the name Afro-American would be wholly adopted. However, the climate of the time made it easy to take the path of least resistance, and so at last to our detriment the name "Negro" became dominant. Still conscious, however, of its degrading use, particularly with a common "n," some of the more thoughtful and manly of our leaders developed a campaign to secure its use with a capital letter.

One of our most influential newspapers still carries at its masthead the proper and honorable name Afro-American. Published first in Baltimore but extending its circulation on a national scale, this journal carries forward some of the best traditions of the press which came into being to voice and to defend the rights of a minority people suffering unjust oppression. This newspaper should now logically be in the forefront of the endeavor to get this name established on a national and international scale.

The chief organization, defending and promoting the general human rights of our people, appears to have been purposely named the National Association For the Advancement of Colored People. Its national organ, *The Crisis* magazine, was founded by the dean of Afro-American letters, Dr. W. E. B. Du Bois, who significantly projected this journal as "A Record of the Darker Races." This organization could ably serve the cause of removing prejudice by playing a leading role in the campaign to change the name "Negro." For such a change would direct thought to the vital aspects of this question, and help to create a state of mind and the social climate, which would certainly make easier the practical realization of the democratic rights of our people, and consequently those of all other citizens.

Allow me to consider the names which have been proposed as an alternative to "Negro." We have heard Ethiopian mentioned, but Ethiopia is now the recognized name of a specific nation and area in Africa and is not applicable to the whole of Africa. The term "colored" is vague, associated with false notions of "race," and lacking any definite connection with the good earth, or with an extensive historical record, or with a significant group culture. The names "Black Man," or "Black Race," have been suggested, but these are also loose, racist, color designations which have no basic, obvious or unmistakable linkage with land, history, and culture. The name "African-American," although expressive of the essential fundamentals, is rather long and does not sound well. The repeated "eecan-eecan" sound diminishes its euphony.

There remains the name Afro-American. Please note that Afro-American could be written as one word without any hyphen, so that the objection to "hyphenated Americans" would not apply. A similar usage has been followed for some time now by enlightened Latin Americans who have fittingly replaced the noxious name "negro" with the names Afroamericano, Afrocubano, Afrobrasileiro, and similar names compounded in the same way.

The name Afro-American properly recognizes and expresses our origin and connection with land, history, and culture. The word Afro-American proclaims at once our past continental heritage and our present national status. Besides being pleasant to the ear, this name Afro-American was devised by ourselves and is already in use to some extent. It should therefore be most easily and readily adopted by everybody.

All other minority groups in the United States of America are generally recognized in terms of the land or nation whence they came—all but the misnamed and proscribed "Negro." Thus we hear of Anglo-Americans, Franco-Americans, Italo-Americans, Irish-Americans, Spanish-Americans, Chinese-Americans, and so on. Standing out alone and shamefully among all these Americans from these several countries and nations are the misnamed "Negro" Americans. They have come from nowhere!

All too often the desire to rid ourselves of this belittling name "Negro," is blocked by the defeatist thought: "How shall we ever be able to change it?" But this is not so difficult as it appears at first. In our time we have seen important changes made in the names of several peoples.

As Bishop Reginald Barrow has pointed out, the name of the people of Ghana was changed upon regaining their independence, and the name which had been imposed by European rulers, "Gold Coast," has been buried with the subject past. For centuries the Ethiopian nation was tagged "Abyssinia" by European powers and publicists. When the proper name Ethiopia was registered with the League of Nations, this misrepresentative "hybrid" name was decisively changed.

Similar changes of name have occurred among the Asian peoples. To mention only two: The people of Iran have put aside the name Persia. The name "Dutch East Indies" has been appropriately cast off and the honorable name Indonesia is now the accepted and proper name.

In our own hemisphere, it has been noteworthy that when the slaves of the former French colony of Saint Domingue succeeded in throwing off their yoke of subjection and emerged as a new nation in 1804, they took as a fitting name one which the indigenous people of that island had used in freedom and honor—Haiti.

The name "West Indies" was almost changed to "Caribbean." The organization which initiated the movement for "federation with complete self-government" called itself the *Caribbean* Labour Congress. The name Caribbean, derived from the indigenous people now almost wholly and sadly extinct, was projected in the draft for the constitution of the new nation. Unfortunately, however, the misnomer due to the error of Colón in assuming that he had reached the Indies has been reverted to and independence has not yet been achieved wholly.

It may still be objected, nevertheless, that all these examples of change of name do not really apply, since people of African origin in this country now lack the political power to enforce such a change. That is mistaken. Once this change of name is insisted upon by a majority of us, it will be accepted generally. The basic principle involved is actually the determination of any group of people to rid themselves of the stigma which a bad name carries and the recognition of their right to do so by other people. Directly in point is the change in the use of a common "n" to a capital "N" in writing the word "Negro" in English. This has been achieved widely, though not completely, as the result of effective action. Among the first important newspapers to adopt this change was *The New York Times.*

What is needed now is a clear recognition by the majority of American citizens of African ancestry that it is imperative to take a further and final step. By united action we must register this desire and will with those most influential in such a matter—the managers of the press and the directors of radio and television communications, educational institutions, religious bodies, fraternal, trade union, and other organizations, and governmental agencies. Fair-minded European-Americans will readily accede to such a request and others will be compelled to follow the decent and proper usage—Afro-American. Let us now call upon all who mould public opinion to reject the name "Negro" as wholly unsuitable, offensive, and insulting.

We are entitled to be called Americans, but some people desire to differentiate. If they must distinguish us, then in accordance with our human right, we will tell them what to call us—Afro-Americans. When all is said and done, dogs and slaves are named by their masters; free men name themselves!

BOOK REVIEW OF *MAN'S MOST DANGEROUS MYTH: THE FALLACY OF RACE,* BY ASHLEY MONTAGU; *RACE: THE HISTORY OF AN IDEA IN AMERICA,* BY THOMAS F. GOSSETT; AND *THE RACES OF MANKIND,* BY M. NESTURKH

Liberator, June 1964, p. 22.

Today the question of "race" has taken on an urgency which requires that this idea with all its results be freshly examined and clearly understood. What is still more necessary is the due realization of the possible dreadful effects of this concept "race" in the minds and on the behavior of most human beings at this decisive moment. For we are caught in a grave dilemma.

It is just about five centuries ago that this notion of "race" appeared full-fledged in the consciousness of man. Like the cloud "no bigger than a man's hand," which appeared in the sky and soon spread till the whole sky was overcast and darkened, so this potent idea of "race" has spread until it has come to becloud the view and to condition the responses of most people today.

Three books just published consider this agitating and threatening question. Ashley Montagu in *Man's Most Dangerous Myth* reveals the origin of the dangerous myth of "race" as "the direct result of the trade in slaves by

European merchants." The idea of "race" thus emerged as a means to attempt to justify and to maintain colonialist enslavement and oppression. Whatever the changing form, whether of the system of oppression or in its supporting ideology, "race" has always served, and still serves, to brand the slave and the oppressed as degraded, inferior, sub-human creatures, fit only to toil for European overlords who assumed dominance over the whole world.

Tracing the historical development of the idea of "race," Thomas F. Gossett in *Race: The History of an Idea in America* goes back to the early perception of certain physical differences by the Indians, Chinese, Egyptians, Jews, Greeks, and Romans. Though there is a tendency to confuse these early perceptions with the later full-blown "race" theories, these last are finally recognized as significantly different and rooted in modern chattel slavery.

Treating the scientific revolt against racism, Dr. Gossett shows how the critical studies of Jean Finot, John Oakesmith, Theodor Waitz, and E. B. Tylor were carried forward by scholars in America, outstanding among whom was Dr. Franz Boas. The professional work of scientists like Kroeber, Benedict, Garth and others is cited, as well as the stand taken by writers such as Cable, Twain, Howells, Crane, Higginson and the artist Winslow Homer.

In *The Races of Mankind* the Soviet anthropologist M. Nesturkh stresses "the gradual obliteration of racial differences in the course of historical development, the racial mixtures that make up modern nations and the absolute invalidity of racism." Refuting theories of racial inferiority, this book points to statesmen of Asia and Africa and declares:

> Special mention must be made of Patrice Lumumba, who gave his life in the struggle for the liberation of the Congolese people. Many representatives of the Negroid race have reached the topmost heights of culture—the scientist Dr. William Du Bois, the famous singer and fighter for peace Paul Robeson, the Australian artist Academician Albert Namatjira.

It is to be noted, however, that while the term "Caucasoid" has been replaced by "Europoid," the loaded term "Negroid" is still used. Nevertheless, growing awareness seems apparent in the statement that "representatives of this part of the Negroid great race *call themselves Africans.*" (Emphasis added.) While a firm stand is taken for "the biological equality of the races of man," yet it appears that Soviet anthropology still labors under the older notion of "race" classification by measurements of external features. From the differing classifications made by Soviet scientists themselves, it would appear that they have not yet found any firm reality of "race" in nature itself.

This reviewer concurs with the proposal of Dr. Montagu that the term "race," because of its false and harmful connotation, should be dropped. The preference which Dr. Gossett shows for the term "ethnic minority" also points in the right direction. It seems necessary, however, to go further and to urge that all "race" labels be abandoned: "Caucasoid," "Mongoloid," "Australoid," and "Negroid." These might well be replaced by terms denoting simple and natural classification of peoples on a strictly continental basis: "African," "European," "Asian," "American," and "Australian." The indigenous peoples of these continents might be thus designated in order to distinguish them from recent migrants and from oppressive invaders.

It should not be too difficult to understand why it is desirable to dispense with all names like "nigger," "negress," "darky," and such terms as "primitive," "native," "savage," "barbarous," and the opposite "civilized." Despite all attempts to change their connotations, these words convey degrading meanings or implications and set off emotionally conditioned reflexes.

Such books as these here reviewed spread vitally essential enlightenment on the deadly results of "race" feeling. The memory of mass murders in Southwest Africa, Hitler's Germany, apartheid South Africa, Angola, Mozambique and Algeria, as well as the violence and slaughter which has taken place in Mississippi, Alabama, Florida and recently Ohio, should all arouse and alert us. The alternatives before us are thus stark and chastening. For if we plot the curve of racist incitement and mass slaughter, we cannot escape the realization: Either we get rid of the vicious notion of racism or racism will inevitably lead to the wholesale destruction of most, if not all, of mankind.

A NEW LOOK AT AFRICAN HISTORY
(Introduction)

Lecture delivered to the Pan-African Students Organization in the Americas, Horace Mann Auditorium, Teachers College, Columbia University, November 13, 1964. Manuscript, Richard B. Moore Papers.

It has long been the custom of European historians to divide history into Ancient, Medieval, and Modern. But this division of history is in no sense absolute or universal. Such a division can only be accepted as a convenient mode of indicating periods of the continuous stream of history, in order to facilitate understanding and exposition. Moreover, this division is suited specifically to European history, in the consideration of which this mode of division arose.

Hence what is deemed *Ancient History* generally refers to the period beginning with the rise of the Egyptian and Chaldean, latterly Sumerian, cultures and starts some time around 3,000 before the Christian Era on down to the end of the Western Roman Empire about 476 of the Christian Era. What is usually known as *Medieval History,* or that pertaining to the

European Middle Ages, begins rather arbitrarily with the decline of Western Rome about 476 in the fifth century of the Christian Era and covers the period of about a thousand years down to the fifteenth century when Colón, or Columbus, first arrived in the American hemisphere. What is called *Modern History* then begins and continues down to the present.

At this point it should be salutary to heed the warning sounded by Doctor George A. Dorsey in his book *Man's Own Show: Civilisation:* "Divisions, epochs, eras, dynasties, reigns, etc.—which serve book purposes are not necessarily rational or sharp divisions; they are conveniences, like punctuation marks on the printed page or milestones on a pike."

Far less, then, do these arbitrary divisions apply to universal history or to African history. At the most those who have been conditioned to this mode of viewing history might find it useful to approach the continuum of history in Africa by looking *seriatim* at those periods of African history which coincide roughly with the European Ancient, Medieval, and Modern. It is, however, more edifying to recognize that there are other and far more fitting ways of envisaging periods in the on-going process of African history. Such modes would not attempt to force African history into European moulds, nor view the African saga in the light of narrow and partisan European or Euro-American interests.

One such convenient mode of viewing African history might be the following, though in this there is necessarily much overlapping.

First, a *Very Early Period* from the emergence of man himself, which according to all the evidence now available took place 1,750,000 years ago at Olduvai Gorge in Tanganyika, extending down to the agricultural settlements at Merimde and the Fayyum in Lower Egypt and the food-producing Tasian and Badarian cultures of Upper Egypt, which were estimated by the Egyptologist Flinders Petrie at 9,000 B.C.E. and 7,471 B.C.E. respectively, but which are now generally dated at about 5,000 B.C.E.

Next, an *Early Period* following after 5,000 B.C.E. down to the First Dynasty of Egypt, formerly dated at about 4,000 B.C.E. but recently considered to be around 3,000 B.C.E.

Then would come what might be called the *Classical Period* embracing the Egyptian, Kushite, Libyan-Berber, Saharan, and Nok cultures, starting around 3,000 B.C.E. and ending with the closing of the temples of Egypt by the Byzantine or Eastern Roman Emperor Justinian in the fifth century of the Christian Era.

Thereafter one might distinguish the *Median Period*, including the Ethiopian, Sudanic, Congolese, Zimbabwean, and Zanj cultures, extending from the rise of Old Ghana some time about the third century of our era to the decline of the Songhay empire in the sixteenth century.

There would follow the *Colonialist Period* starting with the modern slave trade by the Portuguese in 1441, and entering a new stage of annexations with the Berlin Conference of 1884, which initiated the rapid partitioning of Africa among the European powers. This *Colonialist Period* would draw to its close with the withdrawal of Britain from Egypt, consummated finally by the yielding of the Suez Canal during 1958, and with the independence of the modern state of Ghana south of the Sahara on March 6, 1957.

Then what might be called the *Renascent Period,* or period of re-birth, characterized by the rapid re-emergence of independent African states, would continue from the independence of Ghana in 1957 until the present moment.

It might be well to consider another arbitrary division of history, namely, that into so-called prehistory and history proper. Now if human history is the closest possible recovery, recounting, and reinterpretation of the entire gamut of significant events in the varied experience and achievements of man, then all that can be garnered through rigorous research and rational interpretation, whether from written records, or from the re-discovered remains, artifacts, products, and surroundings of man, or from what has been preserved through oral tradition, ought logically to be considered as history and necessarily included in its scope and sphere. . . .

At the very outset of his book *What Happened in History,* in the first paragraph of the opening chapter, Professor V. Gordon Childe wrote revealingly:

> Written history contains a very patchy and incomplete record of what mankind has accomplished in parts of the world during the last five thousand years. The period surveyed is at best about one hundredth part of the time during which men have been active on our planet. The picture presented is frankly chaotic; it is hard to recognize in it any unifying pattern, any directional trends. Archaeology surveys a period a hundred times as long. In this enlarged field of study it does disclose general trends, cumulative changes proceeding in one main direction towards recognizable results.

It is true that Professor Childe then goes on to speak of "history with its prelude prehistory," but his opening statement had already made it clear how much more vastly extended and basically vital so-called prehistory is than history compiled chiefly from written records. Besides, in his prior volume, *Man Makes Himself,* Professor Childe observed: "By the inclusion of prehistory, the purview of history is extended a hundredfold. And again: "But not only does prehistory extend written history backwards, it carries on natural history forward." From all of this one must conclude that if such divisions are deemed necessary or helpful, then it is far more nearly exact and clear to use the terms *archaeological* history, *traditional* history, and *recorded* history. . . .

Gross misconceptions and false images of the African peoples have prevailed all too generally since the beginning of the colonialist period. In the attempt to justify the conquest and enslavement of African peoples, European rulers and their spokesmen found it expedient to regard and to set forth Africans as beings of a low and brutish order who indeed were hardly human. Such creatures then were deemed to have done little or nothing which could be dignified as history.

The stereotypes or mental pictures of "savage Africa" and the "Dark Continent" were deeply impressed upon the minds of people generally. These false images effectively hindered any realistic, rational, or appreciative thought about Africa, its peoples, and their descendents elsewhere. Doctor Edward Wilmot Blyden in his Inaugural Address as President of Liberia College . . . pointedly observed: "It was during the sixth period [the Modern Age] that the transatlantic slave trade arose, and those theories— theological, social, and political—were invented for the degradation and proscription of the Negro. This epoch continues to this day, and has an abundant literature and a prolific authorship."

Reflecting upon the dire results of this vast modern slave traffic, M. Alionne Diop, President, Société Africaine de Culture, commented significantly in his Preface to *Africa Seen by American Negro Scholars*. At the moment of extending the hand of African solidarity to Afro-American intellectuals, M. Diop remarked wistfully:

> What links us first of all is assuredly our common origin. One still does not know how many men and women were kidnapped by a process unique in history from the demographic, cultural, economic and political vitality of Africa. Surely those who were snatched from the fatherland were healthy men and women, carefully selected. Slavery was one of the principal causes of the devitalization and consequently of the colonization of our continent.

Let us profoundly hope that the total effect of all the mores, attitudes, and racial notions which have developed out of the modern slave system, will now be clearly realized, particularly in viewing African culture and history. Such harmful notions should be fully recognized for what they are and thus counteracted logically and rigorously.

THE PASSING OF CHURCHILL AND EMPIRE

Liberator, March 1965, pp. 8–10.

> The evil that men do lives after them,
> The good is oft interred with their bones . . .
>
> Shakespeare

The last of the great statesmen of empire of our era, Sir Winston Leonard Spencer Churchill, has passed from the scene of life and action.

After lying in state at Westminster Hall, with a great procession of the "highest" and the "lowest" passing before his bier, and following funeral services at St. Paul's Cathedral attended by Queen Elizabeth and the representatives of 110 nations, the last remains of the chief political giant of the Western World have finally been interred in a quiet country graveyard. Long and eventful was his career; his life span covered ninety years, almost a century; his political activity burgeoned as the Empire of Great Britain rose to dazzling heights and then began its inevitable downward decline.

"The sun never sets on the British Empire." This was the proud boast which doubtless delighted the heart of the arch-conservative Winston Churchill, whose chief goal it was to maintain, and to extend this farflung panoply of imperial power and possessions. As this century opened, Britain's global empire reached out from the relatively minute island kingdom of England to Ireland and thence through the Mediterranean to Egypt in North Africa, through several discrete colonies and "protectorates" down to South Africa, thence into the Near East and on to India, "jewel of the British Crown," and to Ceylon, then into the Far East to Burma, Malay, Singapore, and Hong Kong, on to Australia and New Zealand, thence across the Pacific to the Dominion of Canada, and down the Atlantic to colonies in the Caribbean and South America.

Growing up during the early years of this century in Barbados, held and ruled as a colony by Britain, this writer was taught, and so thought, that these oft-repeated words about the never-setting sun were solely true of the great and unique British Empire. For such is the partisan and purblind nature of history as narrowly constricted and tendentiously taught by imperialists. Thus it was not until many years after that by a process of personal arousal and deliberate research, the writer came to learn that the predication had been made much earlier—"the sun never sets on the Spanish empire."

The most able and voluble spokesman of the imperial mode of thought, Winston Churchill was nevertheless its prisoner. As such, Churchill could not envisage the millions of people in the colonies as entitled to the same basic rights and opportunities as all other human beings. Like Rudyard Kipling, his famous compatriot and fellow winner of the Nobel Prize for literature, Churchill viewed colonial peoples as "lesser breeds without the Law." "My thought," he himself said, "was more in accord with Rudyard Kipling than with Mr. Bernard Shaw." Thus the chief bearer of "The White Man's Burden" could not duly appreciate or properly feel the evil effects of empire upon its numerous and necessary victims.

Neither could Winston Churchill perceive the fatal contradictions and inevitable conflict inherent in the system of imperialism. Nor could this most astute scion of empire of our age, because of his very top position and the will to retain it, recognize that empire must come at last to its end. For like man himself, empire by the very law of its nature, may rise and bloom for a time in youthful power and glory, but must just as surely later wither and decay in aged decrepitude.

As a conscious upholder of empire, Winston Churchill, when a young British cavalry officer, could seek "action" in the north of India, where upon encountering a Pathan whom he described as "savage" with others behind him, Churchill would not advance to a conflict with swords but fired his pistol and took off safely. Writing of it afterwards as "fun," Churchill rode with the forces of Kitchener into the battle of Omdurman in the Sudan on September 2, 1898, shooting the indigenous African defenders with pistol in hand, since as it has been recorded "a shoulder injury prevented his wielding a saber."

With good conscience thus, Churchill could join and direct while in office ruthless "punitive" expeditions in which thousands of Asian and African people were massacred in their own countries. Winston Churchill did not scruple to degrade and to persecute the militant leaders of nationalist colonial movements, in the same way that he scoffed at Gandhi and imprisoned Nehru. In British politics Churchill upheld the interests of the reactionary upper class into which he was born at Blenheim Palace, though he took great care to project himself in the image of the Great Commoner. His brief shift to the Liberal Party was soon abandoned when it appeared that this party might truly pursue liberal ends. As Churchill bolted back to the Conservative Party, he condemned liberal policies as "socialistic."

In one great event Churchill's action coincided with the best interests of mankind. This it is, doubtless, which won for him wide appreciation and mourning at his death among most people of the world. This action was his wise and valiant stand against the monstrous Hitler menace. Winston Churchill's sage warnings against the grave danger of enslavement and destruction by Hitler's fascist hordes; his eloquent and inspiring calls to great effort and supreme sacrifice in the hour of deepest crisis; his consummate marshalling of all the forces of Britain to withstand the Nazi attack; the forging of vital alliances with the United States and the Soviet Union—these achievements will always stand out as a great contribution to the welfare of mankind.

Yet this action of Churchill must be recognized as due to a most rare and fortunate coincidence in life and history. That was the agreement at that specific moment and in that particular conjuncture of events, of the vital interests of the British Empire with those of the great overwhelming majority of mankind. For Winston Churchill's prime consideration was the survival of the British Empire. This was made abundantly clear by Churchill himself when he declared in the House of Commons:

> For without victory, there is no survival. Let that be realized; no survival for the British Empire; no survival for all that the British Empire has stood for; no survival for the impulse of the ages, that mankind will move forward towards its goal.

It soon became clear from his deeds that Winston Churchill could not transcend narrow, limited, hidebound imperial views. An illuminating instance was the exchange which he engineered with the United States government for 50 over-age destroyers of several 99-year leases of lands in the Caribbean area. These lands were thus alienated from the Caribbean people without any consultation with them, or with such limited representative governments as had been permitted them by their British rulers.

In August 1941 the Atlantic Charter was promulgated following a meeting of Prime Minister Winston Churchill with President Franklin D. Roosevelt. Great hopes were kindled by the Atlantic Charter for a time in the breasts of millions of oppressed colonial peoples. For among other statements to the same effect, the Atlantic Charter declared in Point Three:

> They respect the right of all peoples to choose the form of government under which they will live; and they wish to see sovereign rights and self-government restored to those who have been forcibly deprived of them.

However, these hopes were rudely dashed to earth when the British Prime Minister declared that the Atlantic Charter applied only to Europe. President Roosevelt on the contrary affirmed that the Atlantic Charter applied to all people. But it was realized that the Atlantic Charter could not become effective if the rulers of the greatest empire extant denied its application. Moreover, Winston Churchill revealed himself as an unchanged, die-hard imperialist when he baldly stated: "I have not become the King's First Prime Minister to preside over the liquidation of the British Empire."

To the millions of people in the colonies who had fought in and supported the war against Nazi tyranny, this statement of Churchill, denying them freedom, appeared as gross ingratitude. For it was in November, 1942, at El Alamein in Egypt, on African soil and with vital African aid, that the first solid victory was won for Britain against Hitler's armies. Nor would there have been any possibility of such a victory if certain African colonies had not withstood the collaborators Petain, Laval, *et al.*, who surrendered to Hitler. The maintenance of Free France in Africa was largely due to the statesmanship of Felix Eboué, born in Cayenne of African descent, then governor of Chad, and later governor-general. The sudden and untimely death of Felix Eboué in a Cairo hospital on May 17, 1944, after conferring and dining with Allied friends, has been widely regarded as due to mysterious, prejudiced, and sinister forces.

Not while Winston Churchill held office as Prime Minister did the liberation of Britain's colonial peoples begin. It was under the Labour Party government of Prime Minister Clement Attlee and Sir Stafford Cripps that the independence of India was conceded. The exigencies of the war in the Far East, the fall of Singapore and the capture of Burma, the threatening advance of Japanese forces, the mutiny of Indian sailors on a British warship and the mounting pressure of the non-cooperation struggle of the

Indian people—all led finally to this breakthrough. The subsequent independence of colonial peoples, Asian, African, Mediterranean, and Caribbean, has been achieved in the main in spite of the opposition of Sir Winston Churchill.

Yet Winston Churchill realized that the British Empire owed a great debt to its colonial peoples. In the case of the Caribbean and Indian peoples Churchill made this clear and voluntary admission:

> Our possession of the West Indies, like that of India, . . . gave us the strength, the support, but especially the capital, the wealth at a time when no other European nation possessed such a reserve, which enabled us to come through the great struggles of the Napoleonic Wars, the keen competition of commerce in the 18th and 19th centuries, and enabled us not only to acquire this appendage of possessions we have, but also to lay the foundations of that commercial and financial leadership, which when the world was young, when everything outside Europe was undeveloped, enabled us to make our great position in the world.

As a thorough-going imperialist, Winston Churchill could see no wrong in such appropriation of the wealth of other peoples, and of maintaining rule over them by force and by mental conditioning which would bring them to submit to colonial bondage and exploitation. Churchill's general reactionary attitude appeared in his role in breaking the General Strike of British workers, in opposing suffrage and equal rights for women, in sanctioning the invasion of Russia after the revolution of 1917, and in endorsing the discharge of atomic bombs on the people of Hiroshima and Nagasaki. In the same reactionary manner Winston Churchill pulled down the "iron curtain" in his speech at Fulton, Missouri and let loose the Cold War, ostensibly to defeat communism abroad and socialism at home, but actually to maintain the system of imperial domination of nation over nation and the exploitation of the many by the few.

Likewise, Winston Churchill also concurred in the military invasion of Egypt launched by Prime Minister Eden together with Premier Mollet of France and Premier Ben Gurion of Israel. Truth compels the recognition of the fact that it was the note of Premier Khrushchev of the Soviet Union warning: "how would you like your cities to be bombed?" and his demand to begin the evacuation of Egypt within 24 hours, which obviously saved the Egyptian people, and very likely other African peoples, from being ruthlessly overrun and again subjugated.

Let not the wish control our thought or influence our judgement. Winston Churchill may be the last of the great imperial political leaders, but the imperial system though dying is by no means dead. There are, and there will be, last ditch neo-colonialists and their tools, as in the Congo, Viet Nam, Guiana, and other areas, who will strive to extend the life and maintain the power of imperial oppression, and exploitation by devious, sinister, and even bloody means.

It should be recognized that this imperial statesman Sir Winston Churchill exemplified and exercised, on behalf of his power group, certain great talents and valuable qualities—alertness to basic interests, insight and foresight, the spirit of defiance, the will to resist, the fortitude to endure, devotion to objectives and the ability to organize and to execute necessary tasks, persuasive eloquence and the ability to inspire, to move, and to lead the multitudes. These qualities are also requisite for the oppressed peoples and groups, if their complete liberation is to be assured.

The publishers of the *Selected Poems of Claude McKay* wrote of the poem "If We Must Die" that "Mr. Winston Churchill filled the House of Commons with its fighting message during the war." Written by the Afro-Caribbean poet in reaction against the horrible lynchings of Afro-American people, but broadly universal and truly human, this heroic poem could well be used in any phase of valiant resistance against vile and murderous tyranny:

> If we must die, let it not be like hogs
> Hunted and penned in an inglorious spot,
> While round us bark the mad and hungry dogs
> Making their mock at our accursed lot.
> If we must die, O let us nobly die,
> So that our precious blood may not be shed
> In vain; then even the monsters we defy
> Shall be constrained to honor us though dead!
> O kinsmen! We must meet the common foe!
> Though far outnumbered let us show us brave,
> And for their thousand blows deal one death blow!
> What though before us lies the open grave?
> Like men we'll face the murderous cowardly pack,
> Pressed to the wall, dying, but fighting back!

It appears that the imperial statesman Sir Winston Churchill appropriated this poem without acknowledgement from his former colonial subject Claude McKay. This seems consonant with a too common practice of literary lifting without even a gracious "by your leave." In keeping with the mores of the imperial acquisitive society, the taking of this poem seems a mere bagatelle and in no wise improper or unethical. For the imperial code of conduct sanctioned far greater expropriation of lands, natural and mineral resources, and even the being, personality, and life of millions of forcibly subjugated colonial people.

Sir Winston Churchill now passes into history, and the system of empire which he served so well moves irrevocably into the limbo of the past. It should here be fitting to recall, albeit with due acknowledgement and with new, penetrating, and critical evaluation, a few lines penned by the British poet and bard of empire Rudyard Kipling in the well-known ode *Recessional:*

The tumult and the shouting dies;
  The captains and the kings depart:
Still stands thine ancient sacrifice,
  An humble and a contrite heart.
Lord God of Hosts, be with us yet,
Lest we forget—lest we forget!

Far-called, our navies melt away;
  One dune and headland sinks the fire:
Lo, all our pomp of yesterday
  Is one with Nineveh and Tyre!
Judge of the Nations, spare us yet,
Lest we forget—lest we forget!

CARIBS, "CANNIBALS," AND HUMAN RELATIONS (Excerpts)

Pamphlet published for the Afroamerican Institute by Pathway Publishers, Patchogue, New York, 1972.

This essay has been occasioned by the impact of a placard which brands the Carib people as fierce and frequent consumers of human flesh. Hanging over a case of artifacts in the Museum at Nelson's Dockyard in Antigua, this placard prominently displayed must affect relations between peoples and individuals, specifically as to whether these relations shall be more respectful and amicable or offensive and hostile.

While on a lecture tour of the Caribbean which included Antigua, this writer visited the Museum and was there confronted by the following statement inscribed on a poster in bold letters:

> The Caribs, unlike the Arawaks from the north, were fierce fighters and cannibals. An old historian records—They have tasted of all the nations which frequented them, and affirm that the French are the most delicate and the Spaniards the hardest of digestion.

Astonishing and distressing, to say the least, is the use and repetition today of the debasing charge made against the Carib people of common and widespread cannibalism. It should never be forgotten that this accusation, originally made by invading Spanish conquistadors, was accompanied thereafter by the wholesale enslavement and genocide of the indigenous Caribbean Peoples. Even now, several centuries later, this abominable charge still defiles their name and defames their memory.

It is true, of course, that Carib peoples fought fiercely to repel European invaders and to defend their lands, homes, and liberties. This they had a perfect right to do as human beings; such valiant defense of hearth, home, and sovereignty has been constantly extolled by Europeans in respect to themselves. Such brave and patriotic defense, indeed, has been held up, especially before the youth, as among the highest modes of human conduct. For example, in his epic poem *Lays of Ancient Rome*, Macaulay roundly declaimed:

> And how can man die better
> Than facing fearful odds
> For the ashes of his fathers
> And the temples of his gods?[1]

But it is a woeful misrepresentation, which this placard proclaims, that Caribs "tasted of all the nations that frequented them." Such an all-inclusive assertion of voracious man-eating is decidedly overstated, unsupported, and unproved. Besides, no *direct* reference has been given on the poster to any *specific, credible, and buttressed historical source of knowledge.*

How can it be certainly known or proven that the Caribs "tasted of all the nations which frequented them"? Where is the roster and the record of their tasting *all* those nations, indigenous as well as foreign? An answer is really required to the following question: What is the specific source and particular ground for the facile assumption, and flippant as well as nauseous affirmation, as to the gastronomic delicacy of French flesh and the toughness of the Spaniards? . . .

Besides, just who was that "old historian," referred to but not identified on the placard, who "records" such loose but damning calumnies against the Caribs? A diligent search has disclosed an author who appears to be responsible for passing on these derogatory accusations, Charles de Rochefort. If it be another source, then the Directors of the Museum are requested to state it so that it may be duly examined.

The book ascribed to Rochefort, published in French during 1658, was rendered into English by John Davies and published in London during 1666. Remarkably, this English edition bears two differing title pages—one beginning *The History of the Caribby-Islands*, etc., and the other *The History of Barbados*, etc., with the author's name omitted.[2] This indicates irresponsibility. R. P. Jean-Baptiste Du Tertre, whose book on the French-ruled Antilles was published in 1654, has charged that Rochefort's book was based chiefly on his (Du Tertre's) writings.[3]

Père Labat also affirmed that Rochefort "has copied Père Du Tertre but he has entirely spoiled his narration by description far removed from the truth, in the attempt to make things more agreeable and better to conceal his larceny."[4] Likewise, Elsa V. Goveia in her study quotes the historian Dampiere as having "established that Du Tertre's charge of piracy is almost certainly true. . . ." Goveia concludes: "His (Rocheforte's) narrative lacks the weight of detailed evidence which makes Du Tertre's so impressive."[5]

Du Tertre had recounted the report of the difference which the Caribs were said to have found between the taste of the French and the Spanish. But that historian expressly acknowledged that it was based on hearsay when he wrote: "I have heard it said many times." . . .[6]

That there should be no mistake about the position here taken, the thesis should now be clearly stated and understood.

It is *not* that people called Caribs have never partaken of human flesh. *Obviously, it could not be stated with certainty, either of Caribs, or of any other large group of people, that none of them ever ate human flesh.*

It is here held that there is no credible evidence *that Caribs ate of all who came among them,* as alleged on the offensive poster.

It is here affirmed also that *the common stereotype which pictures Caribs as customary and voracious cannibals, who made war and hunted down other human beings in order to devour them, is demonstrably erroneous, and has been used to attempt to justify their enslavement.*

It is further held that *comparison with similar deeds, especially in ritual and religious ceremonies practiced by other known peoples, does not logically nor justly permit the singling out of Caribs as typical and beastly "Cannibals."* . . .

In the *Encyclopedia Britannica,* Eleventh Edition, 1910–11, along with much that is by contrast lurid and questionable, there appears the following: "CARIBS, the name used first by Columbus (from Cariba, said to mean 'a valiant man'), of a South American people, who at the arrival of the Spanish, occupied parts of Guiana and the lower Orinoco and the Windward and other islands in what is still known as the Caribbean Sea. . . ."[7]

In like manner, Amos Kidder Fiske stated in *The West Indies,* New York, 1899: "Spanish writers used to say that Carib meant man-eater, and was synonymous with cannibal; but it meant nothing of the kind, and it was they who derived 'cannibal' from it by an ingenious variation from caribal or calibal, injecting into it a suggestion of canine origin."[8]

The term "cannibal" does indeed go back to Cristóbal Colón or Christopher Columbus, who shortly after he arrived in the Western Hemisphere, projected the word connected with certain false and vicious notions. It is known that he had travelled before to Guinea on the West Coast of Africa and certainly knew of the slave marts of Portugal and Spain. Columbus had thus become well acquainted with the modern slave trade, its stratagems, and attempted crafty justifications.[9]

Upon his first landing in the Bahamas, as quoted in his *Journal of the First Voyage* and similarly in his *First Letter,* Columbus said that the indigenous people "should be good servants, of quick intelligence, since I see that they very soon say all that is said to them and I believe that they would easily be made Christians."[10] In the entry of three days later, Columbus declared: "These people are very unskilled in arms, as your Highnesses will see from the seven whom I caused to be taken. . . . However, when your Highnesses so command, they can all be carried off to Castile or held captive on the island itself, since with fifty men they would be all kept in subjection and forced to do whatever may be wished."[11]

Upon considering the foregoing statement of Columbus, a discerning biographer Salvador de Madariaga has concluded: "Here is the beginning of the new slavery which the Christians introduced into America. Colón's idea was to triumph in the end, being more in harmony with the economic and social forces of the time. . . ."[12]

The "discoverer" also declared that he heard some of the indigenous people using Carib and kindred names to indicate powerful enemies whom they feared. Under the influence of the medieval mythology and travel accounts he had read in *The Book of Marco Polo* and Mandeville's *Travels*, Columbus confused such indigenous terms as *caritaba, cariba,* and *caribal* with *canima, caniba,* and *canibal*.[13]

Columbus [stated] in his *Journal:* "And so I repeat what I have said on other occasions, the Caniba are nothing else than the people of the Grand Khan, who must be very near here and possess ships, and they must come to take them captive, and as the prisoners do not return, they believe that they have been eaten. . . ."[14] Such a belief, however, was false.

At first the indigenous people believed the same of the Spanish invaders. For instance, Pedro Aguado stated that in New Granada the native inhabitants fought strenuously against the Spanish newcomers, because they believed these to be man-eaters looking for food.[15] A similar belief that European slave raiders were wholesale man-eaters was held in West Africa, because those taken were not known to return. . . .

Columbus himself soon adopted the notion, which he said before he did not believe, that the Caribs were cannibals. This notion he claimed to have heard from the indigenous people, whose language he did not know but was informed at times by signs! Apparently, too, Columbus had come to realize that this charge of cannibalism might well be used to justify his project of wholesale enslavement of the indigenous people.

The myth of ferocious man-eating commonly practiced by Caribs developed apace when Columbus assured King Gucanagari "that the Sovereigns of Castile would order the destruction of the Caribs and would have them all brought with their hands bound."[16]

The "discoverer" persisted in the false notion that he had reached the Indies of Asia, and also had encountered the "eaters of human flesh," as related by Marco Polo. Having assumed the titles which he had insisted upon in the capitulations or agreement with the Spanish sovereigns in case of "discovery"—"Don," "Admiral of the Ocean Sea," and "Viceroy"— Columbus, now "The Very Magnificent Lord Don Cristóbal Colón," presumed to call the entire area roundabout the "Indies" and the indigenous inhabitants "Indians."

Hence arose the misnomers "West Indies" and "West Indians," which deplorably have been allowed to remain. Imposed by colonizers, these misnomers definitely mark the Caribbean peoples as still thus culturally subjugated. Some perception of this appears to be emerging, as in the statement made by Carter Harman and the editors of *Life* in the book *The West Indies:* "When he [Columbus] called the islands the Indies, he set in motion a pattern of misunderstanding which still continues, and which is aggravated by a welter of historical confusion."[17]

It has been pointed out by Dr. Julio C. Salas, Professor of Sociology at the University of Mérida in Venezuela, in his book *The Carib Indians: Study of the Origin of the Myth of Man-Eating:* "Carib signifies in the language of the Antilles and of the continent, brave, daring."[18] The Venezuelan scholar, Gabriel Espinosa, in his study *The Conquest,* confirmed the meaning of Carib to have been "extraordinary man, valiant man."[19]

But Columbus, connected Carib, the name of the people, to cannibal, meaning inhuman man-eater, which would serve as a pretext for enslavement and severe ill treatment. To overcome the religious qualms and moral scruples, especially of Queen Isabella of Spain, Columbus portrayed Caribs as repulsive cannibals, hardly human and therefore deserving of slavery and rigorous treatment. Again and again, Columbus used this pretext of cannibalism while urging the Spanish rulers to sanction Carib slavery.

In his letter to the King and Queen of Spain, 1494, Columbus wrote: ". . . these [are] cannibals, a people very savage and suitable for the purpose, and well made and of very good intelligence. We believe that they, having abandoned that inhumanity, will be better than any other slaves."[20] Clearly, the myth of ferocious Carib man-eaters is now full blown, its pernicious purpose is plainly apparent.

Again, in the Memorandum sent by Antonio de Torres during 1495, Christopher Columbus instructed: "You shall say to their Highnesses that . . . there are now sent with these ships some of the cannibals, men and women and boys and girls . . . it is thought here that to take some of the men and women and to send them home to Castile would not be anything but well, for they may one day be led to abandon that inhuman custom which they have of eating men, and there in Castile, learning the language, they will much more readily receive baptism and secure the welfare of their souls."[21] Columbus further urged the Spanish sovereigns to "give license and a permit" for a regular traffic which would supply "cattle and other supplies and things for the colonisation of the country. . . . Payment for these things could be made to them in slaves, from among these cannibals, a people very savage and suitable for the purpose. . . ."[22] To this suggestion of enslavement the Catholic rulers replied: "As to this the matter has been postponed for the present."[23]

Despite this official postponement, Columbus sought to foster the development of a slave trade by sending to Spain ships laden with hundreds of supposed "cannibals." Among these were women and children; the great majority were captured not from the Caribs but from among the "meek and friendly" Arawaks or Tainos.

Addressing the Spanish monarchs once more in 1496, Columbus urged: "We can send from here in the name of the Holy Trinity all the slaves and brazil-wood which could be sold . . . we can sell 4,000 slaves, who will be worth, at least, 20 millions. . . ."[24] "Frightful project," later commented Alexander von Humboldt upon considering this vast and ruthless slave scheme.[25]

The Spanish monarchs in June 1500, doubtless because of Queen Isabella, ordered that all slaves "who were brought from the Indies" should be liberated and returned. Three years later, however, the crafty appeals of Columbus and other advocates of slavery had prevailed. Salvation of souls was to be accomplished through forcible enslavement of the bodies of all who were said to resist subjection and to practice cannibalism. . . .

This sanction of the Catholic rulers made it possible for Spanish colonizers to label the indigenous people "cannibals" and proceed to enslave them. Arthur Helps in his study *The Spanish Conquest in America* has observed tersely: "As was to be expected, this permission led to great abuse."[26] True, but a great understatement indeed. . . .

The permission of the Spanish monarchs to enslave "cannibals" was thus the death-knell of millions of the indigenous peoples of the Circum-Caribbean area—Arawaks, Tainos, and others, besides Caribs. Driven to death in the mines, in diving for pearls, and on the fields, hunted by ravenous dogs trained for the purpose, and mowed down by the Spanish cross-bows, swords, and firearms, the native peoples were rapidly exterminated. The appalling genocide has been described by Las Casas in the *Shortest Account of the Destruction of the Indies;* an English translation appeared under the title *The Tears of the Indians.*

The broad pattern of colonialist conquest, of the frightful displacement and destruction of aboriginal peoples, and of their replacement by others, was now thoroughly developed and became ever more rapidly extended. Some fifty years after the Portuguese began the modern slave trade in Africa, the demand for slave labor in the Americas spurred the seizure and transport of millions of Africans across the Atlantic into hapless and brutal bondage in the "New World." Nine years after the first arrival of Columbus, the Spanish monarchs gave permission to colonizers in America to import African slaves "such as were born under the power of Spain." Soon slaves could be brought directly from Africa; the Spanish settlers held that as laborers "one Negro was worth four Indians."

As the Spanish conquistadors invaded the mainland and spread over Central and South America, penetrating also into North America, the gruesome pattern of oppression was ever more widely adopted and practiced. The pattern initiated and imposed by the Portuguese in Africa and further developed by the Spanish in the Americas, was followed and carried forward by the English, French, Dutch, Danes, and Germans. The "civilization" thus brought by European colonizers has spelt, and still spells, bondage, misery, and genocide—the ruthless destruction of the lives and cultures of the colonized peoples.

Several students have recognized the horrendous result of the appalling combination of religious zeal with personal gain. A biographer of Columbus, Marcel Brion, in reviewing this development has pointed out: "Carried away by their zeal to exploit the Indians, the conquerors took advantage of everything that would cause the anger and distrust of their compatriots. The great majority at home . . . believed implicitly in the accuracy of these tales and held legitimate slavery imposed on such barbarous people, really more like beasts than men."[27]

The false nature of the accusation of savage and common Carib man-eating is shown by Marcel Brion thus:

> The general aversion of the Indians to human meat is confirmed by the fact that in periods of famine and during the sieges they preferred to die of hunger than touch the bodies of their companions. This reduces to nothing the legend that cannibalism was habitually practised by the Indians.[28]

In his study *Illusion in the Conquest,* Dr. Federico Fernández Castillejo showed the following: "It was Christopher Columbus himself who was the creator of the myth of the existence of Caribs [as man-eaters] in the Antillean Islands . . . the myth created by Columbus was shortly adopted by all and repeated by historians and geographers." "Las Casas and other chroniclers of the epoch," he continued, "explain to us how the early conquerors, imbued with the myth already created, saw as remains of cannibal feasts the human bones that the Indians conserved as relics of their dead kinsmen." . . .[29]

Among Spanish colonizers few ever questioned the destructive slander of "cannibalism" against the Caribs, or any phase of the frightful oppression of the indigenous peoples. Las Casas was the outstanding exception who challenged the false branding of "cannibals" directly in specific cases. The Dominican Antonio Montesinos was the first known openly to castigate the Spanish settlers and to affirm the human rights of their victims. The Pope and the hierarchy of the Roman Catholic Church sanctioned the enslavement of Caribs as "cannibals."

The priest Fray Fernando de Carmellones, however, wrote a letter to the Council of the Indies which declared: "If anyone says he has seen the Indians eat Friars, the Council should consider it a joke."[30] A literary Spanish conquistador Juan de Castellanos, in his epic *Elegies,* was compelled by the facts finally to admit:

> they were called Caribs
> not because they would eat human flesh
> but because they defended their homes well.[31]

Though the Spanish were the first Europeans to encounter the Caribs, the French lived in the same island areas with them the longest. From the most probable source of the statement on the placard, which has previously been attributed here to Charles de Rochefort, there is a very similar statement. However, this ends with a sentence *not* on the placard in the Museum specifically, "But now they do not feed on any Christians at all." *Here is clear evidence that neither the wholesale cannibalism, nor the specific tasting of French and Spanish as charged, existed when that particular accusation was written.* Rochefort thus makes it known, perhaps unwittingly, that he wrote from hearsay and not as an eyewitness. . . .

A subsequent investigator in the Antillean Islands, Jean Pierre Labat, affirmed pointedly:

> It is an error to believe that the Savages of our Isles are man-eaters, and that they go to war to make prisoners in order to satiate their hunger, or that having taken them without such intention, they use the occasion with those in their hands, in order to devour them. I have proofs to the contrary clearer than day.[32]

The foregoing citations appear to be quite conclusive as to the falsity of the repulsive brand "cannibal" as put upon the Caribs. The term "savages," however, should be illumined by the profound observation made by Père Du Tertre:

> By this word savage alone, most people of the world conjure up in their minds, a sort of men, barbarous, cruel, hairy like bears, finally more of monsters than of reasonable human beings: *but in truth, our savages are savages in name only.* (Emphasis added).[33]

Most modern writers on the Caribbean uncritically copy the statements of chroniclers partisan to and allied with the self-centered conquerors. Foremost among these is the former colonial administrator Sir Alan Burns. In his *History of the British West Indies* Burns recounts every possible scrap of hearsay and rumor reviling the colonized peoples, even extending the charge of cannibalism to the "mild and pacific" Arawaks or Tainos.[34] Some rather recent inquirers, however, have begun to pierce through the fog of ignorance, misrepresentation, and deliberate lies. . . .

In the current edition of *All the Best in the Caribbean*, 1972, Sidney Clark with Margaret Zellers, concludes: "Spanish lust and ruthlessness *erased* the gentle Arawaks from the face of the earth, but the Caribs put up a much stronger fight and were often tough customers. Their aboriginal habits are suggested in the etymology of the word cannibal, which is a Spanish corruption of their name, *but this was a contemptuous word of a hostile race and may cast a needless slur upon the Indians.*" [Emphasis added—RBM].[35]

The former current statement coincides with the estimate made by Philip Ainsworth Means in *The Spanish Main Focus of Envy*, 1931. Never once did he repeat the canard of Carib cannibalism. Instead, he affirmed forthrightly:

The Caribs, truth to tell, were remarkable and respect-compelling people. ... To this day a remnant of them survives in proud isolation on some of the least attractive islands. Neither Spaniard, Englishman, Frenchman, nor Hollander has succeeded in breaking their fierce hearts; rather they have been brought low in the world by the insidious forces of imported disease, by miscegenation, and by economic oppression. Hail to their gallant and freedom-loving spirit.[36]

The culture of the Caribs has been noted, from the time of their first encounter with Europeans, as advanced in that area which still bears their proud name. Their self-esteem has been remarked; French writers report them frequently saying, with pronounced self-respect and human dignity, "Moi Caraibe, toi Français." Their bows and arrows and clubs were far superior to the weapons of Arawaks or Tainos. This Carib song reflects their development, strength, and valor:

I am the force of the spirit of the lightning eel, the thunder axe, the stone. I am the force of the firefly, thunder and lightning I have created.[37]

Looking lastly at general charges of cannibalism, it becomes apparent that such have been made widely against peoples of Africa, Asia, and Australia, as well as indigenous America. ... [Consider the distortion used to justify] the continued massacre of the indigenous people while despoiling them of their lands in what is now the U.S.A. Such common and persistent sayings speak volumes: "The only good Indian is a dead Indian!"

Obviously, such lethal characterizations and attitudes projected by conquerors, enslavers, and traducers should now be counteracted and eliminated. For these fan the flames of hatred, hostility and conflict. In this age of "overkill," such smears could readily cause conflict which might lead to dire consequences, even the destruction of mankind.

This question should not be lightly dismissed as just a thing of the past of little consequence for the present and the future. Gerard Piel, publisher of *Scientific American* and author of the current book *The Acceleration of History*, presents a striking example of how the legacy of the past may seriously damage our present and menace our future. Piel wrote:

The ugly transactions involved derive their ethical justifications from the deep unconscious of society—from the institutional memory of the days when the slavemaster drove 80 percent of the population to work in the fields and mines in order that the few might get on with the high occupation of making history and civilization. The cruelty and inhumanity that persist in our system from those days must be extirpated if we are to resolve successfully the issues that confront us.[38]

This essay, therefore, emphasizes the urgent request that the offensive placard directly smearing Caribs as cannibals, and indirectly besmirching other indigenous peoples, should be removed by the Directors from the Museum in Nelson's Dockyard in Antigua.

The request is also made to all to whom this may come, especially to public officials, educators, and all who mold public opinion, to expunge all such debasing names, labels, and statements from the media of communication, especially from books for the instruction of youth.

It is requested finally that all loaded, odious, and degrading terms such as "cannibal," "savage," "primitive," "barbarian," "uncivilized," "native," "negro," "mulatto," and the like be rejected and avoided in the interest of amicable and healthy human relations.

The foregoing request is in accord with recommendations made in the *Report of the Meetings of Experts on Educational Methods Designed to Combat Racial Prejudice.* This report was issued during 1968 by the United Nations Educational, Scientific and Cultural Organization, or UNESCO. These recommendations concerning proper terminology follow:

> The experts agreed that a special precision and prudence should be encouraged among teachers and educationists, authors and publishers of textbooks and other teaching materials and those concerned with the mass media in the use of terminology to describe people of differing ethnic, religious, or other groups, especially former colonized peoples. It was stressed that terms such as "tribe," "native," "savage," "primitive," "jungle," "pagan," "kaffir," "bushmen," "backward," "underdeveloped," "uncivilized," "vernacular," "Negro," "coloured," and "race," *inter alia,* were so charged with emotive potential that their use, with or without conscious pejorative intent, to describe or characterize certain ethnic, social or religious groups, generally provoked an adverse reaction on the part of these groups. . . .
>
> In addition, it was agreed that much of the current terminology used with reference to "race" questions was a heritage of a colonial past and often perpetuated feelings of superiority and prejudice.[39]

Finally, this essay is by no means to be considered as an academic exercise. Rather, this has been a quest for truth in order to expose the harmful use of debasing terms like "cannibal," "savage," "barbarous," "uncivilized." It is clear that by such means human beings have been prejudiced and pitted against each other in deadly conflict. Consequently, the attempt has here been directed toward achieving a climate of regard for others which will make the co-existence of peoples possible and secure. For mankind now appears to be faced with the alternative—co-existence or no existence.

NOTES

1. Thomas Babington Macaulay, *Lays of Ancient Rome,* Horatius XXVII, quoted in *Oxford Dictionary of Quotations,* 2nd ed. 1955, p. 323.

2. John Davis, trans., *The History of the Caribby-Islands,* etc. (London, 1666), Title page. Also by the same author, *The History of Barbados* . . . (London, 1666), Title page.

3. R. P. Jean-Baptiste Du Tertre, *Histoire générale des Iles de S. Christophe, de la Guadeloupe, de la Martinique, et autres dans l'Amerique*, (Paris, 1654); also by the same author *Reédition Executée d'Apres L'Edition de 1667–1671 aux Frais de la Société d'Histoire de la Martinique*, 1959.

4. Père Jean-Pierre Labat, *Nouveaux Voyages aux Iles de l'Amerique* (Paris, 1722).

5. Elsa V. Goveia, *A Study on the Historiography of the British West Indies* (Mexico, 1956), pp. 21–24.

6. Du Tertre, *Reédition Executée*, op. cit.

7. *Encyclopaedia Britannica*, Eleventh Edition, 1910–11.

8. Amos Kidder Fiske, *The West Indies* (New York, 1899), pp. 31–33.

9. Salvador de Madariaga, *Christopher Columbus* (London, 1949), pp. 138, 216–17.

10. Christopher Columbus, *The Journal of Christopher Columbus*, Cecil Jane, trans. (New York, 1960), p. 24.

11. Ibid. p. 28.

12. Salvador de Madariaga, op. cit. p. 138.

13. Justin Winsor, *Christopher Columbus* (Boston & New York, 1896), p. 166; Leo Weiner, *Africa and the Discovery of America*, 3 vols. (Philadelphia, 1920–22), Vol. 1, p. 20 and p. 43.

14. Columbus, op. cit., p. 62; Winsor, op. cit., p. 224.

15. Jerónimo Becker y González, ed. *Historia de Santa Marta y Nuevo Reino de Grenada* (Madrid, 1916–17), Vol. II, pp. 38–39.

16. Columbus, op. cit., p. 125.

17. Carter Harman, *The West Indies* (New York: Life, 1966), p. 10.

18. Julio C. Salas, *Los Indios Caribes: Estudios Sobre el Mito de la Antropofagia* (Madrid, 1920).

19. Gabriel Espinosa, *La Conquista, Vida, Política, Social e Intelectual de Venezuela* (Caracas, 1940), p. 43.

20. Christopher Columbus, *Letter to Ferdinand and Isabella, King and Queen of Spain*, 1494, quoted in Eric Williams, *Documents of West Indian History, 1492–1655* (Port-of-Spain, Trinidad, 1963), p. 54.

21. Christopher Columbus, *Memorandum to Spanish Sovereigns sent by Antonio Torres*, January 30, 1495, quoted in *Select Documents Illustrating the Four Voyages of Columbus* by Cecil Jane, 2 vols. (London, 1930), pp. 88–92.

22. Columbus, quoted in Eric Williams, op. cit. p. 56.

23. Ibid., p. 57.

24. Ibid.

25. Quoted by André Marius, *Columbus*.

26. Arthur Helps, *The Spanish Conquest in America and its Relation to the History of Slavery and to the Government of Colonies*, 4 vols. (London, 1855–61, revised edition, London, 1900–04), p. 141.

27. Marcel Brion, *Bartolomé de las Casas* (New York, 1929), p. 16.

28. Ibid., p. 14.

29. Federico Fernández Castillejo, *La Ilusión en la Conquista: Génesis de los Mitos y Leyendas Americanas* (Buenos Aires, 1945), p. 60.

30. Lewis Hanke, *Aristotle and the American Indians* (Bloomington, Indiana, 1959), pp. 18–19.

31. Castellanos, quoted in Julio C. Salas, *Los Indios Caribes* (Madrid, 1920), p. 135.

32. Labat, *Nouveaux Voyages*, Tome IV, p. 321.

33. Du Tertre, *Reédition Executée*, op. cit., Tome II, p. 337.

34. Sir Alan Burns, *History of the British West Indies* (London, 1965), pp. 40–45, 80, 90, 120, 121.

35. Sidney Clarke, with Margaret Zeller, *All the Best in the Caribbean* (New York, 1972), p. 3.

36. Philip Ainsworth Means, *The Spanish Main Focus of Envy* (New York, 1935), p. 153.

37. Elizabeth Chesley Baity, *Americans Before Columbus* (New York, 1954), p. 50.

38. Gerald Piel, *The Acceleration of History* (New York, 1972), p. 139.

39. UNESCO. *Report of the Meeting of Experts on Educational Methods Designed to Combat Racial Prejudice* (United Nations, 1968), pp. 24–27.

XI

THE PAN-CARIBBEAN
MOVEMENT IN HARLEM

*Although there was early agitation for federation by unusual leaders like
Andrew Cipriani in Trinidad and T. Albert Marryshow in Grenada, the
insular isolation had not produced an enduring Pan-Caribbean movement.
The uprisings of 1937 that inspired Reginald Pierrepoint to bring together
a group of determined activists in New York marked a turning point. They
sounded a cry that would never be silenced until independence was
achieved. The seven documents that constitute appeals addressed to the
British and United States governments, Pan-American Foreign Ministers,
Caribbean leaders, delegates to the founding of the Charter of the United
Nations, and an American political party need to be viewed as a whole.
Each is a significant link in the story of a struggle carried on by a small
cadre of Afro-Caribbean expatriates in New York to alter the flow of history
by speeding the process of independence and channeling it into the desired
form of federation. While the documents were released by organizations and
reflect the perspective of many individuals, they represent Moore's philosophy, commitment, and proficiency in writing resolutions and appeals.*

DECLARATION OF RIGHTS OF THE CARIBBEAN
PEOPLES TO SELF-DETERMINATION AND
SELF-GOVERNMENT

West Indies National Emergency Committee, submitted to the Pan-American Foreign Ministers' Conference, Havana, Cuba, July 1940. Richard B. Moore Papers.

There comes a time in the affairs of every people when it becomes
imperative for them to examine their conditions of existence and to take
such steps as they deem necessary for the protection of their vital interests
and for the enjoyment of their unalienable rights to "life, liberty, and the
pursuit of happiness."

Such a time has arrived in the history of the peoples who have for
centuries inhabited the Caribbean colonies of Britain, France, and the

Netherlands. These peoples, whose total aggregate is over three and a half million and who occupy territories approximating 231,314 square miles, are specifically designated in an appendix to this declaration.*

The war now raging in Europe has brought to the fore the question of basic political and economic adjustments for the peoples of the West Indies and of both American continents. This grave situation has compelled the democratic and peace-loving nations of the Western Hemisphere seriously to consider the best possible collective measures for their mutual defense, security, and welfare.

The existence of strategically situated and economically important European colonies in the New World constitutes, and will always constitute, a basis for aggression and a threat to the security of the nations of Pan-America.

For many years responsible statesmen of the Americas have enunciated the doctrine that this hemisphere should be kept immune from the rivalries and wars of the Old World. The vital interests of the inhabitants of the Caribbean regions, as part of the Americas, are indissolubly bound up in the practical establishment and actual maintenance of this basic principle.

The political control of the peoples of these territories by non-American powers is now recognized to be a menace to the safety and security of all American nations. Opinion is being developed in the United States of America appealing to this sentiment and advocating the sale, transfer, forcible seizure of, or establishment of trusteeship or mandate over these Caribbean areas. But any such menace can best be removed only by the integration of the West Indian peoples into the Pan-American family of nations strictly on the basis of the right of self-determination. Only thus will it be possible to create an enduring foundation for genuine "Good Neighbor" relations.

Taking full cognizance of the grave nature and the serious implications of these proposals for change of sovereignty, the West Indies National Emergency Committee regards it as its solemn duty to present the case and the cause of the peoples most directly involved to the Pan-American nations and to the entire world.

The Committee identifies itself with and whole-heartedly supports every effort honestly directed towards keeping the continents of America out of war. It realizes and submits that conflicts over colonies constitute the major source of war in the modern world. Therefore, the assurance of the right of self-determination and self-government to the West Indian peoples is unquestionably necessary to remove this major danger of war from the Western Hemisphere. Reflecting and expressing the profound sentiments of the peoples of these Caribbean areas, this Committee declares that it is firmly and irrevocably opposed to any sale, transfer, mandate, trusteeship,

---

*Appendix not included in this volume.

or change of sovereignty of these peoples without the exercise of their inalienable human and democratic right of self-determination.

On behalf of the peoples of the West Indies and the adjacent Caribbean areas concerned, whose human aspirations and political interests it expresses, the Committee solemnly protests against any action on the part of Britain, France, and Holland or any other power that would in any way abridge or deny them their indefeasible right to a dominant voice in the shaping of their own destiny. The Committee insists that the will of these peoples must be fully ascertained, in accordance with genuine democratic principles and processes, in respect to any change whatever in their political status.

Fully conscious of the fundamental justice of their cause and reposing confidence in the democratic sentiment of the Pan-American peoples, the peoples of the West Indies and the adjacent Caribbean territories involved openly proclaim their right to untrammeled self-determination. Any denial of this right to them will be opposed by every legitimate means and any attempt at such denial will constitute irrefutable evidence of imperialistic motives and designs on the part of every power involved in any change of sovereignty or establishment of military, naval, or aerial bases in these territories without the consent of the peoples immediately and most vitally concerned.

Moreover, any abridgement or denial of this fundamental democratic right of self-determination would be none other than a flagrant violation of the principles of democracy so long proclaimed by the nations of Pan-America. It is self-evident also that any such denial would weaken, undermine, and destroy the democratic structure which must underlie and sustain all Pan-American nationality and concert for defense.

It is unquestionable, furthermore, that any refusal to recognize and to respect the national aspirations of the Caribbean peoples would be a clear denial and an unmistakable repudiation of the very principles of democracy and the rights of small nations for which the sympathies of the American and Latin American peoples are being solicited in the present crisis. This grave crisis in world affairs only raises most sharply the basic question of self-determination and self-government which had already been raised by the peoples of these territories.

The West Indies National Emergency Committee recognizes the imminent probability of changes of sovereignty in colonial territories in the New World and presents its case for the rights of the peoples, whose just cause it advocates, to autonomous national existence. The Committee draws attention to the fact that every nation in the New World developed from the status of a colony or colonies to its present position as an independent nation and declares that this historical circumstance should justly render every Pan-American nation sympathetic to the aspirations of the West Indian and Caribbean peoples for self-government.

The Committee points to the fact that the inhabitants in these areas have long since reached that stage in historical evolution where they have demonstrated their capacity for practical administration of government in accordance with modern democratic technique. West Indians participate in every department of government—legislative, executive, judicial—to such an extent that only a few posts are administered by Europeans solely because of the existing imperial connections.

The Committee further points to the fact that the peoples of these areas exhibit all the characteristics of nationality and that vigorous movements for self-government have existed for a considerable period and have now reached a stage for full realization. Evidence of this is adduced in several instances and representations cited in the statement appended hereto.

The recent world-shaking military events in Europe and the resulting critical situation for the West Indian peoples have heightened their insistent demand for self-determination and self-government. The declaration hereafter quoted, made by elected members of the Jamaica Legislative Council as reported in the press of that country on May 27, 1940, is typical of the prevailing sentiment of the Caribbean peoples on this crucial question of sale, transfer, mandate, trusteeship, or change of sovereignty: "Should circumstances ever arise as to include the possibility of such a change then the people of this island would claim the right to determine their own destiny, and not be handed over as a piece of chattel to any foreign nation."

Such a realization of self-government has long been recognized as the goal towards which all Pan-American nations should inevitably move. In a message delivered to the Congress of the United States of America on December 6, 1869, President Ulysses S. Grant, speaking on the future of European colonies in the Western Hemisphere, declared: "These dependencies are no longer regarded as subject to transfer from one European power to another. When the present relation of colonies ceases, they are to become independent Powers, exercising the right of choice and of self-control in the determination of the future condition and relations with other Powers."

At the recent Inter-American Conference held at Panama, in September, 1939, Foreign Secretary Eduardo Hay of Mexico presented the statement hereinafter quoted.

"Because of the war some regions of America controlled by non-American states may cease depending on the authorities of those countries.

"That if it appears that some change in sovereignty is about to occur, a consultation meeting should be convoked in order to aid that region freely to determine its own political destiny.

"That it would be unjust to consider the American subjects of non-American nations simply as merchandise.

"That they should be given an opportunity to decide their own political destinies."

A resolution adopted by the official delegates of all the Pan-American nations at the American Scientific Congress, held in Washington in May, 1939, solemnly affirmed that the American republics were "all adherents to the principle of the right of each nation to determine its own destiny."

In pursuit of this high purpose of self-determination, self-government, and the democratic concert of the peoples of the Western Hemisphere, the West Indies National Emergency Committee wholeheartedly subscribes to every sincere effort for the extirpation of all forces hostile to democratic institutions. It solemnly pledges its fullest cooperation with all the American nations in every action necessary to defend, to preserve, and to extend democracy in the Western Hemisphere and to uphold democratic principles throughout the world.

The Committee appeals to all who uphold democracy and to every true lover of liberty in all the Americas and indeed throughout the world to support the rightful claims and just cause of the peoples of the West Indies and the adjacent Caribbean areas to self-determination and self-government.

Let the solemn warning of events be heeded and the inexorable logic of the present critical situation be squarely and fairly faced. Then the justice and wisdom of this earnest appeal will be acknowledged and support and recognition of these rightful claims will be duly accorded as absolutely essential to the mutual defense, security, welfare, peace, and progress of all the peoples of the Americas to the end "that government of the people by the people and for the people, shall not perish from the earth."

A REPLY TO CORDELL HULL

Statement of the West Indies National Emergency Committee on the Address Delivered by Secretary of State of the United States of America, Cordell Hull, to the Pan-American Foreign Ministers' Conference at Havana, Cuba, July 22, 1940 in Respect to the Status of European Possessions in the Western Hemisphere. Richard B. Moore Papers.

The important declaration of Secretary of State, Cordell Hull, on the momentous question of the future destiny of the Caribbean Peoples now held as colonial subjects of the European Empires of Britain, France, and Holland, deserves the most serious consideration.

All who are concerned about the preservation of democracy and peace will welcome the unequivocal statement of the Foreign Minister of the United States of America thus repudiating and opposing any aims at annexation or barter of these peoples and countries:

We have no desire to absorb those possessions or to extend our sovereignty over them, or to include them in any form or sphere of influence. We could not, however, permit these regions to become a subject of barter in the settlement of European differences, or a battleground for the adjustment of such differences.

Nevertheless, a full realization of the fundamental factors involved in this crucial question must compel all democratic and peace-loving people deeply to deplore the endorsement by the Government of the United States of the suggestion for "the establishment of a collective trusteeship, to be exercised in the name of all the American republics."

For, however well-intentioned such a proposed collective trusteeship might appear, it cannot be forgotten that this device of trusteeship or mandate has been used and is now being used by imperial governments of the Old World as a means of maintaining control over various peoples and of subjecting them to tyrannous oppression and unbridled exploitation.

It cannot be conceded for a moment that this discredited formula of trusteeship could be successfully employed in connection with the Caribbean peoples, when it is well-known that it has signally failed either to ensure the democratic rights or to preserve the vital interests and welfare of the many down-trodden peoples to whom it has been applied.

In the light of these indisputable facts, it is difficult and indeed utterly impossible to reconcile this onerous reality of trusteeship with the lofty definition of trusteeship as proclaimed by Secretary Hull in the following terms:

> The purpose of a collective trusteeship must be to further the interests and security of all the American nations as well as the interest of the region in question.

But the most distressing utterance is the extensive and ominous undertaking made by Secretary Hull, without any known solicitation from any competent source or any consultation whatever with the peoples of the Caribbean areas, that:

> As soon as conditions permit, the region should be restored to its original sovereign or be declared independent when able to establish and maintain stable self-government.

The West Indies National Emergency Committee has solemnly avowed its "pursuit of the high purpose of self-determination, self-government, and the democratic concert of the peoples of the Western Hemisphere." This Committee would be disloyal to these principles of democracy and derelict in the discharge of its sacred duty, if it failed to register its emphatic protest against this proposed custody of these peoples and regions and their subsequent restoration to the sovereignty of any non-American powers.

In the name of justice and democracy, this Committee must firmly oppose any plan whereby the Republics of the Americas, at the behest of the United States of America, shall act as custodians, receivers, and bailiffs for European Empires now tottering, bankrupt, or definitely fascist. For such "collective trusteeship" qualified with an undertaking that "the region should be restored to its original sovereign," implies recognition of the sovereignty of non-American powers, which have already submitted to and adopted fascism or have steadily appeased and aided fascist aggression and conquest.

The immediate menace of any recognity of sovereignty of such Empires is real and obvious. Events have demonstrated that no imperialistic power can be depended upon to safeguard peoples under its rule from fascist suppression. High-sounding declarations and lofty assertions are followed by base betrayal and the millions of colonial peoples are in fact only pawns to be sacrificed in predatory warfare or bartered in nefarious deals without their consultation or consent.

It is indisputable that this is the actual policy of all imperialistic powers, and that none of the non-American powers claiming sovereignty over the Caribbean peoples is in any way excepted from this pernicious policy. History attests this and so does the statement of a profound British student of colonial policy, W. M. Macmillan, made in the Preface to his book *Warning From the West Indies*, written in August 1938:

> As a result of the general lack of interest in the colonial peoples, for their own sakes, the disillusioned school which has come to the front in the discussion of the 'colonial question' gains many followers. There are those who . . . would make over control of 'backward peoples,' and a share of their territory, to the very different racialist Germany of 1938.

It is necessary to recall once more the resolution unanimously adopted by the official representatives of all Pan-American Republics in Washington in May 1939, which solemnly affirmed that they were "all adherents to the principle of the right of each nation to determine its own destiny."

The Committee is compelled to ask: "Have not the Caribbean peoples this democratic right to determine their own destiny? How can this basic human right be denied to these American peoples by nations of our hemisphere which claim this fundamental right for themselves? And how can the continued recognition of sovereignty of European Empires, as expressed in this proposal of Secretary Hull, be squared with the historical development of all the American peoples in the path of freedom, or with the interest and security of all the American nations as well as the region in question?"

It is an axiom of American democracy that sovereignty resides in the people. Therefore, the sole paramount sovereignty which is now properly to be recognized is that of the peoples who inhabit these Caribbean regions. It is self-evident also that to keep these peoples any longer in the status of colonial subjects is directly opposed to their vital interests and to their

expressed demands and explicit strivings for the realization of the democratic rights of self-government and self-determination. Moreover, such an
imposition of continued colonial subjection under any form or device
would not only mean the negation and spell the doom of democracy, but
would also preserve that very condition of conflict between Empires which
is the major source of war and of the present grave danger to the "security
of all the American nations."

In respect to the other alternative presented by Secretary Hull that the
region "be declared independent when able to establish and maintain
stable self-government," the Committee re-affirms and emphasizes the
incontestable facts presented in its "Declaration of Rights of the Caribbean
Peoples to Self-Determination and Self-Government" and in the Appendix
containing "Evidence of the Widespread and Urgent Character of the
Demands of the Caribbean Peoples for Self-Government and Self-
Determination."

The Committee affirms again without fear of successful refutation that
the Caribbean peoples have long been prepared and have practically
demonstrated their complete competence and present readiness for full
self-government and free national existence. No basis exists, therefore, on
these grounds for any question whatever as to their present ability "to
establish and maintain stable self-government," or to postpone to some
indefinite, nebulous, and questionable future forthright recognition of
their right to free and independent national existence.

It is an old device of tyrants to traduce the peoples whom they oppress
and to seek to justify their predatory domination over these down-trodden
peoples by declaring them to be unfit to govern themselves. The whole
specious theory of modern Empire, of spurious trusteeship, and indeed of
fascist domination, is founded upon this false and monstrous denial of the
fitness and ability of people to govern themselves. But it is a basic democratic American principle, enunciated by the immortal Abraham Lincoln
precisely in respect to such pretensions whereby "self-government" is
transformed into "despotism," that "no man is good enough to govern
another man without the other's consent. I say this is the leading principle,
the sheet-anchor of American republicanism."

The Committee further directs attention to the statement of principle
affirmed by Secretary Hull in this challenging address:

> Mankind can advance only when human freedom is secure; when the right
> of self-government is safeguarded; when all nations recognize each other's
> right to conduct its internal affairs free from outside interference. . . .

The West Indies National Emergency Committee earnestly submits that
if these words have any significance, substance, or reality, they can only
mean concretely in application to this momentous question, the immediate,
unconditional, and actual recognition of the rights of the Caribbean Peo-

ples to govern themselves, to determine their own destiny, and to join voluntarily as free national entities, in the concert of Pan-American nations. It is crystal clear also, that such recognition is the only way to achieve a just, democratic, peaceful and lasting settlement of this grave question, and guarantee "the interests and security of all the American nations, as well as of the region in question."

APPEAL TO THE UNITED NATIONS CONFERENCE ON INTERNATIONAL ORGANIZATION ON BEHALF OF THE CARIBBEAN PEOPLES

West Indies National Council. Submitted to the United Nations Conference at its founding, San Francisco, May 25, 1945. Richard B. Moore Papers.

To this historic Assembly of Delegates of the United Nations met to lay the foundations of World Security and Peace, the Caribbean Peoples which are still held as colonial dependencies now look with eager hope and confident expectation. In this Conference these peoples see the great opportunity never before afforded by history for the adoption at last of those democratic principles and the establishment of effective means of enforcement which will enable them to realize their long sought goal and inalienable human rights to freedom, security, and self-government along with all the liberty-loving nations of the world.

Events preceding and during this war have shown that security and peace depend upon organization which will ensure justice, equal rights and protection to all peoples, to small and weak nations as well as to great and strong, and which will provide guarantees for the effective exercise of genuine democratic rights by all people who cherish and defend democracy.

It is therefore essential that the voice of dominated peoples, seeking justice and the exercise of those democratic rights for which they fought and bled, should be heard and accorded due consideration by this World Conference upon which the solemn responsibility rests to rescue mankind from the ravages of war, insecurity, and slavery.

Colonial Status Renders Appeal Necessary

Because the very status of colonial dependency imposes onerous restrictions which render it extremely difficult if not impossible for these peoples to make direct representation, it is necessary for the West Indies National

Council to present this Appeal on behalf of the peoples of the British, French, and Dutch West Indies, the Guianas and British Honduras. This Council, organized by natives of these areas, and supported by liberty-loving individuals and organizations irrespective of nationality, creed, or race, reflects the fundamental aspirations of these peoples based upon original ties, constant contact and knowledge, and the statements of responsible democratic representatives of the peoples of these areas.

This Appeal is therefore respectfully and earnestly presented together with seven proposals, adopted by this Council and endorsed by a public meeting assembled on April 16, 1945, at the Renaissance Casino in New York City and further endorsed by the Paragon Progressive Community Association, Inc., the Congress of Dominated Nations, and other organizations and prominent individuals. The Council requests that this Appeal be duly considered and urges this World Conference to adopt its recommendations and proposals in the form appropriate to secure their enforcement. The Council further desires to assure this World Conference that the peoples of these Caribbean areas may be depended upon wholeheartedly to support every measure necessary to the establishment of security, peace, and democracy, as their record amply demonstrates, and also to assume and discharge all duties and responsibilities in furtherance thereof.

Declaration of Rights—Act of Havana

The Declaration of Rights of the Caribbean Peoples to Self-Determination and Self-Government was presented by the West Indies National Emergency Committee to the Pan-American Foreign Ministers' Conference at Havana in July 1940. As a result, the Act of Havana while providing for concerted action by American Powers, recognized certain democratic rights of the Caribbean peoples.

Nevertheless, the Act of Havana was never invoked, though the French and Dutch Empires failed to provide protection and ceased in fact to exist as effective governing heads for these colonies. For a period indeed the people of the French West Indies and Guiana found themselves subject to the control of the fascist Vichy regime against their will and profound democratic conviction.

Vital Support Rendered by Caribbean Peoples

Despite the debilitating hindrances and galling yoke of colonial domination, the Caribbean peoples have loyally and unstintingly supported the United Nations in the present war against Nazi barbarism and fascist domination. In proportion to their size and numbers and the meager actual resources left to them after centuries of colonial retardation and impoverishment, they have made notable contributions to the armed forces and in labor power, finance, and essential materials such as oil, bauxite, etc.

Situated around the approaches to the Panama Canal, which was built mainly by their labor, at the strategic center of the defenses of the Americas, the peoples of the West Indies have suffered and withstood savage attacks by German submarines. Sites for vital bases and labor for their construction have been willingly furnished for the defense of the Americas and the United Nations, even though the rights of these peoples to consultation were not considered.

The Anglo-American Caribbean Commission has conducted broadcasts, made studies, and held conferences, but has done nothing practically to implement the rights of these peoples to self-government and self-determination. These fundamental rights are contravened by the very composition of this Commission which does not include a single direct representative of the Caribbean peoples or any one allied with them by ties of origin, feeling, and contact, in spite of repeated requests for such representation.

Colonial Conditions Menace World Security

The economic and social conditions prevailing in these areas are inhuman, tragic, and unbearable. The overwhelming majority of the population must labor when employment is available at wages far below the level of human subsistence. Housing and health conditions are among the worst in the world; illegitimacy, illiteracy, and the death rates are appallingly high. These dire conditons, resulting directly from centuries of slavery and colonial rule, have been intensified by the war to the point of "almost famine conditions in some places," as acknowledged in a recent bulletin of the British Information Services. Yet the Secretary of State for the Colonies of Great Britain in a recent statement publicly laments that the British taxpayer will be called upon to contribute to a small proposed fund for social development in the colonies.

The West Indies National Council respectfully but firmly submits to the United Nations' Conference that such colonial conditions constitute a major menace to World Security and Peace. The resolute liquidation of these menacing economic conditions should therefore be begun immediately. For this is imperative to raise the level of living standards and purchasing power of the Caribbean peoples, as of all peoples still subjected to colonial rule, in order to transform them into free and valuable participants in that increased production and exchange of goods and services which is no less essential to the security and peace of the people of the industrially advanced nations than it is to the welfare and progress of these now retarded colonial peoples.

Abolition of Imperialism Essential to World Peace

The Council also submits that such economic rehabilitation and progress, so essential to World Security and Peace, can be achieved only by breaking the fetters of imperialist domination and colonial dependency. For in no other way can the free political relations of mutually co-operating, self-governing peoples, fully respecting the democratic rights of each and all, be realized as the indispensable condition for social development and for the full release and stimulation of the energies of all in that increased production and exchange so vital to the security and peace of all mankind.

The Council further submits that the abolition of imperialist domination and colonial dependency will at the same time eliminate those conflicts over colonies which constitute the major source of war in the modern world. The logic of history now demands that imperialist control and colonial subjugation must cease that men may live and attain security and peace. A definite time in the immediate future should therefore be set in agreement with these peoples for the realization of full self-government and democratic rights for the Caribbean peoples and for all other colonial peoples.

Recommendations for Economic Rehabilitation

In accordance with the foregoing, the West Indies National Council earnestly recommends that a Fund adequate for the economic rehabilitation and social development of the Caribbean areas should be established under international supervision through the proposed International Bank for Reconstruction and Development or some similar agency. This Fund should be open to private and government subscription and substantial contributions to this Fund should be made by the British, French, and Dutch Empires. Since a large share of the vast fortunes and immense wealth of these Empires has been derived from the forced labor of the Caribbean peoples, these contributions would not only be in accord with justice but would also materially spur the increase in production and exchange which is recognized to be necessary to world prosperity, security, and peace.

Oppose Any Change without Self-determination

In respect to their readiness for self-government, it is undeniable that the Caribbean peoples possess all the characteristics of nationality and have many times proclaimed their demand for self-government. To settle this question it is necessary only to point to the numerous West Indians who have occupied and now hold administrative posts in every branch of government and to the late Governor General of Free French Africa, Felix

Eboué, a native of the West Indies, whose administrative genius and timely action saved the greater part of Africa, and perhaps all Africa, from falling into the barbarous hands of the Vichy regime and the Nazi hordes in the darkest hours of the present war for the United Nations.

Present discussion and renewed proposals affecting the sovereignty of the West Indian peoples render it our duty to call attention to the following statements affirmed in the Declaration of Rights presented to the Havana Conference and to the supporting evidence adduced therein.

> Reflecting and expressing the profound sentiments of the peoples of the Caribbean areas, this Committee declares that it is firmly opposed to any sale, transfer, mandate, trusteeship, or change of sovereignty of these peoples without the exercise of their inalienable human and democratic right of self-determination.

Trusteeship Thoroughly Discredited

In view of the urgency with which various proposals for mandates and trusteeship are being pressed upon this World Security Conference, it is imperative to affirm with renewed emphasis the following protest contained in the Statement of the West Indies National Emergency Committee on the Address delivered by Secretary Hull at the Havana Conference:

> For, however well intentioned such a proposed collective trusteeship might appear, it cannot be forgotten that this device of trusteeship or mandate has been used and is now being used by imperial governments of the Old World as a means of maintaining control over various peoples and subjecting them to tyrannous oppression and unbridled exploitation.
>
> It cannot be conceded for a moment that this discredited formula of trusteeship could be successfully employed in connection with the Caribbean peoples, when it is well known that it has signally failed either to ensure the democratic rights or to preserve the vital interests and welfare of the many down-trodden peoples to whom it has been applied.

International Commission Acceptable

In the opinion of this Council however, no truly representative objection might be expected from the Caribbean peoples to an International Commission specifically established to supervise the transition from colonial dependency to full self-government, provided their rights to self-government and self-determination were unequivocally recognized and a definite time mutually agreed upon for the realization of such complete self-government, and provided also that adequate and effective representation on such an International Commission were accorded to bona fide natives of these areas truly representative of the majority of these peoples.

Action Requisite against Prejudice and Terror

This Council would fail in its sacred duty if it did not urge this World Security Conference to give serious consideration to the grave menace to world security and peace which stems from racial, national, and religious prejudices. This venomous ideology was developed to its monstrous height in the "master race" mania with which the Nazi imperialist butchers, the Italian fascist slaughterers, and the Japanese military war mongers incited their followers to plunge the world into the present holocaust of slaughter and terror. Full cognizance must therefore be taken of the existence of racial, national, and religious prejudices and of the fact that such poisonous prejudices have already reached alarming proportions within most of the democratic nations themselves, with dire results to minorities therein and to colonial peoples controlled by these states.

Moreover, it is imperative to be aware of the fact that these vicious prejudices are inherent in the system of imperialism in which they are rooted and from which they inevitably develop. It is likewise salutary to mark that the horrible atrocities perpetrated at Belsen, Buchenwald, Dachau and elsewhere, at which mankind is now properly aghast, differ only in detail and degree from similar atrocities perpetrated upon colonial and semi-colonial peoples. The security and peace of mankind require that the lesson of history be now practically drawn that terror and torture developed first in colonial areas inevitably reach back to the dominating peoples and menace all mankind.

The resolution adopted at the Chapultepec Conference, recognizing the existence of racial, national, and religious prejudices within the frontiers of any country to be a matter of international concern, is an important step forward. This Council earnestly recommends that this World Conference adopt such a resolution, as a vital principle for the organization of world security and peace, requiring that all nations shall enact and enforce laws with adequate penalties against any and all overt manifestations of such racial, national, and religious prejudices, and shall undertake a vigorous campaign of education for the extirpation of such prejudices and animosities.

Urges Adoption of Seven Point Proposals

The West Indies National Council earnestly and finally urges this World Security Conference to consider and to adopt the following seven proposals in the interests of the Caribbean peoples and of World Security and Peace.

1. Forthright recognition of the inalienable right of the Caribbean peoples to self-government and self-determination.
2. Practical recognition of the age-long objective of the West Indian peoples for voluntary federation.
3. Integration, on the basis of equality, of the Caribbean peoples into the regional organization of the American nations and for their representation in the making of all plans for the political, military, economic and social security of all the peoples of the Americas.
4. Specific inclusion of the Caribbean peoples in the plans of the Conference for post-war rehabilitation and social security in view of the dire economic conditions of these peoples, resulting from colonial rule, which have been intensified by the war and which have reached almost famine conditions.
5. Recognition of the right of the Caribbean peoples to representation at the United Nations' Conference by delegates of their own choosing, as a matter of democracy and justice and by virtue of the vital contribution which the Caribbean peoples have made to the war effort and to democracy in this hemisphere and to the world.
6. Guarantees for the abolition of all discriminatory laws and practices based on race, religion, color or previous condition of servitude or oppression, and for the assurance of full protection of life and liberty for the Caribbean peoples, for the African peoples, and for all peoples without regard to race, creed, or color.
7. Genuine equality of rights both in fact and in law for all peoples everywhere and full democratic citizenship rights, including universal adult suffrage, for all people.

The West Indies National Council sincerely hopes for the success of this World Security Council and for the adoption of these measures which will enable the Caribbean peoples to take their rightful place among the nations of the world in a new era of freedom, security, peace and prosperity.

WEST INDIES NATIONAL COUNCIL
RICHARD B. MOORE
Vice-President and Chairman Conference Committee
LEONARD LOWE
Secretary
CHARLES A. PETIONI, M. D.
President

REPLY BY RICHARD B. MOORE TO
MR. SABBEN-CLAIRE

"Memorandum on Federation and Self-Government of the West Indies Addressed to the Caribbean Labour Congress," September 2–9, 1947, Appendix II, American Committee for West Indian Federation. Richard B. Moore Papers. (Statement made at a conference with Mr. Ernest Sabben-Claire, Colonial Attaché of the British Embassy, in New York, 1947, following his response to six questions raised by the delegation.)

These questions were put solely for the purpose of discovering, if we could, just how far the British government is ready to go to facilitate federation and self-government for the West Indian people.

We know that federation as such, federation by itself, is not the answer to the pressing problems of the people of the West Indies. Although federation is unquestionably an essential factor in that program which is necessary to meet these needs and aspirations, it is and can be such only if it is accompanied by full responsible self-government based on free, elective institutions and universal adult suffrage.

The obstacles to federation are mainly two: first, the fear in the minds of the West Indian people of resulting diminution of those partial democratic rights which they now possess, and, second, the fear that they will simply be left in their present plight of poverty and lack of finance without the necessary means to rehabilitate and re-build their economy.

If, then, His Britannic Majesty's government will have the grace to make a declaration that it is ready to accord full responsible government based on free elective institutions and universal adult suffrage and that it will extend financial assistance to aid in re-building their economy on a sound basis, it is certain that the path will be made smooth and easier for federation.

The present crisis in the affairs of the people of the West Indies cannot be met by small and halting steps but only by a statesmanlike program which deals with the basic issues and covers the over-all requirements. The fitness and the need of the West Indian people for full, responsible self-government are clearly evident. Their contribution to the accumulation of British capital is a matter of indisputable record.

The time is here and now for the British government to fulfill those hints and promises that at some time in the future self-government would be accorded to the West Indian people.

While the process of federation has to be accomplished through democratic processes and the people of the West Indies have their part to play, the British government can guarantee full self-government at a stated time within the immediate future. The British Parliament has the power and can act to accord this, as it has recently done in the case of India.

The British government found it necessary to use its power to curb the depredations of the slave holders in the West Indies and to abolish chattel slavery. It is now necessary for the British government to use its power to curb the depredations of the financial, planting, and big commercial interests in Britain and the West Indies in order to free the people of the West Indies from their present intolerable plight.

I feel certain that I speak the sentiments of the overwhelming majority of thinking, responsible persons of West Indian origin in this community and this country, when I say that we are interested in federation of the West Indies, and are ready to accord our full support to it, solely on the grounds that the inalienable right of the people of the West Indies to self-determination be unequivocally recognized, and that they be accorded full, responsible self-government with control over external and internal affairs, based on free elective institutions and universal adult suffrage.

Such a declaration, recognizing and according these basic, democratic rights, should be made by the British Parliament and a time set within the very near future for the convoking of a broad, representative Constituent Assembly of the West Indian people to frame and adopt a Constitution based upon and guaranteeing these rights.

Every effort should be made to include the Bahamas in the federation and Bermuda as well. The historical development and cultural structure of the people of these islands are basically the same as that of the other Caribbean areas. The distance of Bermuda is quite small when compared to that of other areas which have been federated. It is reasonably certain that the majority of the people of the Bahamas and Bermuda would favor joining in a free federation when the advantages are made clear and they are freely allowed to express their choice.

All the peoples in the entire Caribbean area, still held as dependencies by Great Britain, inhabit territories in a common Caribbean zone; they speak a common language; they already engage in some respects in a common economic life which is possible of far greater development; their culture is common in its fundamental patterns. These people thus possess the characteristics of developing nationality and should now be encouraged by the British government and people to federate voluntarily in a free Caribbean Commonwealth with full control over their internal and external affairs.

This is necessary not only to facilitate genuine federation of the West Indies but also to carry out the guarantees of self-government for all peoples solemnly made in the Atlantic Charter and re-affirmed at Teheran and elsewhere. This is requisite in order that the West Indian people shall take their rightful place among the nations of the earth as a free people and thereby be enabled to make their full contribution to the economic, political, social and cultural progress of themselves and of the world at large.

MEMORANDUM ON FEDERATION AND SELF-GOVERNMENT OF THE WEST INDIES

American Committee for West Indian Federation, submitted to the Caribbean Labour Congress, Coke Hall, Kingston, Jamaica, September 2–9, 1947. Richard B. Moore Papers.

This Committee hails this conference of the Caribbean Labour Congress and extends warm fraternal felicitations and fervent wishes for the successful accomplishment of the work which history has placed before you.

It is with great joy and high hope that we mark this meeting of your Congress as a body broadly and basically representative of the needs, aspirations, and endeavors of the workers, whether by hand or brain, who constitute the overwhelming majority of the people of the West Indies, and whose task it is therefore to consider, to propose, and to strive for solutions for all those vital problems affecting the welfare, progress and destiny of all the Caribbean peoples.

On this occasion when the question of West Indian Federation has been placed on the agenda for practical settlement, there are again raised to the fore all the basic questions concerning the political, economic, and social life, status and future of the peoples inhabiting the entire Caribbean area. In such a momentous hour, our Committee feels it to be an inescapable duty to address to your Conference a few considerations for your deliberation.

This Memorandum is another tangible expression of the deep and abiding interest of West Indians, who have been compelled in quest of wider opportunities to migrate from the several islands and areas washed by the waters of the beautiful Caribbean and to live, work and settle in the United States of America. Yet along with their devotion to the best traditions and highest interests of the country of their adoption, they have never lost their feeling of solidarity with their brothers in the Caribbean, nor their sense of obligation to render every possible aid toward the development and advancement of the people of the lands of their birth and origin.

This Address also testifies to the growing interest and solidarity of persons of African descent born in this Republic, who are increasingly conscious of the ties of common interest which link their destiny with that of their brothers in the Caribbean. It demonstrates, likewise, the developing sense of solidarity of the organized labor movement in this country with their brother toilers in the West Indies as demonstrated by the support to this Committee given by the National Maritime Union of the Congress of Industrial Organizations.

Such interest has led to action on many occasions, notably the presentation of the Declaration of Rights of the Caribbean Peoples to Self-Determination and Self-Government to the Pan-American Foreign Ministers' Conference at Havana, Cuba, in July, 1940; the Statement of the West Indies National Emergency Committee on the Address by Secretary of State of the U.S.A., Cordell Hull, to the Havana Conference in Respect to the Status of European Possessions in the Western Hemisphere; and the Appeal to the World Security Conference of the United Nations on Behalf of the Caribbean Peoples made at San Francisco in May–June, 1945. See Appendix I.*

Our concern likewise caused the participation by members of this Committee in the Conference, arranged by Mr. A. M. Wendell Malliet, recently held with a representative of the British Government on the Caribbean Commission, Mr. E. Sabben-Claire, to whom several questions were put. These questions, together with his answers and the reply made to him by Mr. Richard B. Moore, are stated for your information in Appendix II.

It is important to note these answers, particularly that the objective of federation includes "participation in international bodies such as the United Nations" [and] "the West Indies might look forward to a form of self-government similar to that of Ceylon." It was also his personal opinion that the British Government would be willing to assist the West Indies with a reasonable financial settlement. "It is not possible to set any date. . . . further developments depend largely upon action from within the West Indies." The reply made to his answers will no doubt receive your consideration and, it is hoped, will merit your approval.

Your Congress will doubtless recognize that a clear view of the most important historical, political, economic, and social aspects of federation and self-government, is essential to a realistic approach, to adequate action, and to successful achievement of the goals projected thereby. An endeavor in this respect is made in Appendix III as an aid to general clarity, pending the more thorough résumé and analysis which our Committee expects to receive from you.

Although the West Indies are among the oldest colonies of Britain, they have not gone forward to full responsible self-government and federation. On the contrary, they have either been retarded or thrust backward by the surrender of almost all of those approaches which had been made toward self-government. This surrender was made by the absentee financial interests in Britain and the planters and the big commercial classes in the West Indies. Although the majority of the people have sought and labored for federation and self-government, only very recently have they succeeded in securing some reforms in this direction.

Yet the advantages of genuine federation are obvious, since this is the means by which most peoples have achieved the power to establish themselves as nations in the modern world and to develop their economic life and social welfare. Switzerland, Germany, the United States of America, Mexico, Brazil, Venezuela, Argentina, Canada, Australia, The Union of Soviet Socialist Republics, and India are outstanding examples.

*Appendixes I and III are not included in this volume.

The following pertinent statement of D. G. Karve, Professor of History and Economics, Ferguson College, Poona, India, in *Federation: A Comparative Study of Politics, 1932,* merits due consideration.

> Federation is a form of government wherein for the purpose of administering some important governmental functions local governments are recognized as independent, free from any interference at the hands of the common government except in a manner predetermined by the constitution, and wherein the common government is constitutionally empowered to administer the field allocated to itself without any hindrance from the component states and with the direct support of the citizens.

Federation is the union of independent sovereign states, hence there can be no federation worthy of the name where there is no recognition or achievement of actual independence and sovereignty. In respect to the West Indies, however, there has existed and still exists a misleading concept of federation. A statement of this is made in the section on West Indian Federation in the *Handbook of the British West Indies, British Guiana, and British Honduras, 1926–1927,* by Algernon Aspinall, the West India Committee:

> The terms "confederation" and "federation" are strictly only applicable to the federal union of independent sovereign states: *but they have been freely used to indicate the policy of bringing together colonies and groups of colonies into some form of union.* (Emphasis ours.)

The results of the application of such a false conception of federation in the West Indies are known and warn against any such repetition now. These dire results have been noted by C. S. Salmon, an able British official who was President of Nevis and Colonial Secretary and Administrator of the Government of the Gold Coast, in his work entitled *The Caribbean Federation. A Plan for the Union of the Fifteen British West Indian Colonies,* Cassell and Company, Limited, 1887, in the following excerpt.

> The so-called confederations of the Windward and Leeward Islands (in 1882) being mere mockeries; the only thing abolished by the term being the local self-governments or partly elected assemblies which cost nothing. On the contrary, expenditure on official salaries has increased, expenditure for public purposes has decreased, and the condition is more intolerable than before. It is true there are two Governors-General that did not before exist. In no country in the world is there anything like the same proportion of the public taxes eaten up by salaries as in the British West Indies.

> The Leeward Islands had a sad fate indeed. They were asked to confederate, and, all the world over, confederation usually confers strength. They had each little Assemblies of their own, with elective elements that were not very valuable, but they could have easily been made most valuable by reform. Some of these islands were induced to surrender their elective Assemblies

and local self-governments. When they were confederated they found themselves bound up together no doubt, but their head, feet, and hands, had been
chopped off. They found themselves all welded and hammered together
into a single government with a pure bureaucratic despotism at its head. The
word 'confederation' was never before perhaps in the history of the world,
used for such a purpose. *Confederation means the possession of a local self-
government by the several constituent parts, and a general government for the purposes
of all; any other use is a misnomer.* (Emphasis ours.)

Thus was the mockery of West Indian Federation revealed in the
nineteenth century.

This Committee, therefore, hails the stand taken by your Congress, at its
first conference in Barbados, in September, 1945, as cited by your Secretary in an article entitled *Colonial Office and Federation.*

> Caribbean Labor demands federation with Self-Government, not without it,
> and further made it plain that each unit of the federation must be advanced
> to a status consistent with a Self-Governing federal constitution: "This con-
> ference advocates the granting to all the units of the British Caribbean area
> of wholly elected legislatures based on Universal Adult Suffrage, with policy
> making Executive Councils responsible to the Legislatures, and of wholly
> elected local government authorities."

It is our confident expectation, therefore, that your Congress will hold
firmly to this correct and basic position and that the present conference will
implement this in concrete proposals which will be placed before the
conference called by the Secretary of State for the Colonies to meet at
Montego Bay, in September.

It is not our intention to propose any blueprint for West Indian federation; we have confidence in the ability of the people of the West Indies to
work out their own detailed plan for federation. We desire to suggest the
following observations for your consideration. Federation should be based
on:

1. Full responsible self-government based on free elective institutions
   and adult universal suffrage.
2. Complete control over external and internal affairs.
3. Wholly elective federal and local legislatures, functioning through
   ministers wholly responsible to the legislatures and the people.
4. The Constitution of the Commonwealth of Australia appears to be
   most suitable with modifications in keeping with conditions obtaining in the West Indies.
5. A wholly elected bi-cameral federal legislature shoud be duly considered.
6. The principle of including nominated members in the federal and
   local legislatures is considered inconsistent and unacceptable.

7. The principle of appointments of administrative officers by the Crown should not be admitted.

8. The provision for reserved powers, which may be employed to negate self-government and to override the will of the people, should be uncompromisingly rejected.

9. The suggestion to use the present Jamaica constitution, with its broad reserved powers as a model for a federal constitution, cannot be entertained.

10. Every effort should be made to secure the adherence of the Bahamas and Bermuda to the Federation.

11. A definite date should be set for the recognition of the Federated Caribbean Commonwealth as a free nation as in the case of India.

12. Any such federation should be included as a member of the United Nations.

Our Committee is certain that your Congress will give due consideration to such questions as a Plan for Economic Rehabilitation and that the vital issues involved in federation will be taken to the broad masses of the people.

This Committee emphasizes the urgent necessity for terminating the status of the Caribbean peoples as the last still to be held in colonial dependency in the Western Hemisphere. We further stress that the Caribbean peoples "have long since reached that state in historical evolution where they have demonstrated their capacity for practical administration of government in accordance with modern democratic technique, and that the peoples of this area exhibit all the characteristics of nationality."

To the announced objectives of your Congress in this Conference, we pledge continued support. The organization of an American Association for West Indian Advancement is projected as a further means of fulfilling this pledge. We conclude with sincere fraternal wishes for the success of your Conference.

AMERICAN COMMITTEE FOR WEST INDIAN FEDERATION
AUGUSTINE A. AUSTIN, Chairman
RICHARD B. MOORE, Secretary.

STATEMENT BEFORE THE PLATFORM COMMITTEE OF THE NEW PARTY

July 21, 1948. Richard B. Moore Papers (Manuscript).

As Secretary of the American Committee for West Indian Federation, it is my privilege—for which I thank you—and my duty to present this statement on behalf of over six million Caribbean people. I speak more specifically for the three million people still suffering colonial enslavement under British rule in the West Indies, Guiana and Honduras. But I must also speak a word for the complete freedom of three million colonial subjects of the Netherlands, France, and the United States in the West Indies and Guiana.

A statement made some time ago by Henry A. Wallace, simple but significant for its broad human spirit, is still vivid in my mind. It is to the effect that there should be jobs and bread and milk for all including every Hottentot child. This has encouraged me to appear here and to believe that this same human consciousness will actuate this Committee to include in the platform of this historic New Party necessary declarations for the welfare and liberation of the Caribbean, the African, and all other oppressed colonial peoples.

In order to answer any questions which may arise in your minds, permit me to state briefly a few salient facts about the Caribbean peoples, their importance and contributions and their present miserable plight and urgent need.

Like a curving shield around the Panama Canal, the Caribbean islands stand as outposts in the approaches to the Americas. Their strategic and political importance were accordingly demonstrated during the war against Nazi Germany. The attack of German submarines upon Aruba brought the war directly to American soil and the Caribbean peoples suffered the first casualties in this hemisphere in that crucial conflict to preserve democracy.

Despite their colonial subjection and impoverishment, the Caribbean peoples contributed military and labor powers, financial support, and supplies of oil, bauxite, and other materials vitally needed for the winning of the war. They provided land for bases for the defense of the Americas though they were not consulted. The Act of Havana, solemnly enacted by the Pan-American Foreign Ministers in July, 1940, which called for "taking into account the desires of the inhabitants of the said islands or regions," was never invoked. Instead the governments of Britain and the United States by themselves decided upon the exchange of over-age destroyers for 99-year leases for lands for these bases.

Immense contributions of labor and wealth have been made by the Caribbean peoples, during three centuries of imperial subjection and exploitation, to the development of the peoples of Britain, France, Spain, the Netherlands and the United States. This historical fact has been tersely stated by Prof. Eric Williams in *The Negro in the Caribbean:*

> Tremendous wealth was produced from an unstable economy based on a single crop which combined the vices of feudalism and capitalism with the virtues of neither. Liverpool in England, Nantes in France, Rhode Island in America, prospered on the slave trade. London and Bristol, Bordeaux and Marseilles, Cadiz and Seville, Lisbon and New England all waxed fat on the

profits of the trade in the tropical produce raised by the Negro slave. Capitalism in England, France, Holland and colonial America received a double stimulus. . . .

The Caribbean people have also made outstanding contributions to democracy, notably their struggle for the abolition of chattel slavery which paved the way for a similar beneficent achievement in the United States and Latin America. In the building of the Panama Canal, West Indian migrants furnished the vital labor power for the accomplishment of that great enterprise, though they were compelled to work under onerous and discriminatory conditions. Thousands of Caribbean immigrants to the United States have contributed and still contribute to the economic, social, and political advancement and to the cultural enrichment of this their adopted land.

Yet the plight of the people throughout the Caribbean areas is tragic and inhuman. Low wages, unemployment, malnutrition, vile housing and health conditions, illegitimacy and illiteracy are forced upon the majority of the population through continued colonial subjection. During the last world war the British Information Service admitted the existence of "almost famine conditions in some places."

Today hundreds of thousands are slowly dying from hunger. The *Barbados Observer* recently carried the headline "Starvation Stalks The Land" and reported the march of thousands to the governor's house to demand relief. Thousands are homeless and hungry in St. Lucia following the recent destruction of the capital city, Castries, by fire. Still the governments refuse to lift restrictions and to remove high import duties which hamper the sending of such relief as is attempted by Caribbean Americans. But bundles for Britain are facilitated and duty free.

Every effort on the part of the working people to increase their miserable wages and to improve their conditions is met by brutal repression. On June 16th five peaceful unarmed striking workers were killed, two of them shot in the back, and eleven injured by police on the sugar plantation of Enmore in British Guiana.

In view of this dire situation the following proposals are submitted for inclusion in the platform of the New Party:

Urge the immediate provision of relief by the people and government of the United States and the lifting of all export and import restrictions and duties.

Voice support to the demand expressed through the Caribbean Labour Congress last September for federation with complete self-government based on universal adult suffrage for all the people still subjected to British rule in the West Indies, Guiana and Honduras.

Call for support to a Plan of Economic Rehabilitation with funds provided by contributions and loans from Britain, France, the Netherlands and the United States of America, in view of the vast wealth drawn from the Caribbean people historically by these great nations.

Demand that adequate representation be immediately accorded the Caribbean peoples on all agencies and bodies acting upon questions affecting their life and destiny. Press for their inclusion in the United Nations as speedily as possible.

Call for an end to police terror and repression in the Caribbean areas and the enforcement of full democratic civil liberties.

Urge the abolition of the discriminatory practice in immigration which limits the entire Caribbean area under British rule to only sixty persons a year to enter the United States, despite the large frequently unused quota for Great Britain.

Demand full civil liberties and equality for Caribbean Americans; an end to the deportation proceedings against Ferdinand Smith of the National Maritime Union and Claudia Jones; the halting of the intimidation and the deportation drive against all foreign born Americans.

Freedom for the Caribbean peoples is imperative to end the menace of the liberty and security of the Americas and the world. This grave danger arises from their intolerable position as the last peoples in this hemisphere still subject to colonial domination by European Empires and imperialist forces of the United States.

The people of the Caribbean have thus become the crucial touchstone of American democracy. Good neighbor relations with the Latin American peoples hinge upon what the United States of America does to insure justice and freedom to the Caribbean peoples. The demand of the representative of Venezuela at the Pan-American Conference at Bogotá is the most recent of numerous forceful expressions of the profound feeling of Latin American nations for freedom for the Caribbean peoples and independence for Puerto Rico. This they regard as a necessary guarantee of their own security from domination and aggression by imperialists of the United States and of Europe.

Caribbean Americans join with our American brothers in urging the adoption of a strong plank in the platform of the New Party to guarantee full civil liberties and equal rights for all the people of this republic regardless of race, color, creed, sex, national origin or political belief; to end the vicious discrimination, segregation, disfranchisement and lynch terror against fifteen million Americans of African descent, from which oppression most Caribbean Americans also suffer; to abolish the discriminatory practices in the Panama Canal Zone and wherever such flagrant violations of democracy exist.

We unite with all who urge complete self-government and independence for the African, Asian and all other colonial and semi-colonial peoples striving to be free.

Finally, in view of the present frantic drive to war with its menace of atomic destruction, the position of the Caribbean peoples in the vanguard of the Americas makes it especially imperative that we urge the adoption of the most vigorous prosecution of the struggle for peace.

SPEECH ON CARIBBEAN FEDERATION AT THE LUNCHEON MEETING FOR LORD LISTOWEL

February 3, 1953, Hotel Theresa, New York. Richard B. Moore Papers.

I should like to make a few observations so our distinguished visitor will realize the trend of thought among people of Caribbean origin here, and also among other interested persons born in these United States, in respect to the important question of Federation of the Caribbean People in the islands and mainland areas now governed as colonies by the British government.

This question of federation now assumes very great importance in view of the forthcoming Conference scheduled to be held in London during the month of April.

The view prevailing among the majority of those especially interested here has been set forth in a Memorandum addressed to the Caribbean Labour Congress which convened in Kingston, Jamaica, on September 2nd to 9th, 1947. This Memorandum I shall now present to Lord Listowel so this more ample statement will be before him and may reach those of weight and influence to whom it may come.

Federation is here considered in its proper meaning and strict sense. As stated in the Memorandum, "federation is the union of independent sovereign states, hence there can be no federation worthy of the name where there is no recognition or achievement of actual independence and sovereignty."

It is recognized, of course, that the term federation has been loosely applied to denote the bringing together of colonies for the purpose of administering them as a single political unit. This improper and misleading usage has been noted by Algernon Aspinall as quoted in the Memorandum:

> The terms "confederation" and "federation" are strictly only applicable to the federal union of independent sovereign states: but they have been freely used to indicate the policy of bringing together colonies or groups of colonies into some form of union.

It should be clear, then, that when we speak of federation, this term is used only in its proper, precise, political significance as the union of sovereign, independent states. This excludes altogether any process of joining together colonies in what Mr. Malliet has referred to as "a glorified crown colony," a phrase which I first heard in this connection from an elder statesman of the Caribbean, the Hon. T. Albert Marryshow of Grenada, when he visited us here a few years ago.

Those of us who have given serious thought to this paramount question are deeply interested in genuine federation with complete self-government. This means that the Caribbean people would then enjoy the status of a self-governing Dominion within the British Commonwealth of Nations. By self-governing Dominion is meant a political status such as that of Canada, Australia, or India. I do not speak of Ceylon, because while there are those who deem Ceylon to be a fully self-governing Dominion, there are also those who hold that there are treaty agreements and other arrangements which detract from the status of full self-government.

From this clear and precise view, federation is the *sine qua non* of progress for the Caribbean people. It is the essential means whereby they can move forward to a solution of the many and grievous problems of economic poverty, political retardation, and social depression with which they are now gravely confronted, and in fact, seriously menaced. Moreover, from any adequate view of the situation, such genuine federation of the Caribbean people is clearly and palpably long overdue.

It is the stated aim and proclaimed purpose of British colonial policy to prepare and to fit the peoples whom they rule for self-government. Quite obviously, the Caribbean people are among the oldest colonies ruled by the British government. Standing high upon the list in point of time are such colonies as the Bahamas, Barbados, St. Christopher, and the other colonies of the Caribbean and mainland areas. After several centuries of such rule, the people of the Caribbean must certainly now be ready for self-government.

Still more important is the fact that the indigenous people of these Caribbean areas, for a considerable period, have been executing most of the work in the actual administration and government of these colonies, except for the few topmost officials appointed by the British government and the overriding control of the British colonial office. There can be no valid question, then, as to their ability or fitness for self-government.

Considerable confusion has arisen, though, over this vital question of federation, chiefly because of the Rance Report, or to give its formal title, the British Caribbean Standing Closer Association Committee 1948–1949 Report. This Report proposes to reserve large powers to the Crown on the score of finance. Significantly, this Report also fails to approach the question of finance with any consideration of the historical flow of wealth from the Caribbean people to Britain. So great are the powers reserved to the British Crown, that the people of some areas in the Caribbean would lose important powers that they have already gained and now possess.

As a result, and because of certain propaganda also, there has developed considerable reluctance in British Guiana and British Honduras, as well as decided reservations in other areas, toward joining in what is misnamed a "federation" in view of the proposals of this Report. For such proposals do not constitute a plan for genuine federation on the basis of full self-government, nor even any appreciable advance toward self-government, but in fact a retrogression for some areas in very vital aspects of political and financial power.

A plan for genuine federation, however, would dispel this confusion, reluctance, and reservation. There are those, we know, in positions of power who still question the ability of the Caribbean people to govern themselves. But in addition to what has already been said in refutation of this purblind notion, which arises only out of partisan and short-sighted self-interest, it should be obvious that as it is only possible to learn to swim by striking out in the water, so it is possible to learn to govern only by actually governing.

Besides, it is well known that the majority of the people in the Caribbean areas are the descendants of people brought from Africa. It is not so well known, but nevertheless an established fact of history, that the African peoples governed themselves for centuries before the European invasion of Africa which began in the middle of the fifteenth century. Any unbiased estimate, based upon the facts of that historical situation, must acknowledge that over vast areas and from remote times the Africans did quite well at the task of governing themselves.

The distinguished anthropologist, Leo Frobenius, and several other scholars have pointed to the facts which demonstrate that Africans had achieved great cultures. They had developed powerful states well organized and administered, flourishing industries, exquisite crafts, great arts. If, on the other hand, we consider objectively the record of the results of government by external imperial powers whether in Africa, the Caribbean, Asia, or anywhere else in the world, and if we accurately assess the plight of the world today, we cannot but conclude that government imposed by any nation upon another people has in no case been just, or alike beneficial, or conducive to the peace and progress of mankind.

Despite all this, there still remains this meretricious theory of the necessity of continuing "guardianship." But the question arises: Who will guard the guardians; who will civilize the civilizers?

The right of the Caribbean people, as indeed of all peoples, to self-determination and self-government is an inalienable, human, democratic right. This fundamental right is deemed to be most vital for themselves by powerful nations which proclaim democracy while imposing imperial rule upon other peoples. Clearly, there is a gap and a contradiction between the theory and the practice.

It is evident, however, that we have now reached a stage in human affairs when the denial of these democratic rights can no longer be maintained with any prospect of peace, security, or well-being for any of the peoples of the earth. Any attempt forcibly to retain the Caribbean people, or any other peoples, in the status of colonial subjection, can only engender hostility in the minds of these peoples against those who impose such imperial rule.

The forthright recognition of this right to self-determination, and to federation with self-government, is the primary condition for that voluntary union which is the only basis for peaceful relations and mutually beneficial advancement. The Caribbean people will thus be enabled to take their rightful place among the other nations of the Commonwealth, and so achieve amicable, proper, and mutually advantageous relations with the people of the United Kingdom, with the other nations of this hemisphere, and with all the peoples of the world.

XII

CARIBBEAN FREEDOM AND NATIONHOOD

During his last forty years, Richard B. Moore was continually involved in advocating the building of Caribbean independence, nationhood, and economic security. "Culture, College and People in the Caribbean," written on the eve of Barbados independence, is a brief admonition on the importance of education to the development of a people. Moore's growing disappointment with the performance of local leaders and dismay with the course of the ill-fated West Indies Federation are revealed in several articles. Yet throughout his writings there is the consistent conviction that federation is essential for the economic and political development of the area and optimism that true self-determination will ultimately bring the people to a unified Caribbean nationhood.

INDEPENDENT CARIBBEAN NATIONHOOD— HAS IT BEEN ACHIEVED OR SET BACK?

Manuscript (c. 1962), Richard B. Moore Papers.

Many of us have joined in or noted the recent celebrations first of Jamaica and then of Trinidad and Tobago. But those who have long given thought to the liberation movement of the Caribbean people could not rejoice over these partial concessions of independence. Though conscious of deep fraternal feelings toward our fellow Caribbeans in Jamaica and in Trinidad-Tobago, we could not take part joyously in these independence celebrations, because of the awareness that almost as many people in the various Caribbean Islands and continental areas yet remained colonial subjects of Britain, still denied the basic human rights of self-determination and self-government.

Even while these independence celebrations were ringing in our ears, we could not but remember the celebrations held here in New York around the inauguration of the Parliament of the West Indies Federation on April

22, 1958. We recalled the Thanksgiving Service attended by a mammoth crowd which filled to overflowing the spacious Cathedral of St. John the Divine. Organized by the Caribbean League of America through its secretary, Dudley E. Barrow, this service was followed by the Federation Banquet and the well-attended dance also given by this body. We recalled as well the dinner sponsored by the Jamaica Progressive League. At all of these affairs rejoicing and merriment reigned supreme.

These recollections were painful now, since in the sequel it had become fully evident that we had been the victims of a great deception. For the much heralded and celebrated West Indies Federation was not at all a genuine federation, since the British colonial rulers had in fact withheld independence and the hope held out that independence would soon come was without any foundation whatever.

Federation is first of all the union of sovereign independent states. Federation properly exists also when former colonies achieve union and independence. Canada, Australia, the United States of America, and such states are veritable examples of genuine federation.

But deception, deprivation, and a whole train of political and social evils inevitably result when this term federation is falsely applied to a bringing together of colonies "into *some* form of union." (Author's emphasis.) Thus all the celebrations of "West Indies Federation" were vain and illusory. For the first time in history there was enacted the farce of a flag without sovereignty—the blue flag of the so-called West Indies Federation.

With the recollection of this hoax and delusion before our minds, it was impossible to be other than reserved, critical, and questioning. What is to be the lot of the people of Jamaica–the Caymans-Turks and Caicos Islands and that of the people of Trinidad-Tobago in these two small fragmented states? What, indeed, is to be the fate of the other thousands of Caribbean people in Antigua-Barbuda-Redonda, the Bahamas, Bermuda, Dominica, Grenada, Guiana, Honduras, Montserrat, St. Kitts-Nevis-Anguila, St. Lucia, St. Vincent, and the Virgin Islands? How and when are those Caribbean people to become independent? Are they to be united or still further fragmented?

The basic question naturally arose: "Has the National Liberation Movement of the Caribbean People been accomplished or set back by the withdrawal of Jamaica from the Federation?" To answer this vital question is the purpose of the present discussion. But in order to find the correct answer, it is necessary first of all to know the historical development and thus to envisage clearly the nature and the goal of the Caribbean National Liberation Movement.

Those who are in the least familiar with the history of the Caribbean People know that there has long existed a national liberation movement whose goal has been the achievement of one federated, united, free, and independent Caribbean nation, constituted out of all the people and areas ruled by Britain. Time now permits the presentation of only a few forth-right expressions of this Caribbean national movement and its objective.

A penetrating political analyst, the Jamaican-born Caribbean, Dr. Louis S. Meikle, gave the following expression in his book published in 1912 on *Confederation of the British West Indies versus Annexation to the United States of America:*

> Confederation would centralize the administration, lessen the expense of running the government, and, as a result, bring relief to our overburdened taxpayers: but confederation and centralization without responsible government, (this means independence—explanation mine—R.B.M.), would work more harm than good and place additional obstacles in our path, rather than prosperity. The one without the other as a necessary part would be tantamount to placing a double-edged sword in the hands of the colonial office and the 'West Indian Committee.'

One of the greatest political leaders of the Caribbean, Arthur Andrew Cipriani of Trinidad, was likewise an ardent advocate of a free federated Caribbean Nation. In a biographical study made by C. L. R. James, and published in the Independence Supplement of the *Sunday Guardian* of Trinidad on August 26, 1962, the following clear and emphatic statement appeared:

> Cipriani was a most ardent federationist and I would not be surprised to learn that the impetus to this came from his experience with West Indians in the British West Indies Regiment.
>
> The point I wish to emphasize is that when he advocated self-government, independence and federation, the advocacy was based on very solid experience: it was not a historical point to be made or a logical argument to be won. He would not tolerate arguments about it. That was where he began. . . .
>
> But he was no backward colonialist politician nor narrow minded egoist. He kept his organization in close association with the Labor Party in England. He became one of the stalwarts and for many years president of the Caribbean Labour Congress. He did not only make speeches about the West Indian nation. He actively worked at it.

Often called the "father" of Caribbean Federation, A. A. Cipriani was a leading figure among the delegates to the Dominica Federation Conference in 1932. Fortunately, the names have been preserved of these early Caribbean patriots who came together to plan for a free, federated, Caribbean nation. . . .

Another step toward a federated Caribbean nation was taken when the first Caribbean Labour Conference met in Barbados in 1945. This assembly declared: "Caribbean Labour demands federation with Self-Government not without it." Delegates from almost all of the Caribbean areas participated. Prominent in the leadership of this Conference were Grantley Herbert Adams of Barbados and Norman Washington Manley of Jamaica.

Broadly based and wholly representative was the following resolution and basic Declaration of the Second Caribbean Labour Congress. This was unanimously adopted at its meeting in Coke Hall, Kingston, Jamaica, in May 1947. Mark this declaration well:

> The Conference is convinced that the development of West Indian nationhood, the evolution of our cultural standards, the expansion and stability of our economy . . . can best and most fully be secured by the Federation of the Territories concerned.

> That the Federal Constitution must provide for Responsible Government equivalent to Dominion Status.

Here then is ample evidence of this broadly based Caribbean national liberation movement with the clearly stated objective of accomplishing the union of all the British-ruled units, insular and continental alike, into one free, federated Caribbean nation.

In support of this declared, specific goal of federated Caribbean nationhood, Caribbean Americans and their friends here in the United States of America have given of their time, energy, counsel, and money. . . . For example, the request for aid made to federation exponents in the United States by Caribbean leaders, headed by Norman W. Manley and Grantley H. Adams, led to the setting up of the American Committee for West Indian Federation. The chairman, Augustine A. Austin, who made one of the largest contributions himself, was effective in raising the required Caribbean Fund of $10,000; the present writer was chiefly responsible for the *Memorandum on Federation and Self-Government* sent to the Caribbean Labour Conference. This Memorandum concluded with twelve specific observations on Federation. It stressed the drawing up of an Economic Rehabilitation Plan, and urged "that the vital issues involved in federation will be taken to the broad masses of the people."

Sincere upholders of Caribbean nationhood joyfully greeted the decisions of the Second Caribbean Labour Conference in 1947. Especially were we moved to great expectations by the resounding Declaration for Federation with Dominion Status as the best way forward for all the Caribbean People.

Unfortunately however, the chief political leaders of that Conference showed themselves thereafter to be more concerned about political preference in their respective areas, than in building a strong, viable, united Caribbean nation in accordance with the Conference decisions to which they had solemnly pledged themselves. As a result, the Standing Closer Association Committee set up by the Montego Bay Conference called by the British Government in 1947 was practically left in the hands of its British-appointed secretary, a former colonial governor, Sir Hubert Rance. The Report of this Commission questioned the economic competence of Caribbeans and put off independence. Yet this "Rance Report" was accepted by the chief Caribbean political leaders as the basis for the Constitution of the ill-starred "West Indies Federation."

Concern had been aroused here over the Draft of the Bill for the proposed Caribbean Federation prepared by Chairman Grantley H. Adams for the Second Caribbean Labour Conference. That draft began by designating officials for the Federation with their respective salaries. But how could money payments for officials be the first consideration instead of the general welfare of the Caribbean People?

This concern deepened into reluctant disavowal when Grantley H. Adams accepted the role of spokesman for imperial domination as alternate delegate of the United Kingdom to the United Nations meeting in Paris in October 1948. The president of the Caribbean Labour Congress declared before that international assembly that the British Government was giving self-government to its colonies just as soon as they were ready for it. The colonial labour leader further endorsed the discriminatory wage system under which Africans were paid a small fraction of the salaries paid to Europeans for similar work.

Conferences on Federation subsequently held in London and the Caribbean were marked by conflict over the capital site, competition for office, and the like, instead of the development of an adequate plan agreed upon in common. Most of the Caribbean leaders favored a so-called "loose federation," while Grantley H. Adams stood for a strong centralized overall government. Summoned finally by Britain to the Lancaster House Conference of February 1956, the Caribbean leaders agreed to and signed a miserable compromise plan for "federation."

The resulting Constitution of the "West Indies Federation" postponed to the future all the essential requirements of nationhood such as independence, a common customs union, free movement of the people, basic economic integration and development, and elimination of costly unit governors, and other similar administrative offices and bodies. Besides, no basic education of the people on the vital issues of federation was conducted; no plan for the economic rebuilding of the entire Caribbean was ever brought forward.

The lack of such a specific economic Caribbean Plan was constantly deplored here. Nevertheless, when in 1957 the Caribbean request for two hundred million pounds was denied by Britain, the Caribbean and Associated Advocates here issued a supporting *Statement on British Secretary's Rejection of Federation Committee's Request For Financial Aid To Caribbean People*. Documenting the need, this statement showed such a sum to be but a small part of the wealth drawn out of and therefore due by Britain to the Caribbean people.

During 1957 the Standing Federation Committee demanded the return of the Chaguaramas site used as a base by the United States of America. The Caribbean League of America reprinted the *Report Presented By Hon. Eric Williams To The Trinidad Council.* Through the Hands Across The Seas

Rally and resolution adopted at the Abyssinian Baptist Church, the Caribbean League of America further supported the request for return of this site. This site, comprising many acres of the best land, had been alienated through the exchange for fifty over-age destroyers made between the imperial government of Britain and the United States of America, without any consultation or agreement with the people of Trinidad.

Again and again during all these developments, conscious supporters here had urged Caribbean political leaders to press for the essential requirement of viable nationhood. But all warnings against delay and departure from their declared goal were ignored or brushed aside. . . .

It is important to know why Guiana did not go into the Federation. Because of its great area and vast untapped natural resources, Guiana has always been recognized as the necessary natural base of a truly independent, viable, and prosperous Caribbean nation. The fact must be faced that the people of Guiana were driven away from the Federation, when Bustamante, Manley and Adams obligingly rushed telegrams to Britain condemning their government in the political crisis of 1953.

This government had been democratically elected by the people under the limited "measure of self-government" then accorded them. Undoubtedly, these telegrams from Bustamante, Manley and Adams helped to make it possible for the British invaders and destroyers of this Guianese government to secure a majority vote in Parliament, thus upholding that military aggression and tyrannical suspension of the constitution of Guiana. Quite obviously, thereafter, the great majority of the Guianese people wished to have nothing more to do with these Caribbean leaders, whom they could no longer regard as trustworthy or fraternal.

Shortly after the setting up of the West Indies Federation, the opportunity was afforded to those in the New York area to question the Chief Minister of Jamaica, Norman W. Manley, then also president of the West Indies Federal Labour Party. That opportunity came after the report on the violent attacks upon Caribbeans in England which Manley gave at the Renaissance Casino here in September 1958. . . .

Our reaction to Manley's answers of avoidance and disdain was given in the article, "Revelations and Reflections on Caribbean Federation." We re-affirmed our continuing interest in Caribbean affairs "despite discouraging expressions." Studied observations on the "Federation" and Caribbean freedom were then summarized in twenty-one specific points for consideration of the Caribbean people.

In an address made here about a year later, Sir Grantley Herbert Adams, then Knighted by Britain and Prime Minister of the West Indies Federation, deferentially absolved Britain of any responsibility and blamed the people of the West Indies, "if the West Indies Federation is not further along."

However, the Prime Minister's statement differed from the British pronouncement which pointed not to the Caribbean people, but to the leaders.

This statement appeared in the booklet, *Introducing the British Caribbean Colonies,* issued in 1956 by Her Majesty's Stationery office:

> There are, of course, a few West Indian leaders who would like the various steps toward complete self-government to be taken even more rapidly; but most of the political personalities seem in full agreement with the British Government that there are limits to the rate at which people can take over the management of their own affairs.

The ensuing division and damaging remarks of the Prime Minister about the greater intelligence and industry of Barbadians, the higher illiteracy of Jamaicans, and the tendency of Trinidadians to sing a calypso rather than work, could not be allowed to go unchallenged. My query was: "how can you as Prime Minister foster the development of Federal National Consciousness when you make such insular comparisons?"

Instead of correcting these errors at once, the Prime Minister inferred that the man who sought to put a stop to such woeful insularity was a bad "Barbadian." Following the question and later press statement of W. A. Domingo, who challenged the accuracy of the statement as to the extent of illiteracy in Jamaica, Sir Grantley used his immunity in the Parliament of the West Indies Federation to attack and to smear Domingo, Pierrepointe and myself as "Communists." Moreover, the Prime Minister's concern about salaries and his rash announcement of retroactive federal taxes gave the arch foe of federation, the British Knighted Sir Alexander Bustamante, the long awaited opportunity for attack against the Federation.

During the Montego Bay Conference, Bustamante had been outspoken against federation. This, he saw as putting a burden on Jamaica to carry the small islanders, who, he said, could hardly creep. Later, however, Bustamante gave formal endorsement to federation. This temporary espousal of federation was apparently due to the influence of the Jamaican and American journalist, A. M. Wendell Malliet, who spent some six months in Jamaica during 1951.

But now, Bustamante saw his main chance to regain office in Jamaica by arousing and playing upon the most rabid fears and selfish passions of the people. Repeatedly he charged that Jamaica did not have enough representation in the Federation, although his own party had agreed to the number of seats and other provisions of the Federal Constitution. Adroitly, Bustamante held before the people's eyes the spectre of increased poverty and certain ruin, declared to be impending from the supposed ever-increasing drain upon their financial resources by the "West Indies Federation."

Caught between the inept blundering of his Federal Party colleague, Sir Grantley Herbert Adams, and the scare-raising demagogy of the Bustamante opposition, Manley proved unable to muster the strength for the necessary fight on two points. Yielding apace to Bustamante, Manley retreated from every basic principle of federation until there appeared hardly any difference between these two cousins. In this game of opportunistic power-politics, Bustamante could easily master Manley.

Taunted by the demand of the Bustamante opposition for a referendum on federation, Manley agreed with confident bravado. But this was Manley's greatest, most direful, and fatal error. This meant turning backwards and opening the door to secession. For both the Jamaica Labour Party and the People's National Party had already unanimously voted for federation in the Jamaica legislature. Both parties had as well participated in the shaping of the "Federal" constitution. Besides, in a prior election of the People's National Party to office, with a plank in its program for federation, the people of Jamaica had also already given a mandate for federation through a clear majority vote.

One of the worst things that happened was the distribution in Jamaica of two pamphlets written and sent from here by W. A. Domingo. In these pamphlets this former progressive advocate of federation now opposed it by appealing to the worst reactionary narrow, insular, and base passions of the most backward of the people of Jamaica.

Unfortunately, no counter action was taken by any Jamaican-born supporter of federation here to mitigate the effect of Domingo's harmful propaganda. Some Caribbeans born elswhere hesitated to intervene, lest they be attacked as partisan and alien and thereby rendered ineffective. This was a mistake; the effort should have been made despite such probabilities.

Once Jamaica had seceded from the federation, the Trinidad legislature then voted to withdraw. This action was regrettable, but not difficult to understand. The Prime Minister of Trinidad, Dr. Eric Williams, apparently realized that it was hardly possible to reconstitute the Federation properly and at once. Besides, it is quite likely that it seemed to Dr. Williams that his experience with Sir Grantley H. Adams had not been such as to encourage the undertaking of this difficult task. Better then to let the slate be wiped clean, so a fresh start might be possible when conditions would be more favorable.

Of the Caribbean leaders then foremost, Eric Williams had been the latest to emerge when elected to chief office in Trinidad in 1956. But even before this, Williams had journeyed to England where he pressed for independence for the projected federation. Thereafter, he called repeatedly for independence but could not succeed without support from the leaders then recognized by Britain as paramount.

It should be helpful now to consider the situation of the Caribbean people in terms of the larger world context. It will thus be seen that the political division of the Caribbean people shows the pattern and policy of neo-colonialism or the new imperialism.

Stated succinctly that policy, conceived and employed by the colonial powers, is seen to be the following: When difficulties multiply in keeping subject peoples in outright colonial bondage, then let these peoples have "independence," but in such a form and manner as to keep them from achieving vital power. This policy of neo-colonialism thus dictates division, partition, balkanization, and fragmentation into petty and powerless states. Along with continuing economic dependence, these measures constitute the new means of maintaining domination which is less onerous and less costly. . . .

Let us consider conditions in Jamaica. The economic and social situation in Jamaica is undeniably grave. The Report of the International Bank for Development made this finding in 1952:

> . . . Jamaica suffers from chronic unemployment and widespread poverty. . . . The future does indeed pose serious questions. Jamaica, which does not adequately support its present population, must provide for an additional 18% by the end of the next decade.

The situation in Jamaica is no better today. Theodore Sealy, editor of the Jamaica *Gleaner* and the chairman of the Independence Celebrations Committee, made this acknowledgement in the Special Supplement to *The New York Times* of August 5, 1962: "The country is relatively poor. Poverty is evident." He pointed out that in Kingston the shanty areas are expanding, the ravages of starvation being frequently stilled by the smoking of the ganja weed, and some women have only one cotton garment to cover their nakedness. So alarming is this social decline that even while preparations were being made for the independence celebration, an outburst was feared. The sale of machetes had risen extraordinarily, and most people who were aware breathed a sigh of relief when this celebration passed without any violent eruption.

Just how independent Jamaica actually is has been shown in the attitude of its Prime Minister. Before taking office even, Sir Alexander Bustamante declared his intention to enter into a defense treaty and total alignment with the United States. On assuming office he speedily offered sites for bases to the United States Government without any pay therefor. It might have been expected that the Prime Minister would at least have asked for a few billion dollars to put some food in the pot bellies distended by hunger.

Besides, has the Prime Minister considered to what extent bases of another power, however friendly, would delimit the sovereignty of Jamaica? It might be well for Sir Alexander to recall that one of the primary causes of the American Revolution of 1776 which led to the independence of the United States of America was the opposition of the people to the quartering of British troops on what they deemed to be their soil.

Moreover, this is the atomic age and the decisive weapon is the nuclear bomb. With the development of long-range missiles, such a base is unnecessary either for the defense of the United States or that of the Caribbean. In fact, such a base could become a grave danger, since it might attract attack as a possible hostile and offensive force. Apart from limited local defense, what surer defense could now be secured than that of all friendly powers and the United Nations?

In his message to President Kennedy, published in the costly special section of *The New York Times* of August 5th, the Prime Minister of Jamaica showed what really comes first with him. Sir Alexander stressed that "our determination to protect and expand American capital investment . . . is the motivation for our acceptance of the great responsibilities of nationhood. . . ." That no specific mention was made by him there of the interests of the people of Jamaica is at once self-revealing and ominous.

Trinidad is in a better position economically because of its oil wells and pitch lake. Yet its proper and necessary development is far from assured standing by itself alone. Increased power and prosperity for the people of Trinidad also depend upon union with other Caribbean people.

A foremost fact of geography and politics has now to be stressed. This cannot be too often repeated and its significance duly realized and acted upon—*Guiana is the natural baseland for the development of a powerful and prosperous nation in the Caribbean.* Guiana's vast sparsely inhabited domain of almost wholly virgin soil and its rich and varied undeveloped natural resources call for the enterprise, industry, skill and labor power of people to come in from other densely populated areas of the Caribbean. At the same time the other Caribbean units need to be buttressed economically and politically by union with the people and land of Guiana.

Recently, large deposits of oil and of copper, said to equal in quality fine "Rhodesian" copper, have been found in Guiana. *The New York Times* of September 6th reported that oil fields covering an area of 15,000 square miles had been discovered by Soviet geologists, "after British and American experts had failed to find it." Perhaps these last mentioned experts were none too diligent in their search.

The vital importance of Guiana as baseland to the entire Caribbean people is underscored by the increased need for suitable outlets for Caribbean people needing to migrate. Drastic limitation of immigration to Caribbean and other *dependent peoples* by the United States of America has been followed by the practical closing of the door by Britain to her Caribbean colonial subjects or little Commonwealth partners. . . .

From this analysis of the situation now obtaining in the Caribbean, certain conclusions may be made. Independence, as it has been granted to Jamaica and Trinidad by themselves and under prevailing conditions, is too partial to be powerful and too limited to be thoroughly effective. No additional new means have been thereby provided for the solution of the economic ills, political weaknesses, and social problems which are rife throughout the Caribbean.

It should be clear that if the Jamaican government fails to establish a sound economic basis for the welfare of its people, and political instability thereby ensues, the British government, and possibly others, will not hesitate to step in and to take over control again in one way or another. . . .

Time and again liberties granted by British imperialists to colonial peoples have been taken away at will. Any incident of any gravity may be seized, or pretext found, to re-assert control and rule when that is desired by powerful imperial States. The landing of British troops in Guiana in 1953 and the annulment of its Constitution and political powers, have already been cited. The recent suspension of the Constitution of Grenada and the re-establishment there of virtually direct imperial rule should yet be fresh in our minds. These are the signal warnings of life and history. They must be blind indeed, who do not heed such warnings. . . .

It is possible now to give a realistic and definite answer to the question at issue: "Has the National Liberation Movement of the Caribbean People been accomplished or set back by the withdrawal of Jamaica from the Federation?" The answer clearly is: The National Liberation Movement of the Caribbean People has not been accomplished, since all these people are not yet free and independent nor united. The Caribbean National Movement has indeed been seriously set back by the withdrawal of Jamaica from the "Federation."

Is the present state of affairs final? Obviously not. For this vital question of Caribbean National Liberation can only approach settlement when the entire Caribbean people have been set firmly on their way towards freedom, prosperity, and power *through Union with Complete Self-Government.*

CULTURE, COLLEGE AND PEOPLE IN THE CARIBBEAN

Caribbean Luncheon Annual Journal, Association for the Advancement of Caribbean Education, January 24, 1965.

> But Knowledge to their eyes her ample page
> Rich with the spoils of time did ne'er unroll;
> Chill Penury repress'd their noble rage
> And froze the genial current of the soul.

In his justly famous and deeply moving *Elegy Written in a Country Churchyard,* Thomas Gray thus mused on the enforced ignorance and wretched lot of most of his fellowcountrymen. The poet in these lines reflected with truth and pathos upon the mentally deprived condition of the serf, peasant, and worker in the England of the eighteenth century. How much more then did the poet's just and compassionate thought apply to the still more deprived and woeful state of the African slave, freedman, and toiler on the plantations of the Caribbean?

For it was an axiom of the modern chattel slave system that learning was the very last thing which the slave should be allowed to secure. This differed from slavery of ancient Greece and Rome, where among the most highly educated and keenest thinkers were found men who were or had been slaves, like the famous fashioner of fables Aesop and the renowned philosopher Plato in Greece, or the slave secretaries, librarians, and tutors in Rome. With European colonialist expansion in the fifteenth century, there had developed new racist notions of white supremacy which grew out of modern chattel slavery based on the production of commodities for a world market.

The masters of this modern European chattel slave system, which dominated the Caribbean, were fiercely opposed to any education of the slave. These slave-holders held that knowledge, beyond the requirements of the simple laborious task, would surely unfit, and indeed ruin, the slave for his specific function as a vital labor force and an essential instrument of production. How the slave avidly longed to learn has been told by the English missionary John Smith who labored in Guiana during 1817–1824.

Seeking to satisfy this thirst for knowledge, John Smith conducted a night school by candle light and refused to stop teaching as required by the planters. But John Smith was charged with inciting the insurrection of 1823; he was unjustly condemned and thrust into jail where he died shortly thereafter. The martyr Smith had recorded in his journal the distress of an old African slave woman who pleaded thus:

> O Massa, Massa, rat eat all my book. . . . When me go look for my book, me find it so; then me cry, and me go show Massa what the rats done; then me beg Massa give me one book for this.

A change for the better came with the abolition of chattel slavery in 1834–1838. Schools were then increasingly provided due to the labors of such men as Bishop Coleridge and Samuel Jackman Prescod in Barbados and William Menzie Webb in Jamaica. But these schools were still quite inadequate, and higher learning was largely limited to the European planters and merchants, still ensconced at the top of the Caribbean social structure. Some phases of higher education were allowed to a few of the more prosperous middle class, under the covert color-class system of "race" restriction, which too long plagued and retarded the people of the Caribbean.

Even so late as 1878 Bishop Mitchinson of Barbados, speaking at the Pan-Anglican Council in London, could baldly declare:

> Experience in my diocese has taught me to be mistrustful of intellectual gifts in the coloured race, for they do not seem generally to connote sterling work and fitness for the Christian ministry. . . . I do not think the time has come, or is even near, when the ranks of the clergy will be largely recruited in the West Indies by the Negro race.

Progress has been made since then but there is no room for complacency or self-praise. A giant step forward was made with the founding and growth of the University of the West Indies, notably with its Extra Mural Courses of Adult Education. The recent launching of the College of Arts and Science in Barbados promises to fill a great and pressing need for extending education to the people broadly, that is, to all who desire it and demonstrate the ability to profit thereby.

One of the chief requirements in the education of a people is certainly that of providing the means of self-knowledge, as the essential prerequisite to self-development and self-fulfillment. "Know thyself" was a principal maxim inscribed in the temples of ancient Egypt and later in Greece. This maxim has been ably applied by a greater educator born in St. Thomas but matured in Africa. In his Inaugural Address as President of Liberia College in 1881, Dr. Edward Wilmot Blyden keenly observed: "The true principle of mental culture is perhaps this: to preserve an accurate balance between the studies which carry the mind out of itself, and those which recall it home again."

Thus the history of a people, knowledge of its origin and development in the past, is vital to its essential equipment in the present, and its continued progress in the future. Especially for a people just emerging from colonialism, such history is of prime importance. For history as conceived and taught by imperial overseers is of necessity focused upon events significant for themselves rather than for the people governed.

The Caribbean people in the past, therefore, have been given accounts mainly of historical events and deeds glorifying the peoples of the metropolitan powers, Spain, France, Holland, and England. But little or nothing was done to set forth the history and achievements of the Indian, Chinese, and African peoples. Yet a considerable number of Caribbean people are of Indian and Chinese origin, and the great majority is of African origin and descent.

It is therefore heartening to observe the progress already being made in teaching Caribbean history, particularly in the developing College of Arts and Science in Barbados. That the interest of the people has made it necessary to open these Caribbean history courses to the public is very significant. The announced three-volume history of the Caribbean will be eagerly awaited by many Caribbean migrants abroad. From the perspective of distance, it would appear that the question of reconciling Caribbean regional coverage with "national" island treatment might well be resolved by producing a good overall Caribbean history first, and then following, as deemed necessary, with specific area treatment.

For it is not at all improbable that the people of the various island and mainland areas of the Caribbean region, in the not too distant future, will indeed learn to work together for the greater good of all. A very great need appears to be to set forth the *background history of the Caribbean people, particularly the history of Africa.* This is required not only to fill in the gaps and round out the picture, but also in order that knowledge of the achievements of all the component groups should foster great respect for one another and lead to more equitable and harmonious relations between them all.

Moreover, the "winds of change" now herald the continuing emergence of independent African states and their growing importance in world affairs. Hence, African studies departments and programs are now functioning in the largest and topmost universities of the United States. Northwestern, Johns Hopkins, Howard, the University of Pennsylvania, Yale, Boston, Roosevelt, Duquesne, the University of California, the Kennedy School of Missions—all have African Departments or Institutes. Expanding African programs are in progress at Columbia, the University of Rochester, Smith College, Massachusetts Institute of Technology, New School for Social Research, Lincoln, Fisk, and Atlanta Universities.

An essential feature of these African studies programs is the specialized library of books and other material on African history, life, and culture. Such a library on the history and achievements of Africans, and their dispersed descendants in the Americas, would consequently seem to be a matter of prime consideration for those who preside over the development of the College of Arts and Science in Barbados.

Noteworthy in this connection is the relevant observation in *A University in the Making* made by the Vice Chancellor of England's latest giant University of Essex, Dr. Albert E. Sloman. While emphasizing the self-education of the student in "the Fulfillment of Lives," the Vice Chancellor counselled thus:

> Here we come to one of the thorniest problems of a new university. Old and new books, current and back numbers of periodicals, are a prime need for teaching and research in all subjects. . . . A library is the university's heart.

In the Special University Section of the *Barbados Advocate* of March 15th last year, Clennell Bynoe wrote "these islands still look to the UWI as 'the repository of the hopes and aspirations of the peoples of the Caribbean.' " Obviously fulfillment of these hopes and aspirations will depend upon the degree of concentration, on the development of the University and the provision of the necessary funds. This requires, too, close cooperation between all concerned. So also there may thus be nurtured the "Men of Ideas" pointed to by the Jamaican poet Roger Mais as the necessary architects of progress.

It should not be forgotten, but instead underscored, that the University of the West Indies is the prime, promising and enduring result of the past endeavor toward federation. The advancement of the University, like that of the people whom it must serve, and especially the progress of the College of Arts and Science in Barbados, appears to depend for the future very largely upon the successful achievement of the Eastern Caribbean Federation. The delay in accomplishing this is now a matter of deep concern, since so much certainly depends upon the establishment of this necessary firm foundation for united and independent regional Caribbean self-direction and mutual advancement.

As interested sons of the soil, thoughtful Caribbean Americans earnestly hope that nothing will now be permitted to stand in the way of speedy and firm accord in building the Eastern Caribbean Federation, and in fostering the progress of the Barbados College of Arts and Science and the advancement of the University of the West Indies as a whole. The situation in Guiana, where disunity and division have been used to set back independence and to threaten chaos, is a storm signal which should be heeded by immediate united action of all the Eastern Caribbean units and people.

From this observation point the statement made by Philip M. Sherlock in *West Indian Story* appears still pertinent, true, and compelling: "Through federation the widely scattered people of the West Indies can work together to improve their conditions, and to win for themselves a place of dignity and respect in the world." In fine, it is our fraternal hope and fervent desire that in the present decisive conjuncture, every leader of each Caribbean area, and of all integral parts, will now pursue and achieve the goal indicated by the Barbadian-born Caribbean poet Vaughan as quoted in *Caribbean Citizen:*

> Far-seeing statesman, born to lead,
> And worthiest of the people's trust.
> And barb the word with wisdom fit,
> And build, oh build, where we but dream. . . .

REMARKS AT GUYANA INDEPENDENCE CELEBRATION

United Nations Plaza, New York, May 27, 1966. Richard B. Moore Papers.

In the five minutes allotted me, I am happy to answer present and to join with you in this celebration of the recently declared independence of the people of Guyana. Perhaps my limited time may duly militate to prevent any eruption of forensic thunder. Accordingly, then, I am constrained to adopt the mode of the still, small voice which may yet express something of what should be said on this historic occasion.

Let me now hasten to felicitate you on the achievement of the political independence of Guyana. For none but the stony-hearted tyrant could fail heartily to greet the breaking of the bonds of alien rule and colonial bondage. Especially so, when by viture of birth in the Caribbean, specifically in Barbados, relatively just a few miles due north of Guyana, I am thus closely related by bonds of similar origin, culture, historical development, migration and intercourse, common oppression, and therefore by consequent conscious fraternal attachment to the people of Guyana.

Besides, my present participation here is all the more fitting because of my past activity through the years in the common struggle for human rights and for the liberation and advancement of the entire Caribbean people, which we have broadly interpreted to include the people of Guyana. Specifically, too, when issues have arisen affecting the rights and welfare of the Guyanese people, such as the suspension of their Constitution and their subjection to alien military intervention and rule, I have taken my stand with those of us here in New York who have rallied to and staunchly supported the fundamental rights of the people of Guyana. At the very founding of the United Nations, it was my function to present an Appeal On Behalf of the Caribbean People which demanded Complete Self-Government and admission to the United Nations. This Appeal to the United Nations specifically included the People of Guiana then still held as a colony of the British Empire.

As we now rejoice that the political independence of Guyana has been formally recognized, we cannot fail, nevertheless, to be mindful of the realities of the world in which we find ourselves. We must be concerned about certain developments prior to and in connection with the accession of independence. We dare not overlook the attempts which have been made to divide and to array Afro-Guyanese and Indo-Guyanese against each other. Nor can we forget the maneuvers with "proportional" representation and otherwise to remove and to supplant the then democratically elected governmental representatives of the people of Guyana. Though we cannot altogether dismiss our concern in this respect, we hope that an incident in the recent independence ceremonies in Guyana augurs better for the future—this you may have recognized as the reported embrace of the present Prime Minister, Mr. Forbes Burnham, with the former Chief Minister, Dr. Cheddi Jagan.

Of even greater concern is the fact that there has developed in the world of today a new force which threatens to overshadow and to render formal political independence an empty facade. We dare not dismiss such concern when we bear in mind the dismemberment of the Congo Republic and the murder of Prime Minister Patrice Lumumba and other ministers, and the subvention of puppets, in order to maintain the practical rule of colonialist oppressors and the continued appropriation of the rich mineral wealth of the Congo by alien financial syndicates. Nor can we ever forget the deposition of the most dedicated advocates of African unity and independence, such as the former Premier Ben Bella of Algeria and the Osagyefo of Ghana, Dr. Kwame Nkrumah.

Consequently, we are compelled perforce to recognize that there are grave dangers in the way of maintaining genuine political independence and economic freedom by the leaders and people of Guyana. There looms too a menace to the territorial integrity of Guyana. Old claims to the land of Guyana have been revived and are being pressed now by forces dominant in Venezuela with the aim of severing territory from the just emerged and comparatively weak state of Guyana. The entire land area of Guyana, formerly held by the British Government, must be maintained as a sacred trust and indefeasible right of the people of Guyana.

Moreover, it must be recognized that Guyana is the natural baseland of what may well become a significant, united Caribbean-Guyanese nation, that would thereby possess the power to build a strong political and economic structure for the welfare of its people, which could not otherwise be achieved.

Congratulations and fraternal best wishes to the people of Guyana! May closer fraternal relations be achieved not only within Guyana but also throughout the entire Caribbean, as the indispensable guarantee of full freedom and genuine economic advancement!

THE SECOND INDEPENDENCE ANNIVERSARY

Journal of the Barbadian Ex-Police Association, Barbados Independence Second Anniversary Celebration, New York, November 30, 1968.

An anniversary, especially of birth or marriage, is usually the occasion of joyous celebration. So surely should this second anniversary of the Independence of Barbados be an event of proud and happy commemoration. What son or daughter of Barbados, who had the pleasure of witnessing it, can ever forget that moment at midnight between the old colonialism and the new nationhood, when the flag of free and independent Barbados was hoisted and at last fluttered from the masthead at the Garrison Savannah in the renewed glare of floodlights, as the climax of a series of commemorative exercises?

However long absent through enforced exile in order to earn a livelihood as an "awayman," as indeed this writer had been for fifty-eight years, compelled by circumstance to "hive off" from the old, beloved island home, the "Bajan" fortunate enough to be able to return at that glorious moment, experienced the same thrill of love for the motherland and exultation over the achievement of independence, as did the citizen happily enabled to remain at home. All were united at that historic moment in memories of the past, joy in the present, and hope for the future.

But anniversaries are not only times of rejoicing and congratulation, these events are also periods of assessment, when the record is examined in order to evaluate past accomplishment or shortcoming, with a view to present welfare and future progress. This, of course, is the task in the main of those directly on the spot. However, some considerations from this distance might add a dimension to the view in this respect.

From the perspective of his long-range view, it would appear to this son of the soil that the fledgling island-nation of Barbados is developing rapidly, assuming her responsibilities, and facing up to the tasks with which she is inevitably confronted. We have seen Barbados take her place in the United Nations. We have also witnessed the admission of Barbados into the Organization of American States. Very recently also the Prime Minister of Barbados was entertained by President Johnson at the White House. All these events and others indicate growing national recognition and function. In this as in other important phases of activity, we hope and believe that the statesmanship requisite to safeguard independence, and to enhance the welfare of the people generally, is present and will continue to be forthcoming.

In the relations of Barbados with other nations and peoples, a vital problem still pressing for settlement is that of closer association with other Caribbean peoples. Some progress is to be seen in the endeavors to establish a Caribbean Common Market. That rapid progress will be made toward such a Caribbean Common Market, and that still closer cultural and political association will also follow, is our present wish. This is the fervent hope of those Caribbeans here, who have realized that small nations and peoples can achieve the power requisite for essential economic growth and political influence in this modern world only through achieving effective alliance and united strength.

Due consideration of the concrete means of participating in the economic development of Barbados appears to be urgent for Barbadians, their fellow Caribbeans, and Afro-American friends here. This would mean, of course, stimulating the increase of tourists to the island and the purchase of more Barbadian products. But there is still the far more basic matter of the purchase of land in Barbados and of hotel and industrial development there.

From Selden Rodman's just published book *The Caribbean*, the statements quoted below should certainly arouse response and activity. "I've heard that the planters still own 75 per cent of the land. . . . The absentee owners are selling out to local groups or the government." Immediately preceding these significant statements, an account is given of the purchase and remodelling of Sam Lord's Castle by Kenneth Coombes and his Euro-American partner, George J. Stewart. It should not be overlooked that these promoters are reported to have spent "an initial $200,000 for the dilapidated mansion and the 100 acres that went with it. But after only five years, the value of the land has increased to $3 million." Why not similar activity by Afro-Barbadians abroad and their associates? Indeed, such purchasers might more likely be possessed of greater interest in the welfare of the people and better guard against certain evils, now developing with tourism, which are exposed in Rodman's book.

The example of united action and concerted effort might well be set by Barbadians and by all other Caribbeans here, who have before them the object lesson of certain results achieved through the "more perfect union" striven for in these United States of America. While we now participate in these commemorative exercises with the Barbadian Ex-Police Association, we must look forward to the coming together again of this organization with The Sons and Daughters of Barbados and all such other groups in a united observance next year and the following years. Such a united observance was conducted through the Barbados Independence Committee at the time of the achievement of independence. This could well be the continued pattern and salutary example for the future.

This second anniversary statement might now be concluded with "The Exiles' Anthem," penned by this writer on the occasion of the island's independence:

> Beautiful mother, forgotten never,
> Barbados our own, our native land;
> Your children abroad will hail you ever
> Radiant in freedom, always to stand.

XIII

IN CONCLUSION

Throughout his many years of struggle on behalf of the oppressed workers and victims of imperialism, Richard B. Moore proved himself an unrelenting driving force. To many who witnessed the heat of the fire that burned within him, he seemed to have cast aside all else to serve "the cause." Late in life he wrote two brief pieces that reveal much of the inner man. To overlook them would cause one to miss a tenderness and sentiment that were important to other achievements. This section includes a letter to his granddaughter, in which we see not only a caring tenderness but his firm position on rationalism. It is interesting to note that about thirty years earlier he had written a similar letter to his daughter, dispelling the notion of a mystical Santa Claus. The second piece, a rare venture into poetry, is a tribute to Lorraine Hansberry. His selection of this form is in keeping with his appreciation of poetry, which he frequently quoted in his polemical discourses, and his sense of loss at the untimely death of the young writer. It also reveals his view of celebration for one who "bared the ugliness she strove to change while yet she lived," and his conviction that "others now shall surely carry on."

DEAR SYLVIA

Letter to granddaughter, Sylvia Joyce Turner. Original in editors' possession.

December 25, 1960

Dear Sylvia,

Once again it is the Winter Solstice—the sun has gone as far southward as it *seems* to those who live in certain areas north of the equator, and will soon start returning northward again. The Winter Solstice, now commonly called Christmas, was celebrated in Ancient Egypt and in some other countries long before there was any Christian in this world. The Winter Solstice is a fact of nature but the Christians, particularly the priests, have woven stories and myths about it until now most people who have been taught by Christians believe many fanciful and false things about a child being born in a manger, who had no natural father, and who was sent to die upon a cross to satisfy a vengeful father for the wrong things, called sins, which all human beings have done or will do.

However, it is far better not to do wrong or harmful things than to expect such fanciful forgiveness. What one does surely makes one what one comes to be; therefore, strive to do that which is helpful, good, and kind, and you will thus become a fine person.

Let it not appear that I write this to give you a lecture. I write to greet you as my little fan No. 1, so you will have this, if you keep it, even when you no longer remember what I would tell you by word of mouth. It certainly made me feel happy that at your age, just 8, you should show so much interest in "Grandpop's book." Lodie told me how delighted you were when you first saw it on the book table at the Book Review Program. Your mother has told us how you sold a copy of the book to your teacher, and also of your effort to sell the book through your classmates to their parents.

I'm happy, too, that you liked the West African dress which you saw worn by Mrs. Sweeting. As you grow, I hope you will continue to appreciate the fine things of art and other expressions of African culture. As some of your fore-parents many generations ago were Africans, you should learn to know and to value the fine things of your African heritage, as well as those of others now more prized in the society in which you are growing up now.

In this society, my dear granddaughter, you will have to make your way often against odds. Nevertheless, along with others who will be helpful, you must always strive for a just, proper, and honorable position in this society or wherever you may happen to go.

You will understand more of this as you grow and learn. So keep your mind open and alert, try to learn ever more and more, and so to grow in understanding of the world about you.

With love and best wishes, in which Lodie joins me, for your growth in every good way.

[signed] Grandpops

FOR LORRAINE HANSBERRY

Caribbean Luncheon Annual Journal, Association for the Advancement of Caribbean Education, January 24, 1965.

Blow the trumpet blow
On a frenzied note of anguish
Keen and shrill and piercing
With a long loud wail

Of rending-agonizing blues
For sadly now we mourn
The great deep loss
Of one so young and beauteous
Yet filled with deepest feeling
For her crushed and struggling people
And for all who toil
Beneath the weight, the hate,
The scorn, the bludgeoning
Of a predatory soulless world.
So talented withal she wove
With skillful plot and moving scene
With winged word and trenchant dialogue
A Raisin In The Sun
That bared the ugliness she strove
To change while yet she lived.

Blow the trumpet blow
A booming peal triumphant
Resounding far and long
In exultation mighty and melodious.
Let the sweet strings sing
And the deep bass boom
Let the cymbals clash
And the drums of Africa erupt
In vibrant repercussion.
Hers was a life well lived
And such a life is never lost.
Who can forget her tripping to the stand
A radiant beautiful brown form
To speak her word of tribute
To Du Bois—great man of letters
And the fight for freedom?
Luminous and brave she showed the way
And others now shall surely carry on
The work she did so well advance
To man's great victory in unison at last.

BIBLIOGRAPHY:

THE WRITINGS OF RICHARD BENJAMIN MOORE

(The Richard B. Moore Papers are available at The Schomburg Center for Research in Black Culture, New York.)

"Bogalusa." *The Emancipator*, March 13, 1920, p. 4.

"Call for Working Class Unity." *Daily Worker*, October 31, 1925, p. 2.

"Statement by Richard B. Moore and Common Resolution on the Negro Question at the Congress of the League Against Imperialism and for National Independence, Brussels, February, 1927." See *Das Flammenzeichen vom Palais Egmont. Offizielles Protokoll des Kongresses gegen koloniale Unterdrückung und Imperialismus, Brüssel, 10.–15. Februar 1927*, translated by Ingeborg B. Knight, pp. 126–30. Berlin: Liga gegen Imperialismus, 1927. The Resolution may also be found in *The Crisis*, July 1927, pp. 165–66, and in *A Documentary History of the Negro People in the United States 1910–1932*, edited by Herbert Aptheker, vol. 3, pp. 539–43. Secaucus, N.J.: Citadel Press, 1977.

"An Open Letter to Mr. A. Philip Randolph." *The Negro Champion*, August 8, 1928, p. 11. Also in *Daily Worker*, August 9, 1928, p. 2.

"The Negro: The Acid Test." *The Negro Champion*, August 8, 1928, p. 12.

"Housing and the Negro Masses." *The Negro Champion*, September 8, 1928, p. 8. Also reproduced as "Housing Vital Problem of Negro Workers." *Daily Worker*, September 17, 1928, p. 6.

"Moore Hits Misleader." *Daily Worker*, September 17, 1928, pp. 1, 3.

"Tenants Urged to Organize Against Tenement System." *Daily Worker*, April 15, 1929, p. 1.

"Problems and Struggles of the Negro Workers." Parts I and II. *Daily Worker*, June 6, 1929, p. 6. Parts III and IV. *Daily Worker*, June 7, 1929, p. 6. Part III reproduced in *The Black Worker*, edited by Philip Foner and R. L. Lewis, vol. VI, pp. 459–60. Philadelphia: Temple University Press, 1981.

Mr. President! Free the Scottsboro Boys! Pamphlet. New York: International Labor Defense, probably 1934.

"The Political Crisis of the Negro People." Broadcast, Station WAAB, Boston, October 13, 1936. Manuscript, Richard B. Moore Papers.

"The Great Douglass Celebrations for Queens." *Economic Adviser* 1, no. 2 (August 15, 1938): 1, 6.

"Frederick Douglass." *The Crisis*, February 1939, pp. 39–40, 50, 61.

Declaration of Rights of the Caribbean Peoples to Self-Determination and Self-Government. Presented at the Pan-American Foreign Ministers' Conference at Havana in July, 1940. Pamphlet. New York: West Indies National Emergency Committee, 1940. Richard B. Moore Papers.

"Statement of the West Indies National Emergency Committee on the Address Delivered by Secretary of State of the United States of America, Cordell Hull, to the Pan-American Foreign Ministers' Conference at Havana, Cuba, July 22, 1940 in Respect to the Status of European Possessions in the Western Hemisphere." (Reply to Cordell Hull.) Richard B. Moore Papers.

"The Frederick Douglass Centenary." *The Crisis*, March 1941, pp. 80, 90–91.

"The Negro in Freedom's Wars." *The Fraternal Outlook*, August 1941, pp. 6, 7, 23.

"Richard B. Moore Raps Hitler Article; Calls Fascism Negro's 'Most Deadly Foe.' "
    The New York Amsterdam Star News, November 1, 1941.
"Appeal to the United Nations Conference on International Organization on Be-
    half of the Caribbean Peoples." New York: West Indies National Council,
    May 1945. Also reproduced in *A Documentary History of the Negro People in the
    United States, 1933–1945*, vol. 3, pp. 561–67. Secaucus, N.J.: Citadel Press,
    1974.
"The Fate and Future of the Colonial Peoples." *New Voice* 1, no. 2 (September
    1946): 2, 7.
"Human Rights and National Independence." *New Voice* 1, no. 2 (September 1946):
    3–4.
"Memorandum on Federation and Self-Government of the West Indies Addressed
    to the Caribbean Labour Congress Convened in Conference at Coke Hall,
    Kingston, Jamaica, September 2–9, 1947." Mimeograph. New York: Ameri-
    can Committee for West Indian Federation, 1947. Richard B. Moore Papers.
"West Indies Federate for Nationhood." *New York Amsterdam News*, September 27,
    1947, p. 11.
"Statement Made by Richard B. Moore, Secretary of The American Committee for
    West Indian Federation Before the Platform Committee of the New Party,
    July 21, 1948." Richard B. Moore Papers.
"Statement of Richard B. Moore, Secretary, United Caribbean American Council
    on Delegation to the British Embassy, March 24, 1949." Mimeograph.
    Richard B. Moore Papers.
"Joint Statement Submitted on Behalf of the United Caribbean American Council
    and The American West Indian Association of Chicago at the Public Hearing
    Held Before The Subcommittee on the Judiciary, Washington, D.C. July 20,
    1949." Mimeograph. Richard B. Moore Papers.
Memorandum Submitted by the Committee to Act Against the McCarran and Walter Bills.
    February 15, 1952. Pamphlet. Richard B. Moore Papers.
"Speech of Richard B. Moore on Caribbean Federation at the Luncheon Meeting
    for Lord Listowel, February 3, 1953, at Hotel Theresa, New York, N.Y.,
    U.S.A." Richard B. Moore Papers.
"The Trinidad Elections and the Caribbean Scene." Press release distributed by
    West Indies News Service, New York, c. 1956. Richard B. Moore Papers.
"Some Writings by and about Caribbeans." *A Salute to the Federated West Indies*. April
    22, 1958. Also in *La Voz de Puerto Rico* 3, no. 2 (May 1958): 14–16.
"Revelations and Reflections on West Indies Federation." *The Sunday Gleaner*
    (Jamaica), November 2, 1958, p. 8.
"Visions of Nationhood Must be Recaptured." *Spotlight* (Jamaica) 21, no. 5 (May
    1960): 17, 19
The Name "Negro"—Its Origin and Evil Use. New York: Afroamerican Publishers,
    1960.
"No New Africa?" Manuscript, c. 1961. Richard B. Moore Papers.
"An Open Letter to Max Lerner, Columnist of *The New York Post*." February 19,
    1961. Richard B. Moore Papers.
"An Appeal to Save the Frederick Douglass Home as a Fitting Historical Memorial."
    Manuscript, c. 1962. Richard B. Moore Papers.
"Independent Caribbean Nationhood—Has It been Achieved or Set Back?" Manu-
    script, c. 1962. Richard B. Moore Papers.
"The Foreign Policy of Jamaica After Independence." *Barbados Daily News*, April
    24, 1962. Also in *Freedomways* 2, no. 3 (Summer 1962): 313–16, as "The
    Foreign Policy of an Independent Jamaica."
"A Further Approach to Caribbean Literature." *Association for the Advancement of
    Caribbean Education Luncheon Annual Journal* (New York), January 27, 1963.

"Frederick Douglass and Emancipation." *Liberator* 3, no. 2 (February 1963): 6–9.

"Letter to the Editor." [Review of *And Then We Heard the Thunder*, by John Killens.] *Liberator* 3, no. 4 (April 1963): 16.

"Federation Without Independence?" *Barbados Observer*, June 7, 1963, p. 2.

"Africa Conscious Harlem." *Freedomways* 3, no. 3 (Summer 1963): 315–34. Reprinted in *Harlem. A Community in Transition*, edited by J. H. Clarke, pp. 77–96 (New York: Citadel Press, 1964); *Harlem U.S.A.*, edited by J. H. Clarke (Berlin: Seven Seas Books, 1964); *Old Memories, New Moods*, edited by Peter I. Rose, pp. 385–403 (New York: Atherton Press, 1970); and *Black Brotherhood*, edited by Okon E. Uya, pp. 241–56 (Lexington, Mass.: D. C. Heath, 1971).

"Lighting up Man's Early Culture." [Review of *The Dawn of Civilization*, edited by Stuart Piggott.] *Freedomways* 3, no. 4 (Fall 1963): 569–73.

Africa Lost and Found. Recording by J. H. Clarke, Richard B. Moore, and Keith E. Baird. New York, 1964. (Available from the editors, P.O. Box 2484, Patchogue, N.Y. 11772.)

"The Tragic 'Race' Concept." [Review of *Man's Most Dangerous Myth: The Fallacy of Race*, by Ashley Montagu.] *Freedomways* 4, no. 2 (Spring 1964): 267–71.

"Books." [Review of *Man's Most Dangerous Myth: The Fallacy of Race*, by Ashley Montagu; *Race: The History of an Idea in America*, by Thomas F. Gossett; and *The Races of Mankind*, by M. Nesturkh.] *Liberator* 4, no. 6 (June 1964): 22.

"Caribbean Unity and Freedom." *Freedomways* 4, no. 3 (Summer 1964): 295–311.

"A New Look at African History." Lecture delivered at Columbia University, November 13, 1964. Richard B. Moore Papers.

"Culture, College and People in the Caribbean." *Association for the Advancement of Caribbean Education Luncheon Annual Journal* (New York), January 24, 1965.

"For Lorraine Hansberry." *Association for the Advancement of Caribbean Education Luncheon Annual Journal* (New York), January 24, 1965.

"Du Bois and Pan-Africa." *Freedomways* 5, no. 1 (Winter 1965): 166–87. Also reprinted in *Black Titan. W. E. B. Du Bois*, edited by J. H. Clarke, et al., pp. 187–212 (Boston: Beacon Press, 1970); and *Black Brotherhood*, edited by Okon Uya, pp. 154–71 (Lexington, Mass.: D. C. Heath, 1971).

"The Passing of Churchill and Empire." *Liberator* 5, no. 3 (March 1965): 8–10.

"Du Bois' Mature Work on Africa Republished" [Review of *The World and Africa* by W. E. B. Du Bois]. *Freedomways* 5, no. 4 (Fall 1965): 532–34. Reprinted in Clarke et al., *Black Titan*, pp. 126–28.

"Basic Views on: Image of the AfroAmerican in Literature, Related Thoughts on Image and Independence and the Independence of Guyana." Mimeograph. New York: Afroamerican Publishers, 1966.

"Remarks of Richard B. Moore at Guyana Independence Celebration, United Nations Plaza, New York, May 27, 1966." Richard B. Moore Papers.

"Some Contributions of Barbadians Abroad." *Salute to Barbados Independence, November 30, 1966*, pp. 22, 24, 44, 50, 52, 54, 56. New York: Barbados Independence Committee, 1966. Excerpted as "On Barbadians and Minding Other People's Business," *New World Quarterly* 3, nos. 1 & 2 (Dead Season 1966 and Croptime 1967): 69–75.

"Stolen Legacy Again?" Manuscript, c. 1967. Richard B. Moore Papers.

"The Significance of African History." *Amsterdam News*, August 12, 1967.

"Disturbances Anniversary Now Awarded Recognition." *Barbados Observer*, August 19, 1967, p. 3.

"Reactions to Riots Against Racism." *Liberator* 7, no. 10 (October 1967): 17–19. Also as "The Century of Color Conflict," *Negro Digest* 17, no. 2 (December 1967): 4–7.

"Afro-American Awareness." *53rd Annual Convention Souvenir Journal and Program,* Association for the Study of Negro Life and History, October 3–6, 1968.

"The Second Independence Anniversary." *Barbados Independence Second Anniversary Celebration Journal.* New York: Barbados Ex-Police Association, Inc., USA, November 30, 1968.

"Afro-Americans and Third Party Movements." WCBS-TV, Channel 2, New York, Black Heritage Series Broadcast, March 18, 1969. Manuscript, Richard B. Moore Papers.

"Afro-Americans and Radical Politics." WCBS-TV, Channel 2, New York, Black Heritage Series Broadcast, March 19, 1969. Manuscript, Richard B. Moore Papers.

"The Anatomy of Slavery as an American Institution." Lecture at Columbia University, July 17, 1969. Manuscript, Richard B. Moore Papers.

"A Name of Human Dignity." *Afro-American Historical Association 34th Annual Luncheon Journal* (New York Branch of the Association for the Study of Afro-American Life and History), February 13, 1971, and February 12, 1972.

"Open Letter On Our People's Name." Reply to Bayard Rustin. Mimeograph. New York: Afroamerican Institute, February 26, 1971.

"The Origin of Man." *The Barbados Observer,* November 27, 1971, p. 3.

Caribs, "Cannibals" and Human Relations. Patchogue, N.Y.: Pathway Publishers, 1972. (Available from the editors, P.O. Box 2484, Patchogue, N.Y. 11772.)

"Editor's Foreword" and "Biographical Sketch of the Author." In T. Albert Marryshow, *Cycles of Civilization.* Patchogue, N.Y.: Pathway Publishers, 1973. (Available from the editors.)

"Carib 'Cannibalism': A Study in Anthropological Stereotyping." *Caribbean Studies* 13, no. 3 (October 1973): 117–35.

"The Critics and Opponents of Marcus Garvey." In *Marcus Garvey and the Vision of Africa,* edited by John H. Clarke, pp. 210–35. New York: Random House, 1974.

"Highlights of the Museum Concerts." *Advocate News* (Barbados), April 1, 1974, p. 6.

"A Note on Racism in History." *Freedomways* 14, no. 4 (1974): 347–49.

"Bicentennial Reflections on Afro-Americans in the Revolutionary Period, 1770–1831." Lecture at Nassau Community College, Garden City, New York, October 2, 1975. Manuscript, Richard B. Moore Papers.

"Hubert Henry Harrison." In *The Dictionary of American Negro Biography,* pp. 292–93. New York: Norton, 1983.

INDEX